"This book is about a community of people who experience the joy, fulfillment, and sheer fun of throwing caution to the wind and themselves into a life of unabashed passion. It's a crash course on management and entrepreneurship showing what risk taking and ingenuity combined can accomplish. *NUTS!* is about people who dare to love and who, in their loving, have found an aliveness that makes them more fully human. Light reading, but profound content."

**TONY CAMPOLO**
Author of *Everything You've Heard Is Wrong* and *Carpe Diem*

"An inspiring tale of the remarkable results possible when employees are liberated to take charge of the rules and have fun on the job. Herb Kelleher's bold innovations stand out from the pack. This down-to-earth book offers valuable lessons about leadership—and profitability—to all who care about the future of their companies."

**ROSABETH MOSS KANTER**
Author of *World Class: Thriving Locally in the Global Economy*

"I'd like to make a power pitch for *NUTS!* It does a great job of telling the inside story of the best bigger-than-Texas success story I know. All of us can learn from Southwest's fiercely competitive spirit and the way it treats employees and customers. Kevin and Jackie Freiberg have hit a home run."

**NOLAN RYAN**

"A wonderful book about spirit. The fighting spirit that kept Southwest going during the tough early years. The enthusiastic spirit that fuels the positively outrageous service by anyone who flies Southwest. The loving spirit that comes from the heart and enriches all they touch—employees, customers, and the communities they serve. Read and tap into the power of the Southwest spirit."

**WALLY AMOS**
Author of *Watermelon Magic: Seeds of Wisdom, Slices of Life*

# NUTS!

## Southwest Airlines' Crazy Recipe for Business and Personal Success

### Kevin Freiberg
and
### Jackie Freiberg

## Broadway Books
NEW YORK

**BROADWAY**

A hardcover edition of this book was published in 1996 by Bard Press.

Broadway Books titles may be purchased for business or promotional use or for special sales. For information, please write to: Special Markets Department, Bantam Doubleday Dell Publishing Group, Inc., 1540 Broadway, New York, NY 10036.

BROADWAY BOOKS and its logo, a letter B bisected on the diagonal, are trademarks of Broadway Books, a division of Bantam Doubleday Dell Publishing Group, Inc.

Company Club, The Company Plane, Heroes of the Heart, Home for the Holidays, Southwest: THE Low Fare Airline, and Southwest Airlines are registered trademarks of Southwest Airlines Co. Where designations used by other manufacturers and sellers to distinguish their products are claimed as trademarks and Bard Press was aware of a trademark claim, the designations have been printed in initial capital letters (e.g., Wild Turkey).

First trade paperback edition published 1998.

Library of Congress Cataloging-in-Publication Data

Freiberg, Kevin, 1958–
    Nuts! : Southwest Airlines' crazy recipe for business and personal success / Kevin Freiberg and Jackie Freiberg ; foreword by Tom Peters. — 1st trade pbk. ed.
        p.   cm.
    Originally published: Austin, Tex. : Bard Books, c1996.
    Includes bibliographical references (p.   ) and index.
    ISBN 0-7679-0184-3 (pbk.)
    1. Southwest Airlines Co.   2. Airlines—United States—Management.
I. Freiberg, Jackie, 1963–   .   II. Title.
HE9803.S68F74   1998
387.7'06'573—dc21                                                      97-50102
                                                                            CIP

99  00  01  02  10

*A wise and trusted friend recently told us,*

*"You have the rest of your lives to change the world,*
*but you've only got one shot at raising these girls.*
*Make the most of it!"*

*To Taylor Grace and Aubrey Hope,*
*who have contributed more to our lives*
*than we could ever express:*

*You give us reason for hope and cause for celebration.*

# CONTENTS

About the Authors  /  *xiii*

Foreword *by Tom Peters*  /  *xv*

Prologue  /  *xvii*

**1** NUTS? . . . YOU DECIDE  /  2

## PART I  A LEGEND TAKES OFF
### The Southwest Spirit Is Born

**2** GOLIATH MEETS DAVID  /  14
*The Battle to Get off the Ground*

**3** THE BATTLE HEATS UP  /  28
*Innovations Forged in the Fires of Competition*

**4** A MAVERICK EMERGES  /  36
*The Creation of a Corporate Personality*

## PART II  BASICS GONE NUTS
### Doing Business Basics with a Southwest Twist

**5** FLYING IN THE FACE OF CONFORMITY  /  48
*Dare to Be Disciplined, Reap the Rewards*

**6** "PROFESSIONALS" NEED NOT APPLY  /  64
*Hire for Attitude, Train for Skills*

**7** KILL THE BUREAUCRACY  /  74
*Think Small, Act Fast*

**8** ACT LIKE AN OWNER  /  96
*Ask Questions, Think Results*

**9** LEARN LIKE CRAZY  /  112
*Stay Fresh, Stretch to Grow*

**10** DON'T FEAR FAILURE  /  128
*Be Creative, Color outside the Lines*

## PART III  NUTS GONE BASIC
### Doing the Extra Special Exceptionally Well

**11** ONE GREAT BIG FAMILY  /  144
*Create a Legendary Culture*

**12** KEEPING THE SPIRIT ALIVE  /  156
*Preserve What You Value*

**13** THE ART OF CELEBRATING MILESTONES  /  174
*Revel in Your Accomplishments*

**14** CELEBRATING PEOPLE WITH BIG HEARTS  /  190
*Honor Those You Love*

**15** STILL NUTS AFTER ALL THESE YEARS  /  202
*Make Work Fun*

**16** LUV  /  216
*More Than Just a Ticker Symbol*

**17** COMPASSION FOR THE COMMUNITY  /  234
*Give Back—It's the Right Thing to Do*

**18** UNCONVENTIONAL ADVERTISING  /  246
*Bending the Rules to Break a Great Story*

**19** CUSTOMERS COME SECOND  /  268
*And Still Get Great Service*

**20** EMPLOYEES COME FIRST  /  282
*Great Service Begins at Home*

## PART IV  THE LEGEND LIVES ON
### Leadership Spices It Up

**21** LEADERS LEADING LEADERS  /  298

**22** LEADERSHIP FROM THE INSIDE OUT  /  312

**23** GO NUTS!  /  320

Epilogue  /  328
Notes and Sources  /  330
Acknowledgments  /  347
Index  /  352

# ABOUT THE AUTHORS

**KEVIN FREIBERG** is a popular speaker known for delivering hard-hitting messages that move people emotionally and inspire them to make long-term, substantive changes in their personal and professional lives. Since beginning his speaking career in 1986, Kevin has challenged corporate leaders all over the world to create unmatched productivity, customer service, and profitability by becoming faithful, devoted, hardworking servants of the people they lead. His philosophy is based on the idea that change comes from the inside out.

Kevin addresses more than one hundred corporations, professional associations, government agencies, and national and international business conferences a year. He is famous for using powerful stories to illustrate how, in a do-more-with-less-world where change is constant and competition relentless, it is still possible to go home at the end of the day emotionally charged instead of emotionally drained. Kevin believes that we teach what we most need to learn, so he is dedicated to helping people find the heroism in their work and rediscover the joy of living life with purpose, principles, and passion.

Kevin is the president of San Diego Consulting Group, Inc., and also serves as executive coach and strategist for the leaders of its client organizations. Before becoming a full-time speaker and consultant, Kevin taught eight years at the University of San Diego and at San Diego State University, where he met his wife, Jackie. He received his bachelor's degree in English literature and master's degree in speech communication from San Diego State; he earned his doctorate in educational leadership at the University of San Diego.

In addition to his other activities, Kevin is being tutored full time by his daughters, who practice the Southwest Airlines' credos of lighten up, be more playful, don't take yourself too seriously, and remember to have fun!

**JACKIE FREIBERG** is also a popular speaker known for delivering messages that are power packed with unconventional business best practices. Her audiences walk away with sound business solutions, a passion to take action, and a refreshing sense of hope and personal commitment to lead more purposeful lives. In addition to speaking Jackie is an owner and the managing partner of

San Diego Consulting Group, Inc. Besides speaking and juggling the multiple priorities of marketing the firm's services, overseeing its daily operations, and managing client relationships, she is the Freiberg family anchor. Jackie is the chief choreographer of the schedules of two very active daughters and all of the duties that come with trying to be loving parents and good friends. Within their firm and family, Jackie is the chief advocate of the conviction that love and life must be thoroughly integrated with making a living.

Through her work as a feedback consultant, she debriefs executives, managers, and front-line professionals on the results of the firm's organizational and 360-degree leadership assessments. Jackie is dedicated to helping working professionals and their families improve the quality of their lives and better understand the impact of their behaviors on organizational performance.

Jackie is the cofounder of the Family Business Institute at the University of San Diego, where she was one of the creative forces behind the development of practical, research-based educational programs for closely held family businesses. She also worked with MassMutual Life Insurance Company to design the first-ever CD-ROM training tool for family businesses and provided expert commentary on the complex business and personal issues family businesses face today.

Before joining the San Diego Consulting Group full time in 1993, Jackie was manager of corporate and professional programs for the University of San Diego. She taught public speaking and business communication as an adjunct professor there and at San Diego State University. She received her bachelor's degree in communication from the University of New Hampshire and master's degree in speech communication from San Diego State University; she earned a doctorate in educational leadership at the University of San Diego.

Jackie and Kevin live in San Diego with their daughters, Taylor Grace and Aubrey, and a golden retriever disguised as a Persian cat named Carlos. Contact them at:

San Diego Consulting Group, Inc.
4110 Palisades Road
San Diego, California 92116-2043
Phone:     (619) 624-9691
Fax:        (619) 624-9695
E-mail:    SDCGI@aol.com

# FOREWORD

## BY TOM PETERS

In 1987, a couple of years after *A Passion for Excellence* was published, I received a letter from Kevin Freiberg telling me that I had missed the boat with my critical comment about Southwest Airlines' customer service. Fresh from finishing his doctoral dissertation about Southwest's chairman, president, and CEO Herb Kelleher, Kevin was convinced that I needed to take a closer look at the inner workings of the company.

If you've read *The Pursuit of WOW!* (1995) or seen *Service with Soul* (1995) you know I took Kevin's advice. I found an absolutely amazing company. I was overwhelmed by the atmosphere and character of the airline. Southwest is "Air Travel's Greatest Show on Earth" because of its on-time service, baggage handling, low fares, no assigned seats, and no heartburn from typical airline food. While most organizations are boring and rigid, Southwest is just the opposite. What I discovered is an organization that dares to unleash the imagination and energy of its people. They make work fun—employees have the freedom to act like NUTS. There is a spirit of entrepreneurship—much more than a decentralized organization chart—an attitude that extends to every corner of the company.

Why has Southwest captivated the interest of *Forbes, Business Week,* the *Wall Street Journal*—a virtual "who's who" of the business press? Because this band of mavericks started a revolution—a revolution whose impact is spreading far beyond the boundaries of the airline industry. In a 1994 cover story, *Fortune* asked its readers: "Is Herb Kelleher America's best CEO?" I believe he may well be.

Newspaper and magazine articles have given us bits and pieces of the Southwest picture, but never the whole story. Now, for the first time you have it in *NUTS!* Kevin and Jackie Freiberg take you inside this crazy company and conjure up the sights, sounds, and feelings of everyday life at this legendary airline. Besides describing how and why the company is successful, they show you the heart and soul of Southwest, and do it in living color.

If you don't already know it, Southwest reinvented air travel twenty-six years ago with its low fares and zany, irreverent style. These NUTS made flying an event. Today, Southwest keeps air fares rock bottom by keeping costs low, satisfies customers by getting people and baggage to their destinations on time (and gives them some fun along the way), practices the Golden Rule at work and in the communities it serves, and has the best productivity and safety records in the industry.

How has Southwest done all this? It's not rocket science—keep costs low, productivity high, service

positively outrageous, and black ink on the financial statement. Three extra special things I see: being crazy enough to follow an unorthodox vision, being courageous enough to allow people to have fun and be "real" people who love and care at work, and being smart enough to recognize that their most valuable assets are their people and the culture they create. Southwest never forgets it is in the people business—the company just happens to operate an airline.

So, what can you expect to take away from a book about a great customer service organization that just happens to be in the airline business? Not just stories (though there are lots of very good ones). Examples. Success tips. Hundreds of practical ideas—most of them refreshingly unconventional—to make your business and personal life fun and rewarding. Like what? Celebrate like crazy. Put employees first and customers second. Forget fancy plans. Love one another. And—even if you have a smart, strong, and passionate (not to mention wild and crazy) leader like Herb Kelleher at the top—instill leadership in every nook and cranny of your organization.

If you take time to read only one business book this year, I strongly encourage you to read *NUTS!*

*Tom* ∿ →

We started on the path to this book in 1986, when Kevin was working on a doctoral dissertation about leadership at the University of San Diego. Kevin wrote to Colleen Barrett, Southwest's corporate secretary and then vice president of administration, to ask if Herb Kelleher would agree to an interview. Barrett's answer: "Herb loves to participate in these types of projects, but if he honored every request he received he would spend all of his time doing interviews instead of running an airline." The answer was no. Kevin wrote back to tell Colleen that she would be halting the advancement of leadership studies and letting the world down if people were not able to learn about Herb Kelleher's extra-ordinary leadership qualities. To this day we're not sure why she finally said yes. Colleen does not wear down easily, so it must have been an act of grace.

After spending several weeks at Southwest Airlines, Kevin was struck by the interest, enthusiasm, and respect he was shown by Southwest employees. Their hospitality and good humor were remarkable and very, very contagious. It was certainly clear that a different kind of leadership was practiced at Southwest Airlines, one that had created a culture unlike anything Kevin had ever seen before. After a year of research and writing, Kevin completed his dissertation describing leadership at Southwest Airlines and Herb Kelleher's passion for the company and its people.

Four years later Jackie began her doctoral work, also at the University of San Diego. She believed that although the media had kept its focus on Herb, there was much more to the story of leadership at Southwest Airlines. She would get no argument from Herb Kelleher on this issue; he is always the first to give Southwest employees credit for the company's tremendous success, and he genuinely believes that leadership is more a function of people's relationships than position. Colleen said yes again, and Jackie began her study of how employees form and carry out leadership relationships at Southwest Airlines.

Since our doctoral work, we've continued working as consultants to Southwest, developing close working relationships with many of the company's talented employees and gaining new insights into the main

can keep setting performance records on so many fronts: financial performance, work force productivity, safety, customer service, and more.

When we proposed our book to Colleen, she said no, the timing wasn't right—they had just begun the Morris Air joinder. Nine months later, Colleen said okay, she and Herb—and more than one hundred other Southwest employees—would now have the time for the interviews and surveys this project would require.

It was time for the Southwest story to be told. In digging into the company's background and inner workings, our aim was to learn all we could about a genuine American success story. How did Southwest's early struggle to get off the ground spark that special spirit that still sustains it today? How does a company that seems obsessed with having fun keep earning the industry's highest awards for customer service and on-

*How can a company that defies conventional wisdom, industry norms, and fashionable management programs keep setting performance records on so many fronts?*

ingredients of the company's phenomenal success. The more we learned about its inner workings, the more excited we got about sharing with others the principles behind Southwest's success. We started planning a book that would reveal how a company that defies conventional wisdom, industry norms, and fashionable management programs

time performance? How does a company headed by a media focus like Herb Kelleher get beyond a "Lone Ranger" mind-set about leadership? How might people in other businesses put some of Southwest's secrets to use in their work and personal lives?

We were also intrigued by the mounting inquiries that Colleen and

Gary Kelly, v.p. of finance and CFO, were receiving from reporters about succession planning. "Is there life for Southwest Airlines after Herb?" they all wanted to know. We thought it was important for people to know that while Kelleher's enormous intellectual capabilities, love for people, playful spirit, and commanding personality all play a vital role in the company's success, leadership at Southwest Airlines doesn't just revolve around Herb.

Ferreting out the answers to these questions, and many others,

and CEO of General Electric, which manufactures its jet engines, for example—for their thoughts on what makes this wacky company tick.

To help you begin to understand why the people of Southwest Airlines are nuts, we describe in chapters 2, 3, and 4 the series of events and the cast of people that shaped the culture, character, and personality of the company. What these people went through in the early years is enough to make anyone nuts. The roots of the revolu-

## It was time for the Southwest story to be told.

took almost two years of inquiry in addition to research through our ongoing consulting projects. We conducted more than 75 face-to-face and telephone interviews, surveyed 166 station managers, provisioning managers, and Culture Committee members across Southwest's route system, and reviewed thousands of pages of internal documents, plus hundreds of studies of Southwest Airlines written up in books and articles since 1971. We talked with Southwest employees at all levels, at headquarters and in stations from coast to coast. We also asked people outside the company—Bob Crandall, chairman and CEO of American Airlines, who has a commanding influence in the U.S. airline industry; Phil Condit, CEO of Boeing, which supplies Southwest's aircraft; and Jack Welch, chairman

tion that Southwest created in the airline industry go back to the company's very beginning. It is impossible to fully grasp the recipe for Southwest's success without understanding where the ingredients for this recipe come from.

In parts II and III, we describe the ingredients in Southwest's recipe for positively outrageous business success. There is no one thing that makes Southwest Airlines so successful. Like a great bowl of chili, Southwest's success comes from the interaction of both ordinary and exotic ingredients. The problem with trying to understand why this company is the envy of businesses all over the globe is a bit like trying to understand which piece of a gorgeous mosaic is responsible for its striking beauty. Nevertheless, in chapters 5 through 20 we have tried to capture the main elements in Southwest's success. Each chapter addresses a different ingredient and explains how it is applied in Southwest Airlines' business. These chapters conclude with prescriptions for business and personal success in a very brief segment titled "Success in a Nutshell." We've also included lots of pictures and stories to help make this company's unconventional way of doing business come alive.

As any master chef will confide, following the recipe and using high-quality ingredients are not all that's required for a culinary masterpiece. Five different people can make the same recipe using the same ingredients and get five different results. In part IV we explain this effect in business. Here we define the model of leadership that makes the pot at Southwest Airlines hot and spicy. While we have the highest admiration for Herb, we now know that leadership doesn't reside in just one person—even if his name *is* Kelleher.

It would be impossible to write a book about Southwest Airlines without writing about Herb. His influence on the organization is powerful, provocative, and profound. Yet, contrary to what the business press would have us believe, no single person influences significant organizational change alone, and Kelleher has surrounded himself, at all levels, with very talented people. In chapters 21 and 22 we explore the way leadership is practiced at Southwest Airlines, and in chapter 23 we leave

you with a challenge: "Go nuts!" Finally, in the epilogue, we address the question "Is there life for Southwest Airlines after Herb?"

It is our hope that Southwest Airlines' crazy recipe for business and personal success will inspire you to become more focused, more fun, more creative, imaginative, and daring, and, in the end, more profitable—even at the risk of being seen as a little bit nuts!

In telling the Southwest story, we write from a perspective on the company, its people, and its practices that is more intimate than most. Having known and worked closely with the people of Southwest Airlines for more than twelve years now, we have an insider's sense of what makes the company tick. Let us say up front that *NUTS!* is not an exposé of Southwest Airlines. Our aim is to describe and explain how the company has achieved a phenomenal track record of success. We make no apologies for presenting a very positive and optimistic view. In terms of doing the right things and doing things right, Southwest Airlines excels on both counts, and we've let the facts speak for themselves. So if you're looking for a tabloid-style, tell-all look into the world's most intriguing airline, you won't find it here. Even if we had the inclination to write that kind of book, we don't know what we would say that isn't already known. The people of Southwest Airlines are about as open and authentic as they come. In the years that we have been watching this company, we have never known anyone to be bashful about divulging his or her shortcomings and mistakes.

We also write as outsiders. Speaking engagements and consulting assignments through our firm, San Diego Consulting Group, Inc., take us into organizations all over the

balanced form of existence. We meet business people almost every day who are saying similar things: "How can we make work more fun and exciting? How can we avoid burnout in a do-more-with-less environment?"

Organizationally, the challenges are no less daunting. Learning to adapt quickly, embracing change as

*The more we saw people searching for meaning in their work, the more we wanted to share the principles behind Southwest's success.*

world, giving us an excellent vantage point for comparing Southwest with other businesses. Observing a lot of different companies in a wide variety of industries gives us many opportunities to see, firsthand, the personal and business challenges facing people today. The themes are very consistent.

On an individual level, there is an emptiness, a lack of spiritual and psychic gratification, that stems from meaningless and exhausting work. This is evidenced by the mass exodus out of big corporations. People are trading in high-pressure, high-paying jobs for a simpler, more

an opportunity instead of a threat, keeping up with the mind-boggling explosion of information and technology, teaching the organization to be more creative, and motivating people to take personal ownership for the success of the business are all issues with which our clients are dealing.

With most of these people we have shared some part of the Southwest Airlines experience. Feeling uplifted, inspired, and challenged, they always react the same way: "How can we learn more?" This says to us that the story of Southwest Airlines is indeed worth telling.

# CHAPTER 1

# NUTS? . . . YOU DECIDE

Isn't it nuts for a company to

. . . like to keep prices at rock bottom?

. . . believe that customers come second?

. . . settle a major legal dispute by arm wrestling?

. . . loathe the titles and trappings of "terminal professionalism"?

. . . run recruiting ads that say, "Work at a place where wearing pants is optional"?

. . . paint its $30 million assets to look like killer whales and state flags?

. . . avoid TQM, reengineering, and other trendy management programs?

. . . spend a lot more time planning parties than writing policies?

. . . avoid formal, documented strategic planning?

. . . make the "Lone Ranger" leadership mentality a thing of the past?

*No in-flight meals, just nuts. Southwest Airlines serves more than sixty million bags of peanuts a year.*

## ARE THESE PEOPLE NUTS?

Well, if being nuts means they are crazy about the company they work for, the answer is a resounding yes! If being nuts means they are extremely enthusiastic about what they do, the answer is again yes! If being nuts means being intensely involved, even obsessed, these people are definitely nuts about providing legendary customer service. If a nut is someone who is fanatically committed to a cause, these people clearly fit the description. The people of Southwest Airlines are radicals and revolutionaries—committed to the cause of keeping fares low to make air travel affordable for everyone.

These people are scrupulous about working hard and zealous about having fun—so much so that many people want to know, "Who *are* these nuts?" They are impassioned about treating each other like family. They hug, kiss, cry, and say, "I love you" on the job. For this reason alone many outsiders think they are hokey and unquestionably nuts. The people of Southwest Airlines also maniacally avoid following industry trends. Until the late 1980s, people in the airline industry rarely took them seriously. Why? Because they considered them to be unmistakably nuts.

Since 1971, this eccentric and outlandish company has established a consistent pattern of deviating from convention. When other airlines were creating big hubs, Southwest was flying point to point. Instead of serving expensive meals, flight attendants pass out nuts. Instead of wearing stuffy uniforms, they sport polo shirts and shorts. For these departures from convention, and many others, the world has become fascinated with these zany people whose irrepressible enthusiasm comes from the desire to make their lives and their company extraordinary.

CBS's *60 Minutes*, CNN's *Pinnacle* and *News Network*, *The Today Show*, *This Week with David Brinkley*, *Fortune*, *Business Week*, *USA Today*, *Working Woman*, and the *Wall Street Journal* are just some of the places the Southwest Airlines story has received major play. Why? One reason is that the media love stories that are out of the ordinary about people who are striking and unusual. Convention is boring. Nuts are exciting. Convention is old news. Nuts raise ratings. Every major newspaper in the United States has tried to help readers uncover the inner workings of Southwest's crazy approach to low costs and legendary customer service. The company has been praised for its leadership and customer service in over a dozen business bestsellers. Management gurus like Tom Peters bring their clients to observe Southwest because they are intrigued with this wacky airline's way of doing business.

## A GENUINE SUCCESS STORY

Another reason everyone's so interested in Southwest Airlines is simple: Southwest is a genuine American success story. See for yourself.

### Profitability

In an industry that is still reeling from the $12.8 billion loss it posted between 1990 and 1994, Southwest was the only airline to be profitable each year during that period. During this time the airline industry lost more money than it had made in the previous sixty years. Southwest Airlines is the only U.S. airline to earn a profit every year since 1973. Its net profit margins—averaging over 5 percent since 1991—have been the highest in the industry.

### Steady Growth Rate

Since deregulation in 1978, when the airlines began competing freely, 120 airlines have gone bankrupt. Since 1990, the commercial airline industry has seen the collapse of Eastern, Pan Am, and Midway Airlines. America West went into Chapter 11, and Continental and TWA both went into Chapter 11 for the second time. Meanwhile, Southwest Airlines continued to expand. The company has experienced 139 percent traffic growth over the last five years, ranging from 8 to 36 percent annually.

### Conservative Balance Sheet

Airline debt has recently reached astronomical and unsustainable levels, more than $35 billion as of 1996 year-end. This financial weakening prevents many airlines from embracing commercial opportunities that could be critical to their success. While balancing the pressures to grow from investors, customers, and competitors, Southwest has maintained a conservative amount of debt in an industry that is very capital-intensive. Gary Kelly, vice president and chief financial officer, says, "Our target is to do at least 50 percent of our capital spending with internally generated funds." As of the end of 1996, Southwest had *29 percent* leverage, or *58 percent* considering operating leases. Because of its conservative balance sheet, Poor's and Moody's give Southwest credit ratings of "A– and A3," respectively, the highest in the U.S. airline industry.

### Outstanding Stock Performance

Investment guru Peter Lynch lauds Southwest as "the only U.S. airline to have made money every year since 1973." Up 300 percent since 1990, Southwest's stock has performed formidably. While airlines typically trade at approximately ten times earnings, Southwest has generally traded at twenty times earnings. "For return on capital," Lynch says, "Southwest has yet to be outdone."

### Lowest Fares

Although there are fewer carriers in the industry, there are over four thousand more competitive routes today, after deregulation, than when regulation ended in 1978. With the lowest fares in almost every market it serves, Southwest Airlines is the driving force behind the steady decline of ticket prices since deregulation. According to

Patrick Murphy, deputy assistant secretary for aviation and international affairs, U.S. Department of Transportation (DOT), in 1988 Southwest Airlines alone was driving fares down to the extent that 15 percent of all U.S. commercial air travelers were benefiting. By the first quarter of 1995, 37 percent of all domestic passengers were benefiting from the reduced fares charged by Southwest and other new low-fare carriers. In 1993, the DOT Office of Aviation Analysis found that "the principal driving force behind dramatic fundamental changes that have occurred and will occur in the U.S. airline industry over the next few years is the dramatic growth of low-cost Southwest Airlines."

### Market Dominance

As a result of low fares, high frequency, and excellent customer service, Southwest Airlines has achieved significant market penetration. The company's shorthaul dominance is evidenced by a consistent market share of at least 60 percent in almost every nonstop city-pair market it serves.

*Southwest flight attendants make flying fun with comical PA announcements and preflight tricks like popping out of overhead bins.*

## Most Productive Work Force

At a five-year annual average of twenty-four hundred customers served per employee, Southwest has the most productive work force in the U.S. airline industry. The company services twice the number of passengers per employee of any other airline, according to customer service expert Richard Whiteley. It also gets more daily departures per gate and more productive hours out of an airplane than anyone else in the industry. For equivalent aircraft stage lengths, Southwest also has the lowest cost per available seat mile.

## Low Turnover

Southwest Airlines has one of the lowest turnover rates in the airline industry, approximately 6.4 percent per year. Southwest is considered by many to be one of the best companies to work for in the country; Robert Levering and Milton Moskowitz put the company in their top ten in *The 100 Best Companies to Work for in America*. Southwest people love working in an environment that encourages them to be themselves—even if they are nuts!

## No Furloughs

As the airline industry has sprinted to reduce costs, highly skilled workers who contribute to the nation's economy and technological strength have been displaced by the thousands. In fact, more than one hundred twenty thousand employees lured by the romanticism and sex appeal of the airline business have been laid off since 1989. Except for three employees who were laid off in a cash crunch in the early 1970s and immediately rehired, Southwest has never furloughed anyone. During the jet-fuel crisis of 1979, the recession of 1982–1983, and the recession of 1990–1994, Kelleher wouldn't even discuss the possibility of furloughing people: "It never entered our minds. Our philosophy very simply is that it is a very short-term thing to do. If your focus is on the long term, the well-being of your business and its people, you don't do it." In an age when people say job security is a thing of the past, Southwest employees have good reason to think differently.

## Highest Customer Service Ratings

If you talk to the person sitting next to you on a plane or just listen as you stand in line to board your next flight, you will quickly conclude that fliers, particularly business fliers, aren't very happy. For many, flying is a significant emotional experience because it feels like they're handing control of their lives over to the airline. Passengers with high expectations are fed up with oversold flights, crowded seating, indifferent flight attendants, late arrivals, and congested airports. The perception of people who travel frequently is that most people in the airline business do not consider themselves to be in the customer service business—at least not in a demonstrable way.

Based on baggage handling, on-time performance, and customer complaint statistics reported by the U.S. Department of Transportation, Southwest Airlines has the best customer service record in the airline industry. Southwest Airlines is the only carrier in the United States to win the industry's "Triple Crown" since DOT started keeping these statistics in 1987.

## Highest Completion Factor

The Federal Aviation Administration (FAA) indicates that air travel in the United States will double by 2005 to more than one billion passengers annually. Delays from congestion at twenty-three of the nation's busiest airports (more than twenty thousand hours annually at each) will cost the airlines and their customers at least $5 billion each year. As more and more people travel, the airlines must find innovative ways to cope with the congestion created by inefficient operations and inadequate facilities. In the midst of this challenge, Southwest has the highest completion factor in the industry; that is, compared with the number of flights it schedules, Southwest cancels fewer flights than anyone.

## Youngest Fleet, Best Safety Record

As of July 1996, the average age of Southwest's 237 airplanes is 7.9 years. This makes Southwest's fleet—50 percent of which the company owns free and clear—the youngest among the major carriers. In terms of the number of flights operated and the number of customers carried without a major accident (let alone fatalities), Southwest has the best safety record in the industry—"the safest airline in the world," according to *Condé Nast Traveler* magazine. The company's rigorous standards for aircraft maintenance and flight operations exceed FAA requirements. Southwest's excellent maintenance standards also contribute to its extremely high completion factor.

*Herb Kelleher, Southwest's chairman, president, and CEO, arm wrestles Kurt Herwald, chairman of Stevens Aviation, Greenville, S.C., instead of going to court over an advertising slogan.*

**Most Emulated**

Since 1992, an avalanche of start-ups such as Kiwi, Reno Air, Western Pacific, and a reborn Pan Am have filed applications to enter this volatile and sometimes unforgiving industry. Most of these new

*Southwest Airlines is definitely nuts, but they've been hugely successful and had fun along the way!*

entrants have adopted some version of Southwest's strategy—offering frequent flights or charging low fares. The major carriers have launched counteroffensives by charging low fares on overlapping routes. United and Continental have introduced their own low-fare clones, United Shuttle and Continental Lite. Today even American Airlines (a carrier with seven times the revenue of Southwest) and Delta (five times as large) are contemplating such experiments.

So, is Southwest Airlines nuts? Without a doubt. But this company is living out one of the greatest success stories in the history of commercial aviation. And it's had fun along the way! Wanting to know how Southwest Airlines achieves these incredible results is certainly a major reason why so many people are interested in this extraordinary company. But there is another reason—one that is perhaps less understood and yet is every bit as powerful. People are drawn to Southwest Airlines because, intuitively or otherwise, they want to be part of a cause that gives them a sense of meaning and significance; they want to belong to something larger than themselves.

### IT'S NOT A JOB, IT'S A CRUSADE

If you look deep enough, behind most great companies there is a moral imperative, an obligation or sense of duty, that compels the company to operate in certain ways. Southwest is no exception. The people of Southwest Airlines are crusaders with an egalitarian spirit who truly believe they are in the business of freedom. Their mission is to open up the skies, to give ordinary people the chance to see and do things they never dreamed of. This is why Southwest is relentless about keeping costs low.

## *"What Southwest has done is create democracy in the airline business."*

Anyone who has ever met Herb Kelleher will tell you that whether he's talking to a U.S. Supreme Court justice, a member of his board of directors, or a hotel valet, he displays the same level of genuine interest and intensity. He's there and he's engaged, regardless of whom he's talking to. Herb Kelleher doesn't have a patronizing bone in his body, and this is the way he runs Southwest. The company's whole business strategy is egalitarian. Roy Spence, president of GSD&M, one of Southwest's two advertising agencies, says, "Herb has always been a populist in terms of the way Southwest is run. He is a very inclusive marketer. He would rather have a full plane at $49 [per ticket] than a half-full plane at $200. What they've done is create democracy in the airline business."

Ron Ricks, Southwest's vice president of governmental affairs, often invokes a slogan Southwest people hold dear: It's not a job, it's a crusade. He says, "The principle, the higher calling if you will, that drives Southwest employees is 'How can we protect the people who fly our airline? How can we protect small businesses? Are we doing what's best for the senior citizens who count on us for low fares?'" This is why the people of Southwest Airlines have become politically active over the years. They believe that politics is the business of protecting people's freedom.

When you look at this company's success, it's important to understand that Southwest employees have bought into the company not only in terms of stock; they have also bought into the principles for which the airline stands. A piece of legislation that advocates higher landing fees, for example, isn't seen just as an affront to their profitability; it's also an affront to their idealism. Ricks explains, "If you accept the notion of what Southwest Airlines stands for in terms of this crusade, then you are going to have a visceral reaction to things that adversely affect your customers."

Billions of dollars of annual fare savings would not have been realized by U.S. consumers had Southwest Airlines not stuck to its principles. Southwest's executive vice president of corporate services, John Denison, says, "The product we deliver is a wonderful contribution to society. We make it possible for people to fly who could never afford to fly in the past." "This isn't just a business that makes money," says Jim Parker, vice president and general counsel. "What's so exciting about Southwest Airlines is that it is a company that changed the business environment in America and continues to change it every time we enter a new market."

There is no question that the people of Southwest Airlines are driven by the desire to make money. They are firmly entrenched in the idea that profitability is the precursor to job security, shareholder return, and investment in the community. But when you really get to know them, you learn that they are also in business to make a difference.

# PART I

# A LEGEND TAKES OFF

The Southwest
Spirit Is Born

CHAPTER 2

# GOLIATH MEETS DAVID

## THE BATTLE TO GET OFF THE GROUND

The history of Southwest Airlines is a story of courage and perseverance. It is the tale of a group of pioneers who beat incredible odds to realize their vision. No carrier in the history of the U.S. airline industry has survived quite the dramatic struggle that Southwest went through to get off the ground. The company's character is rooted in its legendary beginnings; in fact, it is virtually impossible to understand the people, the culture, and the inner workings of Southwest Airlines without first understanding its past. The spirit and steadfastness that enabled the airline to survive in the early years is what makes Southwest such a remarkable company today.

### THE DREAM AND THE PIONEERS

Southwest Airlines was the brainchild of Rollin King, a San Antonio entrepreneur who owned a small commuter air service, and his banker, John Parker. Parker had complained to King that it was inconvenient and expensive to travel between Houston, Dallas, and San Antonio and suggested starting an intrastate airline.

In late 1966, King marched into Herb Kelleher's San Antonio law office with a feasibility study and the grandiose idea of starting a new airline using larger planes to serve these three major cities in Texas. Kelleher, a New Jersey native and graduate of New York University School of Law who had moved to San Antonio with his wife, Joan Negley, to continue his law practice, had done legal work for King's air service. While pitching his dream, King pointed out that the Golden Triangle of Texas was perfect for the kind of service he envisioned. Houston,

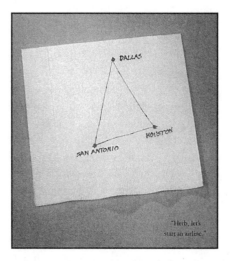

*Among the many wall hangings in Southwest's board-room is a beautiful wooden plaque inlaid with the famous symbol of Southwest's visionary beginning: a cocktail napkin with a sketch of the three-city route Rollin King proposed to Kelleher after talking to John Parker. Etched into the plaque are the words "Herb, let's start an airline" and "Rollin, you're crazy. Let's do it!"*

Dallas, and San Antonio were experiencing rapid economic and population growth. They were also far enough apart to make travel by bus or automobile inconvenient.

## "Herb, let's start an airline." "Rollin, you're crazy. Let's do it!"

Kelleher initially thought the idea was crazy, but he was intrigued enough to discuss it with King over cocktails at San Antonio's St. Anthony Club. King had studied another intrastate carrier, Pacific Southwest Airlines (PSA) in California. It was the perfect model. PSA was a successful intrastate airline operating in a state much like Texas—commercially booming, with cities far enough apart to make air travel an attractive alternative to cars and buses. He had also talked with and involved the founders of another intrastate airline, Air California. The success of these two carriers made it seem likely that King's idea could work.

On March 15, 1967, Kelleher filed the papers to incorporate Air Southwest Co. (later Southwest Airlines Co.). King, with a contribution from Kelleher, raised the initial seed capital and made most of the presentations as he, Kelleher, Alfred Negley (Kelleher's brother-in-law), and San Antonio lawyer, businessman, and politician John Peace set out to raise the necessary second-tier capital, and political support, for the new venture.

Kelleher suspected that this new venture would lead to a highly charged political and legal battle with other airlines operating in Texas, so he and King doubled the amount they thought they needed from their second private offering. Kelleher says, "We initially figured we needed around $250,000, but we doubled it because I was aware there was going to be a fight and it was going to be a prolonged fight. But it turned out to be a much longer vendetta than I had anticipated." King, Kelleher, Negley, and Peace knew not only that they would have to raise a lot of money, but also that they would have to raise it from some of the most influential political and business leaders in Texas, people whose names would lend credibility to their endeavor. In the second round of financing, the four entrepreneurs raised $543,000.

On November 27, 1967, Kelleher filed Southwest's application to fly between Dallas, Houston, and San Antonio with the Texas Aeronautics Commission (TAC). On February 20, 1968, the TAC approved Southwest's application to fly between the three cities. In doing so, it unwittingly started a war that would last more than three years, severely test Herb Kelleher's litigation skills, and almost drive Southwest Airlines out of business before it put a plane in the air.

## FIGHTING TO FLY

The day after the TAC voted unanimously to approve Southwest's application, Braniff, Trans Texas (later Texas International, TI), and Continental aimed their first blow at the little upstart—a temporary restraining order that prohibited the TAC from issuing Southwest a certificate to fly. In the summer of 1968 the case went to trial in state district court in Austin.

From the beginning, the odds were stacked against Southwest. In addition to the legal proceedings, there was also a behind-the-scenes political contest going on. "Before we went to hearing," Kelleher recalls, "the director of the commission, Charles Murphy, told the newspapers that he really couldn't see any need for a new carrier in Texas."

The trial was a volcanic proceeding characterized by uncontrolled tempers and emotional outbursts. Braniff, Continental, and Texas International argued that the markets Southwest wanted to serve were already saturated, that there was no room for another carrier. The litigation was so bitter that at one point the *Texas Transportation Report* told its readers to save their entertainment money: the best show in town was watching Herb Kelleher and the lawyers for the other carriers cut each other to bits every day in the courtroom. The trial wouldn't cost them anything to get into, and it was better than any movie they would ever see. The entertainment was also comical at times. Kelleher remembers: "Braniff's lawyer had Ned Heizer from Allstate Insurance [then Southwest's prime potential investor] on the witness stand and asked him to speak louder. Ned told him that it wasn't possible because he was choking from the collar of a shirt, borrowed from Rollin King, that was too small. When he explained that Braniff had lost his luggage, the courtroom was aroar with laughter."

## *"Gentlemen, let's go one more round with them."*

The trial court ruled that Dallas, Houston, and San Antonio were adequately served by the existing carriers and that the cities Southwest proposed to enter could not support a new carrier.

It took seven months for Southwest's appeal to make it to the state court of civil appeals. In a two-to-one decision against Southwest, the intermediate appellate court upheld the trial court's ruling. The members of Southwest's board of directors were growing tired and frustrated. The original investors' $543,000 had been eaten up in legal expenses, the corporation's liabilities grossly exceeded its assets, and there was no prospect of raising new capital without the TAC certificate in hand. Several directors felt that the economic and political strength of the major carriers was insurmountable.

While the board generally agreed that King and Parker's idea was a good one, some members thought it would be wise to cut their losses. At this point, Kelleher's street-fighting spirit surfaced. "Gentlemen, let's go one more round with them," he remembers saying to the directors at a board meeting in 1969. "I will continue to represent the company in court, and I'll postpone any legal fees and pay every cent of the court costs out of my own pocket." After much debate, the directors agreed to bet on Kelleher and give it one more shot.

Kelleher argued Southwest's case before the Texas Supreme Court, which overturned the lower appellate court's decision. Southwest would get its certificate to fly.

But the fight wasn't over. Braniff, Texas International, and Continental appealed to the U.S. Supreme Court. In late 1970, the Court refused to hear the appeal. Southwest had won a major victory, but over the next several years it would face repeated lawsuits—some again going all the way to the U.S. Supreme Court.

## ENTER THE FLAMBOYANT AND
## COLORFUL LAMAR MUSE

Four years after its incorporation in 1967, Southwest was finally ready to fly. Now the company needed someone who could organize and run the operation. Enter the bold and brazen Lamar Muse. Muse had worked for Trans Texas, Southern, Central, and Universal Airlines; he was the industry veteran King and Kelleher had been looking for. He

*"Lamar was exactly what we needed. He was tough and he was iconoclastic in his thinking."*

loved the airline business, he knew it well, and he had the kind of tough, entrepreneurial character that could stand up to the pressures of starting an airline. Recently retired from Universal Airlines at age fifty, Muse was aggressive, self-confident, and restless—and not one to shy away from a good fight. Becoming the chief executive officer of an upstart airline competing fiercely with the big carriers was the kind of challenge that excited him. In January of 1971, Muse came to work for Southwest Airlines as CEO. "The directors hired Lamar and he was just perfect for getting it started," Kelleher remembers. "He was exactly what we needed. He was tough and he was iconoclastic in his thinking."

Muse joined a company that had $142 in the bank and $80,000 in overdue bills. "It was like we had to start over financially," says Colleen Barrett, then Kelleher's legal secretary and now Southwest's executive vice president of customers and corporate secretary. "Originally, we had money and no certificate. Then we had a certificate and no money."

Muse wasted no time. He started raising money, buying airplanes, and hiring the right people. Figuring he needed to raise well over $7 million to buy equipment and get through the first year, Muse called on his own circle of friends and contacts in the airline business. The $300,000 he raised out of this network (including the $50,000 he put in himself) wasn't nearly enough to prepare Southwest for operation, however.

Then Muse went to Houston to see Wesley West, an old business acquaintance who came from one of the most colorful families in Texas. (West's brother, "Silver Dollar" Jim West, was known for driving through the streets of Houston with bags full of silver dollars and throwing them out to people on the sidewalks.) In pitching the Southwest deal, Muse explained to West that Braniff and Texas International had filed complaints with the Civil Aeronautics Board (CAB) suggesting that Southwest might start flying interstate passengers and thus violate its status as an intrastate carrier. Kelleher says, "Lamar tried to explain to Mr. West that if the CAB didn't rule in our favor, we wouldn't have any right to do business at all." "West said, 'Mabel, bring my checkbook in here,'" Barrett recalls Muse telling her, "and Wesley wrote out a check, on the spot, for $750,000."

With some new financing secured, Muse set out to buy airplanes. He negotiated a deal for three brand-new 737-200s that Boeing hadn't been able to sell because of overproduction during the airline slump in the early '70s. Boeing offered to sell the planes for $4 million each (comparable new aircraft would have cost $5 million apiece at that time) and finance 90 percent of the deal.

## THE OVER-THE-HILL GANG

One of Muse's greatest contributions to Southwest Airlines was hiring the right officers. The recession of the early '70s had put some very talented people out of work; other industry veterans were seeking a change. With King's assistance, Muse assembled a senior staff that included some of the most seasoned pros the industry had to offer.

First on the list was Dick Elliott, a particularly imaginative marketing guru who had worked with Muse at other airlines. He became Southwest's first marketing vice president. Next, Muse hired Jack Vidal, who came from Braniff to be vice president of maintenance and engineering. Vidal, who had served nineteen years at Hawaiian Airlines, developed many of Southwest's trademark safety and maintenance procedures.

To make sure Southwest would have no trouble complying with FAA regulations, Muse brought in Donald G. Ogden, a highly respected pilot and flight operations executive. Ogden had worked in the business since 1936, most recently as chief of standards at American Airlines. The FAA's rule against pilots over age sixty flying commercial jets had forced him to retire. Ogden set up Southwest's original flight procedures. His cockpit procedures were easily approved by the FAA and became the envy of the industry. Besides King, who served initially as executive v.p. of operations, the final member of Muse's original management team was Bill Franklin, another airline veteran who had spent twenty-two years at Trans Texas before going to Frontier Airlines in Denver. As Southwest's first vice president of ground operations, Franklin established some of the industry's most revolutionary procedures for maximizing aircraft utilization. Southwest still follows the fundamental procedures he and Don Ogden created. It was Franklin who coined the affectionate nickname for the original group: "The Over-the-Hill Gang."

## GOLIATH STRIKES AGAIN

While Muse was putting his management team together, Braniff and Texas International kept Southwest grounded. The two carriers filed complaints with the CAB to protest Southwest's start-up, and Braniff also put pressure on some of Southwest's underwriters to withdraw from Southwest's initial public stock offering. Through an acquaintance of King's, however, Muse managed to find another brokerage firm to take a large share, and Southwest's first public stock was sold on June 8, 1971.

Two days before Southwest's inaugural flight, Kelleher received word that the CAB had thrown out the Braniff and Texas International complaints. He also learned that the two carriers had launched yet another attack to keep Southwest grounded; they had secured a restraining order enjoining Southwest from initiating service. Muse and Kelleher knew that Southwest's stock trading would be suspended if its flights were canceled, so Kelleher flew to Austin and headed straight to the Supreme Court Building to ask Judge Thomas Reavley, who had written a 1970 opinion in favor of Southwest, to throw out the restraining order. Worn out from the long hours of the past few weeks, Kelleher looked as if he hadn't been to bed or changed clothes for a couple of days when he arrived at Reavley's office. Kelleher remembers: "When I told Judge Reavley what was happening he said, 'There's going to be a reception this evening. All the justices will be there. I'll ask them to be here at ten o'clock tomorrow morning, and, Herb, you've got to figure out what you're going to do.' I guess Judge Reavley felt real sorry for me because I looked so dilapidated."

> *Just as the CAB threw out Braniff's and TI's complaints, they launched another attack to keep Southwest grounded.*

Kelleher went straight to the law library in the nearby attorney general's office and worked all night to decide how to proceed and to prepare the necessary papers. Absent a formal appeal, an appellate court ordinarily won't order a trial court to dissolve an injunction, so Kelleher had to come up with an extraordinary rationale. He decided on a writ of mandamus. "I think it had been done once before in the history of Texas," he quips.

Kelleher finally found a precedent and presented his argument to the court the next morning. The Texas Supreme Court ruled in Southwest's favor and ordered the lower court judge not to enforce the injunction. Kelleher telephoned Muse and told him to put the planes in the air. When Muse confided that he was still concerned about the sheriff showing up to enforce the injunction, Kelleher didn't mince any words: "I told Lamar, you roll right over the son of a bitch and leave our tire tracks on his uniform if you have to." The very next day, June 18, 1971, Southwest Airlines was finally off the ground.

## A BOLD AND BRILLIANT MOVE

Through private investors and the public stock offering, Muse had managed to put $7 million in the till, but Southwest was bleeding money. Passenger loads were inconsistent; on some days Southwest would carry as few as 150 passengers total on its eighteen daily round-trip flights among the three cities. At one point Kelleher got a phone call from his sister-in-law, who raved about the magnificent service she had received on a Southwest flight. When Kelleher asked how many people were on the flight, she told him there were two pilots, three flight attendants, and herself. Kelleher knew Southwest had to find a way to begin turning a profit.

One of the biggest breakthroughs came when Southwest began service to Houston's Hobby Airport. All of the major carriers had vacated Hobby in 1969 and moved to the new, outlying Intercontinental Airport. Hobby was close to downtown and perfectly suited to Southwest's shorthaul, frequent-flying business passengers, but no one knew whether people would use an airport served by only one carrier. Southwest was failing miserably at Intercontinental, so it gambled and began service from Dallas to the barren Houston Hobby

*Southwest finally takes off on June 18, 1971, with six roundtrips between Dallas and San Antonio and twelve between Dallas and Houston Intercontinental.*

on November 14, 1971. The results were spectacular. Almost overnight the passenger load factor doubled, and Southwest quickly moved all its Houston service from Intercontinental to Hobby.

Braniff and Texas International matched Southwest's bet by transferring some of their Houston service back to Hobby. Having just slugged it out with these giants in the courtroom, Southwest would now go head-to-head with them on the marketing and customer service fronts. Braniff came back to Hobby with an aggressive campaign advertising fares as low as Southwest's. Southwest countered by reminding fliers that the other two carriers would never have reduced their fares if Southwest hadn't come to Hobby with its low fares first. Braniff's plan backfired. Houstonians flocked to Southwest because it gave them more than just low fares: its planes were on time and there were no slow lines at the ticket counter. Southwest emerged triumphant. By the mid-'70s, Braniff and Texas International had thrown in the towel and discontinued service to Houston Hobby.

## NO LOVE LOST

Brilliant marketing and better service enabled Southwest to turn the corner on profitability in March 1973. But while the company worked hard to maintain its competitive edge in the Dallas, Houston, and San Antonio markets, another battle was looming, one that would again take Southwest Airlines all the way to the U.S. Supreme Court.

As construction of the new Dallas–Fort Worth Regional Airport (DFW) neared completion, Southwest Airlines notified the DFW Board that it would not transfer its air service to the new airport—that it would remain at Love Field. A 1968 bond ordinance required the airlines serving DFW to help fund the new facility through landing fees and space rentals. It also made them responsible for any losses incurred by the airport. Love Field is only ten minutes from downtown Dallas and ideal for shorthaul passengers who need easy access to the city. Transferring its service to an airport that was thirty minutes from downtown didn't make sense for an airline that catered to business travelers who wanted to get into and out of the city quickly. Southwest's position was that it was not required to move because it had not agreed to do so nor had it been ordered by the Texas Aeronautics Commission to move. DFW, Dallas, and Fort Worth officials, counting on the airlines to pay off the enormous bonds for the new facility, became livid when they learned that Southwest had no intention of leaving Love Field, but Southwest stood its ground. The DFW airlines, still smarting from Southwest's move from Houston Intercontinental to Hobby Airport, were also outraged at the airline's refusal to join them at the new regional airport. A joint suit was filed against Southwest Airlines on June 6, 1972, by the cities of Dallas and Fort Worth and the Regional Airport Board.

Kelleher enlisted Jack Hauer, an outstanding Dallas trial lawyer, to join a small team of lawyers who would try Southwest's case. The hearings began on March 26, 1973, in Judge William Taylor's federal district court. After thirty-two days, Judge Taylor ruled that Southwest Airlines could stay at Love Field. Fourteen months later, the case was heard on appeal in the U.S. Fifth Circuit Court of Appeals in New Orleans. The lower court's decision was upheld. Finally, Southwest's opponents took the case to the U.S. Supreme Court, where it was denied a hearing.

On February 14, 1975, Braniff and Texas International were indicted by the U.S. government for conspiring to put Southwest out

*In the thick of the fight to remain at Love Field in 1973.* **Left to right:** *Lamar Muse, Rollin King, Colleen Barrett, Herb Kelleher, Dallas attorney Jack Hauer*

of business. In a sixteen-page bill of particulars accusing the two car-riers of violating the Sherman Antitrust Act, a federal grand jury alleged that they had chased Southwest's investment bankers out of its underwriting syndicate, boycotted Southwest's vendors, kept South-west from using the fuel hydrant system at Houston's Intercontinental Airport, and blackballed it from membership in the airline credit card system. Both Braniff and Texas International pleaded "no contest" and were forced to pay $100,000 in fines.

In 1977 the five-year legal fight for Love Field seemed over. During thirty-one judicial and administrative proceedings, Southwest had been dragged through every level of court and administrative agency in the country. With its opponents legally out of the way, the young airline thought it could finally shift its attention from the courtroom entirely to the runway.

## THE "WRIGHT" STORY

Unfortunately, the specter of opposition to Southwest and its service from Love Field would soon reappear. Southwest was only an intra-state (Texas) carrier when the federal Airline Deregulation Act was passed in 1978. The company quickly took advantage of the interstate freedom afforded by deregulation by applying for and receiv-ing authorization from the CAB to fly between Houston and New Orleans—Southwest's first interstate route. But when Southwest applied for authorization to fly from Dallas to New Orleans, DFW supporters opposed the application vehemently. Among the opposi-tion was the powerful majority leader of the U.S. House of Represen-tatives, Fort Worth congressman Jim Wright.

Although Wright testified against Southwest's application, the CAB gave Southwest the go-ahead, and Dallas–New Orleans service began in September 1979. But Wright was not about to give up. He went straight to the floor of the House and in one day persuaded the House to ban all interstate air service into and out of Love Field. Kelleher and Colleen Barrett haunted the Senate Office Buildings and, with the able advice, help, and guidance of J. D. Williams, one of Washington's foremost lobbyists, managed to garner support for Southwest from some influential senators. Jim Wright fought back, though. Only after months of intense lobbying did Wright finally agree to changes in the original legislation.

Under the terms of the Wright Amendment of 1979—the so-called Love Field Compromise—no airline may provide nonstop or through-plane service out of Love Field to any city in any state beyond the four states immediately bordering Texas: Louisiana, Arkansas, Oklahoma, and New Mexico. The amendment means that Southwest cannot advertise, publish schedules, check baggage, or publish through fares with respect to travel from Dallas Love Field to any city it serves outside Texas and the four bordering states.

*"The Wright Amendment is an unjustified pain in the neck, but not every legislative pain in the neck amounts to a constitutional infringement."*

Instead of letting the Wright Amendment debilitate the company, Southwest has turned an obstacle into an opportunity. One of its first tactical responses was to originate many of its flights from Houston's Hobby Airport, El Paso, Albuquerque, Las Vegas, and Phoenix's Sky Harbor International Airport—all of which are unaffected by the Wright Amendment and permit flights to any destination. Via these cities, Southwest linked up service to all of its cities beyond the bordering states.

Kelleher's stance today on the Wright Amendment is "passionately neutral," he says. "The Wright Amendment is an unjustified pain in the neck, but not every legislative pain in the neck amounts to a constitutional infringement."

## TURNING THINGS INTO A CAUSE

Colleen Barrett believes that the seemingly insurmountable obstacles thrown at Southwest by Braniff, Texas International, and Continental and then by the DFW airport officials, supporters, and carriers are what created Kelleher's passionate love for the airline. "They would put twelve to fifteen lawyers on a case and on our side there was Herb," she recalls. "They almost wore him down to the ground. But the more arrogant they were, the more determined Herb got that this airline was going to go into the air—and stay there!"

Herb Kelleher is a master at turning things into a cause. Anyone who knows Southwest Airlines well understands that its survival is *the* cause Kelleher has been fighting for since 1971. Everything about Southwest's struggle to get off the ground challenged his beliefs about what America stands for. "It was an affront to my idealism," he says. "If you're going to let these guys get away with this, it's a radically different type of country from the one I wanted to believe in. The system gave them their opportunity to attack us and the system was very slow in rectifying it. But never forget that the system did rectify it."

The legal battles Southwest fought in the early years also created the esprit de corps for which the airline is so well known. The indomitable spirit of courage and perseverance that Kelleher displayed in the courtroom and Muse displayed during early operations was contagious. Waking up every morning to discouraging stories in the *Dallas Morning News* and the *Dallas Times Herald*, Southwest employees knew they were fighting for their survival. The battle over Love Field was a life-and-death situation for Southwest: had it been forced to move to DFW, it would have gone bankrupt. Southwest employees knew it, the cities of Dallas and Fort Worth knew it, and the other airlines knew it. As they watched the legal drama unfold and read the newspaper accounts, all two hundred employees were caught up in the cause. "The warrior mentality, the very fight to survive," Barrett says, "is truly what created our culture."

**CHAPTER 3**

# THE BATTLE HEATS UP

## INNOVATIONS FORGED IN THE FIRES OF COMPETITION

Starting with its early survival strategies, Southwest has always been known as a maverick and an innovator in the U.S. airline industry. The company's creative roots go back to the early days, when employees came up with clever ideas for keeping the business alive because Southwest had no choice but to become inventive in order to compete with the established carriers. The company simply didn't have the money to go head-to-head with the majors—particularly those that were absolutely committed to its demise. To survive, Southwest would have to outthink and outmaneuver Braniff, Texas International, and Continental not only in the courtrooms, but also in the air, on the tarmac, and in the customer service arena.

### *THE* LOW FARE AIRLINE

Before Southwest capitalized on the idea of offering permanent low fares, the U.S. airline industry as a whole charged the uniformly high fares approved by the CAB. The airlines operated as though there were only two market segments: those who could afford to fly and those who couldn't. This assumption guided the operating strategy of the major carriers, which reasoned that, given their costs, permanently reduced fares would only cut revenues. When problems arose or costs went up, they would simply raise fares. Southwest, however, believing that it could stimulate a tremendous amount of new travel with low fares and superior service, challenged this assumption from day one.

In 1973, when Muse began thinking about expanding the now-profitable little airline, the question was where to expand. Muse thought it was possible to serve some of Texas's smaller cities profitably. Setting its sights on the Rio Grande Valley, Southwest filed an application with the Texas Aeronautics Commission to fly into Harlingen.

Southwest knew it would have to prove to the TAC that the Rio Grande Valley needed additional service. King, Kelleher, Muse, and Gary Barron, now executive vice president of operations but then the newest member of Southwest's legal team, launched a campaign to garner local support. At the TAC hearings in early 1974, TI vehemently argued that the Valley was adequately served and there was no room for another carrier. It took nearly a year, but the TAC ruled in Southwest's favor, granting it permission to fly into the Rio Grande Valley via the Harlingen Airport. Within two weeks, TI sought an interim restraining order and moved to have the TAC's decision reversed. By this time, however, TI was absorbed by a bitter strike

*From day one, Southwest challenged the assumption that permanently reduced fares would cut revenue.*

that had grounded its air service to the Valley. Southwest quickly gathered additional support from unhappy Valley passengers, who were also grounded. TI didn't get its restraining order, and while the proceedings dragged on for almost two years, Southwest kept flying into Harlingen.

Muse was right about serving the Valley. In 1974, the year before Southwest initiated service, 123,000 passengers flew between the Valley and Houston–Dallas–San Antonio. By the end of 1975, just eleven months after Southwest started flying into Harlingen, the market had expanded to 325,000. Why the dramatic increase? One reason was that Southwest's consistently low fares enabled more people to fly.

The Rio Grande Valley case eventually became another legal victory for Southwest Airlines. More importantly, the Valley experience was a signal that people in smaller cities would support Southwest's low-fare, high-volume type of service. As Gary Barron says, "It opened the door for us to go into other cities such as Midland-Odessa, Austin, El Paso, Lubbock, and Corpus Christi." By 1977, Southwest had begun serving these five airports. The outcome of the battle for the Rio Grande Valley proved to Southwest that its operating strategy of low fares and prompt, efficient service was the right foundation upon which to build a successful airline. This is why Southwest is not bashful about reminding customers that it is *The* Low Fare Airline.

## A GAME OF HIGH–LOW

Southwest Airlines perfected systemwide two-tier—peak and off-peak—airline pricing, a pricing structure that eventually reshaped the industry. It fundamentally changed the economics of passenger flight. To do this, Southwest applied the concept of price elasticity to the economics of passenger flight, further cutting fares on off-peak flights to fill more seats and thus achieving higher revenue than with fewer seats sold at a higher price. Like many of its innovations, Southwest's two-tier fare system was not the outcome of a sophisticated, long-range planning retreat; it was the result of good, old-fashioned trial and error.

Just five months into operation, in late November 1971, one of the 737s Southwest had in Houston was needed in Dallas for routine maintenance over the weekend. Rather than have a crew just ferry the empty plane to Dallas, Muse came up with the idea of offering passengers a seat on the Friday-night flight from Houston to Dallas for $10. With 112 seats on the plane at $10 a seat, Muse figured he could at least break even. Even if only a few seats were sold whenever a plane had to go to Dallas for maintenance, generating some revenue to offset the cost of ferrying an empty plane was better than nothing. Passengers quickly caught on. With absolutely no advertising, Southwest was turning people away only two weeks into the offer.

Southwest had started off by charging $20 to fly between the three Golden Triangle city pairs, undercutting the $28 and $27 fares charged by the other carriers. This lower fare had expanded the markets—but not enough to make Southwest profitable. Then it occurred to Muse that there were really two types of travelers that an airline had to satisfy if it were to cover the entire market spectrum: the convenience-oriented business traveler, who was more time- than price-sensitive and wanted lots of business-hours flights, and the price-sensitive leisure traveler, who primarily wanted lower fares and had more flexibility about when to fly. Based upon his success in filling the ferry flights for $10, Muse devised the Executive and Pleasure Class systemwide two-tier fare structure, in which *all* seats on Executive Class flights, departing on weekdays until 7:00 P.M., were sold for $26 (a 30 percent increase over Southwest's original $20 fare), and *all* seats on Pleasure Class flights, departing after 7:00 P.M. on weekdays and all day Saturday and Sunday, were sold for $13 (a 35 percent reduction from Southwest's original $20 fare). Passenger traffic skyrocketed. In effect, Southwest had first defined a special market niche, consisting of shorthaul passengers, and then further segmented those shorthaul passengers, by need, into time-sensitive business travelers and dollar-sensitive leisure travelers. In looking for a way to fill an empty ferry flight, Southwest, through improvisation, had given birth to what would become one of the most widely emulated marketing innovations in airline history—systemwide peak and off-peak pricing.

## THE $13 FARE WAR

In an attempt to improve low load factors between San Antonio and Dallas, on January 22, 1973, Southwest cut its fare in half, to $13, with no restrictions—any seat, any time, any day. On February 1, Braniff launched a counterattack by slashing in half its fare between Dallas and Houston. Full-page ads in the Dallas newspapers announced that Braniff passengers could fly from Dallas to Houston for just $13 to "get acquainted" with the airline.

Muse learned about Braniff's get-acquainted deal while reading his morning paper over breakfast. Since Braniff had been in the market for forty years, an angry Muse thought they needed a "get-acquainted" sale like Southwest needed another lawsuit. He was furious.

Braniff had struck what appeared to be a lethal blow. While Dallas-Houston was a relatively small part of Braniff's operations, it was Southwest's only moneymaker. Losing the Love-Hobby market

"NOBODY'S GOING TO SHOOT SOUTHWEST AIRLINES OUT OF THE SKY FOR A LOUSY $13."

President, Southwest Airlines

*Muse fires the return shot in the 1973 David-and-Goliath duel with Braniff. National media attention and grass-roots support in Texas helped Southwest post the first in its still-unbroken string of profitable years.*

to Braniff would mean the end for Southwest. With very low cash reserves, Muse knew that matching Braniff's fares would bankrupt Southwest. Muse also knew that Southwest was about to turn the corner on profitability. After all the company had been through, he wasn't about to give up.

Lawyers for Southwest's advertising firm, the Bloom Agency, nixed an ad Muse angrily wrote as a counterattack. The wording was somewhat brash, coarse, and perhaps lawsuit-provoking. Kelleher flew up from San Antonio to help rewrite the ad and tone it down.

What finally emerged is one of the most famous ads in Southwest's history.

"Nobody's going to shoot Southwest Airlines out of the sky for a lousy $13" read the headline of the two-page spread in the Dallas and Houston papers on the Monday following Braniff's announcement. The ad explained how Braniff was trying to put Southwest out of business, then went on to say that Southwest would not only match Braniff's fare, it would also offer every passenger a choice. Travelers could choose the $13 fare or buy a regular $26 ticket and receive a complimentary fifth of Chivas Regal scotch, Crown Royal Canadian whiskey, or Smirnoff vodka (or, for the nondrinkers, a leather ice bucket). Business travelers loved it: they could charge the $26 fare to their expense accounts and go home with a free bottle of liquor. It is said that for a two-month period Southwest was the largest distributor of Chivas, Crown Royal, and Smirnoff in the state of Texas!

Breaking the story as a David-and-Goliath duel in which the little airline didn't stand a chance, the media played a critical role in helping Southwest capture the hearts of people all over Texas. To Braniff's dismay, 76 percent of Southwest's passengers paid the $26 and took the gift before corporate controllers caught on to what was happening and insisted that employees traveling on their company's dime take advantage of the lower fare. After two months, as the promotion drew to a close, the number of passengers flying full fare had dropped to about 20 percent, but by then it didn't matter. The damage was done. Braniff's plan had backfired, and Southwest had, once again, outsmarted a more powerful competitor. Braniff terminated its Dallas–Houston Hobby Airport service in December 1975.

## THE TEN-MINUTE TURN

In September 1971, Muse bought a fourth 737 from Boeing to provide out-of-state charter service as well as to fly a stepped-up schedule on regular routes. The plane became a financial burden, however, when a federal district court ruled that Southwest could not fly charters outside Texas. Just eight months after acquiring the aircraft, Muse sold it to Frontier Airlines at a $500,000 profit. While the extra cash gave Southwest a little financial breathing room, the sale of the 737 created a big problem. How was Southwest going to maintain its new schedule with just three airplanes?

Bill Franklin, the man Muse had brought in to run ground operations, knew that Southwest could avoid cutting back its schedule if ground crews kept the three planes' en route stops to ten minutes or less. This meant that the total time at the terminal for each airplane—from the time it pulled into the gate, unloaded passengers, loaded up, and pushed back from the gate again—would be no more than ten minutes. Dennis Lardon, a station manager in 1973, remembers that Southwest was within a week of shutting down in San Antonio when Franklin came down and told him to do a ten-minute turn. Boeing, the FAA, Braniff—just about everybody in the airline industry—thought it couldn't be done, but when Lardon asked Franklin, "Can we turn a plane in ten minutes?" the answer was, "Of course we can!"

## *"Can we turn a plane in ten minutes?" "Of course we can. . . . Most of us had no idea that we couldn't do this, so we just did it."*

Franklin knew from his experience at Trans Texas, where DC-3s were regularly scheduled for fast turns, that a ten-minute turn on the 737 was possible. Franklin, like Muse, was a man of action, a no-nonsense, get-it-done type of guy. He decided it had to be done and directed the station managers to operate the four-airplane schedule with just three planes. Some of the original employees remember Franklin's going down to Houston and telling the station manager, "We're going to do ten-minute turns with this airplane. If you can't do a ten-minute turn, then you're going to get fired and we'll bring somebody else in. If he can't do a ten-minute turn, we'll fire him, too. And we'll just keep firing until we can find someone who can do it!"

"Most of us, not having an airline background, had no idea that we couldn't do this," says Lardon, "so we just did it." "And they did it because they knew our survival was at stake," Barrett adds. Former maintenance and engineering v.p. Jack Vidal told us, "The tough part was getting the fellows who had come from other major airlines to see that changing a tire, checking the oil, and getting the plane turned could happen in ten minutes. We'd get our fastest guys and show them. Ten minutes later the plane is going out, tires have been changed, oil checked, and off it goes—everything in order. And the guys say, 'Oh, it *can* be done.'" Franklin's mandate not only enabled

Southwest to maintain its regular schedule, it was also a key factor in helping the company achieve the best on-time performance in the industry. The ten-minute turn became Southwest's signature.

The legend of Muse's trial-and-error approach to marketing and his shoot-from-the-hip decisiveness has inspired more than two generations of employees to think creatively, to risk intelligently, and to come up with the kind of trend-setting innovations that can change the airline industry. "A combination of low fares, good service, an entirely different culture, and an exclusive on Love Field allowed Southwest Airlines, in the early days, to grow, accumulate capital, make money, and build an asset base," says Bob Crandall, chairman and CEO of American Airlines. "After having built the asset base, it became a substantial company and established a pattern of service with which they experimented and refined. . . . Part of the great strength they've had and the great wisdom of Herb is that they have consistently followed a pattern of keeping costs low in every place they've gone."

# CHAPTER 4

# A MAVERICK EMERGES

## THE CREATION OF A CORPORATE PERSONALITY

Southwest's original cast of characters offers a powerful introduction to the creation of its corporate personality. Like a lot of things about this nutty company, its personality didn't grow out of strategic decision making, but rather from serendipity. Southwest's corporate persona is a maverick personality that has determination, a flair for being positively outrageous, the courage to be different, the vulnerability to love, the creativity to be resourceful, and an esprit de corps that bonds people. These are the qualities that are cherished most by Southwest's spirited employees.

### NEVER GIVE UP

As Kelleher waged war in the courtroom, a team of approximately two hundred was waging a battle for survival in the daily operations of the airline. These original employees came to Southwest Airlines by many different paths, but one thing they all shared was a determination to make the upstart airline work. Their determination was the fuel that inspired the intense work ethic and esprit de corps that drive

Southwest today. At Southwest's 25th anniversary, thirty-six of those original employees are still around to tell it like it was.

These people *believed*. They took a risk and joined a company that had no track record. They bet their careers when the stakes were high; they gave their time when getting a paycheck wasn't guaranteed; they gambled their reputations when the media were doubtful. They were nutty, flashy, and very hip when the competition was conventional, businesslike, and very bland. These originals set the pace and the pattern of Southwest's way of doing business. They believed that if they just worked hard enough, that if Southwest Airlines were just different enough, that if they just cared enough, the company would pull through. Joy Bardo, senior administrative coordinator, believes that it was just a matter of love: "It was a dream that started for all of us. We were focused on trying to do the best job we could because we wanted to see the dream come alive." Karen Ordner, travel agency administrative coordinator, remembers Bill Franklin telling her to think like an owner. "We treated our job like it was our own business,"

*Southwest played its sexy, irreverent "Love Airline" image to the hilt, using the word "love" freely in its ads (up to eighteen times!), putting a red heart in its logo, and serving "Love Potions" and "Love Bites" in flight.*

Ordner says, "and when you have your own business, you work hard and you make sure that things are done right and customers are happy."

## BE OUTRAGEOUS BY ANY STANDARD

Southwest's outrageous personality partially resulted from desperation. During the first year of operation, when half of Southwest's $700,000 advertising budget was spent in the first month, word of mouth became the best and only affordable form of advertising. "For the talk value," says then secretary Sherry Phelps, "we decided that we needed to make our company absolutely outrageous."

The company realized early on that the more outrageous it was, the more people talked. In the three cities Southwest served it was, indeed, the talk of the town. With the help of the Bloom Agency, Southwest's original advertising firm, the company set out to define the airline as a woman—a witty, pert, with-it, startling woman. Southwest then projected that "person" into a "hard-hitting and spectacular campaign," says Kelleher. It was the "love" campaign that successfully defined the airline and gained critically needed free publicity. Its theme was "Now there's somebody else up there who loves you."

Imagine this scene: Three long-legged Raquel Welch look-alikes in hot pants and white, high-heeled go-go boots serving Bloody Marys with a smile to a predominantly male group of wide-eyed, wide-awake commuters on Southwest's 8:00 A.M. "Love Bird" flight from Dallas to Houston.

"The girls are our image," said Dick Elliott, Southwest's original vice president of marketing. Recruitment ads for Southwest's first group of hostesses read: "Attention, Raquel Welch: You can have a job if you measure up." (Keep in mind, the early '70s was a different world; what was outrageous but acceptable then may be shocking by today's standards.) More than two thousand applicants responded! Those who "measured up" were asked to come to their interviews in hot pants to show off their legs. The selection team consisted of Peggy Howze, Southwest's original manager of in-flight services and a former hostess supervisor with an international carrier; Janice Arnold, Southwest's original chief hostess, who had trained the bunny hostesses for Hugh Hefner's well-publicized Playboy jet; and Elliott.

*In 1971, Southwest's low fares and service were as outrageous as its uniforms.*

Each of the forty original hostesses was selected for her own special sparkle. "A cute girl without a great personality was not good enough," said Howze. To add to the sparkle, Southwest commissioned Lorch of Dallas, a chic design boutique, to create uniforms for its long-legged beauties. Braniff may have put its stewardesses in Pucci prints, but Southwest was the first airline to dress flight attendants in hot pants!

Howard Putnam, the former group vice president of marketing services at United Airlines who served as Southwest's president and CEO from July 1978 to September 1981, believes the uniform attracted a special kind of personality. He remembers speaking to a flight attendant graduation class: "We had about forty all lined up in their hot pants and boots and I said, 'How many of you were cheer-leaders, majorettes, or baton twirlers in high school or college?' Eighty percent raised their hands. The uniform attracted the right kind of person. They were extroverts who loved to get out there and perform. They're in the people business."

Outrageously outfitted but thoroughly trained and eager to fly, these women were commissioned to make the usual unusual. An ordinary business trip became a love affair. Aboard the *Love Bird*, drinks were Love Potions, peanuts were Love Bites, drink coupons were Love Stamps, and tickets came from Love Machines. In June 1971, the "Somebody Else Up There Loves You" airline began proudly promoting service within its Love Triangle.

## BE DIFFERENT

What the competition didn't take into consideration very early on is that Southwest had on its side the maverick wisdom of the group known on the inside as the Over-the-Hill Gang. They were the dream makers who would run Southwest Airlines. "In the beginning it took Lamar's guts, his entrepreneurial spirit, and his 'By gosh, we're going to do it' style just to keep us going," says Phelps. From the start, Lamar Muse and Rollin King not only had entrepreneurial spirit and style, they also knew how to stack the deck. Remember, they recruited some of the industry's most seasoned veterans. Those original vice presidents—Bill Franklin, Jack Vidal, and Don Ogden—had esteemed reputations and enormous industry experience. Franklin recruited Carl Warrell, one of Southwest's original station managers, from Texas International. Warrell was a well-connected industry insider in a good position at TI, but when he learned about Southwest's great management team, he decided to risk the move.

These industry veterans brought Southwest much more than reputation and experience; this team brought a spirit of innovation, the inspiration to think like mavericks. Their maverick approach to getting things done produced innovations that are industry benchmarks today.

"Even though they had all been in the airline industry for a long time," says King, "they were willing to adopt a critical philosophy. It was our one chance to do it right. Let's not be lulled into saying, 'This is the way all the other airlines do it, so let's do it this way.' To the contrary, we all understood that this was our opportunity to decide how to do it our way. Our philosophy was, and still is, we do whatever we have to do to get the job done." Scott Johnson, flight dispatch specialist, jokes about the way he responded to questions from flight crews during his first few years in dispatch: "No, I don't think there's a regulation against that. You're doing what?! No, I don't think that's illegal."

And how did Muse, Franklin, and the others play out this philosophy? "They allowed employees to do whatever it took to get the job done. They didn't stand over us with a whip and say, 'I want this done this way,'" says Dennis Lardon, who started as a ramp agent and is now the director of flight attendants. "We improvised and came up with some pretty good innovations back then." Says Karen Ordner, "Both Muse and Franklin were the type of people who looked you in the eye, and whatever they told you, you could take it to the bank."

## FOCUS ON PEOPLE

In the early days it was pretty routine for Rollin King and Lamar Muse to go over to the Flyboy or the old Cockpit Bar and drink beer with employees. Dan Johnson, aircraft dispatcher, describes the reaction of the competitors: "The Braniff pilots practically dropped their beers on the table. 'Holy cow, we haven't got a chance' was written all over their faces when they saw Lamar, Rollin, and a few other people routinely show up to drink beers with Southwest employees."

"Lamar and Rollin encouraged all of us to use our own personalities and to be ourselves on the airplane," says Deborah Franklin, an original flight attendant. "Lamar especially was always interested in what the customers were saying. After each flight he'd ask us what the customers said so we could offer better service for them."

King felt that one of his critical responsibilities was to get out among the troops. He did this by flying twenty-five to thirty hours a month. This gave him the chance to work with the employees, talk to the customers, and check out the stations. King set the standard for getting connected to the front-line people by making a day in the field a common occurrence at Southwest even in 1971.

## BE RESOURCEFUL

The beginning of the first year was tough. Resources were scarce and load factors were very low. Sherry Phelps remembers how rough it was: "We actually bought fuel for a couple of months using Lamar's personal credit card." The company didn't have a lot of ground equipment either, and what it did have was mostly old and dilapidated. Occasionally, employees found used or abandoned equipment to refurbish. "All of our maintenance was done at night," Jack Vidal, former vice president of maintenance, told us. "Of course, early on we didn't have all the parts we needed, so we'd have to scrounge around. Our people would get on the phone and call friends who worked at Braniff and they'd actually loan us parts." Given the fierce battle raging between Braniff and Southwest, Braniff mechanics were afraid of management's finding out that they were lending tools to the enemy—but they did it anyway. Perhaps they did it out of compassion or maybe because they never really considered Southwest a serious competitor.

Although by some standards ground equipment was less than satisfactory and the work environment was less than perfect, morale was high, people were enthusiastic, the work ethic was strong, and employees were willing to make do with what was available. "We had absolute honest communication with employees," King remembers. "We told them from the very outset that we were going to be in a fight for survival and that we really had to be better than everybody else, and they accepted it." Some people just appreciated having a job, while others enjoyed doing something new and innovative. Whatever their reasons, the majority simply believed that they could make it happen and set out to prove to the naysayers that Southwest Airlines was a force to be reckoned with.

"I couldn't understand when I first got there why we didn't have any complaints. Everyone was having a good time," says Howard Putnam. "The employment group worked with the mentality that we hire people who have fun. When I spoke to new employees I'd tell them, 'You've chosen Southwest Airlines and you're going to work harder than at any other airline. You're going to get paid about 30 percent less, but in the long run, when we make this thing work, with your profitsharing you'll be far ahead of anybody else.' And they are! It is one of the best examples of teamwork I've ever seen."

We've been telling corny jokes for 25 years, and so far no one has gotten up and left.

HAVING FUN IN FLIGHT HAS MADE US STAND OUT SINCE DAY ONE. AND NOBODY HAS PLAYED MORE GAMES OR SUNG MORE BOARDING PROCEDURES THAN OUR TEN ORIGINAL FLIGHT ATTENDANTS. TODAY, WE'D LIKE TO SAY THANKS FOR 25 YEARS OF ENTERTAINING CAPTIVE AUDIENCES.

[Left to right top: Brenda Gruslin, Sandra Bogan, Deborah Franklin, Deborah Stembridge, Mary Goins. Bottom: Linda Pinka, Jackie York, Mary Ann Sturdevant, C.J. Bostic, Sandra Force.]

*Ten of Southwest's original flight attendants are still on board for fun and games, but they've changed into khakis and Bermuda shorts.* **Left to right: (back row)** *Brenda Gruslin, Sandra Bogan, Deborah Franklin, Deborah Stembridge, Mary Goins; (front row) Linda Pinka, Jackie York, Mary Ann Sturdevant, C. J. Bostic, Sandra Force*

## BE WILLING AND ABLE

King believes that the original employees' can-do attitude was also a reaction to their previous jobs. A lot of them had been laid off by other airlines. A number of pilots, flight attendants, and mechanics had come from Purdue Airlines, which had just folded beneath them. Other pilots came out of the military, and Southwest was the only ticket to flying because no other carriers were hiring. Some of the flight attendants and mechanics were in airline jobs but anticipating layoffs. All of these people understood that losing a job is a harsh reality.

The ground operations people, for the most part, were not from other airlines, and they came equipped with a refreshing can-do attitude. Ground operations v.p. Bill Franklin had recently been laid off by another carrier, and he brought with him an infectious fighting spirit. "We just had to do it better," says King of the way Franklin and his crew approached their jobs. "The ten-minute turn came out of necessity. That's why pilots, flight attendants, agents, whoever was around, walked through the aircraft and folded seat belts, dumped trash, and picked up newspapers. We simply said, 'We are going to do it,' and, by gosh, we did it."

Dennis Lardon remembers two things that were never said back then: "One, we can't do it; two, it's not my job." Karson Druckamiller, one of the original maintenance crew members, believes that Southwest's singular advantage was in having so many people who didn't know what couldn't be done. "We cleaned aircraft, we changed oil, we changed tires. We did it because that's what it took back then. Some things we did because we didn't know it couldn't be done."

*Putnam got a big laugh out of Kelleher in the late '70s when someone asked, "What was the greatest thing you ever did for Southwest Airlines?" Putnam said, "I didn't implement anything I learned at United."*

"Lamar was ahead of his time," says Ray Phillips, lead line mechanic. "He knew what it was going to take for us to survive and make this airline even bigger than it was. He pushed us to think big and to work smarter." This early fight-for-survival mentality didn't just breed a can-do, inventive spirit; it also brought everyone very close.

## PROMOTE ESPRIT DE CORPS

When people work really hard for something they believe in, a special bond inevitably develops between them. This is what happened with the original employees. From the start, Southwest has always thought of itself as an airline of people who care about people; the original team at Southwest worked hard to uphold that standard. From the very beginning, Southwest was a family. Sandra Bogan, an original flight attendant, says, "You had this little airline that couldn't fly and everyone was working together to get it started—marketing, mechanics, operations people, in-flight. . . . We had this wonderful blend of people who cared." "We were always in the press," Linda Pinka, an original flight attendant, remembers, "constantly thrown into the limelight. We've all turned out to be the very best of friends." "Everybody knew everybody," says Dennis Lardon in remembering the way it was. "Through both the good and bad times in my life, I've always had the stability of Southwest Airlines," says Gene Van

Overschelde, an original pilot. "It's very important to me. It's something that's been very positive for me."

As the original employees of Southwest grew accustomed to doing battle, they learned to team up and enjoy a good fight. Today they seem as energized and closely connected as ever. The esprit de corps the original team felt is still apparent, even to outsiders. Sandra Force, an original flight attendant, says, "People from outside the company tell us all the time that they cannot believe what we have, compared with other companies. They can just see such a family and closeness that's not apparent in other large companies."

Even though it was a shaky trek, Southwest's tenacious mix of determined survivors turned ambitious goals into a highly spirited, innovative company with a very distinct personality. They didn't have many rules back then. In many cases, they were making up the rules as they went along. In many ways, they still are. "With that freedom," says Camille Keith, vice president of special marketing, "I think we'll always be doing something different and new." What evolved out of its litigious start is a maverick, moved by the esprit de corps that comes with the desire to win and the will to stand united against adversarial forces. It is a corporate personality that is tenacious, creative, and very resourceful.

Because of the corporate spirit that developed so many years ago, at Southwest the conventional always plays out as unconventional. There is no doubt that Southwest has stuck with some very basic business practices, but always with an unconventional twist. In part II you'll learn about how Southwest goes nuts in following such basic business principles as staying focused on its fundamental strategy, hiring the right people, and many others. In part III you'll learn how some quite unconventional business practices have become basic ingredients of Southwest's corporate culture. To the people of Southwest Airlines, love, fun, and celebration, for example, are all a part of a typical day at work. In part IV, leadership is described as the catalyst that makes Southwest's special ingredients for success click. We explore leadership as it plays out in the most successful airline in the United States. In the end you'll be challenged to try the unconventional and, perhaps, go nuts.

# PART II

# BASICS GONE NUTS

**Doing Business Basics
with a
Southwest Twist**

**CHAPTER 5**

# FLYING IN THE FACE OF CONFORMITY

## DARE TO BE DISCIPLINED, REAP THE REWARDS

Southwest Airlines' secret recipe for success is really no secret at all. In fact, the ingredient that has catapulted Southwest to the top of the industry is simple, elegant, and well publicized: *discipline.* Throughout its existence, Southwest has consistently adhered to a clearly defined purpose and a well-thought-out strategy for accomplishing it. As simple as it sounds, Southwest Airlines exists to make a profit, achieve job security for every employee, and make flying affordable for more people.

Early on, King, Kelleher, Muse, and others decided that the strategy for achieving their purpose would be to provide the best service and lowest fares to the shorthaul, frequent-flying, point-to-point, "noninterlining" traveler. After deregulation in 1978 Southwest was free to fly interstate routes. The question became "Would the company employ the same low-fare, shorthaul, point-to-point strategy?" Howard Putnam, then Southwest's president and CEO, enlisted Southwest's senior officers for a few days of strategic thinking. In a conference room at The University of Texas, Putnam told them, "We aren't going to leave this room until we can write up on the wall, in a

hundred words or less, what we are going to be when we grow up."
For two days the team focused on the future of Southwest Airlines.
The group decided that the company should stay focused on the fun-
damental strategy that got it off the ground in the beginning.

## No carrier knows its niche as well as Southwest.

"Most companies fail in their growth because they don't have a
vision," Putnam believes. "They don't know where to go. When you
have a vision and someone comes to you with some convoluted idea,
you can hold it up to the vision and ask, 'Does it fit? Does it fly? If
not, don't bother me.' A vision must be so strong that it can outweigh
the egos of managers that might want to take off in a different
direction."

Even at the height of its success, Southwest exercises the discipline not to stray from its strategy. It does not, for example, buy
jumbo jets, fly international routes, or go head-to-head with the
major carriers. While other carriers have been lured by the temptation to step outside their niche, Southwest Airlines has maintained the
discipline to stay focused on its fundamental reason for being.

### SAY NUTS TO MARKET SHARE

In serving its specific market niche, Southwest Airlines is obsessed
with keeping costs low to maximize profitability instead of being concerned with increasing market share. Kelleher believes that confusing
the two concepts has derailed many firms that were otherwise on track
in fulfilling their fundamental purpose. "Market share has nothing to
do with profitability," he says. "Market share says we just want to be
big; we don't care if we make money doing it. That's what misled
much of the airline industry for fifteen years, after deregulation. In
order to get an additional 5 percent of the market, some companies
increased their costs by 25 percent. That's really incongruous if
profitability is your purpose."

Southwest is successful because it is willing to forgo revenue-
generating opportunities in markets that would disproportionately
increase its costs. By focusing on profitability instead of market share,
the company has demonstrated the discipline to do without market

segments that don't fit within its niche. And no carrier knows its niche as well as Southwest.

## FLY LOTS OF SHORT TRIPS

Southwest caters mainly to the shorthaul traveler who wants to choose from a wide range of flying times between two cities that are an average of four hundred miles, or an hour, apart. The company basically exists to serve the business traveler who wants, for example, to leave San Diego at 7:00 A.M. to attend a meeting in Phoenix or Las Vegas at 9:00 A.M. and be back in San Diego for another meeting at 1:00 P.M., or the parent who wants to leave work in Houston at 3:00 P.M. to catch a child's soccer game in San Antonio at 5:00 P.M.

The company has perfected the regimen of flying short trips— lots of them and often. When the company opened its Los Angeles–Phoenix market, it started with 40 daily flights. In the summer of 1994, when Continental and American both increased their daily trips to 15 in one of the busiest markets in the nation—

*Nobody opens a new city like Southwest—lots of flights and fares that are one-third to one-half lower than the going rate. Governmental affairs v.p. Ron Ricks does the honors in Louisville in 1993.*

Dallas-Houston—Southwest was already operating 38 southbound and 41 northbound flights between the same two cities. Southwest averages 10.5 daily flights using each gate, compared with the industry average of 5.0. With this many flights, ground crews are not idle; Southwest maximizes the productivity of its people.

## GET TO THE POINT

After deregulation in 1978, most airlines established hub-and-spoke systems. The idea behind hub-and-spoke is that a carrier flies short-haul passengers into a hub city from smaller outlying cities, then loads them onto one plane that takes them to their final longhaul destination. This means, for example, that if you want to go from Albuquerque or Austin to Washington, D.C., you will first have to go through the Dallas–Fort Worth regional airport. The hub-and-spoke system is an efficient way to fill an airplane, but it usually doesn't offer efficient aircraft utilization.

Airplanes generate revenue only when they are in the air. Simply put, the more flights you can make with each airplane in a day, the more revenue you will produce and the lower your unit costs per flight. The hub-and-spoke system augments costs because airplanes spend more time on the ground waiting for passengers to connect from "feeder" cities. Ground crews that move baggage, operate gates, provision the galleys, and refuel the planes become more expensive when they are idle because a plane is sitting on the ground too long.

*Southwest believes that customers don't want to go out of their way for the convenience of an airline that wants to fill planes.*

Southwest has a very different strategy. The company flies point-to-point between cities, thereby maximizing its use of aircraft. A typical Boeing 737 in the Southwest fleet is used 11.5 hours a day, compared with the average 8.6 hours a day of other carriers. These figures are especially dramatic when you consider that an average Southwest flight lasts just over an hour. The company understands that delays equal more ground time, and more ground time equals less efficient aircraft utilization. Southwest does not interline with other carriers, in part because it is simply unwilling to spend the extra time and money on the ground, waiting to board passengers from connecting flights that are often delayed. Southwest also believes that customers with a choice don't want to go out of their way and travel to a hub city for the convenience of an airline that wants to fill planes. Extra time in the air is just part of it. "Why should we ask a shorthaul customer to wait in a ticket line," Kelleher asks, "while the customer in front of him spends thirty minutes working out a complicated interline route and fare combination with the ticket agent?!"

Phil Condit, Boeing's president and CEO, uses the concept of "average velocity" to explain the difference between the point-to-point and hub-and-spoke systems:

> *In a manufacturing context, you put a part on a machine and machine it like crazy. When you really cut the metal off fast and then put the part on the shelf for a month, and do this repeatedly, the local velocity is very high. You're working on the part very hard when you're working on it, but the average velocity is very low because the parts sit there. In a lean manufacturing system, the key is to drive average velocity up, because you don't want parts sitting around.*
>
> *Let's think about airlines in the same way. What is it that I want as a passenger? I want high average velocity. . . . The fact that the airplane may go fast (local velocity) for the trip isn't nearly as important as achieving high average velocity.*
>
> *What do hubs do? Hubs lower the average velocity. As a passenger, I'm sitting there for an hour and a half, and it's a waste of my time. What do indirect, circuitous routings do? They lower the average velocity. Passengers want good average velocity, but if it's going to cost them three times as much to go straight, they'll go crooked.*

This is the reason Southwest's point-to-point strategy has been so effective: Customers know that when they fly Southwest they achieve high average velocity without paying through the nose.

## DON'T FOLLOW THE CROWDS

Southwest avoids congested airports where it's very difficult to land a plane and get it back into the air quickly. The company's view is: Why work incredibly hard to streamline your system so that you can turn a plane in fifteen minutes, only to sit waiting forty-five minutes on the taxiway for your turn to take off? It just doesn't make sense. Southwest learned this the hard way in Denver. When congestion at Stapleton Airport caused excessive delays across its entire system, the company decided to terminate service in the mile-high city.

The less congested airports Southwest prefers are often closer to downtown areas. The benefit to the customer, especially the business traveler, is less time sitting on an airplane and traveling to and from the airport. A person going to a business meeting in Dallas, for example, can get into and out of the city very quickly because Love Field is only ten minutes from downtown and rarely experiences air-traffic delays. In some cases, Southwest has played a major role in keeping secondary airports open—Love in Dallas, Hobby in Houston, and Midway in Chicago. While the facilities at these airports may not be as modern as at DFW, Houston Intercontinental, or Chicago O'Hare, the savings achieved through more efficient aircraft utilization produce lower operating costs and lower fares.

Although Southwest has been innovative and unconventional in serving smaller airports, where there is less congestion and less competition, it would be a mistake to think that the airline's success has been built solely on this strategy. In fact, some of Southwest's most successful markets are Los Angeles, San Diego, Phoenix, Las Vegas, Oakland, Nashville, and St. Louis, cities where Southwest serves the same airport as everyone else. When an alternative is available, Southwest chooses, then, to operate at airports that allow the most efficient use of its planes.

## OFFER THE LOWEST FARE—EVERY TIME

Southwest bills itself as *The* Low Fare Airline because all its fares are rock bottom. The company's pricing strategy is to keep fares consistently low regardless of what the market will bear.

The conventional wisdom of supply and demand would suggest that, when flights are full, prices should go up. However, throughout its history, Southwest has flown in the face of convention. Instead of raising fares when load factors are up, Southwest increases the number of flights and expands the market. On routes like Dallas-Houston, its discipline in keeping fares low has given the company 69 percent of the market. Once upon a time, when Braniff's coach price between Dallas and San Antonio was $62 and Southwest's fare was a mere $15, one of Southwest's shareholders approached Kelleher and asked, "Don't you think we could raise our prices just two or three dollars?" "You don't understand," said Kelleher. "We're not competing with other airlines, we're competing with ground transportation." In many cases, Southwest makes it more affordable, and certainly more convenient, to fly than to drive.

## DRIVE PRICES DOWN

From the start, Southwest has remained strategically focused on opening markets that are overpriced and underserved because the company is confident that it can bring fares down by one third to one half whenever it enters a new market. Remember, this is the company that didn't have a single fare increase between 1972 and 1978. When

*Southwest Airlines has been the principal driving force behind the steady decline of ticket prices since deregulation.*

the company entered Sacramento in 1991, its everyday unrestricted fare between Sacramento and Ontario was $118 roundtrip, compared with the competition's $440. Southwest entered the Columbus, Ohio–St. Louis market, where the typical roundtrip fare was $672, with its own unrestricted roundtrip fare of $98. When the company opened Cleveland, the unrestricted one-way fare between Cleveland and Chicago was $310 on other carriers; Southwest's was $59 one-way. "Our new customers can't believe these are our regular fares," Colleen Barrett says. "We have to explain that this isn't some introductory promotion."

Southwest's ability to drive prices down has prompted local governments and businesses all over the United States to ask the airline to begin serving their cities. Mitchell International Airport in Milwaukee went so far as to build, paint, and carpet a gate to exact Southwest specifications to entice the airline to begin service there. So far, Southwest hasn't made it into Milwaukee, but you can be assured that the company considers each request very carefully.

## DON'T DIVERSIFY

The clarity of Southwest's purpose and its discipline in maintaining a strategic focus have helped the company make some excellent multibillion-dollar decisions. For example, the mission and purpose of the airline directly influences the kind of equipment it buys. Southwest uses only one type of aircraft—the Boeing 737.

Flying one type of aircraft has a strong impact on the bottom line. First of all, training requirements are simplified. Pilots, flight attendants, mechanics, and provisioners concentrate their time and energy on knowing the 737—inside and out. Thus all Southwest pilots are qualified to fly, all flight attendants are qualified to serve in, all maintenance people are qualified to work on, and all provisioning crews are qualified to stock every plane in the fleet. This makes it easy for Southwest to substitute aircraft, reschedule flight crews, or transfer mechanics quickly and efficiently. With only one type of aircraft, the company can reduce its parts inventory and simplify its record-keeping, which also results in savings. Sticking with the 737 series also helps the company negotiate better deals when acquiring new planes. Southwest was the launch customer on Boeing's 737-300 and 737-500 models, and will be on the upcoming 737-700.

This has enabled the company to buy its fleet of these planes on launch-customer terms.

## KEEP IT SIMPLE

Southwest is anything but traditional. Its unconventional and non-conformist approach has helped the airline simplify its business and stay focused on adding value to the service it gives its customers.

Until 1989 Southwest issued cash-register receipts as tickets. Customers unfamiliar with Southwest's operations started complaining because they lost their tickets among other receipts, ran them through the wash, or inadvertently threw them away. In the meeting where executives were debating the issue, an obvious alternative—to go to a multimillion-dollar system that produced the traditional multilayered airline ticket—was proposed. Then, Gary Barron, executive vice president and chief operations officer, asked, "Why don't we just print THIS IS A TICKET in big, bold, red letters on the receipt?" Instead of spending $2 million to follow the rest of the industry, Southwest modified its ticket stock with the caption, and it worked.

Southwest has never subscribed to the computer reservations systems, owned by its competitors, in the same way as other major

## DEAR MR. KELLEHER

*Another real bonus from flying Southwest is the ease of travel arrangements. I can honestly say I have never used an airline "ticket" to fly your airline. Quite frankly, it wasn't until my sister used one of my free passes that I realized there was such a thing as a Southwest Airlines ticket. Whenever I make my travel reservations, it is so easy. And because my schedule often changes, so do my flight plans. But your people make the changes I need quickly and always with a smile and thanks.*

DUGALD K. WINTER
SAN ANTONIO, TEXAS

airlines. Travel agents wanting to book customers on a Southwest flight have to pick up the phone and call its internal reservation offices instead of having direct access through a computer. Not subscribing to a computer reservations system saves the company $2 for each segment booked. It may not sound like much, but this policy saves Southwest millions of dollars a year.

Southwest still serves no meals. With flights averaging approximately sixty minutes, there is little time for meal service. Instead, Southwest serves peanuts and other snacks and puts extra seats in the empty space that would otherwise be required for food galleys permitting meal service.

And how does the customer respond to this simplicity? If passenger boardings are any indication, people are willing to trade some of the amenities for low fares, on-time performance, better baggage handling, and Southwest's unique brand of Positively Outrageous Service.

## RUN, DON'T WALK

In the early days Southwest learned that it could turn its planes in ten minutes. It also learned that cutting ground time to ten minutes would reduce operating expenses by 25 percent. Even with the dramatic increase in the size of airplanes, the growth in carry-on luggage,

*"Our turnaround time isn't the result of tricks, but the result of our dedicated employees, who have the willpower and pride to do whatever it takes."*

the amount of cargo flying on each plane, and the congestion at many of the airports it serves, the average turnaround time for a Southwest plane is now twenty minutes—still about half the industry average—much faster than anyone else in the business. Two out of three Southwest planes are turned in twenty minutes or less.

Today, when a Southwest plane pulls into the gate, employees in ground operations run for the aircraft like a pit crew scrambling to get an Indy car back on the track. Although 84 percent of the work force is unionized, Southwest has negotiated labor contracts that allow flexibility in the operation of its system. For example, it's not unusual to see flight attendants and pilots working with the provisioning

# MINUTE BY MINUTE AT LAX

*Jim Wimberly, vice president of ground operations, sent us to one of the busiest airports in the Southwest system where ground crews face just about every hurdle there is in turning an airplane on time. With its well-known air-traffic problems, passenger and cargo delays from international flights, limited number of gates, and overcrowded facilities, Los Angeles International (LAX) offers a unique challenge to the people in ground operations. Station Manager Stan Cielak put us in the care of Va'a Mapu ("Boat" as he is affectionately called by his friends), and we ventured out to the tarmac to see how a fifteen-minute turn works.*

**2:45 P.M.**   Like a finely honed pit crew waiting for that Indy car to arrive, Rudy Guidi, Calvin Williams, Kirkland Howling, and Ricardo Pérez prepare to spring into action. Rudy and Calvin go over the bin sheet, which tells the team how much baggage, freight, and mail is on the aircraft, while the rest of the team makes sure the equipment is in position to turn the plane. The ground crew is joined by First Officer Ken Brown, who is there to do a preflight check on the aircraft.

**2:46 P.M.**   The aircraft is in sight, and Ricardo jumps up on the back of the tug to guide the plane into the jetway. Rudy and Calvin each start up a belt loader and begin to move toward the plane as it approaches the gate.

**2:47 P.M.**   The aircraft comes to a complete stop at the gate. The jetway is already moving toward the door of the aircraft. The baggage bins of the Boeing 737 fly open. A fueler pulls up to the aircraft while crew members off-load bags.

**2:48 P.M.**   Ken pauses for a moment from his preflight check to help Kirkland connect the pushback to the nose gear of the airplane.

Provisioning crew members race through the rear door of the aircraft to stock ice, drinks, and snacks and to empty trash. Passengers begin to deplane.

**2:49 P.M.** The freight coordinator pulls up in his tug to ensure freight labeled NFG (Next Flight Guaranteed) makes the next flight.

**2:50 P.M.** First officer completes his preflight check. Flight attendants move through the cabin of the aircraft to reposition seat belts and pick up trash.

**2:51 P.M.** All bags are off-loaded. Ramp agents begin loading bags for new passengers. Provisioning is complete. Current flight crew (pilots and flight attendants) is relieved by new flight crew. Operations agent makes initial announcement calling for preboarders. Several adults with children and a person on crutches make their way to the plane. Fueler is pulling the hose out of the wing of the aircraft.

**2:52 P.M.** Operations agent begins boarding customers in groups of thirty. Bags are loaded and fueling is complete. Most of the ground crew move to another gate to prepare for the arrival of the next aircraft.

**3:00 P.M.** Passenger boarding is complete; operations agent gives weight and balance sheet to pilot. Pilots trim the aircraft according to the load. Ramp agent connects the communication gear to talk to the pilots in the cockpit from the tarmac.

**3:01 P.M.** The jetway pulls back and the door of the aircraft closes. Pushback maneuvers the plane onto the tarmac and turns the plane toward the runway. Ramp agent unhooks the pushback from the aircraft and the plane taxies toward the runway.

*Here is what this ground crew of four accomplished in fifteen minutes: There was a complete change of flight crew; 137 customers came off the plane and another 137 boarded; the ramp agents unloaded 97 bags, 1,000 pounds of mail, and 25 pieces of freight weighing close to 500 pounds. The ramp agents then loaded another 123 bags and 600 pounds of mail (no freight), while the fueler pumped 4,500 pounds of jet fuel into the wing of the aircraft. It's an impressive spectacle. People come out of nowhere and the entire area around the plane is abuzz. Then, in a matter of minutes, their jobs complete, the swarm of people disappears and the plane pulls away.*

and ramp people to stock airplanes, pick up trash, and load bags. Employees have the flexibility and the willingness to step outside previously defined job categories and do whatever it takes to get a flight out on time.

The fifteen- and twenty-minute turns let Southwest use about thirty-five fewer aircraft than an airline with an industry-average turnaround time. With the cost of a new 737 at $28 million in 1995, it's not hard to figure out the savings: $1.3 billion in capital expenditures, which is, in turn, passed on to the customer in the form of lower fares and to the shareholder as profits.

Southwest's fifteen-minute turns are not magic; they are a highly coordinated effort from employees who practice open communication and teamwork every day.

## KNOW WHAT YOU DO BEST

Southwest Airlines has always resisted the temptation to be something it's not. Perhaps this is because the people of Southwest Airlines know that arrogance is the quicksand of success. Kelleher has said to us on many occasions, "A company is never more vulnerable to complacency than when it's at the height of its success." He began his 1993 letter to all employees by outlining the major threat to Southwest Airlines in the '90s: "The number one threat is us!" He went on to say: "We must not let success breed complacency; cockiness; greediness; laziness; indifference; preoccupation with nonessentials;

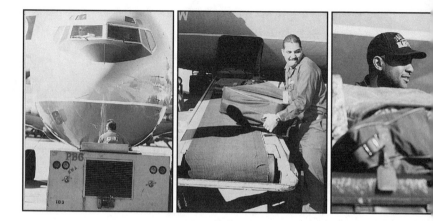

bureaucracy; hierarchy; quarrelsomeness; or obliviousness to threats posed by the outside world."

In exercising a discipline driven by humility, Southwest has never been known for getting too caught up in its own accomplishments or taking itself too seriously. It has successfully remained fixated on purpose and strategic intent. Southwest has had more opportunities for growth than it has airplanes. Yet, unlike other airlines, it has avoided the trap of growing beyond its means. Whether you are talking with an officer or a ramp agent, employees just don't seem to be enamored of the idea that bigger is better.

Looking at it on the surface, one could easily believe that Southwest Airlines is rather loose and frivolous. But a closer look reveals that the company is much more conservative than many realize. Through its disciplined approach to the business, Southwest has done a remarkable job of letting its niche define how it operates. "We don't care whether we fly to Paris. We don't care whether we have a 747," Kelleher says. "What we're focused on is being profitable and job secure. If people didn't pay much attention to Southwest Airlines because it appeared to be a much smaller regional carrier, it was just immaterial to us. We set ourselves up to go into a specific niche in the airline business."

While the company could have ventured beyond the boundaries of its fundamental purpose, it chose not to. Perhaps this is because Southwest has a sense of history; history shows that those who forget their purpose and step outside their niche have a tendency to fail.

## DEAR MR. KELLEHER

*As for "no frills," I'd much rather have reasonable fares and "Friends Fly Free" than such things as meals that are usually worse than prison food and not what the health conscious are eating these days. The sodas, water, and coffee are enough.*

ELIZABETH D. MONTOYA
LAGUNA HILLS, CALIFORNIA

People Express was set up to be a Southwest clone and became America's fastest-growing airline. Then the company began acquiring jumbo jets and competing with the major carriers on longhaul routes such as Newark-London. Pretty soon there was no more People Express. America West modeled itself after Southwest, too, but after yielding to the same temptation as People Express, it went into Chapter 11.

### THINK AHEAD AND BE FRUGAL

Southwest is also very conservative and disciplined with regard to resources. Kelleher's position has always been to manage in good times so that the company can do well in difficult times. He jokingly admits, "Our pilots have accused me of predicting eleven of the last three recessions." The approach has paid off. In the fourth quarter of 1990, when jet fuel prices went sky-high because of the Gulf War, Southwest managed to get by with the smallest loss ($4.5 million) of any major U.S. airline. More importantly, Southwest was the only U.S. airline to make a profit through the Gulf War and the 1990–1994 recession.

There is a flip side to staying purpose-driven and strategically focused. It kept Southwest from becoming a billion-dollar carrier for many years. Had the airline wanted to join the ranks of the "majors,"

it would only have had to raise fares. It took Southwest nearly three times as long to reach the $1 billion revenue mark as it did competitor America West.

John Denison, Southwest's executive v.p. for corporate services, is quick to point out that Southwest has never played by others' definitions of success. Southwest has defined its own targets. Growing market share and becoming a megacarrier have never been the company's priorities. Profitability has been the airline's major focus.

America West grew fast, to be sure, but overblown expansion plans caused it to go through a tremendous struggle before it emerged from bankruptcy in August 1994. Southwest, on the other hand, celebrated twenty-four years of uninterrupted profits at 1996 year-end. The company's discipline has paid off handsomely: Southwest has the strongest balance sheet and the highest credit rating in the industry.

## SUCCESS IN A NUTSHELL

➤ Live within your budget.

➤ Manage in good times for bad times.

➤ Define your own targets. Don't settle for conventional standards; create your own.

➤ Keep things simple. Streamline your systems and your life.

➤ Bigger isn't always better. Don't confuse market share with profitability.

➤ At the peak of success, look for things you can do even better.

➤ Be humble: success is hardly ever all your own doing and rarely irreversible.

**CHAPTER 6**

# "PROFESSIONALS" NEED NOT APPLY

## HIRE FOR ATTITUDE, TRAIN FOR SKILLS

When Kelleher became chairman in 1978, he charged the People Department with the responsibility of hiring people with a sense of humor. "I want flying to be a helluva lot of fun!" he always says. "Life is too short and too hard and too serious not to be humorous about it." Fun is taken very seriously at Southwest Airlines, and the company's recruiting and hiring practices are built on the idea that humor can help people thrive during change, remain creative under pressure, work more effectively, play more enthusiastically, and stay healthier in the process.

In a world where change is one of the true constants, most people are having to work smarter and harder and faster than ever before. As the pace and intensity of our work lives have picked up, it's no wonder we've lost touch with the lighter side of life and become very serious. Many organizations expect their employees to be serious and businesslike, to check their personal and emotional baggage at the door before coming into the office.

"Terminal professionalism" is the term coined by *Lighten Up* authors C. W. Metcalf and Roma Felible to describe the way today's overworked, overstressed, underpaid, and underplaying individuals work. Terminal professionals—and the organizations in which they work—have come to believe that humor is unprofessional and silliness is for children. Southwest Airlines believes that failure to nourish and encourage lightness in the workplace not only undermines productivity, creativity, adaptability, and morale, but also can drive people crazy. By putting humor at the top of its list of recruiting and hiring criteria, Southwest has found a way to nourish joy, pride, and just plain fun in people on and off the job. The company's healthy alternative to terminal professionalism has restored the faded dream of satisfying work and job security for thousands of people.

## A NEW KIND OF PROFESSIONALISM

At Southwest, "professional" and "businesslike" alone just won't cut it. In fact, these are terms Kelleher despises; he believes they have lost their meaning. "Anybody who likes to be called a 'professional' probably shouldn't be around Southwest Airlines," he says. "We want people who can do things well with laughter and grace." The point here is not to offend people who think of themselves as professionals. Southwest Airlines is bursting with professionalism, but it is a unique brand, practiced with flair. The type of professionalism people experience and express within the Southwest culture is not the stuffy, serious professionalism guarded by the philosophy that "the business of business is business." Instead, the professionals that customers encounter at Southwest are remarkably uninhibited and empathetic individuals who believe that the business of business is to make a profit by serving people and making life more fun.

An example of this new kind of professionalism is captured in a customer letter applauding a memorable flight and an entertaining announcement routine:

> *I flew in early May to Albuquerque, on a flight that began with the flight attendant welcoming us and then telling us that we had a VIP on board. He welcomed Leonard Nimoy, the actor who played Spock on "Star Trek." We all clapped and turned to see him—we were told this was all in fun. Instead, we were the VIPs on board! Then he graciously welcomed each of us to Southwest Airlines as the most important person. . . . He then treated us to*

*the most entertaining flight announcement routine, telling us we were flying over 7,943 hot tubs, swimming pools, etc., so here was the water evacuation information. Please wave to his mother on cue. He had a great sense of humor and mixed fun several times into our flight. On arriving, he and the crew sang a song, and he closed by saying if we enjoyed our flight, their names were Reggie, Sam, and Pete. However, if we didn't enjoy his foolishness, their names were Fred, Tom, and Harry. Everyone was laughing and in a great mood by the time we deplaned.*

*Now I realize that not everyone has Reggie's personality and showmanship. But I think many people don't risk this kind of playfulness because they fear that it will be seen as unprofessional. There is a new kind of professionalism that Southwest is becoming known for, all over the world—great service with lots of fun mixed in.*

Southwest's philosophy of professionalism in no way puts a damper on personal style. Employees at Southwest are encouraged to be authentic, to be *real*. They are free to express themselves in real, creative ways and encouraged to influence the uniqueness of Southwest by projecting their own individuality. Perhaps this is one of the reasons customers find themselves drawn to Southwest employees. Somehow they have found a way to make work fun in spite of the intense pace of the airline business.

No one at Southwest doubts that the company's playful work style enriches the lives of customers and employees alike. Fun, humor, and laughter are treated as life-enhancing gifts for everyone. So how does Southwest go about creating the kind of relaxed and accepting atmosphere that grants people the freedom to play and have fun? The company is religious about hiring the right people.

## HIRING FOR ATTITUDE

The People Department is Southwest's equivalent of a human-resources or personnel department. To Southwest, employees are more than just resources; they are real people, with real needs and real emotions, whose satisfaction is valued and respected. Libby Sartain, vice president of people, told us that fun counterbalances the stress of hard work and competition. Fun is about attitude, so Southwest hires for attitude and trains for skills.

## The First Cut

First and foremost, Southwest Airlines looks for a sense of humor. As "The High Priest of Ha Ha"—*Fortune* magazine's nickname for Kelleher—frequently says, "We look for attitudes; people with a sense of humor who don't take themselves too seriously. We'll train you on whatever it is you have to do, but the one thing Southwest cannot change in people is inherent attitudes." Although each department has a unique hiring process, there is one fundamental, consistent principle—hire people with the right spirit. Southwest looks for people with other-oriented, outgoing personalities, individuals who become part of an extended family of people who work hard and have fun at the same time.

Southwest has tailored the general principles of Targeted Selection to hire people with this special kind of spirit. In the interview process, prospective employees are typically asked, "Tell me how you recently used your sense of humor in a work environment. Tell me how you have used humor to defuse a difficult situation." The People Department also looks for humor as well as unselfishness in the interaction people have with each other during group interviews.

*Colleen Barrett and "The High Priest of Ha Ha." Dressing for costume parties—and not just at Halloween—has been raised to an art form by Southwest employees.*

To test for unselfishness, Southwest uses an exercise that's not all that creative in itself; it's the analysis of the applicants' approach to the exercise that makes it a powerful hiring tool. The interviewing team asks a group of potential employees to prepare a five-minute presentation about themselves and gives them plenty of time to prepare. As the presentations are delivered, the interviewers don't watch just the speakers; they watch the audience to see which applicants are using this time to work on their own presentations and which are enthusiastically cheering on and supporting their potential coworkers. Unselfish people who will support their teammates are the ones who catch Southwest's eye, not the applicants who are tempted to polish their own presentations while others are speaking.

### Passing through the Screen

Not everyone makes it through the screening process. Even with pilots, whose technical proficiency is supremely important, attitude also plays a major role. A highly decorated military pilot—on paper, he ranked among Southwest's all-time best applicants—applied for a position. On his way to Dallas for the interview, this pilot was rude to the customer service agent at the ticket counter where he received his transfer pass. When he arrived for the interview he seemed cold and arrogant to the receptionist. These episodes suggested to the interview team that, although the pilot was highly qualified on the technical side, he didn't have the right attitude for Southwest. He was automatically disqualified.

> *"We'll train you on whatever it is you have to do, but the one thing Southwest cannot change in people is inherent attitudes."*

Another example of hiring for attitude involved a group of eight applicant pilots who were being kidded about how they were dressed—dark suits, black shoes, and dress socks. They were encouraged to loosen up by changing into Southwest's standard-issue Bermuda shorts. Six of the applicants accepted the offer and interviewed for the rest of the day in suit coats, black dress shoes and socks, and Bermuda shorts. They were hired.

By hiring the right attitude, the company is able to foster the so-called Southwest Spirit—an intangible quality in people that causes them to *want* to do whatever it takes and to *want* to go that extra mile whenever they need to. In spite of (or maybe because of) such high expectations, people who go to work for Southwest Airlines tend to stay with the company for a long time.

## FINDING THE FUN TYPES

When it comes to hiring, it's not surprising that Southwest gets what it wants. By aiming its recruiting ads to the whimsical, unconventional, even zany streaks in prospective employees, the company attracts applicants who are likely to flourish in its fun-loving culture. If you are outgoing, even a bit off-center, and like to color outside the lines, then Southwest wants you to submit an application.

One ad shows a teacher chiding a boy for coloring outside the lines on a picture of a tyrannosaurus. The message? "Brian shows an early aptitude for working at Southwest Airlines. . . . at Southwest Airlines, you get check pluses for breaking the mold. For 'coloring outside the lines.'" Another recruiting ad has Kelleher dressed in an Elvis suit. The tag line reads: "Work in a place where Elvis has been spotted. . . . Send your résumé Attention Elvis."

## BRIAN SHOWS AN EARLY APTITUDE FOR WORKING AT SOUTHWEST AIRLINES.

Wouldn't you know it. The one who gave Miss Canfield the most trouble ended up working at Southwest Airlines. And he fit in quite nicely, thank you very much. You see, at Southwest Airlines, you get check pluses for breaking the mold. For "coloring outside the lines."

Guess that's why we've ended up with flight attendants who occasionally break into song. Pilots who do halfway decent impersonations. And a CEO who does—well, you never know what he's going to do.

All friendly, motivated people dedicated to hard work and what we call "Positively Outrageous Service."

It's a different way to run a company. But it must be working. Because we've become one of the most successful airlines in the world with the lowest employee turnover rate in the business. And it doesn't hurt any that we also offer outstanding profit sharing and lots of great places to live.

If Southwest Airlines sounds like a place where you'd like to work, call our Jobline at (214) 904-4803. Or complete an application available at a Southwest Airlines airport ticket counter and return it to P.O. Box 36611, Dallas, Texas 75235-1611, Attn: T. Rex. And if you do it in crayon, don't worry about staying inside the lines.

**SOUTHWEST AIRLINES**
Southwest is an Equal Opportunity Employer.

*By making its recruiting ads appeal to the unconventional, Southwest attracts applicants who are likely to "color outside the lines."*

Recruiting brochures encourage you to consider Southwest if you want a future without boundaries, the opportunity to be original, and a chance to work your tail off. These materials emphasize the fact that Southwest is a company that is serious about having fun, cares about making money, and is filled with down-to-earth people. Southwest also holds job fairs in new cities it flies to and in areas where it opens reservations centers. In 1995 Southwest even moved into cyberspace. Southwest's Web site is known by the growing millions of Internet users as "Southwest Airlines' Home Gate—Our Home Away from Home on the Internet" (http://www.iflyswa.com). Its photo galleries, recruitment pitch, and even the welcome message—"Greetings from Our Fearless Leader and Sometime Elvis Impersonator"—epitomize the way Southwest is approaching the Internet to keep its fun and uniquely spirited culture in the minds of potential applicants.

Through all the word of mouth, print advertising, job fairs, Internet hits, and attention in the business press and popular media, the word is out: applicants flock to Southwest Airlines and say, "I want

# FUN FAN MAIL

*Every month hundreds of customers write to say how much they love flying on Southwest because Southwest makes flying entertaining. There is also the occasional complaint. In a 1992 issue of* LUV Lines, *Southwest's monthly employee newsletter, Colleen Barrett helped set the record straight on professionalism, fun, and being yourself at Southwest.*

Yes, we occasionally receive complaints from Customers who feel that joking over the PA system and/or playing/having fun with our Customers is in poor taste—that such activities have no place in an airline environment. But, we get very, very few of these letters. We do, however, receive literally hundreds of letters each month commending us for making flying fun again!

Of course, when we receive these complaints, we usually ask for reports from Employees involved, just so we can have the benefit of your first-hand insight as to the specifics of the situation. However, as long as your response shows us that you were doing what we encourage you to do—for example, you were being creative and showing your individual personality—and that you did not do anything in poor taste, we write back to the Customer supporting you 100% and tell him/her that we ENCOURAGE our Employees to be original and creative in their interaction with our Customers. . . .

Please understand that I am not suggesting that those of you who are not comfortable telling jokes or singing PAs should do so—that would defeat our purpose—because it would be immediately clear to our Customers that this was "not your thing." . . . At SWA, to me at least, being professional means being different; having fun; doing the unusual; offering POS [Positively Outrageous Service]; etc. If you are more comfortable doing everything in a conventional way, that is fine—everyone can't sing, or tell jokes, and I understand that.  But, don't block the way of those who want to give it a try. . . . As the old adage goes, "it takes all kinds to make the world go around," and we have a fairly good history of making that work for us. Let's not get too stuffy or traditional as we enter another year of success! Thanks for listening.

to work for Southwest because it's so much fun." The really tuned-in applicants have sent in applications filled out in crayon, delivered in cereal boxes, mounted on top of pizzas, packaged with confetti and noisemakers, and even done up as labels on bottles of Wild Turkey (Herb's favorite liquor). The company tries to balance the fun image by emphasizing the fact that behind all the fun there's a lot of hard work. Yet the warnings don't keep applicants away. In 1995, the People Department accepted 124,000 external applications, interviewed 38,000 individuals for 5,473 jobs, and actually hired 5,444. Southwest Airlines has created a culture that intrigues many, but it is also a company that exercises the discipline to hire its most valued resources very selectively.

Southwest is a company that rewards, recognizes, and applauds originality and individuality. It doesn't require a particular type of personality as much as it encourages a freedom from inhibition and an opportunity to be liberated through the job experience. Southwest gives employees the freedom to let their personalities shine through. If you happen to be a great singer or a great stand-up comic, or even if you are a quieter type of person, you're encouraged to perform your job through the free expression of your personal talents and gifts.

Southwest wants people to be real. It doesn't want pretentious people trying to be somebodies they aren't. The company believes that employees trying to be people other than themselves will feel too much stress in their lives and that stress will spill over to the customers they serve and the employees they work with. Stress is a serious threat to the kind of culture Southwest has worked so hard to preserve.

# Success in a Nutshell

- ➤ Hire people with a sense of humor.

- ➤ Quit pretending. Give yourself the freedom to be yourself.

- ➤ Train for skill. Hire for spirit, spunk, and enthusiasm.

- ➤ Be religious about hiring the right people. If you make the wrong hiring decision, within the first ninety days make the tough decision to say good-bye.

- ➤ Treat family members as best friends; don't take them for granted.

- ➤ Do whatever it takes. Remember, there is very little traffic in the extra mile.

- ➤ Define your own standard of professionalism.

- ➤ Treat everyone with kindness and equal respect; you never know whom you're talking to.

# CHAPTER 7

# KILL THE BUREAUCRACY

## THINK SMALL, ACT FAST

On November 13, 1990, Jim Parker, vice president and general counsel, along with corporate services executive v.p. John Denison and Southwest lawyers Debby Ackerman and Barry Brown, caught the last flight out of DFW for Chicago. The Southwest team arrived at midnight and turned on the televisions in their hotel rooms just in time to hear Midway Airlines announce that it was out of cash and closing its doors—confirming the rumors that had brought them on this sudden trip to Chicago.

At 9:00 the next morning, the Southwest team started negotiating with city officials for the use of the bankrupt airline's gates at Chicago's Midway Airport. Parker had a group of Southwest's facilities and technical services people on standby at the airport. By 2:30 that afternoon the Southwest team had hammered out a deal with the City of Chicago: Southwest Airlines would spend $20 million to revive Midway Airport and would have immediate use of the gates previously occupied by Midway Airlines.

Mayor Richard M. Daley called a press conference at 3:00 P.M. to announce that Southwest would be the new anchor carrier at Midway

Airport. Parker had just enough time before the press conference to call the facilities and technical services people waiting at Midway: "I told them we had a deal and they should immediately take over those gates and start construction." They had already started rerouting equipment to Midway Airport that had been on its way to other Southwest stations. Parker says, "Imagine this scene: Our people are installing computers, rebuilding podiums, and putting our signs right over the top of the Midway Airlines signs. It was a whirlwind of activity."

After Mayor Daley made his announcement, a reporter asked Parker when Chicago could expect to see some sign of Southwest's commitment to the expansion. Parker's reply? "Go out to the airport; you'll see it right now." As most of the press scrambled for the door in hot pursuit of footage for the five o'clock news, one reporter called Kelleher in Dallas to ask what Southwest was doing at Midway. He said, "If you were from Texas, I'd tell you that we were homesteading, but you may not know what that is."

The speed with which Southwest moved and the flexibility of its people helped the airline garner eighteen new gates at Midway Airport. Today, this translates into 50 percent of the market and almost a hundred flights a day—four times as many passenger boardings as Southwest's nearest competitor. Southwest has also fulfilled its $20 million commitment to Chicago by establishing a reservations center, pilot crew base, maintenance facility, and flight attendant base in the city.

*When a reporter asked Kelleher what Southwest was doing at Midway, he said, "If you were from Texas, I'd tell you that we were homesteading, but you may not know what that is."*

The company was able to capitalize on the opportunity to go to Midway because Southwest was, in the words of Gary Barron, chief operations officer, "nimble, quick, and opportunistic." How did Southwest get that way, and how does the company keep it up? Whenever possible, Southwest flies in the face of bureaucracy: it stays lean, thinks small, keeps it simple—and more.

## STAY LEAN

According to Southwest's corporate philosophy, bureaucracy exhausts the entrepreneurial spirit, slows the organization down, and constrains its competitive position. That is, bureaucracy creates a mindset of dependency, which makes people do what they are told but no more. Rather than encouraging employees to assume ownership and responsibility, bureaucracy teaches them to transfer responsibility. Leanness, on the other hand, gives control, ownership, and responsibility to those who are closest to the action. Southwest allows its people a lot of decision-making power and authority. "I think we are an entrepreneurship within a corporation," says Camille Keith, vice president of special marketing. "We run much more like an entrepreneurship than a corporation." With no more than four layers of management between a front-line supervisor and Herb Kelleher, the leader's span of control is very broad at Southwest.

As any company grows, structure becomes necessary. Yes, there is a hierarchy at Southwest, but the company operates so informally that people are free to go around, over, or under the formal structures whenever they need to. "We've tried to create an environment where people are able to, in effect, bypass even the fairly lean structures that we have so that they don't have to convene a meeting of the sages in order to get something done," Kelleher says. "In many cases, they can just go ahead and do it on their own. They can take individual responsibility for it and know that they will not be crucified if it doesn't work out. Our leanness requires people to be comfortable in making their own decisions and undertaking their own efforts."

*People at Southwest don't have to convene a meeting of the sages just to get something done.*

Kelleher believes that excessive bureaucracy results from the egos of empire builders who try, through title and position, to emphasize their own importance. Lots of assistants and big corporate staffs, for example, create inefficiencies and promote a "My people are here to serve me" attitude that is antithetical to Southwest's family philosophy. Assistants add another layer to the hierarchy, increase overhead, and create more formal communication channels. Instead of just walking up to the second floor to talk with a colleague, an empire builder communicates through assistants, fostering communication that is distant and cold and that increases the probability that information will be transmitted inaccurately. Very few Southwest executives have special assistants. Southwest leaders have traded in the trappings of position for informal relationships that enable the organization to achieve results quickly.

In a bureaucracy that classifies people according to position, power, and capacity, it's very easy for an employee to say, "That's not my job." This undermines productivity and prevents the company from being as nimble and moving as quickly as it might. Leanness helps a company stay alert, think smart, and act fast. It also helps identify nonperformers because, in a lean organization, marginal performance is difficult to hide. Because of its leanness and informality, Southwest has an atmosphere that fosters the active and personal involvement of its managers. When there's a problem with an individual's performance, it can be immediately identified and usually fixed.

What hierarchy Southwest has exists to bring order to a company that has hired over half of its twenty-five thousand people since 1990. But Kelleher is quick to say that the company's structure must always be subservient to purpose: "The bigger you get, the harder you must continually fight back the bureaucracy and preserve the entrepreneurial spirit. Sure, you need more disciplines and more systems, but they're adjuncts. They are not masters; they are servants. You've got to keep that entrepreneurial spirit alive within the company, no matter how big it gets."

## THINK SMALL

One day, Gary Barron caught Kelleher in the hall after a Front Line Forum—a meeting where senior employees get together with Kelleher and other leaders to talk about how to improve the company. Barron told Kelleher that he wanted to talk about the complete reorganization of the management structure of Southwest's $700 million maintenance department. Then he handed Kelleher a three-page memo. Kelleher read it on the spot. When he'd finished, Kelleher raised only one concern. Barron said that he was concerned about that, too, and was dealing with it. Kelleher's response? "Then it's fine by me." The whole conversation took about four minutes.

As in small companies, communication is face-to-face whenever possible and always on a first-name basis. This informality helps employees build more open and direct relationships and make decisions more quickly.

When Southwest had 5,000 employees, Wall Street said the company's success wouldn't last because it depended so greatly on the unique family culture. Skeptics kept saying, "You can do it with a company of only 5,000 people, but wait until you get to be 10,000." When Southwest grew to 10,000 employees, people said, "Well, wait until you have 15,000." Southwest still manages—with over 25,000 people—to maintain a culture where employees and customers feel they're part of an extended family. Herb is constantly telling Southwest employees, "If we think small, we'll grow big, but if we think like we're big, we'll grow small."

*At Southwest Airlines, thinking like a small company isn't just another flavor-of-the-month management philosophy; it's a way of life that has been deeply embedded into the culture from day one.*

Southwest creates its small-company atmosphere in several ways. First, with few exceptions, the company has chosen to grow very conservatively, expanding into only one or two cities each year, so that it can devote the necessary time and attention to creating Southwest's unique culture in each new city. Southwest likes to be considered the hometown airline everywhere it goes and works very hard to earn this reputation.

Second, at Southwest, meetings are action oriented. In a small business, everyone is needed and everyone must contribute because there's usually more work than people. Southwest people leave meetings ready to act on the items they've been assigned. Rarely will you hear them walk away from a meeting saying, "Let's study that."

Third, small companies don't have the time and resources to produce long, drawn-out documents. Neither does Southwest Airlines. When Southwest submitted documentation less than an inch thick to the U.S. Justice Department regarding the Morris Air joinder, investigators were blown away. They assumed something was missing.

# THE HIGHEST FORM
# OF FLATTERY

*In 1981 Southwest's president and CEO of three years, Howard Putnam, resigned to become president and chief operating officer of Braniff International. "One of the reasons the Braniff board of directors came after me," Putnam says, "was they liked what Southwest was doing and their sense was that the only way Braniff would be saved was to simplify and make it a transcontinental Southwest Airlines. Unfortunately there wasn't enough cash to do it." Today, Putnam flies Southwest Airlines a lot, he says. "They don't know who I am, but I watch and I listen. They're still doing some of the same things Southwest did in the very beginning."*

When Justice Department officials implied to Kelleher that the documents were incomplete, he responded, "Well, we're not very big on documents at Southwest Airlines." As it turned out, the Justice Department found everything to be in order and left perhaps more enlightened about the value of operating lean.

## KEEP SIMPLIFYING

As downsizing mania spread through corporate America during the mid-'80s and early '90s, scores of exasperated managers were saying, "We've got to figure out how to do more with less." Southwest is still looking for ways to simplify its operations and get rid of less productive activities, but without eliminating employees.

Sophisticated and complex tasks are harder to understand, take longer to accomplish, and create drag on the organization. By eliminating unnecessary steps in a service process, by making a product with fewer parts, or by handwriting a note, a company can accomplish a lot with less effort. Southwest's simplified boarding procedures require fewer customer service and operations agents to serve customers. The productivity of the company's pilots requires fewer pilots. Consider these productivity and efficiency measures: Southwest serves twenty-four hundred customers per employee; its nearest competitor serves half that number. It takes 84 Southwest employees per aircraft to operate the business; other airlines need anywhere from 111 to 160 employees per aircraft.

"Only self-confident people can be simple," GE's chairman and CEO Jack Welch told us. "Think about it. You get some engineer who is nervous and not too sure of himself. He can't explain his design to you in very simple terms, so he complicates it. If you're not simple you can't be fast, and if you're not fast you're dead in a global world. So everything we do [at GE] focuses on building self-confidence in people so they can be simple." Southwest is an organization of self-confident people who have taken Welch's theme to heart. They are not afraid to keep things simple—even if it means doing things radically differently from the rest of the industry. They understand that simplicity decreases costs and increases speed. Their entrepreneurial frame of mind requires that they look for new ways to simplify operations.

"If somebody is going to turn a plane in fifteen minutes, it can't be complicated," says Boeing's president and CEO, Phil Condit. As the launch customer for the Boeing 737-300, Southwest asked Boeing to make design changes in the new aircraft to help speed up ground operations even more. "They asked us to reposition the service panel for the lavatories so that the equipment used to drain the lavs wouldn't block other equipment," Doug Groseclose, Boeing's sales director in charge of the Southwest account, explains. "They felt the way we originally had it laid out was going to hinder their turnaround time.

## DEAR MR. KELLEHER

*Southwest is without a doubt the most responsive business today. As far as I know, it is the only business where you call and a* human *voice answers on the first ring.*

DONELLE WEISS
HAMMOND, INDIANA

So we listened to them and said, 'You got it.'" From Southwest's perspective, it all boils down to a thousand little things that help people solve the problem of how to turn the planes faster. Condit explains: "The sequence with which you locate ground service equipment around an airplane has a big impact on turnaround time. What's the first thing you put against the airplane? Very frequently, it's the baggage loader, because you've got to start that process first. If that baggage loader blocks access to the lav service panel, then you're going to end up with a real problem that could cost you valuable time." In this case, simplification means good choreography.

Southwest was the first major airline to offer a continental breakfast in its gate areas instead of in flight. The idea was simple: gate areas can be cleaned up after a flight departs; if the food is served on the plane, it is difficult to clean up without extending ground time. Southwest was also the first to eschew the bulky food and beverage carts that inhibit customers from moving about the cabin. Flight attendants serve drinks and peanuts off specially designed trays and finish beverage service quickly so they can spend more time talking to customers.

### *Southwest will not assign you a seat. Your seat is reserved; you just don't know which one it is.*

Boarding passes are another way Southwest profits from simplification. Its plastic boarding passes are reusable, which reduces the cost of materials. But there are two more important reasons for using them, according to Jim Wimberly, vice president of ground operations: "When the employee collecting the passes before you enter the jetway has to read what's on the traditionally printed ticket rather than simply looking at the color of our plastic boarding pass, two problems occur. First, it slows the operation down because it takes longer to read the print. Second, when our employees are focused on reading, they can't do as good a job of welcoming customers on board."

Unlike most airlines, Southwest will not assign you a seat. Your seat is reserved; you just don't know which one it is. Or, as some Southwest flight attendants say, "It's open seating. You can sit anywhere you want—just like at church." Customers are boarded on a first-come-first-served basis, in groups of thirty. If you get to the gate early and receive a plastic boarding card with a low number, you have a wide variety of seats to choose from. Southwest's boarding method is fast and efficient because customers don't have to look for their assigned seat. The process infuriates some customers, who refer to it as a "cattle call," but getting people on and off the plane quickly is essential to Southwest's fifteen-minute turn, and the fast turn helps keep ticket costs low. Southwest prefers to keep the boarding process simple—and thinks most customers do, too.

## STREAMLINE COMMUNICATION

If you've ever watched a documentary where a cheetah is pursuing a gazelle for its next meal, you know what agility is. As the two animals engage in a sixty-mile-an-hour life-and-death race, agility and speed determine how the contest will end. Whether the gazelle can evade the cheetah or the cheetah can feed her cubs will be determined by which animal is faster and more agile. Both animals have skeletal and muscle structures that enable them to be incredibly swift and nimble. Southwest, like the cheetah and the gazelle, is lean and muscular and has quick reflexes. Its agility in quickly mobilizing people and reconfiguring resources comes in part from its streamlined communication style. And its open communication is partly a function of its lean structure and informal code of conduct.

Access to information is essential to agility. Poor communication creates complexity, and the organization becomes sluggish and lethargic while people sort things out. When employees have access to good information and everybody is working from the same page, the company can make decisions and take action more quickly.

Southwest's people go out of their way to make sure employees have access to the information they need. Every issue of *LUV Lines* carries a segment called "Industry News," which keeps employees apprised of what other carriers are doing. A major event—whether it's opening a new city or acquiring another airline—isn't announced without employees hearing about it first. Southwest's results and performance measures are open to any employee. In fact, Southwest is continually educating employees about the company's financial position and its performance with regard to on-time arrivals, baggage handling, and customer complaints. If the company falls below its on-time performance standard for a couple of weeks, employees know about it right away. Southwest believes that when employees have immediate access to critical information, they can make the necessary adjustments to fix significant problems more quickly.

Agility also depends on employees' having access to key people. "I tell people, and mean it, you don't have to have an appointment to see me," says Gary Barron. "The only reason to even call is that I may be out of my office. When I got out of a contract negotiation meeting last week, I got a call from a ground equipment mechanic in Houston. I had never met him before and he just picked up the phone because he wanted to know what was going on with the negotiations. So, I explained to him what was going on to the extent that I could." Decision makers in the corporate office understand that their role is to serve others. This means equipping people with the tools and information they need to do their jobs fast and efficiently. It doesn't take seven signatures to buy a piece of equipment or launch a new program at Southwest Airlines.

With easy access to key people, employees not only stay in the know, they develop the confidence to make decisions, a key factor in Southwest's ability to change direction quickly to address the challenges of an industry that is constantly shifting. When you minimize the layers of management in a company, there are fewer people to congest communication channels and misinterpret what others are trying to say. With fewer filters, information can flow more quickly and accurately. When Phoenix station manager Greg Wells has important news for ground operations v.p. Jim Wimberly, for example, he simply calls him. Southwest's informal atmosphere also helps keep communication uncomplicated and relaxed, as Kenneth Labich illustrates in a 1994 *Fortune* article:

> *A Wall Street analyst recalls having lunch one day in the company cafeteria when Kelleher, seated at a table across the room with several female employees, suddenly leapt to his feet, kissed one of the women with gusto, and began leading the entire crowd in a series of cheers. When the analyst asked what was going on, one of the executives at his table explained that Kelleher had, at that moment, negotiated a new contract with Southwest's flight attendants.*

## ADAPT

"When we look back at the last twenty years, it is obvious that a number of large companies were so set in their ways that they did not adapt properly and lost out as a result. Twenty years from now, we'll look back and see the same pattern," says Bill Gates, founder and chairman of Microsoft. Change has a way of destroying people and organizations that can't or won't adapt.

Adaptiveness is an individual's or a company's capacity to change when forces in the environment threaten the accomplishment of its goals. It is indispensable in a world of perpetual and accelerating change. Kelleher says, "When you're in a business where the capital assets travel five hundred miles per hour, you have to be quick and responsive." Southwest has certainly been alert and adaptable with respect to opportunities in the airline industry. When American Airlines bought AirCal and USAir bought PSA, both carriers scaled back operations in California. Southwest sprang into action by taking over abandoned gates and acquiring more planes. The result? Southwest now has 50 percent of the California market.

*"When you're in a business where the capital assets travel five hundred miles per hour, you have to be quick and responsive."*

The more adaptable a company is, the more freedom it has to seize opportunities that come with change. In this sense, adaptable does not mean wishy-washy or undisciplined; it means open to influence and refusing to get locked into one way of doing things. Like the ligaments of an athlete who hasn't stretched, a company that is rigid and inflexible often tears. In some cases, the organization recovers from its injury; in others, the damage ends a promising career. The idea, then, is to develop the capability of bending without breaking. Southwest has avoided the rigidity some organizations develop because it has never become too comfortable with its success.

Earlier we observed that Southwest's success is largely the result of adhering to a clearly defined purpose and a well-thought-out strategy for accomplishing this purpose. At the same time, Southwest Airlines has demonstrated a powerful drive for progress that has enabled the company to change many things about itself without compromising its fundamental purpose or core values. The ability to stay focused yet flexible has been another key to Southwest's success in an industry where survival depends on agility.

While Southwest is known for its shorthaul niche, the company has stepped outside the boundaries of that niche—but only when there is a significant long-term profit-generating opportunity. For example, the 1,440-mile trip from Nashville to Phoenix is not within the company's defined niche. However, Southwest refuses to become so rigid and narrow in its thinking that it ignores a significant opportunity to increase profits. "You can become a zealot about your niche if you're too confined in your thinking," Kelleher says. "We're not as pure as we often appear to be, but the deviations that we've made from purity have all been very profitable for us."

## EXPECT THE UNEXPECTED

Consider the following scenario: Boeing's employees go on strike and production of the company's 737-300 shuts down. Southwest, planning to implement a critical expansion in Florida, might not be able to take delivery of planes on time. The window of opportunity for expansion could close while the company waits for planes. If Southwest is delayed in the opening of its Florida cities, the people of Florida may mistake the company for a fly-by-night commuter that comes and goes. Another airline facing financial difficulties decides to sell airplanes at a discounted price if the buyer can pay cash. At nearly the same time, American closes its Nashville hub, creating a significant opportunity for Southwest. Where will Southwest get the planes necessary for expansion?

One plan—no matter how well laid—couldn't possibly respond to all of these situations. This is why Kelleher does not put much stock in traditional strategic planning. His concern is that writing something down in a plan makes it gospel. When the plan becomes gospel, it's easy for people to become rigid in their thinking and less open to new, perhaps off-the-wall, ideas. Kelleher explains it this way:

*Reality is chaotic; planning is ordered and logical. The two don't square with one another. When USAir pulls out of six cities in California, they don't call and tell me they are going to do that.*

> *Now, if we have established a big strategic plan that is approved*
> *by our officers and the board of directors, I would have to go to*
> *the officers and the board and tell them we want to deviate from*
> *the plan. They would want to know why I want to buy six more*
> *airplanes. The problem is we'd analyze it and debate its merits*
> *for three months, instead of getting the airplanes, taking over the*
> *gates, and dominating California. The meticulous nit-picking*
> *that goes on in most strategic planning processes creates a mental*
> *straitjacket that becomes disabling in an industry where things*
> *change radically from one day to the next.*

When a financial analyst chided Kelleher about not having a strategic plan, he said, "We do have a plan." When she asked what it was, his response was vintage Kelleher: "It's called doing things." "Then you're telling me that twenty-four years of unbroken profitability is just a matter of luck?" she asked. With a wolfish grin Kelleher quipped, "I *am* Irish."

## *"What if . . . ?" questions get the group thinking about all the possible situations Southwest could face.*

Instead of counting on the luck of the Irish or doing conventional strategic planning, Southwest prepares for the future by practicing the art of "What if . . . ?" *Future scenario generation* is the technical name of the process Southwest Airlines is using to prepare itself for the twenty-first century. The company's executive planning committee meets periodically to create future scenarios in which the airline could find itself. These sessions include a lot of "What if . . . ?" questions designed to get the group thinking about all the possible situations Southwest could face. For example, the group might ask, "What if we open one or two new cities in the New England area? How will the competition respond? How many airplanes will we need and where will we get them? What if Chicago builds a new airport? How will that affect our business?" The result of these discussions is a set of multiple plans. Future scenario generation enables Southwest to prepare for the future in a way that provides direction for the company yet allows it to maneuver on many fronts. This reduces the likelihood that Southwest will get caught off guard.

Before United Airlines announced the launch of its Shuttle, Southwest launched action. Having anticipated United's move in the context of future scenario generation, Southwest quickly responded to Salt Lake City–based Morris Air after the Morris family suggested a joinder. Morris was the perfect acquisition because it flew only Boeing 737s and its route structure covered the Pacific Northwest—a route system that complemented, rather than overlapped, Southwest's. While United was completing its leveraged buyout by employees, Southwest went to work on the deal and joined forces with Morris Air on December 31, 1993. With lightning speed, Southwest fully integrated the new carrier into its system. This enabled Southwest to get a jump on the United Shuttle and establish itself in the very lucrative Pacific Northwest market. In 1994, Southwest added an unprecedented seven cities to its system.

Southwest adapted to United's expected competitive move in another way as well. Through purchasing Morris, it accelerated its acquisition of airplanes so that it could increase the number of flights on anticipated Shuttle routes.

Good preparation can look like prophecy in retrospect. Southwest Airlines is not a company of prophets, however. Rather, it's a company of people who do their homework—thoroughly. Preparation is what makes their decisions intelligent. It is also what makes Southwest a force in readiness. Southwest is always scanning the horizon, trying to anticipate what the other airlines are doing, how they are altering their approaches, and what dominates their thinking. This way, the company will be prepared for any changes in the airline industry.

## PROMOTE ACTION AND FLEXIBILITY

One of the reasons Southwest Airlines can adapt so quickly is that the company trusts its employees and gives them the latitude, discretion, and authority they need to do their jobs. Station managers have tremendous operational responsibilities. Each station functions like an independent business unit, and managers are responsible for setting the tone of the station and ensuring that Southwest's culture is protected and promoted. This includes working with the People Department to recruit and hire employees, as well as scheduling, training, coaching, nurturing, and evaluating an entire ground operations crew. Customer service agents act like department heads—they are given the authority they need to handle oversales, baggage problems, canceled flights, missed connections, and a wide range of other challenges.

Southwest has eliminated inflexible work rules and rigid job descriptions so its people can assume ownership for getting the job done and getting the planes out on time, regardless of whose "official" responsibility it is. This gives employees the flexibility to help each other when needed. As a result, the whole operation becomes more adaptive. Employees adopt a "whatever it takes" mentality. Southwest mechanics and pilots have the freedom and latitude to help ramp agents load bags. When a flight is running late because of weather, it's not uncommon to see pilots helping customers in wheelchairs board the plane, helping the operations agents take boarding passes, or helping the flight attendants clean up the cabin between flights. All of these actions are their way of adapting to the situation and taking ownership for getting customers on board more quickly. "If we see two strollers off to the side on the tarmac that say CLAIM AT GATE," says Captain Terry "Moose" Millard, "we'll walk down the jetway and get 'em. By the time one of us gets back up with the strollers, the ramp agent has thrown twenty or thirty more bags."

## *Southwest employees apply common sense, not rules, when it's in the best interests of the customer.*

Southwest employees can be flexible even when it comes to company policy, if they think an exception is in the best interests of the customer. Rod Jones, assistant chief pilot, recalls a captain who left the gate with a senior citizen who had boarded the wrong plane. The customer was confused and very upset. Southwest asks pilots not to go back to the gate with an incorrectly boarded customer. In this case, the captain was concerned about this individual's well-being. "So, he adapted to the situation," says Jones. "He came back in to the gate, deplaned the customer, pushed back out, and gave us an irregularity report. Even though he broke the rules, he used his judgment and did what he thought was best. And we said, 'Attaboy!'"

Southwest has learned that when employees are trusted to apply a little common sense and ingenuity to a problem, several things happen. First, they come up with far better solutions than the company

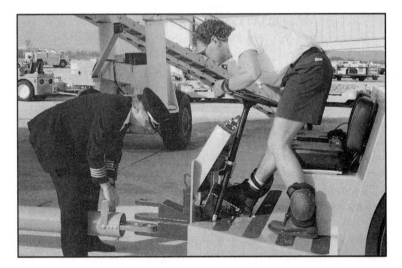

*Everyone at Southwest is fixated on customer service. It's not unusual to see pilots giving ramp agents a hand or vice presidents handling baggage.*

could have dreamed of mandating. Second, they can quickly respond to customers' demands. Finally, they can direct their energies toward seizing unique market opportunities when time is critical. The Southwest story demonstrates over and over that people will act responsibly and do more than expected when they are given the freedom to think on their own.

## BE QUICK OR BE DEAD

At Southwest, speed is about doing things in days that take other carriers months to do. With speed comes the excitement of new challenges, which keep people's hearts inspired and their minds sharp and alert. When people with an ownership mentality advance their ideas only to have them sucked into the black hole of bureaucracy, they become idle and bored. Their hearts grow numb, their minds dull, and apathy begins to take root. If this happens with enough people, the whole organization becomes sedated.

Southwest has learned that speed is both necessary for survival and essential to keeping people inspired and invigorated. In a world where the shelf life of our products and services keeps getting shorter and shorter, we can't afford to be too cautious and play it too safe. Change simply won't wait on those who are afraid of speed.

When Southwest announced service to San Diego, the building permit the company needed to begin construction on its terminal got tangled in the bureaucracy of the Port Authority. Southwest had already published its flight schedule, and time was getting critical. So, rather than complain about things it couldn't control, the company put up a drywall screen and began the necessary construction behind it in a gamble: eventually Southwest would either be granted a permit or have to tear it all down. Two days before Southwest was scheduled to initiate service, the Port Authority issued the permit at 10:00 in the morning. At 10:05 A.M. Southwest took down the drywall, displaying a newly renovated main ticket counter. Kelleher recalls that someone from another airline said, "I heard you guys were fast, but I didn't know you were that fast."

### *In the beginning, Southwest employees learned that there are two kinds of people: the quick and the dead.*

The penalty for being slow and slothful in the early days was not just decreased revenue and a losing quarter; it was the death of the airline and their job security. Southwest employees have chosen to be among the quick because, year after year over the last two decades, they've witnessed the demise of other carriers that were too slow to respond to the challenges they faced.

Kelleher illustrates the alacrity with which Southwest moves by telling a story about Don Valentine, former vice president of marketing. Valentine had just joined Southwest from Dr. Pepper when the marketing group met in January to discuss a new television campaign. Valentine was ready with his timeline for producing the spots: the commercial could be scripted by March, script approval could be completed in April, casting in June, and the company could start shooting in September. When Valentine finished outlining his schedule, Kelleher said, "Don, I hate to tell you, but we're talking about next Wednesday." The new vice president quickly became accustomed to the speed with which Southwest operates.

The sense of urgency that Valentine learned is endemic at Southwest Airlines. Employees are not timid about springing into action

# A BIAS FOR ACTION

*Southwest's bias for action is exemplified in a letter from customer Robert L. Klopfenstein:*

I recently flew from Chicago to Columbus. Upon check-in, we were advised that fog in Ohio was going to delay the flight by one hour, as the needed aircraft was grounded in Cleveland. Because the crew was available in Chicago, someone in your organization [Dispatch] decided to take another aircraft, originally scheduled to go to Kansas City, use it for the Columbus flight, and use the Cleveland aircraft [by now in the air] for the Kansas City trip. You turned a one-hour delay into a fifteen-minute delayed departure and an on-time arrival.

Flying with Southwest Airlines is a pleasure!

*With this kind of freedom, people can adapt as circumstances change. When people are given the freedom and authority to take action and influence change, they will not only assume more responsibility for what they are doing, they will do it faster.*

and doing whatever it takes to help the company accomplish an objective in record time. For example, Southwest can open a station in a new city faster than anyone in the industry. When Southwest decided to expand into Little Rock, a competitor tried to preempt the company by announcing that it was going into Little Rock in a compressed time frame. Forty-eight hours after that announcement, Southwest people flew to Little Rock and quickly obtained a sublease on all available gates from Continental Airlines. Within ten days, Southwest had put together a schedule, laid cable and installed computer equipment, acquired airplanes, and decorated ticket counters. When the competing airline showed up in Little Rock, it was shocked to find that the gates had already been secured by Southwest.

*Southwest employees working in California and at the Albuquerque Reservations Center came out in full battle gear to wage war against the United Shuttle.*

With no time to properly launch a marketing campaign, Southwest got creative. The company introduced itself to the people of Little Rock by offering a $10 fare for ten days. Five days after Southwest initiated service, it had 25 percent of the Little Rock–Dallas market.

## IMPART URGENCY

When it comes to creating a sense of urgency, Kelleher knows how to light a fire in the bellies of his troops. Shortly after United Airlines announced it was launching its Shuttle, an operation created to compete directly with Southwest, Kelleher sounded a call to arms in a letter to all employees entitled "Commencement of Hostilities." These excerpts show the intensity with which he can create a sense of urgency.

> *Since the collapse of Russia's Aeroflot, United Airlines has become the largest airline in the world, approximating seven times the size of Southwest, in terms of gross revenues per year.*

*The world's largest airline has recently announced that it will launch its initial direct assault against Southwest, in the western part of our route system.*

*This initial attack will utilize roughly 25 of the 125 737s that United can devote to its "United Shuttle" operation, signifying that an additional 100 airplanes are in reserve to be hurled against us, at a later date.*

*United has, on hand, over $1,000,000,000 in cash; can cross-subsidize its efforts against Southwest with revenues derived from its worldwide service; and has substantially reduced its costs by recently obtaining substantial wage and benefit reductions from most of its employees.*

*In addition to our stock price, our wages, our benefits, our job security, our expansion opportunities, and, foremost, our pride of accomplishment as our nation's best airline are all on the line, as the war begins with United Shuttle on October 1, 1994, when it first takes to the air.*

*At its beginning, Southwest routed Braniff, Trans Texas, and Continental, with three airplanes. And Southwest can thwart United's actions against us with our 200 airplanes. The crucial elements are the martial vigor, the dedication, the energy, the unity, and the devotion to warm, hospitable, caring and loving Customer Service of all of our people.*

*Southwest's essential difference is not machines and "things." Our essential difference is minds, hearts, spirits and souls. Winston Churchill stated: "Success is never final." Indeed, "success" must be earned over and over again, or it disappears. I am betting on your minds, your hearts, your souls, and your spirits to continue our success. Let's win this one and make aviation history—again!*

There can be security in discomfort. Kelleher's letter made employees uncomfortable, but it also stirred within them the urgency needed to fight the war seriously. Herb understands that job security is inexorably linked to victory and victory belongs to those who fight most passionately. Herb's letter also portrays Southwest Airlines in the role of underdog—a theme that has been rallying Southwest employees (and customers) since the beginning. When you're the underdog, the opponent is Goliath, and your job is threatened, you come out fully armed to defend the cause.

*One of the ads attached to Kelleher's call to arms to spark employee pride and to remind them that, while there are competitors who sometimes emulate Southwest's low-fare strategy, Southwest is the low-fare original*

All over the globe, the pace of change continues to accelerate. There's not a business in the world that isn't thinking about trimming its bureaucracy, moving faster, and adapting better to the demands of an increasingly competitive environment. With deregulation in 1978, change came at the U.S. airline industry much faster than most companies anticipated. With their big, inflexible bureaucratic structures, inefficiencies created by waste and redundancy, and service that seemed to say the customer was a minor consideration, many carriers were ill equipped to deal with warp-speed change. Although the industry as a whole had trouble adapting, Southwest succeeded primarily because it never let go of its small-company attitudes and practices.

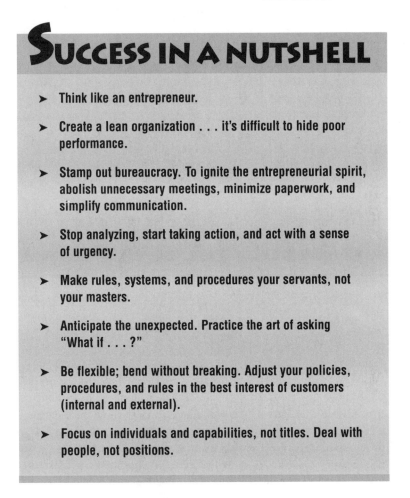

# Success in a Nutshell

➤ Think like an entrepreneur.

➤ Create a lean organization . . . it's difficult to hide poor performance.

➤ Stamp out bureaucracy. To ignite the entrepreneurial spirit, abolish unnecessary meetings, minimize paperwork, and simplify communication.

➤ Stop analyzing, start taking action, and act with a sense of urgency.

➤ Make rules, systems, and procedures your servants, not your masters.

➤ Anticipate the unexpected. Practice the art of asking "What if . . . ?"

➤ Be flexible; bend without breaking. Adjust your policies, procedures, and rules in the best interest of customers (internal and external).

➤ Focus on individuals and capabilities, not titles. Deal with people, not positions.

# CHAPTER 8

# ACT LIKE AN OWNER

## ASK QUESTIONS, THINK RESULTS

People who think like owners have a unique perspective. They ask provocative questions. And the answers they come up with influence their attitudes and behaviors, which, in turn, determine the company's performance. It's not unusual to hear someone who is thinking like an owner ask, "If this were my company, how would I handle a customer in this situation? Would I buy this piece of equipment or make that investment? If I personally owned this business, how would I treat my employees? Would I establish this committee, attend that meeting, or make that trip?"

What does it take to get employees to assume ownership for a business, to truly take personal responsibility for its success? This is one of the most frequently asked questions in business today. Finding an answer to this question is critical because, as Southwest has learned, ownership is a powerful catalyst for organizational change. It seems that if only we could get employees to show more initiative for cutting costs, serving customers, and improving productivity, we could gain the advantage we need to excel in a highly competitive business environment.

## THINK LIKE AN OWNER

Owners think differently from nonowners because ownership is a state of mind. It's about caring, about becoming fully engaged in the active pursuit of organizational objectives. For example, nonowners are more apt to worry about how their actions are being perceived by their superiors. Owners focus on the business results of their actions, regardless of who's watching. Nonowners may be more inclined to protect functional areas, pursue self-interest, and approach the business from a parochial point of view. Owners transcend functional boundaries. It doesn't matter where an idea comes from, owners evaluate its merit based on whether it contributes to the ultimate objective of delivering customer value.

Nonowners have a greater tendency to live by the rules, even when the rules run contrary to common sense. Owners bend, stretch, and even break rules that don't serve the organization's purpose. If breaking the rules is not an option, owners take the initiative to change them. Owners pay attention to details others fail to notice. When people have a vested interest in the outcome of a business, they become more cost-conscious, industrious, and imaginative. Owners are also different from nonowners in their willingness to take action without being asked; they are rarely spectators. An owner takes the time to follow up with a customer who expresses a concern during a casual meeting. An owner picks up the piece of trash that others have been ignoring for hours. An owner makes the extra phone call to pass on a small but important piece of information that could be helpful to another employee.

*"When you talk to a ramper or a flight attendant, they'll tell you what the stock price is that day."*

"Our people think like owners and have for a long time," says Gary Barron, who offers retired skycap Tommy Perryman as an example. Perryman, one of the original employees, worked at Southwest for fifteen years without missing a single day. "When I was in San Antonio back in the early days, I would go to the airport to catch a flight to Dallas. Inevitably, when I got out of the parking lot and started to walk into the terminal, I would run into Tommy. Every time, he would pull clippings out of his pocket about Southwest

*Original employee Tommy Perryman's twentieth anniversary portrait*

Airlines and the legal battles we were having, and there were a bunch of them. Tommy always wanted to know what was going on and how we were doing. He cared and he thought about it. Being a skycap wasn't just a job to him."

What sets Southwest apart from the competition is thousands of employees like Perryman, who exemplify the dedication and consistency that come with ownership. Chic Lang, a Southwest captain, says, "It amazes me how you go talk to a ramper or a flight attendant and they'll tell you what the stock price is that day. There are articles all over the wall about what's going on with the competition and they're all reading them." Ownership is a very powerful incentive because it inspires motivation and encourages the kind of loyalty for which Perryman was so well known. Here are some of the ways Southwest Airlines encourages people to assume ownership of the business.

## HIRE ENTREPRENEURIAL SELF-STARTERS

Southwest not only attracts people who are fun and like to have a good time, the company also looks for self-starters who have an entrepreneurial spirit. Previous airline experience doesn't carry a lot of weight at Southwest. The company is much more interested in ordinary people who are driven to do extraordinary things, people who are not afraid to step outside the routine and use their initiative to challenge the status quo. Southwest doesn't worry about hiring people who are mavericks. A new applicant who didn't fit in a large bureaucracy or who shuns a profession that requires specific, formal education may be just the right fit for Southwest.

The hiring process for pilots is a good example of how Southwest attracts people with an entrepreneurial spirit. Southwest Airlines is the only company in the airline industry that requires a pilot to have a 737-Type Rating before he or she is considered for hire. This rating, given by the Federal Aviation Administration, essentially says a pilot is qualified to be the captain of a Boeing 737. This means that all first officers are qualified to fly as captains.

Terry "Moose" Millard, a Southwest captain, explains how this hiring policy attracts pilots who have an entrepreneurial spirit: "The average person will pay about $10,000 to get this qualification. It's interesting because this is another part of the equation of hiring entrepreneurial people. There is about a one-in-five chance that one of these pilots will be hired at Southwest. Each one of these people is taking a risk. Some of them are borrowing money to get $10,000 so that they can compete—just so they can throw their hat in the ring. That eliminates a lot of contenders at the very outset. Every step of the selection process tends to eliminate those folks who simply want to find job security, for the minimum investment."

When people come to the job with this kind of entrepreneurial drive and enthusiasm, they naturally look for opportunities to assume ownership. Why? Because it's in their very nature. It's who they are. The company's role, then, is to create an environment that nurtures the entrepreneurial spirit. Southwest has been particularly successful at drawing out of its employees the very characteristics for which they were hired in the first place.

## GIVE EVERYONE A STAKE

How many times have you read "People are our most valued asset" in an annual report or heard it in an executive's speech? Yet, employees in a lot of companies will tell you that this oft-repeated phrase is empty. Not so at Southwest Airlines. The words have meaning because the company demonstrates in a very tangible way how much it values people. In fact, Southwest has been putting its money where its mouth is since the beginning.

### Profitsharing for the Right Reason

In 1973, Southwest Airlines was the first company in the airline industry to introduce a profitsharing plan for employees. Today, all Southwest employees become participants on the January 1 following their date of employment. "Profitsharing . . . is an expense we'd like to be as big as possible so our people get a greater reward," Kelleher says. The company invests 15 percent of its pretax operating income, almost $60 million in 1996, in this profitsharing plan. While people can certainly choose to increase the amount, 25 percent of an employee's profitsharing goes to the purchase of Southwest stock. In the 1970s, Southwest was the only airline in the world that had given its people stock ownership without asking for wage concessions. "It's not the only profitsharing plan in the airline business," says Gary Barron, "but, historically, it is the only profitsharing plan that was

*"It's not the only profitsharing plan in the airline business, but it's the only one implemented simply because the board thought it was the right thing to do."*

implemented by a company simply because the board thought it was the right thing to do." Today employees own approximately 12 percent of the company.

Perhaps the point is too elementary, but profitsharing serves as a benefit only when the company makes a profit. Southwest has been profitable every year since 1973. The company's stock price had increased almost 300 percent in the five years ending December 31, 1995. Consequently, profitsharing has had a very positive effect on Southwest's employees. A thousand dollars of Southwest stock bought in 1973 is worth approximately $1.5 million today. One reason Southwest people are so willing to step up and assume ownership for the success of the business is that they personally have a lot at stake. Profitsharing has made millionaires of more than a few employees, and not just the executives. As their profitsharing accounts continue to grow, the concern Southwest employees have for the health and longevity of the company grows as well.

### Assets on the Line
Tammy Romo, director of investor relations, sums up the relationship between profitsharing and ownership quite well: "Profitsharing aligns the employee's interests with the interests of the company. Our people are more conscious about protecting the company's assets and accom-

plishing its goals because their well-being is tied to the company's well-being."

Protecting the company's assets is something Southwest people take very seriously. When a ticket agent from another carrier asked one of Southwest's customer service agents if she could borrow a stapler, the Southwest employee said, "No problem," and proceeded to follow the other agent back to her counter. A bit annoyed, the other agent asked why she was being followed. "I want to make sure we get our stapler back," the customer service agent told her. "It's a part of my profitsharing." Several years back, a new pilot for Southwest was watching a flight attendant picking up trash and cleaning out the ashtrays in the gate area. When the pilot jokingly asked, "Is that in your job description?" the flight attendant responded, "No, but it affects my profitsharing." These stories are not isolated incidents. Southwest employees frequently talk about how pride of ownership affects their attitudes and behaviors.

Southwest pilots are also very conscious of how their daily activities affect profitsharing. Pilots flying for Southwest are much more than super technicians who look out for the safety of the aircraft as they take us to our destinations. They are business owners who understand that they can make a huge difference when it comes to Southwest's financial performance. As a result, they take pride in constantly looking for ways to cut costs and increase the efficiency of the operation without sacrificing customer service. "I like to think that every Southwest pilot knows every possible shortcut in and out of an airport," Captain Chic Lang says. "A little operational knowledge about a particular city tells you which runway to request when you want to taxi more quickly."

Frequent requests for more direct headings and more efficient altitudes are all a part of the Southwest pilot's daily quest to maximize speed and minimize the burn rate of fuel. So frequent are these requests that air traffic controllers have nicknamed Southwest pilots "Requesters." On a recent flight from Phoenix to Tulsa, we left the gate a little bit late because of an unexpected crew change. Captain Jim Yeaton was monitoring the fuel burn rate and watching the computer for our estimated time of arrival. (The onboard computer tells the pilot the weight and balance of the aircraft, the most efficient holding speed if the pilot has to go into a holding pattern, and the most efficient speeds the aircraft can fly given certain other conditions.) Captain Yeaton knew the flight crew needed to compensate for lost time. After a brief discussion with his copilot, First Officer Mike Balfany, he concluded that it wasn't a problem on this particular flight because we had a strong tailwind. So Yeaton requested a different altitude in order to decrease his fuel burn rate and maintain the same speed. The result? We arrived on time and the company saved money.

The results are not inconsequential. Southwest spent approximately $485 million in 1996 to fuel its airplanes. Depending on the altitude at which you fly, a 737 burns approximately 100 pounds, or 15 gallons, of fuel per minute. In 1996, the cost of 15 gallons of fuel was approximately $10. So every time a pilot gets a more direct heading and cuts a minute off flying time, the company saves $10 on that leg of the trip. Southwest has hundreds of pilots flying thousands of legs every week, each looking for ways to operate more expeditiously. The cost savings are significant, particularly when you consider that 20 percent of Southwest's cost structure is in fuel.

## THINK ABOUT EVERYBODY'S STAKE

Southwest pilots see the cockpits as their offices. And out of these offices, they are running a business in which hundreds of daily decisions affect the health and well-being of the company, as well as their profitsharing. Captain Yeaton says, "This is the first job I've had where the company actually encourages the pilot to get involved, to think. We get periodicals and memos on fuel burn and conservation all the time. I was at Eastern Airlines before this, and fuel burn was irrelevant to us. It should have been a factor, but it wasn't, because the relationship between management and pilots wasn't very good. There were a lot of opportunities to save money over there, but it didn't happen because people didn't care."

When Desert Storm broke out, jet fuel prices skyrocketed. Kelleher proudly remembers how quickly the pilots responded to the crisis this created: "I wrote a memo to our pilots and said, 'Fuel is just going sky high, we've got to cut back.' And in one week our costs went down, just like that. Now, let me contrast that with the consultant who wanted to set up an incentive program, whereby pilots' pay would be increased to the extent they conserved fuel. I kept telling the guy we didn't need to do that. Our pilots just did it on their own."

This incident perfectly illustrates the entrepreneurial spirit and ownership mentality Southwest employees bring to the job and the power of their initiative when they know how closely aligned their interests are with those of the company. The real secret to Southwest's success is having one of the most highly motivated and productive work forces in the world. They are motivated by a sense of fairness that says, "We want your well-being to be tied to the company's well-being because, after all, you *are* the company."

## LET EVERY EMPLOYEE MAKE A DIFFERENCE

There is no question that stock ownership is a tremendous incentive for employees, but it doesn't guarantee that they will think and act like owners. In fact, there are a lot of businesses in which employee stockholders are passive and reactive because they don't see how their individual efforts directly affect profitability. Ownership isn't just about having a piece of paper that says, "I own stock." Ownership is the result of believing that you can make a difference, then acting on that belief in everything you do.

When people see that their contributions are valued, their dignity and self-respect are enhanced. Instead of feeling like cogs in a machine or numbers on a spreadsheet, they feel that their work is important. To know that our labor counts is to know that *we* count.

Captain Chic Lang says, "One person can make a difference. A captain can make a whole lot of difference by example. Not because I can sit on the throne and throw around my four stripes, that's not it at all. Every person at Southwest can be a leader because you're given that chance. I love it because I think my little effort can make a huge difference—even as we've grown to two thousand pilots. Everybody feels that way. It's so much fun to go do a series of flights and see all the people working their butts off around you. You make a difference because you're allowed to!"

## ENGAGE EMPLOYEE HEARTS AND MINDS

Ownership isn't just about equity; it's about bringing something to the table—ideas, skills, and talents that others value and appreciate. When people feel involved, they care more. The more they care, the more willing they are to assume ownership. Jack Welch, GE's chairman and chief executive officer, believes that engaging people's hearts and minds is the key to everything: "I think any company that's trying to play in the 1990s has got to find a way to engage the mind of every single employee. If you're not thinking all the time about making every person more valuable, you don't have a chance. What's the alternative? Wasted minds? Uninvolved people? A labor force that's angry or bored? That doesn't make sense!"

At Southwest, people put passion, energy, enthusiasm, and motivation into their work because they truly believe that they are playing a crucial role in shaping the airline's destiny. It's the mechanic who changes a tire on the landing gear in six minutes to turn a plane on time; it's the provisioner who spends his own time designing a new ice chest for the provisioning trucks that will decrease melting and reduce the amount of ice a station needs by 45 percent; and it's the freight coordinator who goes way above and beyond company policy to ensure that a customer who arrives late at the cargo office gets her package to its destination on time. In each case, these people are thoroughly convinced that their efforts directly contribute to the company's profitability, their job security, and, most importantly, a work environment they wouldn't trade for any other in the world.

*Twenty-fifth anniversary ad salutes original employees* (left to right) *Jerry Puckett, lead shop mechanic; Jim Eldredge, lead stock clerk; Bill Lawrence, ground equipment mechanic; Ray Phillips, lead line mechanic; Karson Druckamiller, lead shop mechanic; Tony Gobernatz, supervisor aircraft field services.*

*After 25 years it's nice to take a step back and admire what you've accomplished.*

OUR AIRCRAFT MAINTENANCE TEAM HAS ALWAYS KEPT OUR FLEET IN TOP OPERATING FORM. WE HAVE AS MUCH PRIDE IN THEM AS
THEY HAVE IN THEIR JOB. TO THESE SIX ORIGINAL EMPLOYEES WE WOULD LIKE TO SAY THANKS. OKAY GUYS, BREAK'S OVER.

People will automatically assume ownership for protecting the right to be engaged in work that gives them a sense of meaning and significance. Why? Because there's a tremendous amount of spiritual, emotional, and psychic gratification that comes from meaningful work. Much like the runner who experiences a "runner's high," people who encounter this joy and aliveness in their work become fanatical about the natural high it produces. Once they get a taste of how good it can really be, they assume ownership and take responsibility for doing whatever it takes to protect this euphoric feeling.

> *"Any company that's trying to play in the 1990s has got to find a way to engage the mind of every single employee."*

Do Southwest employees deliver world-class productivity because they own stock and their profitsharing is tied to the company's success? Absolutely. But don't be fooled into thinking that you can run out and institute an employee stock-ownership plan tomorrow and achieve the same results. "If money were the only motivator," Colleen Barrett says, "probably half of our directors and officers wouldn't be here, because most of them could go out and earn more money elsewhere." Employees at Southwest Airlines exhibit a tremendous sense of ownership for the success of the business because they truly believe that what they are doing makes a difference.

## LAY OUT THE GUIDING PRINCIPLES

There is no question that ownership requires faith and confidence. As a leader, you have to be confident that when the decisive moment comes, those who have assumed ownership will exercise common sense and good judgment. As the one assuming ownership, you have to be confident that what you are doing is the right thing because, after all, with ownership comes responsibility and accountability. Exercising good judgment and doing the right thing when the path is uncertain result from a clear understanding of the company's guiding principles. The company's business purpose and strategies, its mission, vision, values, and philosophy, all define those principles. When the principles driving an organization are clear, employees have more freedom to step up, assume ownership, and take action for getting things done. When the principles are fuzzy, people tend to stick to the rules and cautiously gravitate toward the center of the playing field, where things are safe.

Aside from the fact that they are humble enough to admit that they don't know it all and that the company is lean enough that they don't have a choice, Southwest's executives are comfortable giving front-line employees a lot of authority and responsibility. This is because the senior management group trusts its people to make decisions and take actions that are consistent with Southwest's purpose and strategy. For example, former flight attendant Kathy Pettit, now director of customers at Southwest's headquarters, was given the power and authority to negotiate with Boeing on the cabin design of the new 737-700. Southwest was convinced that she would make decisions that were consistent with what the company was trying to accomplish because she understood its purpose and strategy so well. Southwest is not big on throwing around management buzzwords, but there is a deep yet profoundly simple connection between the freedom and empowerment Southwest employees have to assume ownership for the company's success and the clarity they have regarding the company's purpose and strategy.

We would be flat-out lying if we said all twenty-five thousand employees at Southwest Airlines have written on their hearts and in their minds the company's mission, vision, values, and philosophy. Like every other organization, Southwest still struggles to get people to live by the guiding principles that are essential to its success. However, the employees who have trouble embracing the company's values and philosophy are by far the exception. You can ask almost any mechanic, ramp agent, operations agent, pilot, flight attendant, customer service agent, or general office worker to state the mission, vision, values, and philosophy of Southwest Airlines, and the answer they give you will be close to the answer you would get from Herb Kelleher himself. The only difference, Herb says, is that "employees will be more articulate."

## COMMUNICATE, COMMUNICATE, AND THEN COMMUNICATE SOME MORE

One of the reasons Southwest has been so successful in getting people to internalize and embrace the company's principles and priorities is consistent communication. Rather than having the mission statement in one place—the lobby—Southwest displays it everywhere in the system to serve as a performance standard and a constant reminder of what is important for all employees. Like an old bulldog that playfully grabs your pants leg and refuses to let go, the airline tenaciously looks for ways to communicate its mission, vision, values, and philosophy to employees, over and over again. "The only way to change people's minds is with consistency," Jack Welch says. "Once you get the ideas, you keep refining them and improving them; the more simply your idea is defined, the better it is. You communicate, you communicate, and then you communicate some more. Consistency, simplicity, and repetition is what it's all about." Leaders throughout the company simply refuse to let go of the message; they continually find new ways to say it and new means to communicate it, but the core values and basic philosophy remain the same.

Whether it's in a memo, *LUV Lines*, Herb's Message to the Field, a training program, an ad campaign, or an awards ceremony, employees are constantly being exposed to, and challenged with, the guiding principles that have made Southwest great. The guidelines for running the business have been internalized by employees because they've had years of consistent exposure.

## USE TRUST TO INSPIRE OWNERSHIP

In January 1995, Southwest reached another milestone in aviation history. In an unprecedented move, Southwest pilots signed a ten-year contract with the company. Ten years is unheard-of in any collective bargaining situation, but what makes this contract unique is not just its length, but also the fact that the pilots agreed to freeze their wages for the first five years in return for stock options.

Both the company and the Southwest Airlines Pilots' Association (SWAPA) are very proud of this contract. And rightly so. It symbolizes the kind of relationship Southwest has built with its pilots—a relationship built on trust. Reflecting on the significance of the groundbreaking pact with the pilots, Gary Barron said, "To me, the bigger thing was the level of trust that had to exist between management and the employee group to get them to agree to it. It's not just the money. They signed a contract which froze work rules in place for that ten-year period because they believe that we are willing, if things change dramatically, to change something if it needs to be changed. And that takes a lot of trust."

Trust is crucial; it's the foundation of all relationships. Putting our trust in others tells them we think they are trustworthy. It suggests that we have faith in their character and their competence. Trust is a prerequisite to ownership because it strengthens self-confidence. "If you assign people heavy responsibilities, that implies confidence in them, and belief in their ability to deliver the goods," says Price Pritchett, author of *Firing Up Commitment during Organizational Change.* "Such a move stimulates their desire to prove your faith is well-founded." One of the reasons pilots are willing to assume ownership for Southwest's success is that they are confident they will have a crucial role in shaping the company's future.

Trust also opens the door to change. The 1995 agreement between Southwest and its pilots represents a significant departure from industry norms. Southwest pilots would have been unwilling to take the risks associated with such a long-term commitment had there not been years of trust built up between them and management.

Obviously, trust isn't built overnight. At Southwest, union negotiations don't happen only every three or four years; they go on every day, all year long. As Jim Wimberly, vice president of ground operations, puts it, "It's the way you treat people on a daily basis that impacts the degree of success you have when you officially sit down to work out a contract." "You have to work at it continually and demon-

## DEAR MR. KELLEHER

*WOW, I'm impressed! . . . I received the enclosed note along with a new Southwest luggage tag today. I can't tell you how many luggage tags I've lost over the years, and this is the first one ever to be returned, by a pilot no less.*

KATHY CHANCE
SATISFIED CUSTOMER
CHICO, CALIFORNIA

*Hey guys, slow down, we're trying to thank you.*

THESE FOUR EMPLOYEES RESUPPLY AIRCRAFT, BOARD CUSTOMERS, HANDLE ALL THE PAPERWORK, AND STILL TURN OUR PLANES AROUND FASTER THAN ANY OTHER AIRLINE. SO AFTER 25 YEARS, WE'D LIKE TO TAKE JUST A MOMENT OF THEIR TIME AND SAY THANKS.

*uthwest honors original employees for twenty-five years 'on-time performance in a 1996 anniversary ad.* **Left to ght:** *Carl Warrell, station manager; Joy Bardo, senior ministrative coordinator; Frank Martiniano, operations pervisor; Mike Mitchell, operations agent*

strate to people that you have the same interests," Gary Barron adds. "You can't wait until contract negotiations and ask them to trust you and agree to things they don't believe in, and then go out and stab them in the back for the five years of the contract because you got an agreement. Just like any other relationship, it takes a long time."

## USE INTEGRITY TO FUEL TRUST

Trust is fed by personal integrity. Trust grows when we keep our promises and follow through on our commitments. You have to be deadly earnest, completely authentic, and do what you say you are going to do to earn people's trust. When people know they can count on you, your words and actions have more power to influence them. This is why Herb Kelleher and Southwest Airlines have had such successful union relationships. Kelleher is a man of his word. He thinks straight and he talks straight, so people respect and trust him.

Rod Jones, a former union representative, remembers that when he first arrived at Southwest his union's board of directors was in the final phase of establishing a contract with the company. The package had been approved, except for one item. The union had a pilot whom the board thought the company had treated unfairly. Board members wanted this matter taken care of before they recommended the contract to the pilot group.

At dinner on the evening of the board meeting, Kelleher and John Schnobrich, president of the union at the time, discussed the issue over drinks. When the board reconvened the next morning, Schnobrich indicated that the issue had been resolved.

Jones recalls: "As the new union rep, I said, 'How was it taken care of?' Schnobrich said, 'Herb told me it would be taken care of.' I said, 'Do we have it in writing?' I remember Schnobrich looking rather irritated and saying, 'You don't need it in writing. When Herb Kelleher tells you something is going to be taken care of, it's taken care of.' I said, 'So I'm supposed to assume that it's taken care of and recommend this contract to the pilots without it being in writing?'

Again, Schnobrich got kind of red in the face and said, 'I already told you once. Herb gave me his word on it and that's better than any piece of paper.' I looked around at the other people in the room, who had been doing this for a lot longer than I had, and I said, 'Okay, I think I understand now.' And, of course, the issue was taken care of, exactly as Herb said it would be."

It is this kind of integrity, built up over the years, that makes it safe for the pilots to enter into a contract that requires them to express their entrepreneurial spirits and assume ownership for the future of the business.

Kelleher has a unique philosophy about union negotiations, which also contributes to the trust his people have in him. His position has always been to negotiate with an abundance mentality. That is, instead of looking for ways to see how much he can squeeze out of people, Kelleher goes into the negotiation process asking the question, "What's the most we can give without jeopardizing job security and profitability?" During negotiations, Kelleher told Gary Kerans, president of SWAPA, that if the contract went through he would freeze his own salary and bonus for five years. Apparently, what's good for Southwest's pilots is good for its chairman as well.

Kelleher's actions in hundreds of situations like this illustrate one of the most powerful concepts in operation at Southwest: the chairman and chief executive officer owns, passionately and enthusiastically, those ideas he asks his people to embrace. It is his commitment that causes employees throughout the Southwest system to say, "Herb would never ask us to do anything he isn't willing to do himself."

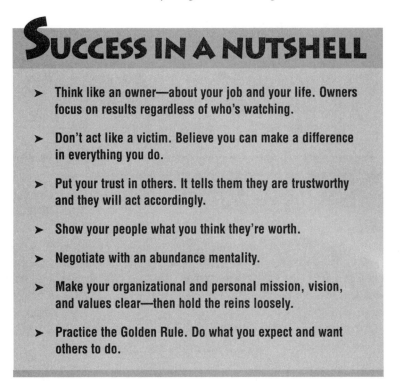

# SUCCESS IN A NUTSHELL

➤ Think like an owner—about your job and your life. Owners focus on results regardless of who's watching.

➤ Don't act like a victim. Believe you can make a difference in everything you do.

➤ Put your trust in others. It tells them they are trustworthy and they will act accordingly.

➤ Show your people what you think they're worth.

➤ Negotiate with an abundance mentality.

➤ Make your organizational and personal mission, vision, and values clear—then hold the reins loosely.

➤ Practice the Golden Rule. Do what you expect and want others to do.

# CHAPTER 9

# LEARN LIKE CRAZY

## STAY FRESH, STRETCH TO GROW

Arthur Schlesinger, Jr., sums up the speed of change in our fast-paced society in *The Cycles of American History* by observing that "a boy who saw the Wright Brothers fly for a few seconds at Kitty Hawk could have watched Apollo 11 land on the moon in 1969." No longer a luxury, learning is essential to staying ahead in a world of high-speed change.

> *"The illiterate of the future will not be the person who cannot read. It will be the person who does not know how to learn."*
>
> —*Alvin Toffler*

In the early days, learning was the key to Southwest's survival. If the people of Southwest Airlines hadn't been willing to learn, they would not have come up with the innovative strategies they used to compete with carriers that had more money and more resources. Today the company still believes that learning is essential to keeping its competitive advantage. Employees who embrace learning as a life-long pursuit are more alert, better informed, and more creative. This translates into new ways to simplify operations and cut costs, and new ways to better serve customers.

## CURIOSITY FUELS LEARNING

Do you ever wonder how little kids learn? They try things. Their curiosity is uninhibited. Free from the constraints of a "We've always done it this way" or "It'll never work" kind of world, they get great joy out of putting the wheels of exploration and experimentation in motion. Their minds are free to wander. Totally enthralled, they exhibit a refreshing sense of wonder while they learn. The people of Southwest Airlines have this same kind of childlike curiosity. Their tremendous sense of adventure makes them more open to learning and trying new things.

Herb Kelleher and Colleen Barrett are both intensely inquisitive. Barrett is willing to try almost anything once and is responsible for bringing many new ideas to the company. Kelleher is a student of life and a voracious reader who digs deeply into issues to understand them thoroughly. It is not unlike him to go on a book-buying binge and spend four or five hundred dollars at his favorite bookstore. When his son, David, was studying physics in college, Kelleher started reading up on the subject so the two of them could converse. Dave Ridley, vice president of marketing and sales, told us that Kelleher once bought a three-hundred-page history of Richmond, Virginia, and read it before speaking there at a symposium for CEOs sponsored by *Fortune* magazine. Ridley says of Kelleher's trip, "He ends up having dinner at some old-line Virginian's home talking about the history of Richmond. They're going around the city and Herb is pointing out where battleworks were set up and other places of historical importance. I don't know where he finds the time. He didn't do it to show off. He did it because he was going to a new place and he loves history."

People who are curious listen more attentively, ask more questions, and display a genuine interest in what others know. They suspend judgment until they have a firm grasp on the issues they are trying to understand. They listen to gain information, not to validate or confirm their own ideas. All of Southwest's officers bring curiosity to their jobs. In their unique ways, each of them balances inquiry and advocacy. As a result, Southwest employees feel that their ideas count. When an officer of the corporation says to an employee, "I don't know; what do you think?" that employee feels respected, and in turn becomes more open to learning.

## EMPATHY STIMULATES LEARNING

It's amazing how much you can learn from simply putting yourself in another person's shoes. Southwest accelerates the learning process by encouraging people to understand other people's jobs. This stimulates cross-functional communication and reminds people that there are perspectives other than their own. Learning, sharing, and understanding are the result.

To help pilots better understand a ramp agent's job, Cliff Slaughter, a Southwest Airlines captain, designed the Cutting Edge program. The idea was to get a group of Southwest pilots to work on

*The Cutting Edge program encouraged Southwest pilots to get out of the cockpit and onto the ramp to promote communication and teamwork between flight crews and ground operations teams.*

the ramp so they could learn more about what goes on around the plane or in its belly while it's at the gate. The team started visiting cities where the communication between ramp agents and pilots seemed to be breaking down. At first, the idea wasn't all that popular with the pilots. Many of them had been helping load bags for years, but a more formal program didn't excite a lot of them.

On the first day the Cutting Edge Team went into the field, Brian Dige, one of Southwest's senior captains, was in the cockpit starting the auxiliary power unit (APU), a small jet engine used to get the power on in the airplane. Dige, however, was in a ramp agent's uniform. As he was standing in the jetway, another pilot with whom he had gone through training walked right by him without recognizing or acknowledging him. The flight attendants with whom he tried to start a conversation appeared indifferent and uninterested. When Dige turned to the first officer and said, "I've got your APU started and I've aligned your IRS [internal reference system] to save you some time," the response was, "Since when are ramp agents allowed to start the APU?" Dige said, "Well, I'm a pilot." "Yeah, well, we've got a lot of guys around here flying light airplanes," the first officer chided. Captain Dige shook the first officer's hand and said, "Have a nice day." A few minutes later Brian Dige again ran into his classmate, the captain in command of the airplane that day. This time Dige's friend recognized him and said, "Brian, what are you doing up here?" Brian said, "You know, I've just been treated like a second-class citizen today because of the clothes I'm wearing, and that's wrong."

A similar incident happened with another flight crew in Austin. Dave "Bubba" Edens, Southwest's chief pilot in Oakland, was working the ramp in a ramp agent's uniform when the captain of the aircraft got on the headset and chewed him out—and engaged in behavior that was totally out of line with Southwest's values. When Edens said to the captain, "I don't appreciate your attitude," the captain replied, "That's your problem." At Phoenix, his next destination, this particular captain was met by chief pilot Jon Tree, who spelled out the Cutting Edge program to him and explained that his rudeness in Austin would not be tolerated again. If there is anything faster than the speed of light, it is the Southwest grapevine. This incident got everyone's attention in a matter of days. More to the point, it validated the need for pilots and ramp agents to improve communication and better understand each others' jobs.

A very enthusiastic captain and Cutting Edge Team member, Mark Boyter, explains that a culture exchange is any two people talking about Southwest Airlines. It doesn't have to be some big event; it's when employees talk to each other and develop a better understanding about what they do. The Cutting Edge program enables pilots and ramp agents to talk about how better to coordinate efficient ground and flight operations. In the course of these discussions, new pilots and new ramp agents get a sense of history from more senior pilots and ramp agents and learn why there is so much hustle on the ramp and in the cockpit.

Southwest employees have developed a greater sense of empathy for their coworkers as a result of the Cutting Edge program. Mark Boyter continues:

> *I remember one time when I was working the ramp in Los Angeles. I was dead tired. I had flown that morning and had a couple of legs in, so I got out of my uniform and jumped into my ramp clothes. That afternoon it was very hot. It was in the 80s— I can't imagine how they do it on a 120-degree day in Phoenix. I was tired and hungry and hadn't had a break. Then I saw this pilot sitting up there in the cockpit eating his frozen yogurt. I said to myself, "Man, I'd like to be up there right now." Then I caught myself. I'm up there every day. Now, I know that pilot has been up since 3:00 in the morning. I know that he's been flying an airplane since 6:00 A.M. I know it's 3:00 in the afternoon and he hasn't had a chance to get off and have a meal yet today. I know all that, and yet, the yogurt still looks really good to me. Then I thought, "How can a ramp agent in Los Angeles who works his butt off for two or three years, working double shifts two or three times a week, understand this?" It hit me that there's a big gap in understanding here.*

The Cutting Edge program built a tremendous amount of goodwill between the people flying the airplanes and the people unloading the bags, dumping the lavatories, and fueling the jets because Cliff Slaughter took the initiative to create opportunities for learning.

## INFORMATION IS POWER

Information that is presented creatively is engaging. Information that is immediate provides a real-time, current perspective and is, there-

# ON THE CUTTING EDGE

*Through the Cutting Edge program, thousands of culture exchanges have occurred on the ramp between ramp agents, operations agents, and pilots. The pilots get the ramp agents up into the cockpit and show them what it takes to get the plane going; ramp agents learn that getting their headsets on thirty seconds earlier enables them to run through their checklists with the pilots earlier so the pilots can push back from the gate sooner. Thirty seconds saved at the gate means that Southwest is ahead of two or three other airplanes. This can make a big difference because FAA regulations require mileage separation between planes going in the same direction. Thirty seconds could mean getting stuck behind other airplanes, which could cost Southwest five or ten minutes at the next city. Thirty seconds on the second flight segment of the day might put the aircraft at number five for takeoff on the runway and cause it to be airborne twenty minutes late. The plane then gets caught in the middle of five or six other planes taking off at the next city. Still airborne, the aircraft goes into a ten-minute holding pattern while traffic clears up. Finally able to land, the plane pulls into the gate, completes a fifteen-minute turn, and then sits on the runway again waiting for three more aircraft to take off. At the end of the day, it's not difficult to see how this aircraft, which started out thirty seconds late, is now forty-five minutes late for the evening shift.*

fore, more useful. Finally, information that is relevant shows us how issues affect our lives and reminds us why things are important to us. Southwest has figured out that when information is creatively presented, immediate, and relevant, it stimulates people to learn. This is why Southwest employees don't mind being flooded with information. In fact, they crave it, because good information is addictive. It satisfies their curiosity and sharpens their good judgment and common sense.

Southwest disseminates massive amounts of information that grabs people's attention and leads to new understanding. When the company drafted its mission statement, the Employee Communications Department came up with a creative way of getting it into employees' hands. Every Southwest employee received a copy of the mission statement disguised as a prize in an oversized box of Cracker Jack. Employees loved it. Not only did they read the mission statement, it became a topic of conversation throughout the company. Many people learn through dialogue. The more Southwest employees discussed the mission statement among themselves, the more they began to understand its meaning.

Another way Southwest disseminates information is through its corporate newsletter, *LUV Lines*. Published by a creative and talented group in the Employee Communications Department, *LUV Lines* is a powerful and effective tool for creating knowledge. A company newsletter alone can't create a learning environment; however, Southwest Airlines does a very good job of using its monthly newsletter to educate employees. *LUV Lines* is filled with information that Southwest employees look forward to. The information is presented in such a way that it causes people to want to learn. In addition to featured topics, the newsletter includes several sections ("The Learning Edge," "How Do We Rate," "Industry News," and "Milestones") that keep Southwest's work force informed on business developments and inspire new ways of thinking about their jobs. By creatively and frequently disseminating information, Southwest is empowering its work force to pioneer innovation and willingly embrace change.

### Learning through Metaphor

"The Learning Edge," a segment that appears frequently in *LUV Lines*, is written by the People Department and provides employees with new ideas or insights that will help them do their jobs better. For example, in a 1991 issue of *LUV Lines*, "The Learning Edge" borrowed from naturalist Milton Olsen's work on the behavior of geese to make an interesting point about teamwork.

> *This spring when you see geese heading back north for the summer flying along in "V" formation, you might be interested in knowing what scientists have discovered about why they fly that way. It has been learned that as each bird flaps its wings, it creates an uplift for the bird immediately following.*

*By flying in "V" formation, the whole flock adds at least
71 percent greater flying range than if each bird flew on its own.*
    **Basic Truth No. 1:** *People who share a common direction
and sense of community can get where they are going quicker and
easier because they are traveling on the thrust of one another.*

*Whenever a goose falls out of formation it suddenly feels the drag
and resistance of trying to go it alone and quickly gets back into
formation to take advantage of the lifting power of the bird
immediately in front.*
    **Basic Truth No. 2:** *There is strength and power (safety, too)
in numbers when traveling in the same direction as others with
whom we share a common goal.*

*When the lead goose gets tired, he rotates back in the wing and
another goose flies point.*
    **Basic Truth No. 3:** *It pays to take turns doing hard jobs—
with people or with geese flying north.*

*These geese honk from behind to encourage those up front to keep
up their speed.*
    **Basic Truth No. 4:** *Those who are exercising leadership
need to be remembered with our active support and praise.*

*Finally, when a goose gets sick or is wounded by gunshot and falls
out, two geese fall out of formation and follow him down to help
and protect him. They stay with him until he is either able to fly
or until he is dead, and then they launch out on their own or with
another formation to catch up with their group.*
    **Basic Truth No. 5:** *We must stand by those among us in
their times of need.*

People learn more easily and retain information longer when the
lesson is housed in a story, illustration, or metaphor. Southwest continually teaches through illustrations like this one so that the learning
process is more interesting and the lesson more memorable for
employees.

### Learning through Life
Another opportunity for learning, called "Scenario," appears in *LUV
Lines* periodically. This part of the newsletter presents "real life"
Southwest stories from which employees can learn. Sometimes

"Scenarios" come in the form of short case studies; other times they are written as anecdotes. The following piece by Jon Shubert, manager of executive office communications, from the December 1992 issue is a good example:

> *It is inevitable that we will not be able to please all of our Customers all of the time. The complaints we receive usually fall into two categories: (1) we didn't do something we should have; or (2) we did something we shouldn't have. So, beware the pitfalls of, respectively,* Omission *and* Commission!

Omission

- *A Customer writes, "Your employees didn't apologize even once!" We've seen that complaint many times. That's Omission, because we didn't do something we should have.*

- *"We waited in the gate area for almost two hours, and no one updated us on our delayed flight." Omission.*

> *Work on empathizing with our Customers. Let them know what, when, why, and how to the best of your knowledge. Keep them informed. Let them know we care and we're sorry. After all, everyone wants explanations—and everyone deserves apologies.*

Commission
*Commission, on the other hand, is when we do too much. How could that upset a Customer, you ask? Well, consider "verbal communication":*

- *Mr. Bigg arrives just as the flight closes and demands that you and your cohorts form a human bridge from the jetway to the aircraft door. This is not a good time to engage in off-the-cuff lecturing: "You should have been here sooner!" That's Commission. (And Customers routinely classify this as "verbal abuse" in their letters.) Save the "tsk, tsk"-ing for Rover when he gnaws on the corners of the Chippendale.*

- *Ms. Haverman's Guccis didn't arrive. Practicing armchair psychology will only make matters worse. "Maybe you just thought you handed them over at curbside to a Southwest employee. Are you sure he was wearing a Southwest uniform?" Commission. Engaging thusly is dangerous, and ranks up there with eating snakes.*

**Bottom Line Literacy**

Continually trying to help employees learn how their individual contributions make a difference is what distinguishes Southwest from a lot of other companies. It is rare for front-line employees to be as well educated and informed as they are at Southwest. Southwest doesn't treat front-line people like second-class citizens; it treats them like owners and partners who not only have a right to this information but, more importantly, *need* to know it in order to do their jobs effectively.

As part of its effort to keep employees informed, Southwest communicates the importance of every single customer by educating employees about how many customers the company actually needs to make a profit. By demonstrating to employees how just a few people can make the critical difference, the company encourages them to think about how their individual behaviors influence customer service. In November 1995, *LUV Lines* put customer service in perspective with the following piece on profitability:

> *How important is every Customer to our future? Our Finance Department reports that our break-even Customers per flight in 1994 was 74.5, which means that, on average, only when Customer #75 came on board did a flight become profitable!*
>
> *Aside from that statistical data, let me share with you a down-to-earth formula devised by our Dallas chief pilot, Ken Gile. It utilizes our annual profit and total flights flown to clearly illustrate how vital each Customer is to our profitability and our very existence.*
>
> *When you divide our 1994 annual profit by total flights flown, you get profit per flight:*
>
> $$\frac{\$179,331,000 \ (annual \ profit)}{624,476 \ (total \ flights \ flown)} = \$287 \quad (profit \ per \ flight)$$
>
> *Then, divide profit per flight by Southwest's systemwide average one-way fare of $58:*
>
> $$\frac{\$287 \ (profit \ per \ flight)}{\$58 \ (average \ one\text{-}way \ fare)} = 5 \ (one\text{-}way \ fares \ [Customers!])$$
>
> *The bottom line, only five Customers per flight accounted for our total 1994 profit! In other words, just five Customers per*

*flight—only 3 million of the 40 million Customers we carried—
meant the difference between profit and loss for our airline in
1994. To take it a step further, to have lost the business of only
one of those Customers would have meant a 20 percent reduction
in profit on that flight. That's how valuable each Customer is to
Southwest and you!*

Every employee at Southwest Airlines understands that the company is in the customer service business. Captain Gile's formula helps make customer service tangible and personal for Southwest employees.

The *LUV Lines* article didn't stop with customer/profit statistics. It went on to educate employees about the importance of recovering from a poor service incident:

*Studies reveal that, on average, for each Customer who was
"wronged," there are 25 others who remained silent. The studies
claim that each person in this silent majority will, by word of
mouth, tell between 8 and 16 people—an average of 12—of their
complaint. (Over 10 percent will tell more than 20 people!) When
you do the math, a potential 300 people can be influenced by just
one negative situation. Here is what that factor means to
Southwest Airlines:*

*Last year, we heard from about 60,000 Customers who were
dissatisfied with some aspect of their experience with us. (Happily,
employee commendations outnumbered complaints by five to one!).*

*60,000 ("wronged" Southwest Customers)*
*×   25 (silent majority)*
*= 1,500,000 possible dissatisfied Southwest Customers*

*Now if those 1.5 million dissatisfied Southwest Customers told 12
others of their experience:*

*1,500,000*
*×   12 (word of mouth)*
*= 18,000,000 potential "influenced" Southwest Customers*

*Do you think that 18 million is enough Customers to put us out
of business? And, when you compare that 18 million potentially
lost or never-reached Customers with the 3 million which*

*accounted for our total 1994 profit, the significance of each and*
*every Customer becomes even more apparent.*
*    There is, however, a positive aspect of Customer complaints!*
*The aforementioned research also indicates that if you make a*
*sincere effort to remedy complaints and regain Customers' good-*
*will,* **82 to 95** *percent of those Customers will stay with you!*

"The company believes that employees who become 'literate' through articles like this are better equipped to provide their unique brand of warmth, friendliness, and hospitality to Southwest customers," says Ginger Hardage, v.p. of public relations and corporate communications. Research on customer service can be found in any number of books on the subject. What makes it so powerful here is that the writers of *LUV Lines* take the time to apply these studies in a way that is relevant and educational to Southwest employees.

### Revisiting Milestones

During the first quarter, *LUV Lines* highlights the previous year's milestones. This is a particularly important recap of its monthly "Milestones" feature for Southwest employees because it shows the company's progress and builds momentum for the new year. We've worked with firms that have done some pretty significant things during a year; unfortunately, the majority of their employees are unaware of these achievements. When we talk to them, it's as if they have no sense of progress or feeling of accomplishment. One of the reasons Southwest employees have so much pride and enthusiasm is because they are continually informed about the company's accomplishments.

### Keeping an Eye on the Competition

Frequently, *LUV Lines* educates employees about their overall performance in a segment called "How Do We Rate." In this part of the newsletter, employees review monthly statistics kept by the Department of Transportation for on-time performance, baggage handling, and customer complaints—the Triple Crown criteria. "How Do We Rate" usually compares the current month's performance with the previous month's performance and shows the company's rank in each of the three categories compared with other carriers. Industry averages are provided so people can spot trends and compare Southwest with the industry norms.

# SO, WHAT WAS HERB DOING ALL THIS TIME?

*"Milestones" usually includes a smaller segment titled "So, What Was Herb Doing All This Time?" to give employees a run-down of the major events in which Kelleher participated. These include station visits, days in the field, Ronald McDonald suppers, conferences, speeches, special employee events such as weddings and birthdays, media interviews, and television programs. This portion of "Milestones" is even more important as Southwest grows because it helps put Herb's job in perspective for employees. People who are disappointed because they don't get to see him as often as they would like develop a better understanding of how he spends his time.*

Southwest employees watch these statistics faithfully because they know that the airline's success depends on how well they do on each of these performance measures. When a major competitor ranks higher than Southwest for a couple of months, word travels through the system in a matter of days. The result is a critical mass of people spread out across more than fifty cities working to make the necessary changes.

If Southwest employees want to find out what another carrier has been up to, "Industry News" is the place to find the information in *LUV Lines.* The company compiles information on all of the major airlines, and in two or three pages employees learn about the financial performance, predicted expansion plans, aircraft acquisitions, and productivity of other carriers.

Between "Industry News" and "How Do We Rate," *LUV Lines* keeps Southwest employees up-to-date. From this foundation of knowledge, Southwest people are better equipped to take risks, try new things, and make fast decisions.

### Learning through Dialogue

The substantive information that comes out of *LUV Lines* does not replace leadership at Southwest Airlines. Learning takes place when leaders at all levels help each other interpret the information they get. We learn when we're drawn into a dialogue about the information we receive. At Southwest Airlines this dialogue almost always results in a better understanding of the implications of the information and its relevance to what people do. At this point information becomes

*It is rare for front-line employees to be as well educated and informed as they are at Southwest.*

knowledge. Once Southwest employees acquire knowledge, it can be used to influence change in their lives and in the organization. When they use the knowledge they've gained, their outlook becomes more focused, their judgment improves, and their discernment sharpens. That knowledge has become power.

## STRETCHING AND GROWING
## ACTIVATE LEARNING

Southwest Airlines is not afraid to give people with relatively little experience big, big responsibilities. Most of these people rise to the

# THE UNIVERSITY FOR PEOPLE

*Southwest's University for People is a multitiered learning facility staffed by the Employee Learning and Development Department. Its primary mission is to equip employees to practice the kind of leadership that Southwest Airlines expects. In addition to facilitating and teaching courses, faculty serve as internal consultants and change agents to ongoing work groups within the company. Because Southwest knows that its growth depends upon the growth of its people, the University offers a full catalog of courses designed to teach people how to lead with integrity, run a profitable airline, practice the principles of stewardship, care for customers, and live the company's core values. The University reinforces the importance of learning as a way of life at Southwest Airlines.*

occasion and grow like crazy. In the process, the company grows. When Southwest Airlines built its new corporate headquarters at Love Field in 1990, one of the company's biggest problems was how to make the interior of the huge 225,000-square-foot box aesthetically pleasing.

The FAA required that the building be low, given its proximity to the runway. A number of architects had come up with round atrium designs for the lobby (the building's main statement) that no one at Southwest was thrilled about. To break through the impasse, Southwest hired Robert Dorsey, fresh out of college at Texas Tech. After getting the lay of the land, Dorsey went home and, over the weekend, came up with a design that was different from any the company had seen. When it was presented to the executive planning committee the next week, the design received a unanimous thumbs up. Dorsey was subsequently charged with the design of the new building—the type of assignment that normally takes years for a junior member of an architectural firm to get. Southwest Airlines demonstrated again that it is not shackled by convention: it didn't operate under the assumption that Dorsey was too young and inexperienced for a project of this magnitude.

## *Southwest really doesn't care how people get the job done.*

Robert Dorsey then became the project manager for building construction. When an interior decorator told him that the lobby needed to make a statement and recommended a $30,000 area rug, Dorsey said, "I think we can do the same thing with carpet squares." And he did! When construction was nearing completion, Colleen Barrett began asking Dorsey for his recommendations on interior decorations. His response was always the same: "Let me sleep on it, Colleen." Little did Barrett know that the young architect (who wanted to make a good impression) was going home and asking his wife, Darla, what he should recommend. The next day he would come back with the perfect answer. Barrett became more and more impressed with his ideas. One day when they were making decisions about accessories for the executive boardroom, Barrett pressed him for an answer. After he gave his usual response, she said, "Robert, I need to know your recommendation today!" Dorsey's day of reckoning had come. When he told Barrett that he had been going home and asking Darla for guidance, she said, "Well, get her in here!"

Southwest really doesn't care how people get the job done. The company is much more interested in people like Dorsey, who can demonstrate the resourcefulness to find out how to do something if they can't do it themselves. The people of Southwest Airlines have chosen to create an atmosphere in which the childlike curiosity and enthusiasm in every employee is not only welcomed, it is sought after and drawn out. In an environment in which intuition is trusted and seemingly crazy ideas are routinely explored, learning has become a way of life.

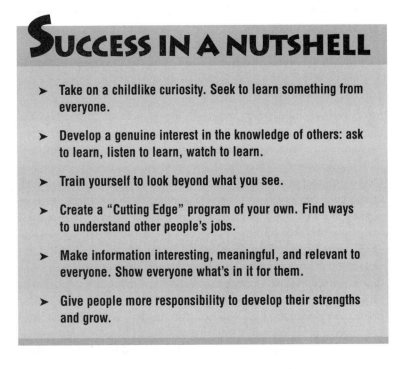

# Success in a Nutshell

➤ Take on a childlike curiosity. Seek to learn something from everyone.

➤ Develop a genuine interest in the knowledge of others: ask to learn, listen to learn, watch to learn.

➤ Train yourself to look beyond what you see.

➤ Create a "Cutting Edge" program of your own. Find ways to understand other people's jobs.

➤ Make information interesting, meaningful, and relevant to everyone. Show everyone what's in it for them.

➤ Give people more responsibility to develop their strengths and grow.

# CHAPTER 10

# DON'T FEAR FAILURE

## BE CREATIVE, COLOR OUTSIDE THE LINES

Southwest Airlines has chosen to fly in the face of convention and conformity. The company deliberately hires people who aren't afraid to express their individuality and color outside the lines. At Southwest there is no socially prescribed role that will gain you acceptance. Certainly, there are values and guidelines: providing Positively Outrageous Service and treating coworkers with kindness are non-negotiable. But the company encourages employees to live these values in their own way.

Once when Colleen Barrett was in an all-day meeting at the Oakland station, a couple of the ramp people interrupted the meeting with a pressing issue. Colleen excused herself from the meeting, and the employees took her out on the ramp to show off a tug with a brand-new paint job. This wasn't any old tug painted with the normal Southwest colors, however; it was painted jet black with an emblem just like the Oakland Raiders' football team logo. While delighted with the magnificent paint job, Colleen was even more impressed with the creativity and maverick spirit it represented. At most other airlines, this expression of creativity might have been seen as a waste

of on-duty time or a desecration of valuable equipment. Colleen applauded it because the company knows that the same ingenuity used to paint that tug is also used to solve problems on the ramp. Now in many Southwest cities with professional football teams, tugs are transformed into billboards supporting the local team.

Just before Vice President Al Gore visited Southwest Airlines in March 1993 in search of ideas for his reinventing government initiative, an advance team was sent to headquarters to establish security and make final preparations. The advance team wanted to give Southwest a list of questions for employees to ask Mr. Gore and suggested that Southwest handpick the people who would ask the questions, to reduce the risk that the vice president or Southwest Airlines would be embarrassed. Kelleher remembers Colleen Barrett saying, "No, our people would be so offended by that. I'm not worried about who the vice president calls on. Our people will be spontaneous; they will ask good, substantive questions; and they *will* be articulate!" The event actually turned out to be like the big, spontaneous town hall meeting the advance team envisioned. More importantly, it showed the trust and confidence Barrett has in Southwest employees, her interest in seeing them express their individuality, and her commitment to protecting that freedom of expression.

## QUESTION AUTHORITY AND
## CHALLENGE CONVENTION

Several years ago Kelleher came up with what he thought was a great concept for a new flight schedule. He got hot on the idea of reducing Southwest's flight schedule to shirt-pocket size, making it less cumbersome for customers to carry around. Although the Marketing Department opposed the idea, Kelleher continued to press for it. This went on until, finally, someone in marketing had the courage and insight to create a prototype schedule the size Herb was advocating. When they presented it to him, the print was so small he couldn't read it. Kelleher remembers saying, "I think I get the message now."

*"We've never tried to be like other airlines. From the very beginning we told our people, 'Question it. Challenge it. Remember, decades of conventional wisdom has sometimes led the airline industry into huge losses.'"*

Southwest employees demonstrate a lot of creativity with regard to cutting costs. But in many situations cost cutting requires someone who is not afraid to challenge the system. One of Southwest's flight attendants, Rhonda Holley, wrote to Colleen Barrett in 1994 suggesting that the company remove its logo from the white plastic bags used for collecting trash at the end of the flight. Her argument was that nobody really cares about a logo on a trash bag. After Joanne Lardon, purchasing manager, and Joyce Rogge, vice president of advertising and promotions, looked into it, they and Barrett decided that Holley had a good point. By using trash bags without logos, Southwest now saves $300,000 a year.

Southwest also encourages employees to challenge conventional wisdom. "We've never tried to be like other airlines," Kelleher is fond of saying. "From the very beginning we told our people, 'Question it. Challenge it. Remember, decades of conventional wisdom has sometimes led the airline industry into huge losses.'"

At Southwest every employee is a steward of the company's mission. If a policy or a practice appears to violate the intent of the company's mission or is inconsistent with its values, people are expected to speak up.

## REMOVE THE FEAR OF FAILURE

Real learning is almost impossible without experimentation, but experimenting is risky business. Anything really worth doing always requires some risk, and with risk comes failure. We vividly remember when our elder daughter, Taylor Grace, took her first steps. Pushing herself away from the wall was certainly a risk—one that involved immediate failure, a face-plant right into the carpet. Without too much initial shock, she pushed herself up and tried again—this time with a much higher degree of success. Rather than focus on her failed attempts, we applauded her small wins. Our encouragement combined with her thirst for adventure and aim to please gave her the courage to try again. If she were unwilling to risk and unwilling to make a few mistakes, Taylor Grace would be out of the walking business. It was uncomfortable to watch her fall, yet essential to her learning a new skill. Encouragement, rather than criticism, gave her the motivation to keep trying.

Somewhere in the journey between childhood and becoming adults many of us lose our tolerance for risk because we can't stand the rejection and lack of acceptance that often come with failure. Remove the fear of rejection and people become less inhibited by the prospect of failure. This is one of the major factors contributing to Southwest Airlines' outrageous business success.

### Eating Crow Is Good for the Soul!

At Southwest, it's okay to make mistakes—really! In 1985, after just three years with Southwest, Matt Buckley had moved from ramp and operations to manager of cargo at corporate headquarters. He proposed an idea that he was convinced would revolutionize the industry and catapult his career at the same time. The idea was a same-day, door-to-door cargo product called RUSH PLUS.

Buckley put together a detailed business plan for his new idea and made a well-rehearsed presentation to Kelleher, Barrett, GSD&M, and some key people in Southwest's Marketing Department. "I boldly promised a 50 percent revenue increase," Buckley recalls. "After all, Federal Express rocked the world in the '70s with its door-to-door service, and it was *next* day. I'll never forget getting the nod from Herb when he said, 'Let's try it!' As my pride swelled, I was overcome with the sensation of sticking a flag in a large mound of dirt at a very high altitude."

Matt Buckley and the people from GSD&M designed a hot new logo for the product and developed an aggressive advertising campaign including full-color newspaper ads. Buckley presented his business plan to senior management, station managers, and the entire field marketing staff at Southwest Airlines. Colleen Barrett wrote each member of the board of directors, urging them to dump Federal Express and use RUSH PLUS instead. Buckley says, "I was so caught up in the hoopla I adopted a proud new battle cry of 'It's Hot, It's Happenin', It's RUSH PLUS!' I felt like I was starring in my own movie. Little did I know, a lifetime supply of humble pie was baking for my consumption."

Southwest had extra phone lines installed to handle the huge demand Buckley anticipated. On the big day the phone rang very little. In fact, the phone didn't ring much the first week or the first month. By the end of the second month Buckley and his peers were convinced that the phone wasn't going to ring. RUSH PLUS was declared a total bust. Buckley remembers, "As far as I was concerned, my life was over and the headstone read, 'Here Lies a Failure. RUSH PLUS Was Not Hot. Nor Was It Happenin'.'"

Matt's sense of failure was more painful than anything he had ever experienced. Humiliated and ashamed, he dodged people in the halls, especially Kelleher, and opted out of company functions to avoid RUSH PLUS jokes. Buckley's depression was eventually overcome by love and support from Southwest people. He says:

> *The more I was exposed to the jokes and jabs, the better I felt. I finally realized that people were actually trying to help me heal. It became easier to look people in the eye as time went on. Despite my overpromising and underproducing, people showed support and continued to reiterate, "It's okay to make mistakes; that's how you learn." In most companies, I'd probably have been fired, written off, and sent out to pasture. But, in this lifetime, I'd be hard-pressed to find the kind of love and forgiveness bestowed upon me by so many to allow me to save face.*

Kelleher remembers that when Vice President Gore met with employees in Southwest's atrium, Buckley stood up and told him, "One thing I like about this company is that I made this terrible mistake on RUSH PLUS and Herb didn't fire me." At the time, Kelleher quickly joked, "Mr. Vice President, what Matt doesn't know is that he's a short-termer."

It's obvious that Buckley has grown from the RUSH PLUS experience. Reflecting on this character-building event, he says, "Eating a little crow is good for the soul when you're in the right environment. RUSH PLUS was initially about me. It was about making my mark in my company. Self, self, self! That's what I was into. Since then I've learned that's not what's rewarded around here. It's not about self. It's about the Golden Rule, and it's about serving rather than being served."

Southwest has promoted Matt Buckley four times since RUSH PLUS. The reasons are pretty straightforward. First, the company values his entrepreneurial spirit and enthusiasm. Second, Buckley was able to turn failure into an opportunity for personal growth and maturity. If we are open to learning from them, mistakes teach us a lot about ourselves and the methods we use for getting things done.

### Forgiveness Transforms Failure

Southwest encourages its people to step out and take risks—knowing full well that some of them will fail. Is it uncomfortable for Southwest executives to watch their employees fail? Certainly. But Southwest has chosen to take a long-term perspective when it comes to developing people. The company understands that part of helping employees like Matt Buckley become seasoned leaders involves giving them the freedom to make mistakes and to learn from them.

While Southwest doesn't encourage people to be reckless and irresponsible, the company recognizes that in an action-oriented, get-it-done culture, where front-line employees have a lot of responsibility and authority, mistakes will happen. In these instances, failure is not fatal. In fact, Southwest does everything it can to maintain the dignity of and respect for employees who make mistakes. "If one of our employees commits Southwest Airlines to doing something," Kelleher says, "we stand behind that commitment—even if it's a bad business decision."

Southwest's properties and facilities people have the authority to negotiate deals regarding construction of new gates and renovation of ticket counters, deals that involve millions of dollars; they don't have to go through the bureaucratic process of seeking approval from the board or senior management. When Bob Montgomery, then

Southwest's manager of properties, was new to the Properties Department, he made a commitment to the City of Austin on a business deal that ended up being a $400,000 mistake. During negotiations, Montgomery made a verbal commitment on behalf of Southwest Airlines to fund some preliminary design work for a new airport the City of Austin wanted to build. From Southwest's perspective, however, the new airport was a mistake. When Kelleher heard about it, he asked if the deal had been signed. When the response came back, "No, but Bob told them we would," Kelleher said, "If Bob represented that we would sign it, then that's what we're going to do."

> *"The costs of getting burned once in a while are insignificant compared to the benefits that come from people feeling free to take risks and be creative."*

Montgomery expected to be fired, but he wasn't. A year later when he and Kelleher were flying back from Detroit together, Montgomery said, "Herb, that was a pretty stupid mistake I made, costing the company $400,000 and all. It should never have happened." Kelleher responded, "Bob, I'm glad you *finally* learned from it." It was a serious message delivered in Kelleher's typical lighthearted way. After that discussion, the issue was dead. Montgomery learned from a serious mistake without losing his dignity in the process; he has since been promoted to director of properties.

Southwest has also learned that when employees are encouraged to take risks and are held accountable for keeping costs low, they may end up doing the wrong things for the right reasons. On November 6, 1995, Jim Wimberly got a call from Dispatch as he walked through the door of his office. "Hey, we're taking delays in Spokane because the first snowfall of the year hit and we didn't have the deicing equipment ready." A few hours later Jim got another call. This time it was from Dave Yarbrough, Southwest's station manager in Spokane: "We got caught with our pants down. We were expecting one to two inches of snowfall and we got four to six inches instead." That morning Southwest took one-and-a-half-hour delays on two of its flights out of Spokane, causing a huge inconvenience to customers and messing up the schedule for the entire day. Wimberly says, "When you get two airplanes that are an hour late, it's not just the

274 people that are on board those two aircraft. You potentially impact 2,500 people that day and maybe even 3,000."

The ramp supervisor on duty and the station manager took a risk and, unfortunately, made a mistake. Because deicing isn't a routine activity in Spokane, Southwest usually calls in additional people to perform the deicing procedures when necessary. This requires paying overtime. Trying to save the company money by avoiding the cost of overtime, the ramp supervisor and the station manager attempted to have the Spokane ground crew conduct their normal activities in addition to deicing the planes. Wimberly says, "I am much more tolerant of those kinds of mistakes because I understand the motivation and decision making behind them. When asked whether they are more interested in saving a few bucks or upsetting the customer, both of these people would say that customer service comes first." Wimberly told the ground crew in Spokane that there was nothing to be fearful about: "You made a decision; it turned out to be the wrong one; but tomorrow is another day. Let's learn from it and push on."

At this point you might be tempted to say, "Southwest Airlines is too lenient; the company has taken forgiveness too far." Has Southwest had to pay a price for encouraging people to take risks? Absolutely. When you allow people to make mistakes, you are going to get burned. But the people of Southwest Airlines would be quick to respond, "The costs of getting burned once in a while are insignificant compared to the benefits that come from people feeling free to take risks and be creative." One of the reasons people like Matt Buckley and Bob Montgomery are so dedicated to the company is that Southwest has treated them with dignity and respect—even when they've made big mistakes. Talk to these two individuals about their enthusiasm for Southwest Airlines and you will be hard-pressed to find two more loyal fans.

## MAKE WORK AN ADVENTURE

Southwest employees are an adventurous bunch. They like to take on new endeavors—particularly if the activity involves some risk. Their adventurousness goes back to the very beginning, when the fight for survival required imagination and ingenuity. Many of the people who launched Southwest Airlines came from companies where their creativity was inhibited. For these employees, Southwest was one big adventure. It represented an opportunity to express their creativity and try things in the airline industry that had never been done before. Each time they tried something new, they learned a little bit more.

The spirit of adventure that brought the company into existence is still alive and well. Most of today's pioneers have different faces, but their desire for adventure is no less passionate and their creativity is no less astonishing than that of their counterparts who blazed the trail. "The spirit of adventure is the fuel that drives the creative engine," says Doug Hall in *Jump Start Your Brain.* "It awakens the imagination, fires up the adrenaline, and ignites the willingness to try." The proof of Hall's statement can be seen in any number of innovations created by Southwest's contemporary trailblazers.

### Go Ticketless

On January 31, 1995, Southwest Airlines became the first major carrier to offer ticketless travel systemwide. This milestone is an example of the creativity and entrepreneurial spirit shown by Southwest employees when they are in a crunch. Southwest had been ejected from three major reservations systems. United's system, Apollo, kicked the company out when United decided to create the United Shuttle; Continental ousted Southwest because of competition with Continental Lite (another Southwest clone); and Southwest was downgraded in Delta's Worldspan because of its entry into Delta's Salt Lake City hub. Conventional wisdom says that if 55 percent of your business comes through computer reservations systems and you get kicked off three of them, you're in big trouble. Unless, of course, you decide to sidestep those reservations systems altogether.

In May 1994 employees from Ground Operations, Systems, Reservations, Finance, Technical Services, Customer Relations, Executive Office, Network Operations, Internal Audit, and Marketing got together to figure out how they could do just that. The group met on their own initiative, without seeking permission from anyone to pursue the project . The original idea was laid out on a cocktail napkin. (Sound familiar?) Bill Lyons, controller, led a core team through the rigors of designing, developing software for testing, and fine-tuning the ticketless system. In just four months the new system was ready. Meanwhile, Kelleher spouted off at an American Society of Travel Agents (ASTA) meeting that Southwest would go ticketless

*Southwest boarded its one-millionth ticketless customer on March 21, 1995—less than sixty days after offering ticketless travel systemwide.*

before he even knew that an entrepreneurial group within the company had been working on the idea.

Ticketless travel allows customers to bypass the computer reservations systems completely; they get a confirmation number from Southwest and show up at flight time. Customers who use a travel agent go through the same process, only now travel agents don't have to hand-write tickets when ticketing Southwest's customers.

The benefits to customers and to Southwest are enormous. Less paperwork to be processed means greater savings. Quicker processing means shorter lines at the ticket counter. Some consultants estimate that an airline's direct costs for issuing a paper ticket are approximately $7. When you figure that Southwest issues forty million tickets a year, the savings are significant. Southwest anticipates that, ultimately, its costs will be reduced by as much as $100 million a year. Customers gain the convenience of ticketless travel and also benefit from the cost savings passed on in continued low fares.

### Make It from Scratch

Another example stars a very enthusiastic trailblazer, Mike Golden, Southwest's current vp of purchasing and former director of technical services and a team of creative technicians. Trained in digital electronics and electromechanics, this group really knows each piece of electronic equipment Southwest uses. When eight hundred computers were needed for Southwest's new reservations center in Albuquerque, Golden decided they could build them more cost effectively than buying them. Jim Parker, vice president and general counsel, remembers: "We had a big internal debate over which computer—IBM, Compaq, or Macintosh—would be the official standard at Southwest Airlines. Mike Golden and his Technical Services Department said, 'Well, we can buy the box; we can buy the parts; we can put the parts together; and we can do all of that for about half of what it would cost us to buy the PCs.'" "Mike's Tronics," as the technical services group is affectionately referred to by Southwest employees, put the word out that if people were willing to join an assembly line, Technical Services would buy the pizza and beer. They got a lot of takers. With computer parts purchased at Sam's Club, Radio Shack, and various wholesalers, Southwest employees, most of whom knew nothing about computers, worked side by side on an assembly line building them. Golden reduced the cost of each computer by 50 percent, saving Southwest Airlines over $1 million.

### A Ticket in a Minute

In early 1979 Bill Franklin, vice president of ground operations, Lowell McAlister, manager of publications and procedures, and Gary Stacy, director of accounting, got together to explore ways to increase customer service agent productivity. The goal was to reduce the time each customer spent in line waiting to be ticketed without increasing the number of customer service agents. Borrowing from the automatic teller machines used by banks, the group came up with an idea for an automated ticket vending machine (ATVM). According to Audy Donelson, a Southwest ground operations employee, "The whole idea was thought up in a bar one night in Denver."

Here's how it works. A customer runs a credit card through the machine, presses the button for the destination city, and then chooses one-way or round-trip. In seconds, the machine spits out a ticket. The whole process takes less than a minute. Customers purchasing tickets with credit cards can be ticketed without assistance and reduce their wait. Customer service agents can spend more time with customers needing assistance. Cash flow is enhanced by credit card transactions that can be billed more quickly.

Cubic Corporation in San Diego was enlisted to build the "Quicket Machines," and the first one was received in 1980. The results have been rather impressive. Billings now total about $62 million annually from sixty-one ATVMs used throughout Southwest's system. Each ATVM conducts as many transactions as two customer service agents per shift. Increased productivity, improved cash flow, and additional options for getting through the airport hassle-free are among the benefits resulting from this kind of entrepreneurial thinking.

After the first Quicket Machines were put in, Southwest Airlines introduced restricted-fare tickets and expanded its routes. As a result, the company outgrew the number of buttons on the machines. Rather than go through an expensive modification from the manufacturer, Mike's Tronics got involved. Using off-the-shelf computer parts, Technical Services built the machines themselves. The per-unit costs fell from $50,000 to $14,000, again saving the company over $1 million. Today, when a Southwest employee orders a new PC, Golden's former team builds it. When a station orders a new arrival/departure screen, Golden's former team builds it. Mike Golden's spirit of adventure is the catalyst that drives his creativity. It's obviously contagious. In the case of Mike's Tronics, a sense of adventure pays off—big time!

## PLAY TO WIN, DON'T PLAY NOT TO LOSE

Whether it's opening a new city, putting on a celebration, or running an ad campaign, when Southwest people go for it, they really go for it. A lot of people in business operate as though they are playing not to lose—there is an attitude of timidity or hesitation in their approach. Sometimes cautiousness smothers creativity. Southwest employees do just the opposite. Their philosophy is jump in with both feet and play to win.

When Southwest wanted to increase the number of its daily flights at Sky Harbor's old Terminal One in Phoenix, the problem was gates. The company had only three, and the terminal simply didn't have the capacity to support any more gate space. Mike Golden, Bob Montgomery, and facilities director Dave Spears weren't constrained by circumstances, though. They devised a plan that would enable Southwest to put up prefabricated modules that looked like mobile homes on the tarmac in front of Terminal One. With working drawings in hand, they went to Kelleher and said, "We think we can build six gates in Phoenix. The manufacturer of these prefabricated modules said they could do it in ninety days." Kelleher asked, "Are you sure you can do it?" When the crew assured him that it could be done, he gave them the go-ahead. What they didn't realize was that, based on their estimate, Kelleher committed a whole new flight schedule to publication two days later.

### *When Southwest people go for it, they really go for it— they jump in with both feet and play to win.*

The plot quickly thickened. When Montgomery called to order the modules in November, the manufacturer told him it had made a mistake. It was now going to take twice as long and cost twice as much to build them. With the printed schedule showing additional Phoenix flights starting up on March 10, the manufacturer's time frame was unacceptable.

Dave Spears rallied the group and said, "We'll do it on our own." The crew hired a construction firm to build the structures conventionally while people from Properties, Facilities, Technical Services, and Telecommunications spent the next three months working eighteen-hour days to build the new gates. The crew even rented an apartment in Phoenix for the duration of the project so that they could work around the clock. Montgomery says, "There were only five or six of us and we were doing things we'd never done before. We

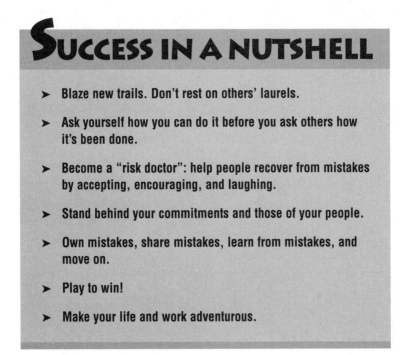

# SUCCESS IN A NUTSHELL

➤ Blaze new trails. Don't rest on others' laurels.

➤ Ask yourself how you can do it before you ask others how it's been done.

➤ Become a "risk doctor": help people recover from mistakes by accepting, encouraging, and laughing.

➤ Stand behind your commitments and those of your people.

➤ Own mistakes, share mistakes, learn from mistakes, and move on.

➤ Play to win!

➤ Make your life and work adventurous.

didn't know anything about the installation of speakers and intercoms, but we figured it out." The crew referred to themselves as the "B Team," which stood for "We be here; we be there; but, mostly, we be behind." On March 10, just four months after the team had approached Kelleher with the idea, six new Southwest gates were up and running at Terminal One in Phoenix.

Stimulated by crisis and their spirit of adventure, Bob Montgomery and his colleagues played to win. They were encouraged to use their imagination and express their individuality. In the final analysis, a creative solution enabled Southwest Airlines to establish a stronger foothold and build momentum in the Phoenix market.

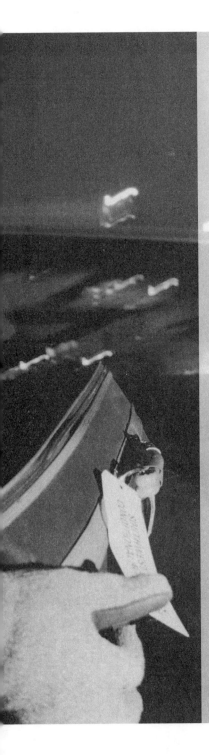

# PART III

# NUTS GONE BASIC

### Doing the Extra Special Exceptionally Well

**CHAPTER 11**

# ONE GREAT BIG FAMILY

## CREATE A LEGENDARY CULTURE

"There is growing concern that companies cannot live by numbers alone." So said *Fortune* magazine to introduce the results of its 1995 Corporate Reputations survey. "The one thing that set the top ranking companies in the survey apart is their robust cultures."

A company's culture, like a person's character, drives reputation. It should come as no surprise that the companies whose cultures honor customers, employees, and shareholders alike have excellent reputations. *Fortune* ranked Southwest number one in the airline industry for 1994, 1995, and 1996.

*Culture is one of the most precious things a company has, so you must work harder at it than anything else.*

The idea of a corporate culture is too important to the effective functioning of today's organizations to be dismissed as a fleeting craze. Culture is the glue that holds our organizations together. It

She says tomato. He says tomato. She says potato. He says potato. She says great airline. He agrees.

FOR 25 YEARS GARY HAS FOCUSED ON THE OPERATION OF OUR PLANES WHILE COLLEEN HAS CREATED A CARING ENVIRONMENT FOR THE PEOPLE WHO WORK AND TRAVEL ON THEM. THANKS FOR FINDING THE CRUCIAL BALANCE THAT MAKES OUR AIRLINE SECOND TO NONE.

*Executive v.p.s Gary Barron and Colleen Barrett featured in a 1996 ad celebrating Southwest's twenty-fifth anniversary*

encompasses beliefs, expectations, norms, rituals, communication patterns, symbols, heroes, and reward structures. Culture is not about magic formulas and secret plans; it is a combination of a thousand things. Kelleher and Barrett believe that culture is one of the most precious things a company has, so you must work harder at it than anything else.

In any organization, culture is the present manifestation of the past: the challenges, successes, mistakes, and lessons learned. Culture becomes the organization's memory; it guides behavior and provides a sense of identity, stability, and organizational boundaries. Within organizational boundaries, people gauge the appropriateness of their thoughts, behaviors, and actions and determine the norms and values from the organization's cultural rules and beliefs. In an organizational culture where values are shared and enthusiastically embraced, employees can make decisions that positively affect the organization.

Southwest's culture is rooted in its early struggle to get off the ground. The shared vision of survival has fostered a close-knit, supportive, and enduring family-like culture. Even though the fight to get in the air has long since passed, it is a very powerful part of the

Southwest lore that has led to the creation of an airline like no other. Southwest's employees all know this story:

> *Well over twenty-five years ago, a couple of guys said, "Here's an idea. Why don't we start an airline that charges just a few bucks and has lots of flights every day instead of what the others guys are doing—charging a lot of bucks and having just a few flights each day?" The rest, as they say, is history.*

Today the Southwest legend lives on in the company's rich culture. Within Southwest's homey work environment, the members of this family have come to realize that Southwest's culture is one of its most important assets.

## THE COMPONENTS OF SOUTHWEST'S CULTURE

In all organizations, formal and informal values, philosophies, and norms interact and overlap to create the fabric we call "culture." Southwest is no exception. Southwest's values, philosophies, and norms are so tightly meshed that they have created a "thick" culture. That is, the culture at Southwest Airlines appears to be a virtually seamless piece of fabric in which the "threads"—the ways in which values, philosophies, and norms interact to make up the company's culture—are often difficult to isolate. In an effort to help you understand the uniqueness of Southwest's culture, we have tried to identify some of the dominant values, philosophies, and norms we've observed in our ten-year association with the company.

### Southwest's Core Values

Values are deep-seated beliefs about the world and how it operates. They are the emotional rules that govern our behavior and attitudes. Values determine our choices, including those we make in an organizational context. Value-driven decisions determine organizational outcomes and a company's operating strategies.

If we wanted to learn more about your values, we would ask to see two things: your checkbook and your calendar. How you spend your money and your time tells us a lot about what you value. The same is true for organizations. Employees, consciously or not, learn about an organization's values by watching how the company and its executives spend company money and use company time.

Unlike many companies, Southwest has never formally documented its principal values. However, we have identified at least thirteen dominant values that drive the company and contribute significantly to Southwest's corporate character:

- Profitability
- Low Cost
- Family
- Fun
- Love
- Hard Work
- Individuality

- Ownership
- Legendary Service
- Egalitarianism
- Common Sense/Good Judgment
- Simplicity
- Altruism

## *How you spend your money and your time says a lot about what you value.*

### *Profitability*
Most of the twenty-five thousand employees working for Southwest believe that profitability is essential. They understand that it drives the company's growth and is directly linked to profitsharing and to job security. Equally important, employees know that profitability is the key to shareholder returns and a huge factor in Southwest's credibility in the industry. Finally, Southwest employees are very proud of the fact that the company invests a lot of time and money in the communities it serves, and they know that Southwest's contributions to the Ronald McDonald Houses and the other charities the company supports would not be possible if the company were not profitable.

### *Low Cost*
So fundamental is low cost to Southwest's operating strategy that without it the airline could not grow the market in every city it serves. The key to Southwest's success is consistently low fares, which enable people, who previously couldn't afford to do so, to fly or to fly frequently. An acute cost-consciousness pervades Southwest Airlines as

employees continually look for ways to save money without sacrificing service.

### Family

The company believes that when you treat employees like family, you foster the kind of intimacy and informality that builds strong relationships and makes work more fun. We tend to support, defend, accept, and love people more easily when they are a part of our family—this is the way Southwest wants it. The company also works hard to nurture and support its employees' families and actively invites them to become a part of the Southwest family. For example, employees are encouraged to periodically bring their children to work and spouses are invited to attend significant company events. The company believes that when an employee's family is involved in the employee's work, the family will be more supportive of the time the employee spends at work.

### Fun

Employees are encouraged to take their jobs and the competition seriously—but not themselves. The company is serious about creating an environment where play, humor, creativity, and laughter flourish. Southwest believes that people having a good time are more stimulated and more themselves. Southwest rejects the idea that work has to be serious in order for people to accomplish great things.

### Love

Southwest encourages its people to conduct business in a loving manner. Employees are expected to care about people and act in ways that affirm their dignity and worth. The company understands that when people feel loved they develop a greater capacity to love others. Employees bear out this belief every day in the kindness, patience, and forgiveness they extend to each other and their customers.

### Hard Work

The pace at Southwest Airlines is fast and intense. Turning planes as quickly as Southwest does requires lots of concentration and a strong work ethic. The company also runs very lean, which requires everyone to do his or her part—and then some. Southwest has the most productive work force in the airline industry; those who shy away from hard work do not fit in Southwest's culture.

## *Individuality*

Southwest's emphasis on fun allows employees to be themselves. The company encourages people to think like mavericks; Southwest is not looking for clones. It works hard to stimulate diversity of thought and opinion, as well as diversity in the makeup of its work force. When people are free to be themselves, they are liberated to express their true gifts and talents.

## *Ownership*

Southwest believes that people take better care of things they own and expects employees to take care of the customers they have earned the right to serve. Thus, Southwest allows employees to participate in the financial benefits of ownership. When the company does well, employees are rewarded for their contributions via profitsharing.

The company also counts on employees to take care of each other. Southwest trusts its people to take special care of the culture they have built. The company values employees with an entrepreneurial spirit who are willing to own their actions and the consequences of those actions.

## *Legendary Service*

Southwest wants its customers to experience service that makes a lasting impression, service that is kind and loving, service that is fun and makes them laugh. The company believes that treating people with respect and dignity is the key to providing its unique brand of Positively Outrageous Service. Thus, Southwest will go a long way to defend and support an employee who may violate a company policy to bend toward the customer. The company instills in every employee the idea that happy, satisfied customers who return again and again create job security.

## *Egalitarianism*

Southwest's ultimate fight is for the common person. This airline has been fighting from day one to make flying affordable for everyone. It is not big on titles because titles give the impression that some people are more important than others. Southwest's executives are expected to do the things they ask others to do. And Southwest's boarding process is fundamentally democratic—those who arrive early are served first.

### Common Sense/Good Judgment

Southwest believes in the people it hires and encourages employees to use their instincts and good judgment on the job. The company wants people who think "service" before adherence to rules.

### Simplicity

Southwest believes that simplicity creates speed, reduces costs, and fosters understanding. People who like to complicate things or become paralyzed by analysis have a difficult time succeeding in Southwest's fast-paced environment. Southwest encourages its people to operate very informally with each other and its customers. The company believes that formality, pretentiousness, and duplicity shackle creativity and innovation. Informality generates speed, increases the flow of information, and breaks down barriers to enable people to engage in more productive and satisfying relationships.

### Altruism

Southwest employees freely demonstrate their love for each other, for their customers, and for the communities Southwest serves through countless acts of goodwill. They not only give money, they give generously of their time and develop long-lasting relationships with those to whom they give. Southwest looks for people who are other oriented, people who give unconditionally, because the company has learned that there is a tremendous sense of joy and satisfaction that comes from helping others.

## Southwest employees seem to passionately follow the Golden Rule, inside and outside the company.

## Philosophy—A Lens on Life

Your philosophy is your worldview or attitude toward life. It is the lens through which you see and understand the world in which you live and interact. Whether we see the glass half-full or half-empty, whether we operate from the standpoint of earning or entitlement, whether we have a victim mentality or a survivor mentality, whether we approach a business as employee or owner—these views are determined by the lenses we use to see the world. The attitude and the feel of corporate communities are determined by corporate philosophy. Southwest Airlines' philosophy includes eleven primary attitudes:

- Employees are number one. The way you treat your employees is the way they will treat your customers.

- Think small to grow big.

- Manage in the good times for the bad times.

- Irreverence is okay.

- It's okay to be yourself.

- Have fun at work.

- Take the competition seriously, but not yourself.

- It's difficult to change someone's attitude, so hire for attitude and train for skill.

- Think of the company as a service organization that happens to be in the airline business.

- Do whatever it takes.

- Always practice the Golden Rule, internally and externally.

## Norms—Values in Action

Norms are patterns of attitude, behavior, and practice. They are the living expression of our underlying values. They govern how we treat people, which affects their attitudes and how we build trust, respect, and relationships with them. Norms influence the vigor and rigor with which we work and how far we are willing to go for a company. They determine the quality and character of our interaction with colleagues and the degree of fun, creativity, and enthusiasm we bring to the job. Norms also influence how we solve problems. The following norms by no means make up a comprehensive list, but we think they will give you the flavor of the Southwest culture.

### *Be Visionary*

Vision is the bigger picture that motivates employees because they understand how their individual efforts contribute to the overall dream. Southwest Airlines was founded by visionary thinkers. Rollin

King's crazy, forward-thinking idea gave the company its start. Over the years visionary thinking and big dreams have encouraged people to enlist in the crusade to provide legendary service and give ordinary people extraordinary opportunities. At Southwest the vision lives, and visionary thinkers continue to provide the inspiration for its future.

### Celebrate Everything
Southwest throws a party whenever possible to honor and reward people and to give them opportunities to experience the Southwest culture. Southwest is also fanatical about documenting its celebrations so that employees and friends can relive the memories.

### Hire the Right People
Although done with an informal and lighthearted touch, hiring is taken very seriously at Southwest. The company is famous for hiring people who are not afraid to express their individuality, take risks, and assume responsibility. Southwest's whole screening process is designed to identify these essential qualities in new applicants.

### Limit Committees and Keep Them Ad Hoc
The use of committees in general is not favored at Southwest because they tend to create complex decision-making structures and chew up time. Southwest has very few standing committees.

### Keep a Warrior Spirit
When it comes to dealing with the competition, Southwest employees mount a good offense. They have a history of aggressively going into battle. In fact, Southwest is half-assed about nothing! The company believes if you're going to do something, do it with intensity and do it right.

### Keep Multiple Scenarios
Southwest rejects formal strategic planning. Things change so fast and so abruptly in the airline industry that the company has learned to forecast and plan by preparing for a variety of possibilities.

### Minimize Paperwork
Southwest encourages simplicity and shies away from paperwork and elaborate documentation. When something can be handled in a brief

face-to-face interaction versus a formal memorandum, Southwest people usually opt to get up close and personal. Don't type a memo—just get it done.

### Feel Free to Be Informal

Employees have earned the freedom to dress comfortably and casually. People frequently show up for high stakes meetings wearing blue jeans. Casual wear facilitates and encourages the playfully creative spirit at work within the company. Agreements are often made with a handshake, and the legal documents to support these agreements are brief and written so a person without a law degree can understand them.

### Move Fast

Getting things done and having a bias for action are norms that play a critical role in Southwest's success. Nowhere is this more evident

*Southwest's work force more than doubled in the first half of the decade, from 8,620 employees at the beginning of 1991 to 19,933 by 1995 year-end. The Professor, the animated character here, is featured in Southwest's video* **Keepin' the Spirit Alive.** *This video is just one of the methods the company uses to bind employees together and preserve its legendary culture.*

than in the airline's commitment to turning planes quickly to get customers to their destinations on time and to give them as many flight options as possible.

### Dare to Be Different

Southwest employees think like mavericks. It is this maverick spirit that pushes them to look for new and unconventional approaches to their work. Southwest employees aren't afraid to be different; every day they prove that there are a variety of ways to combine safety, caring for customers, and fun to achieve Positively Outrageous Service and success.

Much of what the general public knows about Southwest's culture has to do with Herb Kelleher's antics or the company's zany promotions and advertisements. Don't be fooled: Southwest's attention-grabbing antics are supported by a deep-seated seriousness about its core values. Southwest's culture has withstood the test of time because its values are rooted in real life and celebrated day to day. Employees talk about them constantly and practice them fanatically.

The legend and the love, the vision and the values, the philosophies and the principles mixed with, in Kelleher's words, "boundless energy, immense goodwill, and a burning desire to excel" are known in the company as the Spirit of Southwest. "Spirit is engaging our minds and our hearts and our souls to do the right thing. Southwest Spirit is *you*," says the Professor, the animated character who narrates Southwest's *Keepin' the Spirit Alive* video.

The Southwest Spirit, says the Professor, "is the twinkle in your eye, the skip in your step; it is letting that childlike spirit escape and be heard. To know what really makes Southwest Spirit, you have to look beyond the machines and things because running a fun and productive airline defies science; it is an art that comes from working hard with feeling."

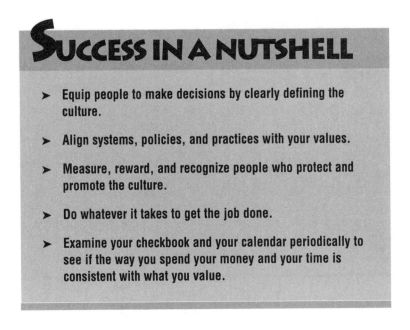

# SUCCESS IN A NUTSHELL

➤ Equip people to make decisions by clearly defining the culture.

➤ Align systems, policies, and practices with your values.

➤ Measure, reward, and recognize people who protect and promote the culture.

➤ Do whatever it takes to get the job done.

➤ Examine your checkbook and your calendar periodically to see if the way you spend your money and your time is consistent with what you value.

**CHAPTER 12**

# KEEPING THE SPIRIT ALIVE

## PRESERVE WHAT YOU VALUE

In early 1990, during the Gulf War crisis, oil prices soared, the American spirit declined, and the economy took a turn for the worse. Employees in most major U.S. corporations were hearing rhetoric about "tightening the belt"; it looked as though tough times lurked just over the horizon. At Southwest, the talk was much the same, but unlike other U.S. companies that chose to "right-size," Southwest's no-furlough policy caused it to refocus its energy. Instead of looking over their shoulders, the employees of Southwest Airlines were rolling up their sleeves and gearing up for a fight for survival.

### *Instead of right-sizing, Southwest refocused its energy.*

In this emergency, one employee in particular, Colleen Barrett, was preparing for more than a fight for survival; she was gearing up for a fight, not just to keep the airline alive, but to keep "the dream" alive. Barrett was laying the groundwork for nothing less than the perpetuation of the values, norms, and philosophy that make up the special Southwest culture.

# DARE TO DREAM

Dare to Dream, *written by John Turnipseed, director of people services, was dedicated to the dream makers of Southwest Airlines and appeared on the front page of the twentieth anniversary issue of* LUV Lines.

*Some people only look at life through eyes that seldom gleam*
*while others look beyond today as they're guided by a dream*
*And the dreamers can't be sidetracked by dissenters who may laugh*
*for only they alone can know how special is their path*
*But dreams aren't captured easily;*
*there's much work before you're through*
*but the time and efforts are all worthwhile*
*when the impossible comes true*
*And dreams have strength in numbers*
*for when a common goal is shared*
*the once impossible comes true because of all who cared*
*And once it's seen reality a dream has just begun*
*for magically from dreams come dreams*
*and a walk becomes a run*
*But with growth of course comes obstacles*
*and with obstacles comes fear*
*but the dream that is worth dreaming*
*finds its way to the clear*
*And the dream continues growing*
*reaching heights before unseen*
*and it's all because of the courage of the dreamers*
*and their dream*

*Long before the twentieth anniversary of Southwest Airlines, the company's dream had indeed become a reality and the reality had turned into a legend.*

## THE COMPANY OF FAMILY

Southwest is an anomaly in the airline industry not only because of its business success but also because, in more ways than one, Southwest is a secure place to work. The security we're referring to has nothing to do with ground operations, maintenance, or in-flight procedures. We are referring to the emotional, psychological, and spiritual security employees feel. Southwest's no-furlough policy, for example, is more than just an executive pronouncement; it is a business principle that says Southwest cares about its people. Countless policies and practices say to employees, "This is more than a company, this is a family." "A family atmosphere simply means, number one, that you're sincerely interested in everyone who's a part of your family," says Kelleher. "Number two, that you forgive some eccentricities, some departures from the norm, because they are a part of your family." Southwest's culture is a nurturing environment within which people are encouraged to grow, prosper, and share their good fortune.

## A MESSAGE TO THE FAMILY

*Employees and visitors entering Southwest Airlines' corporate headquarters at Love Field in Dallas are greeted with this spectacularly displayed message on a window that stands fifteen feet high and twelve feet wide:*

> The people of Southwest Airlines are "the creators" of what we have become—and of what we will be.
>
> Our people transformed an idea into a legend. That legend will continue to grow only so long as it is nourished—by our people's indomitable spirit, boundless energy, immense goodwill, and burning desire to excel.
>
> Our thanks—and our love—to the people of Southwest Airlines for creating a marvelous family and a wondrous airline!

*Kelleher himself wrote this message, which was unveiled in front of three thousand guests and employees at the corporate headquarters open house in 1990.*

### Covenants Inspire Community

Covenants are commitments that join people and provide guidelines for action. They define how we should live and work. For example, when two people commit to the covenant of marriage, their partnership inspires a deep sense of loyalty and the promise of sacred love between the two. In organizations where relationships are based on covenants, people are bound by a deep sense of loyalty to each other; instead of simply trading a fair day's work for a fair day's pay, they share a common set of values, norms, and guiding philosophies. They subscribe to a common purpose and deep-rooted beliefs, and they are willing to subordinate self-interest to the common good.

Southwest is more than just a successful organization, it is a covenantal community. The people of Southwest are a family of employees who are connected by a web of common beliefs, shared commitments, and collective memories. Southwest employees work hard to serve the values, norms, and philosophy that constitute the covenants that define this community. Southwest's covenants have made the company a community instead of an organization.

## THE CREATION OF COMMUNITY

When individuals join Southwest, they join more than a $3 billion corporation; they join a community. Southwest likes to say, "Welcome to our extended family"—a family of people who are committed, invested, dedicated, and passionate about the cause of Southwest Airlines. "The cause of Southwest Airlines is to increase the collective prosperity of all of the employee family," says John Jamotta, director of schedule planning. This fundamental mission has become a covenant that draws employees together in a bond continuously cemented in their minds by vivid reminders of the importance of family and by memorializing the family's history.

### Photos and Memorabilia

Southwest's employees work and play in an environment that nurtures and values family. The sense of family is quickly experienced as one wanders the halls of the corporate headquarters at Love Field. Instead of adorning the walls of its new headquarters with art, the company hung captivating and intriguing photos, news clippings, letters,

*The halls of Southwest's Dallas headquarters are a
life-sized, walk-through album of family memories,
containing photos of every conceivable company
event, large and small. Also on display are letters,
clippings, ads, greeting cards, party favors, and
other memorabilia to evoke the family spirit.*

articles, advertisements, promotions, gifts, trinkets, and mementos, all framed and exhibited in a symbolic display of Southwest's lore.

Most of the photos are of employees at Southwest's numerous celebrations and events—Christmas parties, chili cook-offs, Halloween celebrations, charity benefit games, and Ronald McDonald House dedications. Letters from governors, business associates and competitors, and community leaders are interspersed among the photos. Articles and news clippings about Southwest and its employees are carefully matted and framed to serve as reminders of Southwest's celebrated personality. Advertisements and promotions from Southwest's beginnings call up days gone by and draw attention to the company's business priorities as well as the styles of each era. Like a storefront display, on the third level of headquarters there is a gallery of mannequins modeling the uniforms that employees have worn since the company's beginnings. Gifts and trinkets from customers and friends are displayed in appreciation of their fun-loving spirit. Cards of all sorts—Valentine's Day, St. Patrick's Day, birthday, holiday, Christmas, and many more—are framed and hung to recall the greetings of the season that Southwest faithfully spreads around the country.

Colleen Barrett is the inspiration behind these memory-trimmed walls. She has created a life-sized, walk-through, family photo album. "An employee comes into the building with a friend or family member," Colleen says, "and as they start walking down the hall they see something that reminds them of a fun experience, like a chili cook-off or an Annual Awards banquet. They stand there and start reliving the whole experience. People's spirits are actually lifted as they relive these memories. Pictures create history and memorialize our fondest memories." A walk through these halls is a stroll through a collective and vivid pictorial of Southwest—what it was, what it is, and what it continuously strives to be—a fun, loving family!

### Gifts and Acknowledgments

Memorializing life's events is a passion for Colleen. She sends birthday cards to all the members of the Texas legislature. Herb recalls various legislators saying, "Hey, Herb, thanks for the birthday card!" He also remembers an employee once telling him, "You know, it's the damnedest thing. Every present that Colleen gets for me is just perfect for me."

*Southwest mails more than 75,000 greeting cards a year to customers, employees, and friends to memorialize events like birthdays, promotions, anniversaries, losses, and new babies.*

Terry "Moose" Millard, a Southwest pilot, remembers how the company has touched him and his wife in very significant ways:

> *I'd been with Southwest for two years and I had cancer. The first time I was out for three months, when they removed a kidney. After about six weeks, we received a big package from Herb and Colleen. It was a big cheesecake and some dooda dooda stuff and it was the first major representation that in this company nobody is forgotten. . . . When I was out the second time I was out for nine months, the same thing happened, different package. We know this is a business and chances are these gifts were a part of a bigger system. But the point is, the company cared enough to put in place all the expense and the resources to make it happen.*
>
> *We are continually blown away. I get gifts out of the blue from Colleen. I don't know how she decides, but suddenly this thing will arrive and it's not happenstance. I ask myself how can a company of twenty-five thousand people, and somebody at Colleen's level, remember people so specifically? And I know that I am not the only one. It happens to a lot of people.*

Colleen has a special insight and a deep understanding of giving. "It's just what families do," she says modestly. "If families have cancer you reach out, if families have babies you reach out." But when you are twenty-five thousand strong you have to have some help to make it happen, so Colleen uses the network of people that extends across the entire Southwest system. She is constantly asking employees and friends to help her stay in touch with what's happening in people's lives. When the network learns about events that are worthy of acknowledgment, the word quickly gets to Colleen. These significant events are then fed into her database and tracked.

For Colleen, giving and acknowledging are not just about buying any old gift and sending it off. Giving is about touching the heart of the recipient, about individualizing the gift. She has a remarkable ability to give gifts that connect her with those to whom she gives. Gift giving is her way of saying, "Even though we can't be with you, we are thinking about you." As a result, people feel cared about and important.

Colleen's efforts are supported because Southwest realizes this is also good business. When employees feel they are a part of the family, they see their work as an ongoing effort to protect and preserve the company's sense of community. Consequently, they're willing to work harder and produce more because "it's for the family."

### Storytelling

"Leaders create cultures, but cultures, in turn, create their next generations of leaders," says Edgar Schein in *Organizational Culture and Leadership*. The truth in this insight can put industry analysts' worries to rest. For years, they've been asking, "Is there life for Southwest Airlines after Herb?" Many concerns result from the public's tendency to perhaps somewhat deify Kelleher. While his contributions have been powerful and dramatic, Southwest is much more than a one-man show. The truth of the matter is that the company has developed a generation of future leaders who daily live the core values and business principles that have contributed to creating and preserving the Southwest culture.

Boeing's president and CEO, Phil Condit, describes Herb's role in perpetuating the Southwest culture:

> *If you go back to tribal behavior . . . one of the most critical people in any tribe was the shaman, the fundamental storyteller. Keep in mind, their job was not one of historical accuracy. Instead, their job was to tell stories that influenced and guided behavior. Stories were modified in order to achieve the appropriate kind of culture. I've watched Herb tell stories: he watches the reaction of people and his story then takes on new and different nuances depending upon his audience and the reaction he is hoping for. You see, stories are powerful because we remember them. I think Herb is Southwest's shaman; he is the storyteller, and those stories get repeated and retold and they form the fabric of the Southwest culture.*

Yes, indeed, Herb is a storyteller (read "leader"), but he is not the only one at Southwest. The company has created a tribe of shamans who have woven such a tight culture that it would take years to unravel. When Kelleher does decide to step down, Southwest has this group of highly spirited people ready to carry the stories forward.

### Culture Committee

"Every family, every college, every corporation, every institution needs tribal storytellers," says Max De Pree, former CEO of Herman

Miller. "The penalty for failing to listen is to lose one's history, one's historical context, one's binding values. Without the continuity brought by custom, any group of people will begin to forget who they are."

Southwest instituted a mechanism in 1990 for the sole purpose of perpetuating the Southwest Spirit. The Culture Committee (one of only a very few standing committees) has become an inspired team of more than a hundred storytellers who are the company's cultural ambassadors and missionaries. "We're not big on committees at Southwest," Kelleher states, "but of the committees we do have, the Culture Committee is the most important!"

Southwest's Culture Committee is an example of people working together to create covenantal relationships. Committee members are zealots when it comes to the continuation of Southwest's family feel. The committee represents everyone from flight attendants and reservationists to top executives. It is not a group of headquarters staff and managers who use their power to tell the rest of the organization how they ought to think and behave. Rather, it is a group of shamans, spiritual teachers, and organizational storytellers. "The Culture Committee is not made up of Big Shots; it is a committee of Big Hearts," Roy Spence, an alumnus of the committee and president of GSD&M, the advertising firm that has served Southwest since 1981, has said. Culture Committee members are not out to gain power; they use the power of the Southwest Spirit to better connect people to the cultural foundations of the company. The committee works behind the scenes to foster Southwest's commitment to values such as profitability, low cost, family, love, and fun.

## *"The Culture Committee is not made up of Big Shots; it is a committee of Big Hearts."*

Southwest works very hard to reinforce its history because it doesn't want its more than twenty-two thousand employees to forget that they are a part of a very rich legacy. The Culture Committee was created to pull together people who exemplify Southwest's culture. Most of the original committee members had ten or so years at Southwest and embraced Southwest's maverick, caring, irreverent way of doing things. They were all great in their individual jobs and were handpicked for their creativity, expertise, energy, enthusiasm, and, most importantly, Southwest Spirit.

Southwest's Culture Committee is a group of committed team leaders dedicated to perpetuating the airline's mission, vision, values, norms, and philosophies. They come from different parts and levels in the system and serve on their own time. Union contract employees must arrange for a trade or shift their schedules so that they can attend four all-day meetings each year. Ad hoc subcommittees formed throughout the year meet more frequently. For the two years they serve on the committee, members engage in leadership activities that protect the company's unique and highly valued culture. Committee members have been known to visit stations with equipment and paint in hand to remodel a break room. Others rally at one of Southwest's maintenance facilities to serve pizza and ice cream to maintenance employees. Still others simply show up periodically at various field locations to lend a helping hand.

The power and influence of the Culture Committee comes from members' Southwest Spirit. The "Big Hearts" selected for the committee don't participate for public recognition. Their labor is really a labor of love; their payoff is the relationships they build with other workers, the knowledge that they have sparked worthwhile and fun endeavors, and, most importantly, the satisfaction of having been a vital part of keeping the Southwest Spirit alive.

### Walk a Mile in My Shoes

Have you ever wondered what it would be like to wear someone else's shoes for a day? To help Southwest employees better understand the daily challenges of others, this is exactly what the company asks people to do.

From January to June 1995 the Walk a Mile in My Shoes program helped Southwest employees gain an appreciation for other people's jobs. Employees were asked to visit a different department on their days off and to spend a minimum of six hours on the "walk." Over a six-month period, 75 percent of Southwest's employees participated in the program. Joe Dlouhy, a ramp supervisor in Orange County, California, walked a mile in the shoes of Las Vegas ground support team member Randy Tagorda. Dlouhy's account of the day shows the appreciation he gained for the service Tagorda provides to ramp agents.

*I have to give you guys credit where credit is due! What an experience I had on my "walk a mile."*

*I reported to Ground Support in LAS [Las Vegas] at approximately 11:30 A.M. and started to "walk" in Ground Equipment Mechanic Randy Tagorda's shoes. The soles of my shoes were worn out at 7:00 P.M. Some of the projects I completed included preparing a bag tug for painting; removing a transmission from another bag tug; assisting in removing a transmission from a beltloader; and the finishing touch was painting a bag tug. Amazingly, there were no paint runs!*

*I never really imagined the hard work that our Ground Support Team does. The appreciation to keep our equipment operational sometimes goes unnoticed. This experience helped me understand and take more pride in each piece of equipment that is used daily.*

Southwest employees who participated in the Walk a Mile in My Shoes program were rewarded not only with transferable roundtrip passes, but also with the goodwill and increased morale that comes with taking the time to understand another's job more thoroughly.

## A Day in the Field

Another way culture is reinforced and spirit spreads is through Southwest's Day in the Field experience. Unlike the Walk a Mile program, which was limited to a specific time, this activity is practiced throughout the company all year long. Barri Tucker, then a senior communications representative in the executive office, for example, once joined three flight attendants working a three-day trip and shared highlights of her experience in a letter to *LUV Lines*. Her letter also offers a few examples of why people love this company and feel like part of an extended family.

*Where else could you work that allows you the opportunity to experience all aspects of its operation first hand??? . . .*

*I am, of course, referring to my three-day trip as a flight attendant. I flew with some real veterans! All three flight attendants (Ellen López, Pam Morgan, and Fran Chance) have been flying with us for eighteen years, although you'd never guess it. All three exhibited Southwest Spirit, zest, and passion for their job. Burn out after eighteen years??? Not these women . . . Some of the things that keep spirit up are downright "hokey." Example:*

> *the little sticky notes the provisioners leave for the flight atten-*
> *dants. "Southwest FA's are the best" . . . What a great little thing*
> *to do. The notes are never the same, but they are always there,*
> *at every stop. . . .*
>
> *Our Customers are very responsive and impressed with what*
> *they see. They like us. They are very complimentary. They LUV*
> *the casual uniforms. They thanked us when they deplaned, and*
> *some would just thank us for the service. One guy said, "The*
> *service on this flight was the best I've ever had. You guys were*
> *great." Another guy stopped just to say he thought Southwest*
> *was better than any other airline . . . always on time.*
>
> *The most memorable comment was made by a pilot from*
> *another airline. . . . He looked over at me and just shook his*
> *head. "You guys do a turn faster than anyone. It's amazing;*
> *I've never seen anything like it."*

By spending a day, even a few hours, in the shoes of fellow employees, people see the company from a different perspective. Their relationships with internal customers are enhanced by a deeper sense of appreciation for coworkers' jobs and responsibilities. The other benefit is motivation. Think of the motivation Tucker gained: by spending a few days experiencing the company from a new angle and hearing directly from customers, she was able to see how important it is for corporate headquarters to support Southwest's front-line employees.

### Helping Hands

At the end of 1994, a year of phenomenal growth for Southwest Airlines, the company initiated the Helping Hands program. The idea was to send out volunteers from around the system in the fourth quarter of 1994 to lighten the load of employees in the cities where Southwest was in direct competition with United's Shuttle. Each volunteer worked two weekend shifts pushing wheelchairs, working on the ramp, provisioning the airplanes, assisting at the ticket counter and at the gates, and playing games with Southwest's customers. Both the employees at the stations and the volunteers developed admiration and respect for each other as a result of Helping Hands. The program not only played a significant role in building momentum and strengthening the troops for the battle with United, it also helped rekindle the fighting spirit of Southwest employees. Just read the following letter from then administrative services clerk Larry Coble, and you'll see what we mean.

*Upon my return from weekend warrior duty ("Helping Hands") at the front in LAX [Los Angeles], I am proud to report our glorious troops are doing a hell of a job.*

*As I flew to LAX, I contemplated the reports of troops working double shifts, lack of experience, and a need for larger facilities. Quite frankly, I wasn't sure what to expect. Having spent twenty-three years in the U.S. Army, I have witnessed firsthand battle weary soldiers who display signs of severe stress and battle fatigue. It's hard to imagine Positively Outrageous Service (P.O.S.) being displayed under these circumstances.*

*When I arrived, I was greeted with the same "Southwest Spirit" I have experienced in my many years of flying Southwest as a Customer, and even more as a member of the family. By 1330 [1:30 P.M.] I was on the scrimmage line at the ticket counter. Though I had absolutely no experience, the soldiers quickly trained me on simple tasks and I joined the battle.*

*I was almost dumbfounded as I witnessed how well a brand-new Employee handled the express Customers. She and ALL the Customer Service Agents were armed with the "Southwest Saber," a beautiful smile. Even though several of the Customer Service Agents had been at their posts since 0600 or 0700, with few breaks, at 2300 these LAX Lancers were still attacking with their "Southwest Sabers."*

*I don't know how much help we "Weekend Warriors" were for the Stations, but I thank you for this truly educational and rewarding experience. I have no doubt that I got more out of this than I could have possibly given.*

*As I settled in on my flight home I thought about the war we are in and that small band of soldiers serving us at LAX. My view of the Hollywood Hills as we took off reminded me of tenacious Rangers who took Point du Hoc on D-Day. LAX may very well be our Point du Hoc and those soldiers at LAX are as tough as any Ranger I have ever known. As we gained altitude over the Pacific, I thought of the British and Canadian pilots who fought and won the Battle of Britain; and I could almost hear the grizzly voice of that old British Bulldog, Sir Winston Churchill, when he saluted those valiant airmen, "Never have so many owed so much to so few."*

## Consistent, Ongoing Communication

Southwest also uses the more commonplace methods—in-house newsletters, videos, and annual reports—to reinforce its culture. Its monthly newsletter, *LUV Lines,* gives special attention to the company's core values by celebrating milestones and capturing memories like a family photo album. *As the Plane Turns* is a quarterly news video sent to all stations to share special events or messages with the growing Southwest family.

*Southwest specializes in giving employee newsletters, pamphlets, and videos an unconventional twist. In 1995 the Employee Communications Department took 5,328 photos of Southwest events and published 642 pages of information for employees in its monthly* LUV Lines, *weekly* Employee Update, *and special pamphlets and flyers.*

Southwest goes above and beyond with videos. One of the most memorable is the *Southwest Shuffle*, featuring hundreds of Southwest employees rapping about having fun on the job. In *Keepin' the Spirit Alive*, Southwest uses animation to capture the Southwest Spirit on video. Almost every event at Southwest is videotaped. The company believes that when people share time and energy to craft an event or a celebration, then certainly it's worth capturing on video so those who couldn't make it in person have the chance to join in the experience as well.

The company also uses periodic Culture Exchange meetings all around the system to keep the spirit alive. Employees transform airplane hangars into festive, balloon-adorned celebrations and meet for a day to inspire spirit. Yes, these exchanges are basically pep rallies—people come together for the sole purpose of sharing great ideas to keep the Southwest Spirit in the minds and actions of their fellow employees.

Kelleher's annual Message to the Field is more than the usual speech from a company CEO; it is a celebration of the people and a reinforcement of the culture. Employees, enriched by the care and compassion they show one another, their customers, and their communities every day, come from all over the system to celebrate yet another year of profitability and fun. During the 1996 Message to the Field, Kelleher was escorted to the podium in a straitjacket to celebrate the company's twenty-fifth anniversary theme, "Still Nuts after All These Years." Employees loved it. Amid the celebration, Kelleher invariably manages to convey a serious message to his spirited audience.

An avid student of history, Kelleher once stated that he wanted "a Battle of Britain mentality." What that implies, in essence, is a willingness to make a sacrifice, to be less focused on your own person, and to take joy in the organization's accomplishments. That is a lot to ask, but Southwest has managed to create a community of people who will work their tails off to share in the celebration of the company's success.

Southwest employees have always demonstrated an intense will to succeed. When employees work with a desire to win, it ignites a very powerful competitive spirit. The momentum from the airline's early fight for its right to fly endures today because of this ever-present desire to compete well and succeed. At Southwest, people's will to succeed comes from four commitments: (1) employees' willingness and desire to own their jobs; (2) employees' uncompromising commitment to do more with less; (3) employees' willingness to do whatever it takes; and (4) the corporate and personal pride of belonging that employees feel when they work hard for the good of the entire Southwest family.

As the company continues to grow, the need to perpetuate and reinforce the Southwest Spirit ever more purposefully becomes even more real and more difficult. This is not just an executive responsibility at Southwest; it is a firmly believed and fanatically practiced corporate philosophy. Cultivating the Southwest Spirit happens at all levels of this company. Profitability, low cost, family, fun, and love are key principles deeply embedded within the culture and shared and practiced by the people. These are the principles that employees have used to reinforce the Southwest Spirit since 1971. They have become the benchmarks and hallmarks of the employees' burning desire to succeed.

In truth, what Southwest has done has been to make mission, vision, and values the boss. Its principles are what makes this organization fly. The covenants that serve its principles have glued this culture together so tightly that, even when Herb Kelleher is absent, the dream lives on.

# SUCCESS IN A NUTSHELL

➤ Memorialize and display your fondest memories. Make pictures of people your artwork.

➤ Make the vision the boss.

➤ Develop a sincere interest in every family member.

➤ Building the culture you want doesn't just happen; make it purposeful, not accidental. Create a culture committee that protects, promotes, and projects a purposeful culture.

➤ Do what you value: practice what you preach, walk the talk.

➤ Become a storyteller for your company and your family.

# CHAPTER 13

# THE ART OF CELEBRATING MILESTONES

## REVEL IN YOUR ACCOMPLISHMENTS

On November 7, 1991, we found ourselves in an airplane hangar across from Austin's Robert E. Mueller Municipal Airport at a gala honoring Southwest Airlines' twentieth anniversary. The hangar had been transformed into a colossal music hall, complete with stage, stage lights, and massive video screens—with the feel of an indoor rock concert, although slightly more formal. Texas politicians, employees, and longtime friends, customers, and other supporters mingled at the dozen or so bars before sitting down to a traditional Texas dinner.

You could sense the guests' pride and patriotism as the event kicked off with a spectacular medley of songs about Texas performed by singers and dancers from the Incredible Productions company. The emcee—singer and songwriter Red Steagall—told us that the purpose of the party was to say thank you to the attendees for their support and loyalty over twenty years. During dinner the Kilgore (Texas) Rangerettes entertained and photographs of employees and selected commercials from the previous twenty years told the story of Southwest's unique sense of humor and a dream come true.

Jim Chancellor, Southwest's regional director of ground operations, fiddled his way through the "Orange Blossom Special" as only a five-time Texas state fiddle champion could. Then a talented group of women—appropriately named the Luv Notes—from the company's frequent flier program and the Customer Relations Department brought the house down with new lyrics to Billy Joel's upbeat "We Didn't Start the Fire" that described the major events in Southwest's twenty-year history. As we ate the last bites of pecan pie, Steagall introduced the first of two surprise attractions for the evening—Larry Gatlin and the Gatlin Brothers. The Grammy Award–winning band had entertained us for well over an hour when Herb Kelleher came to the podium to thank over a thousand guests for supporting an airline whose only real asset in the early days was persistence.

After his heartfelt speech, Kelleher invited the Gatlin Brothers back to sing one final song. Joined by a cadre of Southwest employees, the Rangerettes, and Incredible Productions, the Gatlins belted out "The Lone Star Is Flying High," written by Tim McClure of GSD&M especially for the occasion to commemorate the goodwill

*Boarding* **Lone Star One** *to party on to Dallas*

Southwest had built in the heartland of Texas. It was a grand finale that rivaled the close of the Grammys.

Had the evening come to a close right then and there, the celebration would have been the memory of a lifetime. What we didn't realize was that everything up to that point was priming us for a final surprise: the unveiling of Southwest's newest capital acquisition. As Red Steagall directed our attention to the front of the building and the huge hangar doors slid open, a full marching band fired up its instruments and the spotlights focused on a brand-new Boeing 737. The plane, named *Lone Star One*, had been painted in brilliant red, white, and blue, with a giant white star over the front doors, to look just like the Texas flag. The new 737 was, indeed, a graphic symbol of Southwest's gratitude to the people of Texas. Whether it was the unique concept, the creativity of the artwork, or the bold statement that it made, the guests were in awe.

The party continued out on the tarmac for another hour, as dignitaries, friends, and family pressed in to have their pictures taken with the plane in the background. When it was time to say good-bye, Herb Kelleher, Rollin King, the original Southwest employees, and a few family and friends boarded *Lone Star One* and flew the party back to Dallas. It was a continuing celebration, Southwest style!

## THE PARTY NEVER ENDS

True, the unveiling of *Lone Star One* represented a celebration of the highest magnitude, but Southwest Airlines is famous for honoring individuals, groups, significant events, and important accomplishments in creative, festive, and often positively outrageous ways. There are few organizations where people celebrate life as passionately and as consistently as do the people of Southwest Airlines.

All over Southwest's system you will hear people say, "We work hard and we play hard." It's easy to focus on the "play hard" part of that equation—particularly when the media have devoted so much attention to it. But the other half of the Southwest philosophy shouldn't go unmentioned. By any measure of productivity, the evidence indicates that the people of Southwest Airlines are not afraid to work. Every victory has been earned through hard work.

Call it gratitude, a sense of exhilaration, or emotional release, when we work hard and win, there's something inside us that screams out, "Let's celebrate!" When Southwest Airlines has faced negative or difficult circumstances and overcome them, the culture has cried out, "Let's party!" and celebration has become a way of life. Except in companies like Southwest, you don't see much festivity and celebration in the corridors of corporate America. Under the cloak of "professionalism," we've become too serious. Seduced by the mentality that says business, if conducted responsibly and effectively, must always be serious, we have grown heavy-hearted. Oh, we still celebrate, but in many organizations, celebrations lack real impact and joy. Perhaps this is because by *not* understanding the value of celebration we lack the passion for doing it right.

> ## *To deny our need to celebrate is to deny a part of what it means to be human.*

Certainly, Southwest is not the only company that has demonstrated the virtue of hard work and the resulting urge to celebrate. However, the difference between Southwest Airlines and many other companies may be that when the hunger to celebrate is felt, particularly after a stunning victory, rather than ignore it or avoid it, Southwest nourishes it.

After observing the joy and aliveness exhibited by people at Southwest Airlines, we have concluded that the cost of not responding to the human desire for celebration is very high. Celebration enhances our humanity. Without celebration, we are robbed of the life and vitality that energizes the human spirit. Latent and undeveloped though it may be, there is within our nature as human beings an inherent need to sing, dance, love, laugh, mourn, tell stories, and celebrate. Whether we are talking about people in Africa, Australia, Asia, Europe, or the Americas, there is no culture in the world that doesn't embrace some form of festivity. To deny our need to celebrate is to deny a part of what it means to be human. When we work in an environment where we are not encouraged to express this festive nature, part of our humanity is repressed and life becomes dull and spiritless. When this happens, our celebrative faculties, like unused muscles, begin to atrophy. Of course, this has a devastating impact on morale and productivity.

## PAYOFFS FROM HEARTY PARTIES

While it's difficult to draw a direct cause-and-effect link between productivity and profitability, Southwest's experience demonstrates that celebration has a number of benefits.

### 1. Celebration provides an opportunity for building relationships.

Any way you look at it, success in business over the long haul comes from relationships built on trust. Southwest's formal and informal celebrations are opportunities for relationship building. Terry "Moose" Millard, a pilot and alumnus of Southwest's Culture Committee, explains: "If you want your company operating at maximum efficiency, you have to have trust. In order to have trust, you must have some kind of relationship. So all the things we celebrate give us opportunities to establish and strengthen our relationships."

Celebrations provide an opportunity for friends and colleagues to get together more frequently in a company where they might otherwise see each other only once every couple of years. Southwest spends a lot of time and money on celebrations, special events, and other festivities that bring people closer. The average CEO might think this is money and time wasted because it's difficult to measure the return. However, when you look at the relationship Southwest has with its employees (84 percent of whom are union members), customers, and vendors, common sense tells you that the payoff is significant. Most of us would agree from experience that good, solid, healthy relationships are the key to productivity and essential to a thriving business. But good relationships don't just happen. They are created by people who are willing to make an investment in the relationship over time. Celebrations are simply one way Southwest makes this investment.

### 2. Celebration gives us a sense of history.

Celebration helps us remember the past. In remembering the past we develop a sense of history and are linked to the wisdom associated with it. Southwest's twentieth-anniversary celebration in Austin was not just a spectacular and entertaining event, it also reminded everyone of the company's amazing history. The stories and pictures from the early days reminded onlookers of Southwest's fight to survive and its wisdom in staying focused on a particular niche. Twenty years of commercials reminded the audience how Southwest's unique culture and maverick spirit contributed to creating an airline that made flying

*Herb Kelleher (left) and Mayor Richard Daley buckle up to dedicate Southwest's Chicago Midway flight attendant base.*

fun and affordable. This glimpse of history during this special evening firmly connected the people of Southwest Airlines to the remarkable legacy they are charged with upholding.

### 3. Celebration helps us envision the future.

Celebration also connects us to the future. Just as the ritual of a wedding symbolizes our commitment to and hope for tomorrow, certain celebrations can have the same impact on an organization. For example, Southwest Airlines opens each new facility with flair and festivity. When Southwest celebrated the opening of its new flight attendant base at Midway Airport, the company shied away from the traditional ribbon-cutting event. Instead, the dedication featured the ceremonial fastening of a giant, ten-foot seat belt, performed by Kelleher and Mayor Richard Daley, to symbolize bringing the City of Chicago and Southwest's Chicago-based flight attendants together. When Southwest inaugurated service to Baltimore/Washington International Airport in 1993, the company celebrated the event and highlighted its $49 one-way unrestricted fare to Cleveland by treating forty-nine fifth-graders (many of whom had never flown before) to a day at the Cleveland Metroparks Zoo. On January 8, 1993 (Elvis Presley's fifty-eighth birthday), Southwest celebrated expanded service to Las Vegas with fifty-eight Elvises. Sporting jumpsuits, spangled belts, pompadour wigs, guitars, and gyrations, the winners of a look-alike contest sponsored by Southwest entertained customers at the LAX terminal before the inaugural flight.

Celebrations actually help us get a glimpse of the future. Whether it's for a station, maintenance facility, reservations center, flight attendant base, or pilot base, each celebration inaugurating a new facility invites Southwest employees to transcend the mundane and imagine what's possible; it inspires them to participate in making the facility profitable and in owning its success.

### 4. Celebration is a way of recognizing major milestones.

On December 16, 1984, Southwest took delivery of three Boeing 737-300s, a new generation of aircraft that Southwest would incorpo-

*Kelleher* (this page) *and General Chuck Yeager* (opposite) *launch Southwest's first 737-300,* **The Spirit of Kitty Hawk.**

rate into its fleet. At the celebration dinner in Dallas, Bob Hope was the surprise feature entertainer and General Chuck Yeager, first pilot to break the sound barrier, was the honored guest. The following day, Southwest's first 737-300 took off from Love Field at precisely 10:35 A.M.—the day and time of the Wright Brothers' first powered flight at Kitty Hawk in 1903. To commemorate the stunning achievement of Wilbur and Orville Wright, Southwest named the aircraft *The Spirit of Kitty Hawk*. General Yeager accompanied Southwest employees on *The Spirit of Kitty Hawk* as it flew the company's original Dallas–Houston–San Antonio route. Celebrations and public viewing of the aircraft were staged at each city.

Way back on January 23, 1974, Southwest carried its one-millionth customer. Twenty-one years later, on March 21, 1995, less than sixty days after Southwest introduced ticketless travel system-wide, the company carried its one-millionth customer without a ticket. To celebrate this momentous occasion, Southwest threw a party for the customer, Dr. Gregory Doane, at Phoenix Sky Harbor International Airport. The party, complete with balloons, confetti, and champagne, was Southwest's way of thanking Dr. Doane and

# DEAR MR. KELLEHER

*This letter is written to let your company know how pleased we were when we recently flew Southwest from Lubbock, Texas, to Las Vegas, Nevada. . . . This trip was a surprise trip for my husband, as he thought he was traveling with me to El Paso on a business trip. However, I had planned a surprise trip for the two of us to Las Vegas for our tenth wedding anniversary!*

*When Cherry and Robin became aware of the situation, they went above and beyond the call of duty to treat us "special." By the time we arrived in Las Vegas, everyone on the plane knew it was our anniversary and knew my husband had been surprised by the trip to Vegas.*

*These two flight attendants made our anniversary more special and memorable. . . .*

MARTY AND DIANNE SEA
ANTON, TEXAS

recognizing an industry milestone achieved by some very dedicated and tenacious employees. Before boarding a flight to Los Angeles, Dr. Doane was decorated with silly string and serenaded with "For He's a Jolly Good Flier" by Southwest employees dressed in tuxedos.

People like to be associated with winners. There are lots of companies that achieve great things, but you'd never know it by talking to their employees. For one reason or another, the organization has simply failed to inform people about its accomplishments. It's not unusual for employees in a business like this to have little pride in their company; they lack a sense of meaning and significance about what they do. By taking time to celebrate significant accomplishments, Southwest reminds employees that they are part of a winning team. Employees look at the milestones and are reminded that they had a part in achieving them. The self-esteem of the whole organization is elevated. The result? When people feel good about what they do, they try to do more.

### 5. Celebration helps reduce stress.

Celebration is a form of play. It provides a minivacation from the routine. Such minivacations seem to be part of the everyday work life of Southwest employees.

In 1986, when the Chicago Bears went to the Super Bowl, MTV featured them in a hilarious video doing a rap song called the "Super Bowl Shuffle." This inspired the Employee Communications Department to commission Butch Cope, now a customer service agent in Houston, to write a rap song for Southwest Airlines called, naturally, the "Southwest Shuffle" and to immortalize it on video. The video features employees from practically every department in the company rapping, dancing, and being unafraid to look foolish while they tell how much fun it is to work at Southwest. Once featured on the CBS program *60 Minutes*, the video is still used as an orientation tool in Southwest's program for new hires. By watching the video, new Southwest employees not only learn that it's okay to celebrate, they also learn that they were hired because they are the kind of people who don't take themselves too seriously, people who will have fun, capitalize on their individuality, and fully participate in the company's celebrations.

*Warming up for the "Southwest Shuffle"*

*T. J. LUV leading the
Southwest troops in the
Chicago St. Paddy's
Day parade*

Southwest interrupts the daily routine and takes the stress out of work by making a big deal of holidays. When the system grew so large that it was impossible to have just one Christmas party, Southwest decided to throw three company parties. When having all the Christmas parties during December got to be just a bit overwhelming, with all the other year-end activities facing Southwest employees, Colleen Barrett simply decided to hold them at different times of the year. Can you imagine a Christmas party in July? That's what happened in Oakland. Christmas in September? That's what they had in Chicago. At least a thousand employees turned out for an enjoyable evening of Christmas carols and merriment in each location. The parties were such a success that the company plans to keep on having them at oddball times.

Other holidays are celebrated with equal enthusiasm. For several years on Thanksgiving, Southwest devoted a whole issue of *LUV Lines* to employee and customer letters describing the things for which they were thankful. A lot of their gratitude was directed toward the company for creating job security and a fun place to work. Every Halloween, corporate headquarters and each of the stations join in a systemwide costume contest. Awards are given for the funniest, cutest, scariest, most original, and most "spirited" costumes. Each department is decorated in a particular theme and employees go all out to come up with the most creative designs. Judy Jefferson, in Southwest's Treasury Department, says that "departments carry out their themes in such an unbelievable fashion that schoolchildren and family members come and tour the headquarters building all afternoon." With so many members of the Southwest family being full-blooded Irish, it won't surprise you to learn that the St. Patrick's Day parades in Dallas and Chicago each draw two to three hundred employees every year. Equipped with green and white balloons and leprechaun-style derbies, the marchers and the floats are led by Southwest mascot T. J. LUV.

### 6. Celebration inspires motivation and reenergizes people.

Celebrations, even small and spontaneous ones, can recharge people's batteries and leave them feeling refreshed. When people feel renewed, they think more clearly and their attitudes become more positive. Laura Runge, employee communications representative at Southwest's headquarters, told us about a spontaneous celebration in 1995 on the Friday afternoon before the Fourth of July. People at headquarters were busy working when, all of a sudden, there was a lot of noise outside their offices. Employees flooded the hallways to see what all the commotion was. The entire Finance Department, dressed in patriotic costumes, was marching through the halls and riding makeshift floats pulled by bicycles. It was a Fourth of July parade! "It was a perfect example," Runge says, "of how our people can take a tough, serious workday and make it fun by giving everyone an unexpected break in the routine and some laughs."

Southwest has figured out that celebration is indispensable for survival in a world of high-speed change. The company understands that, to succeed, Southwest's people must be innovative and think unconventionally; they must draw from experiences that transcend traditional practices and familiar routines for solving difficult problems. Celebration encourages this nontraditional way of thinking by interrupting routines. When routines are broken, people's minds are freed to entertain ideas that might not have emerged had the routine not been disrupted; their experiences are enlarged and they are less likely to be constrained by conventional thoughts and actions.

## 7. *Celebration builds self-confidence and removes fear.*
Celebrations nourish the spirit of an organization. They cause us to blossom and inspire us to become bigger people.

The people of Southwest Airlines are very proud of what they have created, and this is one of the reasons the company screens potential employees so carefully. Even with the company's tremendous growth, it is not easy to get a job at Southwest today. So, when a new person is hired, the company sees cause for celebration. New hires spend a full day experiencing the You, Southwest, and Success (YSS) program. By participating in fun, games, and Southwest-style celebrations, new hires learn that success at Southwest means hard work and commitment to the mission of internal and external service.

Knowing how difficult it is to make it through the screening process, employees are genuinely excited for newcomers. When new employees are celebrated in an environment that is warm and welcoming, the fears associated with being new soon dissipate. New hires quickly develop the belief that they were chosen for their particular characteristics and the unique gifts and talents they bring to the company. From day one, the YSS program instills the idea "We believe in you" in every new hire. It empowers employees to develop self-confidence, helps raise their motivation level, and inspires them to become better than they thought they could be.

## 8. *Celebration helps us mourn the losses associated with change.*
Celebration is not always festive and it doesn't always have to focus on the positive. Celebration can also help us acknowledge the losses associated with endings and separations. Layoffs, failed projects, and reorganizations where entire teams are disbanded are just a few instances in which celebration can help heal the organization and cement lessons learned, according to Katie Soles, a consultant who helps companies learn how to celebrate.

With the exception of three people who were released and immediately rehired in 1973, Southwest Airlines has never been through a furlough. It has, however, lost employees to terminal illness and fatal accidents. When Southwest employees die, their lives, their impact on friends and coworkers, and their contributions to the company are celebrated. In many organizations, the passing of a coworker is treated rather matter-of-factly; friends are rarely given the opportunity to express their feelings about the person who is gone. Southwest

# FAREWELL TO A FRIEND

*This is an excerpt from the farewell letters published in* LUV
Lines *when San Antonio Customer Service Agent Speedy Paipa
died:*

> *"The better part of life consists of friendships."*

The Employees of Southwest Airlines lost a very special
friend on February 20, 1993, when Oralia "Speedy" Salazar
Paipa died. . . . In a way we feel like Speedy's life was cut
short, but in her own way it really wasn't. She lived life for
every moment to the fullest. She traveled wherever she
wanted; she got whatever she wanted; and she loved like she
wanted. In essence, she lived a whole life in a short period.
Her going has left an ache in our hearts and our arms feel
very empty, but there's a joy in knowing that she is safe. We
are the ones who feel the loss, but we have our loving, funny
memories, and Speedy will always be in our hearts. We
might not ever understand why she left us. You could say
that now she graduated to a better place. Most likely, Speedy
is helping St. Peter check in people at the Pearly Gates!

Thank you, Speedy, for the laughter, the memories, the love,
and the friendship. Maybe it'll be like you're off on a long shift
trade, and we'll see you when it's over.

LUVing Friends at the SAT Station

takes the opposite approach. Employees are encouraged to talk about
their feelings and write down their memories about the person. These
letters, anecdotes, stories, and poems are published in *LUV Lines* so
that people throughout the company can learn more about the person
and the way he or she touched the lives of others. The outpouring can
be enormous.

Southwest does this because people in the company take the concept of family seriously, and that's what families do when a loved one
dies: they reconstruct memories, reminisce, and tell stories. There is,

# IN LUVing MEMORY

*Excerpts from Herb Kelleher's eulogy at a special memorial service for retired Vice President of Maintenance and Engineering Jack Vidal on January 3, 1996, published in the next issue of LUV Lines for all employees to share:*

*"Aloha to a Legend"*

We have great reason to rejoice that Jack was with us, even though he has left us. If one of the true measures of a man's worth is the legacy he leaves behind for others, then Jack was, indeed, a worthy giant, triumphing over the limitations of our mortality to build an earthly monument and to become an earthly legend.

. . . An aircraft named "Jack Vidal" will fly in Southwest Airlines' fleet for as long as Southwest has a fleet that flies— and may that be forever. Thus, the spirit of Jack Vidal will always be flying with us and the spirit of Jack Vidal will always be watching over and inspiring us.

From us to you, Jack, many thanks and aloha, with love.

however, another benefit derived from this deliberate and overt expression of love and respect: it has a healing effect on the organization. When people have the opportunity to express their feelings about loss, they heal more quickly. The other benefit of expressing grief openly is that it helps hold the family together. As people comfort and console each other during a tragedy, they often become stronger and closer. One reason the employees at Southwest are such a tight-knit group is that they have celebrated the bad times as well as the good times together.

Today the employees of Southwest Airlines are not fighting to keep the airline alive; they are fighting to keep the spirit of the airline alive in a company that is growing rapidly. As Southwest continues to expand, leaders throughout the company continue to engage in celebrations that are intended to make big seem small and far seem near. The goal is to minimize the differences and the distance between headquarters and the other stations around the system. Celebrations are one way Southwest differentiates itself from the competition and provides a family-like environment that cares for its people, its customers, and its communities in a fun, loving way.

# Success in a Nutshell

➤ Use celebrations to create memories.

➤ Have celebrations acknowledge what's important, what you value.

➤ Let celebrations give people the opportunity to say hello and good-bye.

➤ Use celebrations to build relationships.

➤ Celebrate to make the mundane fun and unusual.

➤ If you're going to celebrate, do it right.

# CHAPTER 14

# CELEBRATING PEOPLE WITH BIG HEARTS

## HONOR THOSE YOU LOVE

"This is a company created by its people," Herb Kelleher says. "It is a daily celebration here of customers. It is a daily celebration of great employees. It is a daily celebration of positive things that happen." Celebrations are an important way Southwest informs people about the activities, behaviors, attitudes, and values that have made the company great. Values decay without attention; celebrations are one way of raising people's consciousness about the values that drive the business. Celebrating corporate heroes and heroines for their contributions to the business reinforces desired behaviors. "Celebration makes the spirit of the organization visible," says celebration consultant Katie Soles. Celebrations have a way of painting pictures for us, pictures of people heroically, compassionately, innovatively, or entrepreneurially living the company's values.

### WINNING SPIRITS

Every other month, the company honors ten to twelve employees whose actions make them living examples of Southwest's values and

# THE WINNERS ARE . . .

*By way of example, we've included a couple of the nominations from one issue of* LUV Lines. *These stories may sound unbelievable, but they're an everyday occurrence at Southwest Airlines.*

**Eric Brown, Amarillo Ramp Agent—***You'll think Eric Brown's middle name must be "Serve" after reading what Amarillo Station Manager Rusty Arnold had to say in his Winning Spirit nomination:*

> On Tuesday, December 27, 1994, a flight destined for Lubbock diverted to Amarillo due to fog. On this flight was a Customer with no money and no place to go, who had to be in Lubbock as quickly as possible. Without hesitation, Eric offered to take the Customer to a relative's house in Lubbock, driving all night and returning to work at 5:00 A.M.
>
> Eric truly went above and beyond the call of duty, and we are very lucky to have an Employee of his caliber, who is willing to do whatever it takes to get the job done.

**Debra Undhjem, Phoenix Flight Attendant—***The nomination submitted by Phoenix Customer Service Agent J. B. Thomas shows how a senior citizen got the royal treatment from Debra Undhjem:*

> Recently Debra came to the aid of an eighty-seven-year-old lady who misconnected in Oakland. The Customer eventually made it to Phoenix, only to miss her flight to Tulsa. At that point, the Supervisors decided to put her up at a local hotel at Southwest's expense.
>
> That's when Debra stepped in. She offered to take the lady home with her and called the Customer's family to let them know where she was and that she wouldn't arrive in Tulsa until the next day. The next morning, Debra brought the Customer back to the airport and waited with her until the flight left.
>
> I asked Debra what motivated her to do what she did, and she responded by saying that the Customer was diabetic, eighty-seven years old, and she didn't want her staying in a strange city alone in a hotel room. I feel Debra went above and beyond to help one of our Customers.

philosophy. The Winning Spirit Awards are given to employees nominated by other employees (or sometimes by customers) across Southwest's system. Sunny Divjak, manager of culture activities, heads the committee of nine that makes the selections. Each recipient is invited to a presentation held in the executive boardroom at Southwest's headquarters building; Herb reads the letter of nomination sent in for each recipient and gives each a Winning Spirit lapel pin and two positive-space passes on Southwest Airlines. Each honoree gets a framed photo taken with Herb as a follow-up gift, and a group photograph is published in *LUV Lines,* along with an inspirational quote and a summary of each person's "winning spirit."

## HIGHEST HONORS

A night many Southwest employees eagerly await and remember long afterwards is the Annual Awards Banquet. This banquet is more than an opportunity to give out awards—it is one of the company's most festive celebrations and honors the dedication, loyalty, and extraordinary contributions of ten-year, twenty-year, and now twenty-five-year employees. Besides bestowing special service pins on the anniversary employees, the company honors other employees with awards that support Southwest's spirit and its unique culture.

*"This company is a daily celebration of great employees."*

One of these awards, Southwest's highest and most prestigious, is the coveted Founder's Award, given only in years when a continuous history of significant achievement merits special recognition. Kelleher himself selects recipients from nominations submitted by all Southwest employees. This award is reserved for those who go above and beyond the call of duty on a consistent basis—in community service, outstanding job performance, implementation of creative solutions to complex problems, and bringing innovative ideas and programs to the company.

At the Annual Awards Banquet, Southwest also recognizes its people with the President's Award. Winners are honored for demonstrating the virtues and values esteemed by Southwest: showing compassion for customers, untiring support of coworkers, willingness to learn new things, leading by example, practicing the Golden Rule, embracing change, keeping promises and following through, and, of course, bringing a sense of humor and fun to the job.

Founder's Award and President's Award honorees are truly celebrated for making Southwest Airlines a better organization. Each recipient gets a plaque with a personalized inscription written by the vice president for his or her department, a check for $500, and a collage of photos taken during the banquet. Judy Haggard, regional marketing director and 1995 President's Award winner, says, "I can only tell you it was one of the most memorable and humbling experiences I've ever had. It will be a part of my life that I never forget." The company also publishes photos of the winners in *LUV Lines* and puts their names on a plaque that hangs in Southwest's corporate headquarters.

## THE OCCASIONAL AND THE OFFBEAT

In addition to the Founder's and the President's Awards, Southwest creates special awards from year to year to honor other unique contributions. In 1995, Rudy López, former El Paso station manager and now station manager in Houston, received a special Leadership Award for "continually exemplifying and personifying the principles behind our mission statement." Tracie Martin, manager of civic and

## TEN MORE YEARS

*Celebrating his tenth year with the company, Captain Chic Lang said about the 1994 Awards Banquet:*

I couldn't believe what they did for us, and my wife couldn't believe it either. The effort that went into this party, from top down, fired up every person in that room, including the people who didn't work for Southwest Airlines. It's not just slam bam, here's your award, here's your watch, you're out of here. There was a lot of real personal input into it. It made you want to go out and work another ten years just as hard.

charitable contributions, received the Community Relations Extra-ordinaire Award for her "tireless efforts on behalf of the company's various community involvements."

Southwest also recognizes people outside the company who have given their friendship and support to the airline. Jazz musician C. C. Jones, for example, received a 1995 Good Neighbor Award for working so closely, as a customer and friend, with the company's Culture Committee.

Another occasional award is Southwest's Sense of Humor Award, given to an employee renowned for his or her sense of humor, like flight attendant Jan Kegley, who received the award in 1995. Recipients are given a clown figurine and their names go on a plaque, which is often turned upside down in the corporate headquarters hall.

Other occasional—and occasionally offbeat—awards presented at Southwest have included the Luv, Most Spirited In-Law, Heart and Soul, Creativity and Guts, Training Excellence, Tell It Like It Is, Hairdresser of the Year, and Positively Outrageous Customer Service Awards. All give employees an opportunity to see the spirit of the company in a tangible—and usually lighthearted—way.

## HEROES OF THE HEART

Lots of companies talk about the importance of internal customer service, yet many find it difficult to appropriately recognize and reward those behind-the-scenes employees whom customers never see. Southwest appreciates these employee groups and understands just how crucial they are to its daily operations. Just ask any front-line customer contact person at Southwest and he or she will tell you that the people who operate behind the curtain are as much a part of Southwest's success as anyone else.

In 1992, Southwest's Culture Committee wanted to devise a way to honor these unsung heroes for their outstanding efforts. A sub-committee representing a wide variety of departments was formed to find a unique way of saying "thank you" to employees who rarely interact directly with customers. The result was a recognition program called Heroes of the Heart.

Each year, one "behind the curtain" group is selected to be Heroes of the Heart for its outstanding efforts in serving and supporting employees in other parts of the company. The name of the

*Kelleher announcing the 1995 Heroes of the Heart (above) in the headquarters atrium on Valentine's Day. The 1996 Heroes of the Heart (left) were Southwest's customer service coordinators and flight information agents.*

winning group is kept secret until Valentine's Day. On the afternoon of February 14, employees from different locations throughout Southwest's system fill the atrium of corporate headquarters in Dallas and await the big announcement. In typical Southwest fashion, balloons and banners adorn the main lobby, and there is some form of special—usually homegrown—entertainment. The group that receives the award has its name painted on a specially dedicated aircraft that carries Southwest's Heroes of the Heart insignia. The company also runs a one-page article commending the group in *Spirit*, Southwest's in-flight magazine, and *LUV Lines* does a feature article.

The recipients of the coveted award for 1997 were the Reservations Administrative Support Staff. These unsung heroes were nominated by fellow employees and were chosen for their many contribution and their unwavering spirit. Although internal customers as well as external customers may never see these heroes, they play a vital role as the support behind the voices who strive to provide Southwest customers with extraordinary Triple Crown customer service.

## *Celebrations paint pictures of people living the company's values.*

The recipients of the 1996 award were Southwest's customer service coordinators and flight information agents. These two groups work extraordinarily well together, keeping up with each leg of every flight and trying to communicate flight information, protecting Southwest's customers from schedule problems, and providing legendary service every day. These are no small tasks, but no matter how hectic their schedules get, they always manange to have fun together.

The Heroes of the Heart for 1995 were a group who helped Southwest through a time of tremendous growth. That year, Southwest went from 1,883 flights per day, with 199 aircraft in 45 cities, to 2,065 flights per day with 224 aircraft serving 46 cities. The number of pilots jumped from 1,500 to 2,400 and the number of flight attendants increased from 2,400 to 3,200. This could have become a scheduling and planning nightmare, but the flight operations and in-flight planning, scheduling, and payroll employees—the people responsible for staffing flights and making sure each crew member is paid correctly—rose to the occasion with what Paul Sterbenz, vice president of flight operations, called "an excellent display of teamwork, internal customer service, and openness to the daily unexpected challenges they face and overcome." Bill Miller, Southwest's vice president of in-flight services, described this group's magic vividly when he said, "Imagine throwing a puzzle up in the air and then trying to put the pieces back together when the pieces are continually changing shape. This is what this group must do every day, and they manage to do it with a sense of humor. Without them, we would never have a plane take off."

Previous Heroes of the Heart include the Technical Services Department (1994), for their expertise and responsiveness in maintaining electronic equipment for the whole company, and the ground operations and provisioning administrative coordinators (1993). Cookie Hunnicutt, a former Midway Airlines employee, remembers the day in 1993 her group received the award: "They took us to a hangar and everything was hush-hush, so we didn't know why we were there. But when the hangar doors opened and the heart with our title on it was on the plane, it really hit home. That was my second-best day at Southwest Airlines. The first was when I was hired."

## TOP WRENCH

Southwest has very high maintenance standards and celebrates its best mechanics through the Top Wrench program, created in 1989 to reward the efforts of mechanics, whose contributions might otherwise go unrecognized. (There is also a Bottom Wrench Award, bestowed to date only once—on Herb.) To qualify for the Top Wrench award, a mechanic must be trained to work on and taxi every airplane in Southwest's fleet. Daily workmanship and attitude are also taken into consideration by the selection committee, a group of former Top Wrench recipients. Honorees for Top Wrench are selected once a month or once a quarter, depending on the size of the location. Once a year, Southwest invites monthly Top Wrench winners to Phoenix or Dallas for a banquet to honor the Top Wrench of the Year.

In 1994, Phoenix aircraft appearance supervisor Mark Endriss decided to get into the game and initiated a Top Cleaner program to commend the cleaners for their attention to detail in maintaining superior aircraft appearance. Top Cleaners are chosen for perfect attendance, for exemplifying teamwork, and for possessing a "What can I do to help?" attitude toward other employees.

## SOUTHWEST'S GUIDELINES FOR CELEBRATION

They are not written down anywhere and people seldom talk about them, but Southwest follows a number of commonsense guidelines that have contributed to the success of the celebrations that the company holds every year.

### 1. The celebration must be authentic.

Southwest's celebrations come from the heart—they emerge out of a genuine appreciation for people. The company truly values the uniqueness of its employees and what they've accomplished, and the senior executives at Southwest honestly believe that the company's success could never have been achieved without those employees' dedication, commitment, and creativity. Celebrations at Southwest are not superficial. They don't ignore tragedy, because people who know how to rejoice and celebrate with real abandon are usually those who know what it's like to embrace difficult times and tragic events.

### 2. The celebration must raise people's dignity and self-esteem.

The motive behind all Southwest celebrations is to build people up and honor the gifts, talents, and personalities they bring to the job. Poking fun at weaknesses or idiosyncrasies is fair game, even encouraged—but it's done in a jovial, lighthearted manner aimed at helping the person or group not take themselves too seriously. Celebrations at Southwest are never conducted with an intent to harm.

### 3. The celebration must be done right.

Southwest takes the time to make sure any celebration is well coordinated, well timed, and well executed—with classy production all the way. The company designs celebrations so there is a good fit between the event, the reason for the event, the company culture, and the personalities of the people involved. This means a lot of time and energy are invested in a successful celebration.

Whether the event is big or small, three roles help ensure success when Southwest plans a celebration:

*Imagineer.* The imagineer can visualize a future or an event not yet created and engineer its creation. These are the dreamers who have the ability to envision a celebration and its potential impact on participants. Imagineers can see a celebration before it becomes reality. Colleen Barrett, one of the original imagineers at Southwest Airlines, can tell you exactly how she wants people to feel and respond to a celebration, both during the event and long after it's finished.

*Artist.* The artist takes the celebration from concept to reality. Celebrations can be simple or elaborate, but there is always an artist behind the creation who transforms the words into a song, the pictures into a story, and, of course, the balloons into a spectacular arched entryway. One of the very talented artists behind Southwest's celebrations is Tim McClure of GSD&M. McClure and his team are responsible for designing many of the striking elements (songs, painted airplanes, and live productions, to name just a few) that go into Southwest's celebrations.

*Evocator.* Evocators are the catalysts who draw people into a spirit of celebration and invite them to initiate their own celebrations. There are many evocators at Southwest Airlines, but chief among them are Barrett and Kelleher. Nobody likes to party and have fun more than Kelleher. Any of his officers will tell you that he has a way of turning a potentially boring business meeting into a celebratory event. By his very example, Kelleher arouses the spirit of the organization and summons the art of celebration.

### 4. The celebration must appeal to all the senses.

Southwest has mastered the art of balloonery, according to MaryEllen Milano, GSD&M's executive who heads up the Southwest account: "Southwest could single-handedly keep the balloon industry afloat. Ann Hancock, Southwest's senior promotions and events specialist, has perfected the art of the balloon arch, the balloon drop, and the balloon pre-event decorating party. I think she's even held balloon school!" Balloons, banners, flags, floats, and costumes are just some of the ways in which Southwest celebrations are visually appealing. The celebrations usually have, as well, live music that is carefully selected for the audience. The company also uses video and photographs creatively. Clips from commercials, interviews with employees, and snapshots of people being real—usually real funny—are all a part of the way Southwest celebrates.

### 5. *The celebration must be seen as an investment.*
Business people are often reluctant to engage in elaborate celebrations because it's difficult to justify the cost and the return on the investment. What we've witnessed at Southwest Airlines is a deep-seated belief that celebrations are an investment, not a cost. Southwest views celebrations as one way to raise the morale, job satisfaction, productivity, and spirit of its people. When people are celebrated they feel better about themselves and develop more dedication and enthusiasm toward their work.

### 6. *The celebration must be cost-effective.*
Remember that Southwest Airlines has achieved its success in no small part because of low costs, so when it comes to celebrations, the company looks for the least expensive way to do it right. Usually this means capitalizing on the talents of its own people rather than contracting out. When the company does go to an outside vendor for a particular service, it almost always tries to barter positive-space flight passes for services.

The word "family" at Southwest Airlines is not some worn-out cliché or management buzzword. At Southwest, the idea of family is embraced with devotion and sincerity, and no one protects and promotes the concept of family more arduously than Colleen Barrett: "Celebration is what families do. Whether it's an anniversary, a new job, a new baby, a promotion, a birthday, a holiday, or anything in between, families celebrate special events." If you're going to talk about the company as a family, your behavior and activities must demonstrate a commitment to family members. Celebrating the significant events in the lives of family members is one way of doing this. "I have no idea how many different awards and recognition ceremonies we have," says John Farry, one of Southwest's flight attendants, "but it has shown us all that this company is big on 'thank yous.' "

*"Celebration is what families do. Whether it's an anniversary, a new job, a new baby, a promotion, a birthday, a holiday, or anything in between, families celebrate special events."*

Few companies overlook the importance of reward and recognition, but not all companies understand the importance of enveloping reward and recognition in festivity. Southwest makes its special events more powerful and more memorable by adding the dynamic element of celebration. Celebrating people for their accomplishments is not just Southwest's way of saying "thank you," it is also a way the company raises the level of motivation within the organization. Southwest understands that when changes go unrecognized, particularly changes that were accomplished at great personal expense, people lose their fight and relinquish their drive. Saying "thank you" is not just good manners at Southwest, it is essential to creating an organization filled with vitality. Perhaps this is why Southwest people have such festive spirits.

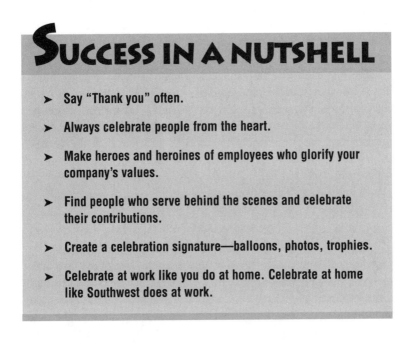

# Success in a Nutshell

> ➤ Say "Thank you" often.

> ➤ Always celebrate people from the heart.

> ➤ Make heroes and heroines of employees who glorify your company's values.

> ➤ Find people who serve behind the scenes and celebrate their contributions.

> ➤ Create a celebration signature—balloons, photos, trophies.

> ➤ Celebrate at work like you do at home. Celebrate at home like Southwest does at work.

# CHAPTER 15

# STILL NUTS AFTER ALL THESE YEARS

## MAKE WORK FUN

Bruce Campbell, one of Southwest's comedians in the sky, and two other Southwest flight attendants boarded a van one very hot day to get to their hotel in Kansas City. They were in uniform—cool and comfortable in shorts, polo shirts, and tennis shoes. Six flight attendants from another airline boarded the van, too, dressed in long-sleeved shirts, suits, and dresses, the women wearing pantyhose. All six of them had sweat pouring from their foreheads. As they headed toward the hotel, the Southwest crew grew uncomfortable because the flight attendants from the other airline were pointing at them and whispering back and forth. At last, one of them said, "We just want you to know . . . we hate your uniforms. Where can we apply?!"

### WORK IN PLAY CLOTHES

"Say farewell to the suit, that once universal emblem of modern commercial life," says William Nabers in a November 1995 *Fortune* magazine article titled "The New Corporate Uniform," "and say hello to an exciting, unnerving, less formal new business world where the right look varies according to where you live and what you do." Employees today are free, even encouraged, to bring into the office all the spontaneity, creativity, and uniqueness that their blue-pinstriped predecessors reserved for their personal lives. We encourage you to experiment for a day if you haven't already. Try working in casual, comfortable "play clothes." You may find yourself feeling more lighthearted, more creative, less stressed, and less serious.

Southwest is one company leading the change to more casual

*Herb in Corporal Klinger costume at a company Christmas party* (above) *and on the custom Harley-Davidson Heritage Softail* (left) *given to him by a group of Southwest and Morris pilots at the company's 1994 Chili Cook-off*

# WORK AT A PLACE WHERE WEARING PANTS IS OPTIONAL.

Not to mention high-heeled shoes, ties, and panty hose. Because at Southwest Airlines, we do things a little differently. And it's obvious just by looking at us. Especially when we don't wear pants. You'll see us in tailored walking shorts and golf shirts. Or colorful pullovers. Plus, the ever-popular tennis shoes. Which not only makes Southwest Airlines people look a little more hip, but feel a lot more comfortable. And when we feel good, it's contagious.

We're always looking for people who take their jobs seriously. But not necessarily themselves. So if you're a bit of a ham and unusually allergic to stuffy uniforms, call our People Department Job Hotline at (214) 904-4803. Or send your résumé to P.O. Box 36644, Dallas, Texas 75235-0644, Attention: No Pants. And come to a place where you'll enjoy working your pants off.

**SOUTHWEST AIRLINES**
Just Plane Smart

Southwest Airlines is an Equal Opportunity Employer.

*Orange hot pants gave way to other outrageous styles for uniformed employees: denim bibbed miniskirts, red-orange- and gold-striped bellbottoms, orange ponchos, and eventually khakis and polo shirts.*

wear in corporate America. "Fun wear"—casual clothing—is the work dress of choice for everyone, from customer service agents working the gates to executives at headquarters. Don't think for a minute it's only flight attendants, customer service agents, and the like who dress casually. Kelleher, too, relishes comfortable, fun, casual wear, even at the expense of executive image—which isn't all that important to him anyway. He has been known to go to board meetings in jeans and a sweatshirt. He has also appeared in front of Southwest's troops and the media as Elvis, Corporal Klinger, General Patton, Big Daddy-O, and a Harley rider (to name just a few).

Over the years, Southwest has become known for eccentricity in its choice of uniforms, from hot pants to fun wear—and beyond. One of the company's recruiting ads captures this spirit quite well: "Work at a place where wearing pants is optional. Not to mention high-heeled shoes, ties, and panty hose." At various times in 1995, employees working at different California stations and the Albuquerque Reservations Center sported painted faces, battle helmets, and camouflage fatigues to symbolize their ownership of the war against the United Shuttle.

Southwest did at one time have a formal uniform, very business-like—jacket, pants or skirt, long-sleeved shirt, and tie—but customers commented that with the more formal uniform the flights weren't as fun and the flight attendants didn't seem as playful and friendly. In 1992, when Southwest won its first Triple Crown for best on-time performance, fewest customer complaints, and smallest number of mishandled bags, the airline gave its formal uniform a rest. For doing such an outstanding job of serving the customer, Southwest employees were rewarded with the option to dress casually for one full year. Southwest won the Triple Crown again in 1993, and casual wear ruled for a second year. In 1994 and 1995, Southwest topped all three performance categories for the third and fourth years in a row. In 1996, after winning the Triple Crown for the fifth year in a row the Triple Crown and formal wear were retired. The Triple Crown remains theirs and casual remains the style of choice.

When the people of Southwest dress in a fun style, their work becomes play. When you're having fun at work, it doesn't feel like work at all; it's better than tolerable, it's enjoyable. Having a job that's fun is certainly worth holding onto; people are more likely to accept ownership of their responsibilities, and much more inclined to go the extra mile and do whatever it takes. Stories of going above and beyond and doing whatever it takes are a dime a dozen at Southwest.

## HUMOR: SOUTHWEST'S "E" TICKET

*Please let your flight attendants and customer service agents know that every time you play games to generate some creative fun with Customers, you get free advertising. I hear wonderful stories about games, songs, poems, and skits on Southwest everywhere I go. I was in Orlando and people were talking about how flying Southwest was more fun than Disneyland and then told about a game of drawing a pumpkin on their head without looking or a scavenger hunt while waiting for a weather delay. You are the talk of the town.*

*Thank you, Southwest. You're terrific.*

*A Frequent Flyer*

Humor starts at the top and cascades across the entire Southwest system. It's practiced on the ground, in the sky, at the gates, and—yes, indeed—within the executive office, not just for the free advertising but because it has become such a standard way of doing business at Southwest. It's almost contagious.

Reporter Jan Jarboe of *Texas Monthly* tells a famous story that illustrates Herb's style. When Southwest became the official sponsor of Sea World of Texas and introduced *Shamu One*—a Southwest Airlines plane painted like the killer whale—to promote vacations to the whale's playland paradise, American Airlines' CEO Bob Crandall called Kelleher to congratulate him for such a clever marketing tactic. Crandall had one question, though: "What are you going to do with all the whale sh—?" Without a second's hesitation, Herb replied, "I'm going to turn it into chocolate mousse and spoon-feed it to Yankees from Rhode Island." The next day, Crandall, a Yankee from Rhode Island with whom Kelleher shares a competitive yet jovial relationship, received a huge tub of chocolate mousse with a king-sized Shamu spoon right in the middle, compliments of Kelleher. People all across the Southwest system feel free to engage in similar playful acts. Southwest Airlines has become masterful in creating an environment rich with humor and good-natured pranks.

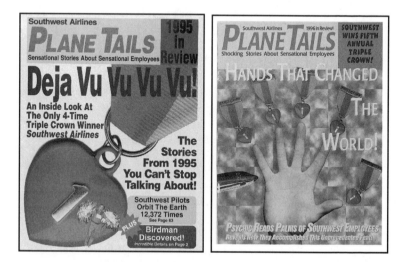

*The 1996 and 1997 issues of* Plane Tails *touts Southwest's fourth and fifth annual Triple Crowns.*

Humor at Southwest is about making life less serious. It is intended to decrease tension, build confidence, and involve others in enjoyment. At Southwest, humor that laughs at others, obscures solutions, increases tension, destroys people's self-worth, and excludes others from the joke is not welcomed. Humor, Southwest-style, is healthy and very often commendatory.

In 1995, Tonda Montague and her Employee Communications Department began a publication called *Southwest Airlines Plane Tails*. This in-house tabloid spoof, modeled after the *National Enquirer*, contains fifty-six pages of sensational stories about Southwest employees. It is loaded with tributes to employees who have found innovative solutions to difficult situations and humorous articles designed to build confidence, decrease tension, and make people laugh. A 1995 article entitled "What's Hot and What's Not" at Southwest gives readers instant insight into the culture:

| What's hot . . . | What's not . . . |
|---|---|
| men in casual attire | men in suits |
| women in comfortable shoes | women in high heels |
| CEOs who ride Harleys | CEOs who ride in limos |
| sweating on the job | sweating at the gym |
| open seating | assigned seating |
| hugs | formal handshakes |
| leaders | managers |
| flexibility | strict policy |

Another article, "How You Eat Southwest Airlines Peanuts Tells a Lot about You," highlights the findings of a "new study." In this witty spoof, "an accredited mastopeanocologist" claims to have analyzed ten types of peanut eaters and what their nutty styles reveal. Next time you're on a Southwest flight, look around and see if you can spot the suckers, pickers, throwers, dunkers, sniffers, holders, gobblers, munchers, tossers, and nibblers, and guess what their peanut-eating style says about their personality.

With more than twenty-five thousand employees in the company today, not everyone gets to mingle with the dynamic leaders of Southwest Airlines on a daily basis. So Montague and the creative editors in Employee Communications created a Southwest-style

## Gary Kelly
### Vice President Finance & Chief Financial Officer

**Began Coloring At Southwest:** June 1986

**Birthday:** March 12

**Job Responsibilities At Southwest:** Finance Department head; member of Executive Planning Committee; CRS Committee; COMPANY CLUB Committee; and Budget Committees.

**The Things I Like Most About Working At Southwest Airlines Are:** The challenges, the fun, the outstanding results, and the people.

**When I Was A Child, I Wanted To Grow Up To Be:** An oceanographer.

**Favorite Toy Growing Up:** Basketball.

**Favorite "Toys" Today:** Hunting and fishing gear.

**As A Child, The First Time I Performed In Front Of A Group, I:** Played "George Harrison" in a third grade Beatles imitation.

**Proudest Moment As A Child:** Being selected third grade "best citizen" by my classmates!

**Proudest Moment As An Adult:** ... grow up.

**First Pet And His/Her Name:** B...

**My Teen Idol:** Roger Staubach...

**Favorite Candy Bar:** Snicker...

**Favorite Book Growing Up...** Puppies bring out the chil...

**My High School Classmat...** A legend in my own mind...

**Something Few Peopl...** play the electric guitar...

**When I Want To Hav...** friends.

**The Person Who M...** course!

"A Southwest Employee who 'colors outside...
who has the courage to dream radically, b...
rationally."

## Jim Wimber...

## Jim Parker
### Vice President General Counsel

**Began Coloring At Southwest:** February 1986

**Birthday:** January 1

**Job Responsibilities At Southwest:** Our Department has responsibility for managing the legal affairs of Southwest Airlines, the acquisition of airport and other properties owned or leased by the Company, as well as airport lease negotiations (Properties); the design and construction of facilities and improvement thereto (Facilities); the repair, maintenance, installations, and design of the Company's electronic equipment (Technical Services); and the operation of our Headquarters Building and related facilities (Building Services).

**The Thing I Like Most About Working At Southwest Airlines Is:** Southwest Airlines is the most exciting Company in the most exciting business in the world. It is not a Company built on greed or selfish goals, but... on a shared commitment to be the...

**As A Child, The First Time I Performed In Front Of A Group, I:** Froze up and forgot the speech I was supposed to make (third grade).

**Proudest Moment As A Child:** Winning the citywide elementary school public speaking contest in the sixth grade.

**Proudest Moment As An Adult:** Presenting the 1994 Heroes of the Heart Award to the Technical Services group in our Department.

**First Pet And His/Her Name:** My cocker spaniel, Silver.

**My Teen Idol:** Perry Mason—he never lost a case.

**Favorite Book Growing Up:** "A Tale of Two Cities."

Any competitive game h...

...the child in me.

...ld Describe Me As:

...ut Me Is: My
...se to some
...Mule as a child.
...her Francis the

...hallgame with my
...mily.

...st: Herb.

...mployee
...sense
...adigm
...k

## John Denison

## Libby Sartain
### Vice President People

**Began Coloring At Southwest:** July 1988

**Birthday:** November 2

**Job Responsibilities At Southwest:** A Leader of People.

**The Thing I Like Most About Working At Southwest Airlines Is:** Laughing as loud as I want—with reckless abandon.

**When I Was A Child, I Wanted To Grow Up To Be:** Dale Evans.

**Favorite Toy Growing Up:** Bicycle.

**Favorite "Toy" Today:** Stuffed animal golf club wood covers: a monkey, a skunk, and an alligator.

**As A Child, The First Time I Performed In Front Of A Group, I:** Was singing, of course!

**Proudest Moment As A Child:** The day I finally learned to ride my bike—I was in second grade! It took me a while.

**Favorite Candy Bar:** Hershey's with almonds.

**Proudest Moment As An Adult:** The day my daughter received an outstanding student award in fourth grade for scholarship, leadership, citizenship, and sportsmanship.

**First Pet And His/Her Name:** Candy, a sheltie.

**My Teen Idols:** All of the Beatles.

**Favorite Book Growing Up:** "Little Women."

My child brings out the child in me.

**My High School Classmates Would Describe Me As:** Off the wall, crazy, but a Leader anyway.

**Something Few People Know About Me Is:** I once exposed 34 men to an infectious disease. (I was a Little Sister for a fraternity in college. At a Rush party, I prepared all of the refreshments not knowing that I had hepatitis.)

**When I Want To Have Fun, I:** Go on vacations so I can relax on the beach and drink pina coladas.

**The Person Who Makes Me Laugh Most:** Herb Kelleher. He makes me laugh the loudest, too!

"A Southwest Employee who 'colors outside the lines' is an Employee who is creative, innovative, willing to take risks, off center, and presents arguments in a positive manner. Someone who challenges everyone around them to think outside the box."

***Some of Southwest's leaders showing their colors in* Our Colorful Leaders**

executive yearbook entitled *Our Colorful Leaders*. It is a classic example of Southwest humor put to practical use. The idea was to give everyone a chance to get to know the leaders of the company through zany pictures and fun-filled personal descriptions. If you want to know what they thought they wanted to be when they grew up, what makes them laugh, or what their favorite candy bar is, this yearbook is the place to look. The result is a level playing field, where executives become more real and more approachable.

## LAUGHING ALL THE WAY

With leaders who embrace humor and merriment, is it any wonder the airline allows, actually encourages, flight attendants to add spice to the routine announcements at the beginning and end of each flight? During one of our trips from Dallas to San Diego, Southwest flight attendant Karen Wood captivated the passengers on the Phoenix–San Diego leg with this rendition of the safety announcements:

> *If I could have your attention for a few moments, we sure would love to point out those safety features. If you haven't been in an automobile since 1965, the proper way to fasten your seat belt is to slide the flat end into the buckle. To unfasten, lift up on the buckle and it will release.*
>
> *And as the song goes, there might be fifty ways to leave your lover, but there are only six ways to leave this aircraft: two forward exit doors, two over-wing removable window exits, and two aft exit doors. The location of each exit is clearly marked with signs overhead, as well as red and white disco lights along the floor of the aisle. (Made ya look!)*
>
> *Located in the seatback pocket in front of you or to the side of you in the lounge area, among the peanut wrappers, coffee cups, and newspapers, you should find an emergency information card supplementing our safety features. Take note on the back that in the event of a water evacuation, your bottom . . . your seat bottom, that is, can be used as a flotation device by removing the cushion, holding onto the straps underneath it, and choosing your favorite stroke.*
>
> *Please check at this time to make sure your seat belts are securely fastened, seat backs and tray tables are in their full*

*upright and most uncomfortable position, and all the carry-on luggage you've brought in is crammed underneath the seat in front of you, or in one of the overhead bins.*

*FAA regulations require passenger compliance with all lighted passenger information signs, posted placards, and crew member instructions regarding seat belts and no smoking. In other words do exactly what we say!*

*Speaking of smoking, there's never any smoking aboard our flights. You know what happens if we catch you smoking here at Southwest, don't you? You'll be asked to step out onto our wing and enjoy our feature movie presentation,* Gone with the Wind. *There is never any smoking, even in the lavatories.*

*Finally, although we never anticipate a change in cabin pressure, should one occur, four oxygen masks will magically appear overhead. Immediately stop screaming, please deposit a quarter, and unlike President Clinton, you must inhale! If you're seated next to a child or traveling with someone who is acting like a small child, secure yourself first and then assist him or her. Please continue wearing the mask until otherwise notified by a uniformed crew member—yes, believe it or not, these are uniforms! And we do need to tell you that the bag does not inflate, but you still are receiving oxygen. Sit back, relax and enjoy a one-hour flight to San Diego on the best airline in the universe— Southwest. Southwest Airlines is determined to offer Positively Outrageous Service to customers.*

For the grand finale, the flight was concluded with this:

*Oh, my airline has a first name, it's S-O-U-T-H; my airline has a second name, it's W-E-S-T. Oh, I love to fly it every day and if you ask me why, I'll say, 'cause Southwest Airlines has a way of bringing sunshine to your day.*

The wit and humor that Karen injected into the announcements made a standard procedure seem new and refreshing. It was fun to listen to and it was a flight worth remembering.

The fun doesn't stop with the PA, however. For a good laugh, flight attendants have been known to hide in the overhead luggage compartments and pop out when customers open them to store their belongings. While we were getting ready to board a flight in Reno, the customer service agent came over the public address system to say,

"Southwest Airlines would like to congratulate one of our first-time fliers who is celebrating his eighty-ninth birthday. Ladies and gentlemen, be sure to poke your head into the cockpit and say happy birthday to your pilot, Captain John Smith."

Customer service agents and flight attendants alike have a book of games they use to create a more enjoyable travel experience for customers and help them pass the time. Entitled "T. J. LUV Presents a Guide to Inflight and Gate Games," it serves as an instant source of playful contests, trivia, games, and songs when the urge strikes for offering the "outrageous" in Positively Outrageous Service.

For example, passengers waiting at the gate, or on one of Southwest's longer flights, might find themselves proudly sharing a hole in their sock, or a humiliating driver's license picture, in order to win a $25 gift certificate or a free drink. It's all in an effort to make the Southwest experience more memorable and fun for customers!

Southwest employees don't limit the fun and games to their work with customers. Audy Donelson, then station manager in Dallas, for example, has a propensity for practical jokes. On one occasion, Tulsa Ground Operations thought it might be time to turn the tables and play one on the Dallas station. "One morning," as Greg Golden, Southwest's Tulsa station manager, tells the story,

*a customer checked a large, empty kennel that obviously had been used. There was straw and debris still in the kennel. A light went on. The next Dallas flight, we put the kennel in the doorway of the front bin, opened the kennel door and spread some of the straw out onto the floor of the bin. When we sent the offload message to Dallas, we inserted into the remarks section: "Beware of wild boar in front bin. It belongs to an employee in Dallas. Use caution!" I telephoned Audy to give him a heads-up on what we were doing. After several hours had passed, we hadn't heard anything. I phoned Audy again to see how it had gone—"Oh my gosh," Audy replied, "I forgot to tell anyone!" He quickly conferred with Mike Sand, manager of ramp and operations, to see what had transpired. Every ramp agent who wasn't working another flight had gathered around the front bin to see the wild boar. As soon as they opened the bin door and saw the kennel open but no pig, they scattered like quail and didn't want anything to do with that flight. They were sure they had a wild boar loose in the belly of the airplane.*

## DEAR MR. KELLEHER

*One more thing. I really enjoyed the message and music while I was put on hold. You guys are different, pleasantly different. I wish all of our service industries could emulate your success.*

WILLIS YEH
CUPERTINO, CALIFORNIA

We have observed a childlike quality in the people of Southwest Airlines—not childish behavior, but an attitude of playfulness. Besides the practical jokes, there are hundreds of examples of how fun and humor add spice to the daily routine at Southwest Airlines. It is not at all unusual to find toy boxes, rocking chairs, Ping-Pong tables, and loud music in various departments around the general offices, all used as stress reducers and creativity aids. The goal is to make the work environment as user-playful as possible.

The creativity consultants tell us humor and creativity go hand in hand—"HA HA leads to the AHA!" Southwest employees work very hard and, most of the time, at a grueling pace. In order to perpetuate the Southwest Spirit and continue to take the serious lightly, the company welcomes these playful outlets, even encourages them. At Southwest, not only is it okay to have fun at work, but the company spurs it on. Southwest has realized the benefits of such on-the-job nonsense and truly values humor.

## HARD-LINE BENEFITS OF FUN

### 1. The most productive work force in the industry
Southwest Airlines has the smallest number of employees per aircraft, serves the most customers per employee, and has the most enviable record of profitability in the industry. The company works very lean and reaps the financial benefits.

# THE SOUTHWEST WAY TO A SENSE OF HUMOR

*Think funny.*
People at Southwest are masterful at looking for the flip side of all situations. Try to focus and zero in on your most outrageous thoughts—make these thoughts fun, not embarrassing.

*Adopt a playful attitude.*
Let your mind be open to uncensored, nonconformist, silly, and outrageous behavior and responses to life's daily occurrences. It doesn't mean you have to do outrageous things—but you can always consider them!

*Be the first to laugh.*
At Southwest, it's hard not to laugh at the incongruities in everyday situations involving yourself and others. If you don't, someone else will—and encourage you to join in. Try to be the first to find some humor in an otherwise awkward and stressful situation.

*Laugh with, not at.*
Southwest promotes healthy humor—that is, laughing *with* others about what they do or what you do. Never laugh *at* people because of who they are (unless you are assured that they can laugh at themselves). If and when we do laugh with others about their idiosyncrasies, we should see it as an opportunity to visit our own.

*Laugh at yourself.*
Kelleher is the first to laugh at himself, not in mockery, but with objectivity and self-acceptance. Laughing at ourselves is a great first step in taking life less seriously.

*Take work seriously, but not yourself.*
One of Southwest's mottoes is "Take yourself lightly and take your job and your responsibilities seriously." By adopting this motto, you may soon discover that life's burdens and anxieties are lighter— sometimes even lighter than air. Or, as GSD&M president Roy Spence says, "Take some yeast and lighten up."

### 2. Working for the fun of it

It is not at all unusual for Southwest employees to work without pay on days surrounding the holidays to help the airline maintain its Positively Outrageous Service during its busiest time of year. Employees also participate, again without pay, in "walk-a-mile" programs that give them the opportunity to see how other departments or other stations operate. It is normal practice for employees to go to very busy stations on their days off, just to lend a hand.

### 3. Low attrition and absenteeism

Southwest is known within the industry for its very low turnover rates. When people go to work for Southwest, it often becomes their final career destination. Research shows that when we are having fun and laughing, we produce endorphins—our bodies' natural life-giving, healing medicine. So when work is fun and employees are free to laugh and play, people are healthier. Perhaps the old prescription "Laughter is the best medicine" is true. The evidence is pretty convincing. People want to come to work when they laugh and have fun.

### 4. High creativity and innovation

The toys, games, and other creative outlets so readily available on Southwest's planes, in waiting areas, and in the offices make it easy for employees and customers alike to engage in creative breaks. In many cases, these breaks give them a laugh and a new lens through which they can view a particular situation, problem, or task.

The people of Southwest have created an environment and a style of doing business that is like no other—Southwest is passionate about its pursuit of fun. The company has become known for its zany antics, both on the ground and in the sky. It has inspired business innovators around the world by creating a culture in which fun, humor, and playfulness are the low-cost antidotes for the harmful side effects of the stress and seriousness that pervade much of the corporate community. The bottom line: Fun is hard to avoid at Southwest Airlines.

# Success in a Nutshell

➤ Lighten up: don't take yourself so seriously. Associate with fun people. Identify six ways you can lighten up, then work on them for six months.

➤ Ask family, friends, and colleagues to finish the following: *(Your name) would be more fun if he/she would . . .*

➤ Work in play clothes!

➤ Be the first to find humor in tense moments.

➤ Try to make someone smile or laugh every morning and every night.

➤ Laugh at yourself at least once a day!

**CHAPTER 16**

# LUV

## MORE THAN JUST A TICKER SYMBOL

If you look up Southwest's stock price on the New York Stock Exchange, you'll find it under the ticker symbol LUV. The ticker symbol not only represents an advertising theme that has been a part of the airline since 1971, it also exemplifies the loving character of the company. Southwest has become a loving place to work because of the kind of people who work there. "We are interested in people who externalize, who focus on other people, who are really motivated to help other people," Kelleher once said. "We are not interested in navel gazers, regardless of how lint-free their navels are." If you are careful about hiring loving people, it should come as no surprise that acts of love and generosity will naturally spill out of them. It should also come as no surprise that when you get enough people with these attributes in the same company, a corporate character is created that practices love as a way of doing business.

### THE GREATEST NEED OF THE HUMAN HEART

While macho managers might never use the word "love" in the workplace, most of them would admit that, when it comes right down to it, the deepest need in our human existence is the need to be loved and accepted. Southwest Airlines understands that this need doesn't change suddenly or mysteriously disappear when employees walk through the door at work.

"The greatest disease in the West today is not TB or leprosy; it is being unwanted, unloved, and uncared for," says Mother Teresa in *A Simple Path*. "We can cure physical diseases with medicine, but the only cure for loneliness, despair, and hopelessness is love." The disease of which Mother Teresa speaks is not relegated to the streets; it can also be found inside the corridors of corporate America. We've all seen it. An antidote for loneliness, despair, and hopelessness is found in the lessons we've learned about love at Southwest Airlines and how it is expressed there.

## LOVE IS ACTION ORIENTED

A lot of people confuse love with romanticism and sentimentality. That's not what you see at Southwest Airlines. Southwest people are

sentimental, and the company has its share of die-hard romantics, but at the core of this business, there is something more significant going on than gushy feelings. The kind of love we see at Southwest is action oriented and involved. It operates more as a verb than as a noun.

Love is an act of will. It's something Southwest employees *do*. Sometimes sentiment and affection accompany their actions, but not always. At Southwest, love is some-

thing employees choose to do because they are committed to the well-being of others. In this sense, love is a decision more than a feeling. It isn't an on-again, off-again thing that people do when they feel emotionally inclined. Love is something the employees of Southwest Airlines have decided to practice, regardless of how they feel at any given moment. What we've learned from Southwest is that the power inherent in love is released only when love is shared.

## LOVE IS PATIENT

The degree of patience we exercise with others reveals a lot about how much we care about them. It's easy to take people for granted at work, and irritation and impatience with people—over projects and work routines—can often send a signal that we don't value them. Our ability to put up with the guff and inconveniences caused by others can be an indicator of how much we love them. Love is slow to anger when inconvenienced. When we get in the trenches with people to endure difficulty or hardship, and we do it without complaining, we express our love for them.

Love can be expressed by demonstrating patience and commitment toward coworkers, customers, and the company for the right reasons. In December 1994, the Fleet Services Union (better known internally as ROPA—the Ramp, Operations, and Provisioning Association) began negotiations for a new working agreement. An in-house employee association modeled on the Southwest Pilots Association, ROPA was certified in 1989 after Kelleher told the group he would deal with them in good faith as he had with the pilots. "The ramp, operations, and provisioning union is made up of employees, run by employees, and operated in support of employees," says ROPA President Mark "Squidd" Goodwin.

## DEAR MR. KELLEHER

*We've made several trips on Southwest lately, and I'd like to compliment you on your people.*

*We came to you first because of your prices—and they're still the best incentive.*

*But also your people are so sincerely friendly and helpful. Not only to the passengers. As we've waited in the boarding areas, they seem genuinely happy and friendly toward each other too. To me, this says a lot for Southwest as an employer.*

*Thanks a lot.*

MRS. W. A. RUSSELL
MINDEN, NEVADA

Love was patient during these negotiations, for it took almost eighteen months for the union and the company to forge an agreement they were satisfied with. All during this time, according to Goodwin, ROPA employees continued to do a stellar job even though the negotiations created some pressure. "The ramp, operations, and provisioning group is the only team of employees whose job performance directly impacts *all three* categories of the Triple Crown—customer service, on-time performance, and baggage handling," he notes. ROPA employees demonstrated their patience and commitment to coworkers and the company throughout the negotiation process by continuing to play their part in an all-out effort to keep the lead in these three critical industry measures.

## LOVE IS KIND AND GENEROUS

Love finds one of its greatest expressions in kindness and generosity. People who are kind are charitable, considerate, and humane. They go out of their way to assist others.

*Kind people don't look away; they involve themselves and sometimes inconvenience themselves.*

Several years ago a Dallas television newscast aired a brief documentary about some men who lived in a homeless shelter. Ann Rhoades, Southwest's former vice president of people, watched the program and was intrigued with what she saw in one of the men—intelligence and long-lost pride. Ron Bruner had been out of work for a number of years, and, through a series of events, had lost everything, including his family. Rhoades and Sherry Phelps, director of corporate employment, arranged to visit him at the shelter and discovered a very bright, intelligent man who had had a run of bad luck. Southwest offered Bruner a job as a reservations agent in Grand Prairie, Texas. Southwest employees at the reservations center quickly adopted him. They scrounged up enough furniture, food, and money to help Bruner get an apartment within walking distance of the center, and they covered his first few months of rent until he could get on his feet. They got him a bicycle and, when it was stolen, promptly replaced it. Southwest purchased special hearing aids that allowed the hearing-impaired Bruner to talk on the phone with customers. Today, Bruner still works in the reservations center, has been reunited with his daughter, and is, as you might imagine, a die-hard Southwest fan. Southwest employees' love played a significant role in restoring Bruner's sense of dignity and self-worth. And, in the end, Southwest gained a talented and dedicated employee.

## LOVE IS COURTEOUS

Rather than getting caught up in the bitter dynamics of jealousy and envy, most Southwest people take great joy in seeing others succeed. When someone does something extraordinary, happiness is the emotion and celebration is usually the order of the day. You will rarely find Southwest employees engaged in the kind of backbiting gossip that puts people down. It's as though there were an unwritten rule or cultural norm in the company that says, "We don't talk bad about family members and teammates."

> *Love helps us believe in people and look for the goodness in others.*

People who are respectful are also courteous. "Southwest people have good manners," says MaryEllen Milano, GSD&M's vice president and director in charge of the Southwest account. It's difficult to walk through any station, or through the halls of Southwest's corporate headquarters, without being struck by the courtesy shown by Southwest employees. In many businesses, you're lucky if you can get people to look at you, let alone say "hi," when you walk the hallways. At Southwest, it's more like an ongoing cocktail party without the cocktails. People you've never met will stop, introduce themselves, offer to help you, ask some get-to-know-you questions, and then be on their way. A remarkable courtesy pervades the place. "There is a sense of caring about one another and respecting one another and being sensitive to one another that is extremely refreshing, and it causes you to be happier in everything you do," says Tom Kalahar, president and CEO of Camelot Communications, Southwest's media-buying agency. "It makes me feel good to see my people happy to be working with Southwest. . . . Having Southwest as one of our clients is one of the best benefit programs I have for my people!"

## LOVE IS AFFIRMING

Love believes in people. It chooses to look for the goodness in others. People who have worked in gold mines will tell you that tons of dirt must be removed before the miners hit a vein of ore. The miners go on to say, "But we focus on looking for the vein of gold rather than the dirt." Love makes people say, "I believe in you. I value you. I want you to succeed and be fulfilled in everything you do."

*To some politicians and CEOs, it is inconceivable that Herb won't change his schedule if he has a commitment with Southwest employees.*

Kelleher and Barrett are fanatical fans of Southwest employees. Although we don't know how to measure it and therefore could never prove it, we believe that few work forces in the world receive as much affirmation from their CEO as Southwest employees get from Herb Kelleher. The fact that Southwest employees feel loved and accepted is not surprising when you listen to the way Kelleher talks to them. For example, in his opening remarks at his annual Message to the Field in Phoenix several years ago, Kelleher showed his love for this extended family by talking about their sprightliness, their can-do attitude, their joy, their concern, and their caring for other people. Then he had this to say:

> *And that's the reason why I am so enthusiastic about every oppor-tunity to be with you. I have said on at least a hundred occasions that I would rather be with the people of Southwest Airlines, no matter what the occasion, no matter when it is, than make a trip to Paris or do anything else in the world people think is of an exalted nature.*
>
> *The truth is, you know, there was a Spanish explorer named Ponce de León who was looking for the Fountain of Youth. He believed that if you dipped yourself in it, even for the shortest period of time, you would add twenty or thirty years to your chronological lifespan. Well, I found my Fountain of Youth in the employees, the people of Southwest Airlines. Because every time I have the opportunity to be with you, it reminds me how wonder-ful you are, it rejuvenates me, restores me, and refreshes me.*

While this kind of talk may be passed off by some as merely inspirational rhetoric, Kelleher stands behind his words. When other CEOs ask Kelleher to give speeches or attend executive roundtables, he will send his regrets if he is scheduled to be with Southwest employees. During filming for the *Service with Soul* videotape, Tom Peters asked Kelleher if he had any advice for other chief executive officers. Kelleher's reply? "Spend more time with your people and less time with other CEOs."

Kelleher started writing his "Letter to Shareholders" in the company's *1978 Annual Report*. Since then, he has never failed to close one out with an affirmation of Southwest employees. Perhaps this is because he knows that, unlike those of the Energizer bunny, the batteries of affirmation don't last without being recharged. The constancy of Kelleher's love for employees comes alive in those letters.

**1984.** *As long as the glowing ambiance of our People persists, Southwest Airlines itself will both persist and prevail. Our loving People are the heart and soul of Southwest Airlines—today, tomorrow, and forever.*

**1988.** *1989 could be a "bumper" year. If it so eventuates, the "power and the glory" will belong to the magnificent People of Southwest Airlines who, in their sincerity, striving, and caring, are unequaled elsewhere in our industry and elsewhere in our nation.*

**1990.** *Their feats are legendary; their will indomitable; and their hearts huge. Their caring for the Company has caused them to establish, voluntarily, a "Fuel from the Heart" program, whereby many are incurring payroll deductions in order to purchase fuel for Southwest, demonstrating once more that ours is not just a corporation, not only a business, but a lovely and loving family.*

**1991.** *Our motto for 1991 was: "Only the Strong Survive." Because our balance sheet was conservative; because our operating costs were low; because our Customer Service was legendary; and because our People have the hearts of lions, the strength of elephants, and the determination of water buffaloes, we did, indeed, "survive."*

**1993.** *The excellence of Southwest—in all aspects of its performance—is attributable to the affirmative, caring, compassionate, unified, proud, and Customer-focused dedication of our wondrous People. Thanks to them, Southwest . . . escaped the worst ravages of the economic holocaust that literally decimated our industry during the past four years. Our People are not opportunists focused only on the middle of next week. Our People are visionaries focused on the middle of the next decade. As long as they continue to maintain their long-term vision, Southwest will prosper and succeed, as it has done in the past. I have every confidence in their maintenance of that vision because they are truly superb!*

**1994.** *In 1994, our People made an enormous investment in the future of Southwest Airlines. Only Southwest's People could have effectively handled so much change so successfully. While a number of other airlines may attempt to imitate Southwest, none of them can duplicate the spirit, unity, "can-do" attitudes, and marvelous esprit de corps of the Southwest Employees, who continually provide superb Customer Service to each other and to the traveling public. Just as the past has belonged to Southwest, because of our people's goodwill, dedication, and energy, so shall Southwest seize the future!*

Criticism is easier to accept when an employee knows, beyond a shadow of a doubt, that the boss loves and accepts him or her. When people receive affirmation, they develop the courage to change and the confidence to succeed when they try something new. Ultimately, when people are affirmed, they see themselves as lovable. "Love starts in the heart of the lover," says Dr. Ken Blue. When we know how much we are loved, only then can we love others. It's hard to draw on an emotional bank account that is depleted. People who feel unloved have a difficult time loving others. Kelleher's public affirmations of Southwest's people make them feel special and loved. From this point of validation, they are then free to love and affirm others.

## LOVE IS COMPASSIONATE

Love draws us to get in touch with the condition of other people's lives. When we develop a deep awareness of their suffering, compassion induces us to take action. Compassion consists of the capability

# THANKS, HERB

*Southwest employees appreciate the faith their boss has in them. After fifteen years of reading the accolades Kelleher has bestowed on them, the employees of Southwest Airlines decided to turn the tables. In their own expression of affirmation, and as a surprise to Kelleher, they took out and paid for a full-page ad in* USA Today *to honor him on Boss's Day 1994:*

For remembering every one of our names.

For supporting the Ronald McDonald House.

For helping load baggage on Thanksgiving.

For giving everyone a kiss (and we mean everyone).

For listening.

For running the only profitable major airline.

For singing at our holiday party.

For singing only once a year.

For letting us wear shorts and sneakers to work.

For golfing at The LUV Classic with only one club.

For outtalking Sam Donaldson.

For riding your Harley Davidson into Southwest Headquarters.

For being a friend, not just a boss.

*Happy Boss's Day from Each One of Your 16,000 Employees*

of identifying with the pain of another person coupled with the desire to relieve it. It is this expression of love that causes so many Southwest employees to do such extraordinary things for each other and their customers.

When a Southwest skycap in Tulsa had a financial strain due to an illness in the family, Southwest employees took up a collection and presented him with $200. The entire Dallas Provisioning Department put on a benefit golf tournament for the son of a probationary employee, who had been with the company for only five months. The little boy was three years old and had recently been diagnosed with leukemia. The group raised more than $6,000 to offset the massive medical bills. Pilots at Southwest's Chicago pilot base got behind one of their peers from Phoenix who had been paralyzed in a bicycle accident. The Chicago base alone raised $3,000 for their comrade. "These are regular occurrences," Lisa Weigold, manager of customer service in Houston, points out, "spontaneous gestures you may find at any station."

Watching others be loving and compassionate can give us the courage to trust our instincts when the policy manual fails to provide guidance. There are hundreds of stories that show Southwest employees' instinctive love and compassion for others in action. Rachel Dyer, a customer service agent at Southwest's Los Angeles station, gives a heart-wrenching example in a letter to *LUV Lines:*

*Last Christmas was a very difficult one for me. My family and all of my close friends were back home in Florida. It was cold here in California and I was all alone. I was working so many hours and was very sick, on Christmas Eve in particular. I was working a double [shift] and feeling really miserable inside. Never had I imagined it would be such an important memory for me. I think of this story often in my mind, and each time I feel just as moved as I did when it happened.*

*I was working on the ticket counter, and it was about 9:00 P.M. on Christmas Eve. There were a few of us working and very few Customers waiting to be helped. When it was time for me to call the next person to the counter, I looked out to see the sweetest-looking old man standing with a cane. He walked very slowly over to the counter and in the faintest voice told me that he had to go to New Orleans. I tried to explain to him that there were no more flights that same night and that he would have to go in the morning. He looked so confused and very worried. I tried to find out more information by asking if he had a reservation or if he remembered when he was supposed to travel, but he seemed to become more confused with each question. He just kept saying, "She said I have to go to New Orleans."*

*After much time, I was able to at least find out that this old man was dropped off at the curb on Christmas Eve by his sister-in-law and told to go to New Orleans where he had family. She had given him some cash and told him just to go inside and buy a ticket. When I asked if he could come back tomorrow, he said that she was gone and that he had no place to stay. He then said he*

*would wait at the airport until tomorrow. Naturally, I felt a
little ashamed. Here I was feeling very sorry for myself about
being alone on Christmas, when this angel, "Mr. Christmas,"
was sent to remind me of what being alone really meant. It broke
my heart.*

*Immediately, I told him we would get it all straightened out,
and Customer Service Agent Cynthia Jackson helped to book him
a seat for the earliest flight the next morning. We gave him the
senior citizens' fare, which gave him some extra money for traveling. About this time he started to look very tired and when I
stepped around the counter to ask him if he was all right, I saw
that his leg was wrapped in a bandage. He had been standing on
it that whole time, holding a plastic bag full of clothes.*

*I called for a wheelchair. When the wheelchair came, we all
stepped around to help him in, and I noticed a small amount of
blood on his bandage. I asked how he hurt his leg, and he said he
had just had bypass surgery and an artery taken from his leg.
Can you imagine? This man had heart surgery, and then shortly
afterward was dropped off at the curb to buy a ticket with no
reservation to fly to New Orleans alone.*

*I had never really had a situation like this, and I wasn't sure
what I could do. I went back to ask my Supervisors, Kathy Hooper
and Mercedes Larrea [currently Phoenix operations agent]. I told
them the whole story and asked if we could find a place for him to
stay. They both said absolutely and got a PSO [passenger service
order] for me. We gave Mr. Christmas a hotel room for one night
and a meal ticket for dinner and breakfast. When I came back
out, we got his plastic bag of clothes and cane together and gave
the nice World Services employee a tip to take him downstairs to
wait for the airport shuttle. I bent down to explain the hotel, food,
and itinerary again to Mr. Christmas and then patted him on the
arm and told him everything would be just fine.*

*As he left he said, "Thank you," bent his head, and started
to cry. I cried too. When I went back to thank Kathy Hooper
she just smiled and said, "I love stories like that. He is your
Christmas Man."*

*It's not that I think that every person needs help or that as
a company we could even afford to do for everyone what we did
in this situation. It's just that I do think that life can be very
challenging at times. For some it can be even more difficult, and
I am so proud and happy to work for a company that not only*

*allows but encourages me to help people who really are in need.*
*I truly believe the success of this company has to do with the fact*
*that it was founded and is run by kind, honest, and loving people.*
*Thank you, Herb and Colleen, for being all of these things. I also*
*believe that the success of the LAX Station is a result of the same.*
*May we all find our own "Christmas Man" this holiday season.*

## LOVE EXTENDS GRACE AND FORGIVENESS

Grace is the capacity to accept people as they are and forgive them for the wrong they cause. As a component of love, grace is an act of the will, extended without condition or limitation. When we receive grace, it is always undeserved and usually unexpected. We come by it through no power of our own, but, rather, through the power of love extended from others. It has been said that too much grace and forgiveness in an organization will give people the freedom to act irresponsibly. We don't think so. In fact, the authentic response that usually accompanies the gift of grace is one of gratitude and awe. People who feel an overwhelming sense of appreciation are compelled to act more responsibly.

*A striking difference between Southwest and other organizations is that Southwest has created a culture where the norm is to forgive and forget.*

Several years ago, Colleen Barrett was concerned because one of Southwest's customer service agents had been the subject of a few customer letters that didn't seem as glowing as in the past. Barrett called the employee into her office and asked, "Is everything okay? The letters we've been getting about you don't seem to have that warmth they used to." At that point, the employee started to cry and then went on to describe a difficult divorce, a custody battle over a three-year-old son, and an $1,800 debt for legal fees. Barrett listened and consoled her. A few hours later, the employee received an envelope with $1,800 in cash from Barrett's personal account. There was no note; it simply had the employee's name written on it, in Barrett's handwriting. Needless to say, this employee was overwhelmed by Barrett's display of compassion and grace. More than seven years later, this person remains one of Southwest's true zealots and her responsibilities have been expanded. She says, "At what other company could you walk in thinking you're fired and walk out feeling loved, listened to, and really cared about?" Having experienced the freedom that comes with grace, this person acted more, not less, responsibly. As is often the case when one feels a deep sense of gratitude, her love for the company grew and her commitment to Southwest's success intensified.

There is a spirit of liberty and freedom at Southwest Airlines, and we believe grace has a lot to do with it. However, it would be erroneous to think that Southwest Airlines is a utopia, where nothing goes wrong and everyone loves everyone else all the time. In any organization the size of Southwest Airlines, people frequently make mistakes. When they do, other people get hurt and feel angry. The difference between Southwest and other organizations is that Southwest has created a culture where the norm is to forgive and forget. When people forgive and are forgiven, they are free to move beyond the hardened boundaries of their lives—boundaries that harbor anger, fear, mistrust, and resentment. Southwest employees cherish the culture they've created too much to let bitterness destroy it, so they don't dwell much on the past. They have learned to separate the action from the actor, forgive the person, and move on.

## LOVE DOESN'T GUARANTEE APPROVAL

Although many people equate love and approval, they are not the same. Real love comes without conditions; it doesn't depend on anything. Approval must be earned by our performance. In this sense, you can love a person without approving of his or her performance. As parents, we do this all the time.

As loving people and responsible executives, Herb Kelleher and Colleen Barrett operate this way at Southwest Airlines. We have seen them remove employees from jobs where their performance was hurting the company. However, Herb and Colleen aren't the type of people who would withdraw their deep love and affection from a person simply because they vehemently disapprove of his or her behavior. We've seen them remain friends with people they've had to fire. Herb and Colleen recall a former employee who, after being terminated from Southwest, even named his first child after both of them!

# AMAZING GRACE

*People who are gracious are often individuals who have faced their own inadequacies and weaknesses, felt the need for compassion, and experienced what it is like to receive grace. At Southwest Airlines, one of those people is Matt Buckley, director of the cargo management group. A creative spirit with an entrepreneurial passion, Buckley is one of Southwest's more colorful characters. He also knows a lot about grace and forgiveness and what it means not to take yourself too seriously.*

One day, while Buckley was contemplating his plan for distributing merit increases to the cargo management group, he entered the men's room and bellied up to the urinal next to Jim Hinna, director of ground operations. Knowing that Hinna was going through the same mental exercise for his group, Buckley asked him, "So have you figured out how to allocate your raises yet?" Hinna went on to explain a very thoughtful methodology that seemed equitable for all involved. With more than a hint of sarcasm, Buckley said, "That's interesting; I gave myself a 20 percent raise, so there's not much to go around for anyone else." The two colleagues chuckled at the joke, since their authority does not include awarding their own raises. Then, according to Buckley, he followed the time-honored rule of checking beneath the stall doors for feet before saying, "Seriously, I've got a real tough situation I need to discuss with Wimberly before I can finish the process. But you know, Mr. Accessible isn't available to speak."

The two men yukked it up, finished their business, and started walking back to the office. The next thing Buckley knew, he heard Jim Wimberly's all-too-familiar voice at the end of the hall: "So, you're giving yourself a 20 percent raise, huh? Does anyone need to see Mr. Accessible about anything?" Turning red from head to toe, Buckley immediately started patting his body, concluding he had been bugged! Recounting the story, Buckley says, "Jim Hinna

*Matt Buckley* (left) *receiving his award from Jim Wimberly at the scene of the crime*

involuntarily fell to his knees, doubled over in hysterical laughter. Heads began popping out of offices and cubes. Time stopped as everyone within earshot congregated around Mr. Accessible and me to see what was up."

Here's what had happened. Hearing Hinna and Buckley walking into the bathroom, Wimberly had a hunch he could have some fun. He quickly picked his feet up off the floor of the middle stall. "As you could imagine, I was in kind of an awkward position. My legs were shaking, I started to get cramps, and I was trying to keep my feet from falling down to the floor. When they left, I collapsed in a heap in the stall with my legs quivering."

A few days later, Wimberly rounded up the entire department and brought everyone to the scene of the crime. "As we all piled in, standing room only for men and women alike, I saw my career flushed right down the same toilet my boss had been sitting on when he picked up his feet," Buckley says. "But, much to my surprise, the only negative consequence I suffered was the public humiliation that goes along with being presented the 'Boner of the Decade' award in the men's room." "I could've gotten upset about the Mr. Accessible part," Wimberly told us, "but I took that as something I needed to work on, because Matt genuinely felt he was having a hard time getting in to see me. So I actually took it as a personal wake-up call that I needed to rearrange some things I was doing so there would be more time for my group."

Buckley proudly displays his award in his office to remind him of just how amazing grace really is.

## LOVE IS TOUGH AND GUTSY

Sometimes the most loving thing we can do for people is tell them the truth—even when the truth hurts. Making decisions that hurt people in the present but help them avoid even greater pain and hardship in the future may be the kindest thing we can do for them. This is why love is tough and gutsy. The caveat, of course, is that our actions must be motivated by genuine love.

Often we avoid telling people the truth because, in the name of kindness, we want to spare them the hurt. At other times, we avoid telling people the truth out of self-protection—we hate the thought of being disliked. In either case, we do them no favor. Our evasion of the truth enables employees to continue operating with deficiencies that are detrimental to their success and well-being. That is not love. In fact, the argument could be made that by an act of omission, we exacerbate their problems. Kelleher agrees: "Colleen and I both have told many people, 'You think you are being kind, but you're letting a whole lot of other people down in this particular area.'" Real love says, "I will tell you what you need to know to become a bigger, more authentic person because I want you to succeed in life." People who exercise "tough love" have the courage and strength to say, "At this time I'm willing to trade popularity for the truth because my love for you demands that I tell you the truth." This, of course, is a lot easier if we don't mistake our disapproval for the withdrawal of love.

Colleen Barrett is one of the most loving people we know. She is deeply interested in Southwest employees and very protective of the company. She is also one of the toughest people we know. She has very little patience for habitual mediocrity and simply will not tolerate behavior that compromises the dignity of another person—particularly when it's a Southwest employee or customer. In those circumstances she exercises tough love—even if it means firing someone. Employees are rarely fired for lack of technical competence, but an employee who mistreats someone is history. Like a coach confronting an athlete who isn't playing up to his or her ability, Barrett is not afraid to confront her employees when she feels they are not practicing Southwest's values or living up to their full potential:

> *We talk a lot about treating our people like family, but families are not always filled with good. Sometimes you have to confront family members. Herb and I both will get comments or letters*

> *that say, "My boss fired me and that's not love, that's not family,"*
> *or employees will tell us, "My supervisor had a strong disagree-*
> *ment with me and that's not the Southwest Spirit." We say,*
> *"Baloney! That's tough love." I've had some strenuous disagree-*
> *ments with my son, but it doesn't mean that I love him any less.*
> *We've had to remove people from positions around here whom*
> *I consider close personal friends and it broke my heart. But, by*
> *their own admission, it was the best thing for them and clearly*
> *the best thing for the company.*

While Barrett is certainly willing to make the tough calls when it comes to employees, she rarely does so without feeling the pain and compassion that come with confronting someone she loves. Perhaps this is why it's called "tough love." It not only requires the guts to express our disapproval to people we care about, it also requires that our resolve be stronger than the emotional pain that tempts us not to do it in the first place.

## LOVE EMBRACES HUMILITY

Love is humble. It does not entertain pretentiousness or arrogance. There is a big difference between self-confidence and arrogance. We know a lot of self-confident leaders who don't draw a lot of attention to themselves. They fight like hell to draw attention to the causes they fight for, but they don't become too impressed with their own accomplishments. While the media have always demonstrated a propensity to glorify CEOs, we think one of the reasons they have had such fondness for Herb Kelleher is his rare blend of sheer confidence and utter humility.

Humility is marked by modesty. Like Kelleher, other company executives are quick to point the finger at Southwest employees when they are asked about the key to the company's success. "I probably shouldn't admit this," Gary Barron says, "but I really think we could eliminate all the officers and it would be weeks before they felt any effect from it. I suspect that if you left our people to their own devices, it would run pretty smoothly out there, without us messing with it. Maybe it runs *despite* us messing with it." After pausing for a moment, Barron finishes his thought: "Maybe it would run *better* without us messing with it."

When you are okay with yourself and yet not caught up with yourself, you can focus more on the needs of others. After more than twenty-five years of unmatched success in the airline industry, Southwest people don't seem overly impressed with themselves. Confident about their capabilities? Yes. Jubilant about their accomplishments? Absolutely. But the most refreshing thing about Southwest employees is that they never seem to forget their humble beginnings.

## SUCCESS IN A NUTSHELL

➤ Show love more often.

➤ Make love a decision, not just a feeling; then stick to it.

➤ Recognize other people's need for love—and your own.

➤ Don't be afraid to be vulnerable and express your needs. Love often insists on vulnerability.

➤ Life is short: forgive and forget!

➤ Love people by speaking the truth in loving ways.

➤ Be gracious. Polish your politeness.

➤ Don't withhold love when you disapprove of others. Don't view others' disapproval as holding back love.

**CHAPTER 17**

# COMPASSION FOR THE COMMUNITY

## GIVE BACK—IT'S THE RIGHT THING TO DO

True to its family spirit, Southwest likes to be thought of as the "Hometown Airline" in every community it serves. The company believes that employees who understand this goal will work harder to invest in the communities in which Southwest operates. Not only is it good business, it's good stewardship. Good corporate citizenship is often discussed in terms of doing what's right. Southwest believes that doing the right thing—keeping the moral code, if you will—is a natural by-product of acting out of love. Love chooses, to use Peter Block's words, "service over self-interest." Love uses power to serve and wealth to expand its capacity to serve.

Southwest Airlines has embraced the role of good corporate citizen not just because it's the right thing to do, but because giving something back to the communities it serves is the most loving thing to do. Gary Barron explains how the company's outreach efforts start: "Typically, it will start on a local level. Our people will see something that touches them and then they leap into the breach. All it takes is for somebody to put out the call and say, 'Let's do this!'" What follows are descriptions of the many practical ways Southwest Airlines demonstrates compassion and love for the community.

## THE LOMA PRIETA EARTHQUAKE

In 1989, when the San Francisco Bay area experienced a terrible earthquake, Gary Holloway, then a Southwest employee in Phoenix, thought of a way to help the victims. He called the ABC television affiliate in Phoenix and asked newscasters to tell viewers to take blankets, clothes, and canned food to the Southwest terminal at Sky Harbor Airport. "The community responded in full force," says Karen Hayenga, Phoenix marketing manager. "Southwest Airlines sent flight after flight, with bins full of helpful belongings, to help the Bay Area." The outpouring from Phoenix and other Southwest cities was so strong that, when it was all over, Southwest Airlines had flown in more supplies to relieve the victims than anyone else, including the American Red Cross!

## OKLAHOMA CITY BOMBING

In the aftermath of the horrible 1995 bombing in Oklahoma City, Southwest employees immediately became involved by transporting investigators, rescue workers, and crash-site volunteers at no charge. Stations throughout the Southwest system told officials that Southwest would take paying customers off airplanes if needed to get these people to Oklahoma. Reservations agents offered their personal flight passes to victims' family members needing to get into the city.

*Giving something back to the communities it serves is one way Southwest demonstrates its love.*

When asked if Southwest Airlines could transport five hundred teddy bears to the site of the bombing, the company's governmental affairs v.p., Ron Ricks, said "yes" without hesitation. Remember the televised coverage of family members holding teddy bears during the memorial service for victims? Those bears were flown to Oklahoma City on Southwest. When Oklahoma governor Frank Keating and Oklahoma City mayor Ronald Norick conducted the "Thank You, America" tour to thank rescue workers from around the country for their assistance in the bombing tragedy, Southwest donated a plane and the services of a flight crew.

## THE GRINCH WHO TRIED TO STEAL CHRISTMAS

"The Grinch tried to steal Christmas, but the people of Dallas swiped it back" ran the headline in the *Dallas Morning News* on December 4, 1993. Some of those people who "swiped it back" were Southwest Airlines employees. When the Salvation Army reported that a truck filled with holiday gifts for needy children had been stolen, Ken Gile, then an assistant chief pilot for Southwest, walked into Gary Barron's office and said, "I need $5,000 today." Gile told Barron what had happened and promised that he would lead the charge to raise the money to repay the company. Barron gave him the check and Gile began calling colleagues and asking for support. Then he rounded up Judy Haggard of the Marketing Department and several other Southwest employees, jumped into a pickup truck, and went shopping. By the time they returned with a truckload of three hundred toys to deliver to the Salvation Army that afternoon, other employees had raised the $5,000 and then some. "It just snowballed so rapidly," Gile was quoted in the *Dallas Morning News*. "Everyone's talking about this. I think the idea of children doing without really touched people. All I had to do was put out my hand, and it was there."

## ST. LOUIS FLOOD RELIEF

When St. Louis experienced severe flooding in 1993, the St. Louis station contacted relief centers in the region to determine what supplies were needed and got the word into the Southwest system. Supplies were transported to St. Louis from other stations and donated to the Red Cross for distribution. The Cleveland station got in on the act, too, and raised more than $5,000 for flood victims. It also gathered, boxed, and distributed twenty thousand pounds of goods to St. Louis. Besides collecting over thirty thousand pounds of supplies itself, the St. Louis station provided belt loaders for the sandbagging operation.

## "LET'S PAINT THE TOWN!"

Every year, Southwest's Marketing Department puts on a conference that brings together all the marketing employees from around the system as well as people from the company's ad and media-buying agencies. Several years ago, the meeting was held in San Francisco. "Our theme that year was 'Working Together Sets Us Apart,' because the definitive difference at Southwest Airlines is working together," advertising and promotions v.p. Joyce Rogge told us. So instead of just having business meetings and training sessions, the group decided to engage in a community project they could all do together. Oakland-area marketing manager Cheryl Hansen-Pole arranged with San Francisco city officials to let Southwest employees paint graffiti-covered buildings in four areas of the city. "The city was astounded that we asked to do it," Rogge says, "but our thing was to do a project where we took the discussion of togetherness into action." Over 150 Southwest employees and advertising associates flew to the Bay Area, boarded buses, and headed out to "paint the town." The city supplied the paint, materials, and supervisors; Southwest provided the sweat and enthusiasm. Rogge remembers: "The group I was with just attacked this huge building. We had it done in an hour and a half because so many people pitched in and did their part." The group was so fast that city workers supervising the effort had to call the city to ask for another project. The city had recently received a bid—in excess of $25,000—to paint just one of the buildings the group had tackled!

## HOME FOR THE HOLIDAYS

Southwest reaches into all communities it serves with a program called "Home for the Holidays." Every year during the winter holiday season, the company donates tickets to senior citizens so they can fly home to see their relatives. These are people in every Southwest city who typically can't afford to fly, like Wila Mae Weems, who says, "Had it not been for Southwest Airlines, my husband and I would not have been able to afford the trip which gave us the opportunity to experience the precious moment of meeting our twin great-grandsons." In 1996 alone, Southwest flew 850 seniors to visit their families during the Home for the Holidays promotion. Over the last seventeen years, thousands of senior citizens have enjoyed the opportunity to reconnect with friends and family. In 1986 and 1987, Southwest was cited by President Reagan for this program.

## THE "HOUSE THAT LOVE BUILT"

In 1985, Herb Kelleher sat next to a beautifully decorated Christmas tree with a group of joyful children and their parents in a warmly decorated home. The setting was perfect for one of those precious moments when the radiant smile and touch of a child make all the worries in the world seem insignificant. Such moments can alter a person's life forever. And in Kelleher's case, it did. Choking back tears

for the third take, Herb looked into a video camera and spoke these words: "We're here to spread the word ... about the special kind of love we've found." At that moment five-year-old Shea Runnels, a young cancer patient, approached Kelleher from behind with a Christmas present and said, "Merry Christmas, Herb." Turning toward the little girl for a hug, Kelleher looked into her eyes and replied, "Merry Christmas, Shea." This scene took place in a Southwest-sponsored public service announcement—Southwest employees prefer to call it a "Christmas card"—at the Ronald McDonald House in Fort Worth, Texas. The television spot ended with the narrator saying, "When the airline that love built visits the house that love built, the spirit of Christmas seems to last all year long!" Since then, a "Christmas card" featuring children and their families from the Ronald McDonald Houses and Southwest employees has aired each holiday season.

Southwest Airlines adopted the Ronald McDonald Houses as its primary charity benefiting children in 1985. When a child develops a serious illness, the family almost always incurs tremendous emotional stress and heavy medical expenses. If that's not enough to handle, add to it the challenge of having to live in an unfamiliar city for an extended period so the child can receive specialized medical care. Trying to find suitable housing in a situation like this can be overwhelming. That is why the Ronald McDonald Houses were built—to serve as temporary homes for seriously ill children and their parents. Usually located near major hospitals, the Houses are places where families can come together to comfort and support each other. Each House is equipped with private bedrooms plus common living areas, playrooms, laundries, and a kitchen.

## *Love doesn't just happen. It is a work of art that demands constant care.*

Southwest's interest in the Ronald McDonald Houses began after Captain Dick East lost a daughter to leukemia. Seeing the Ronald McDonald House as a natural tie-in to Southwest's family spirit, East went on a one-man crusade to recruit the people of Southwest to the cause. His first ally was Colleen Barrett. "It probably took him a year to get me to a House," Barrett remembers. "He kept wanting me to go, but my idea of a night out was not to spend it with very sick children. I said, 'I'll give you money,' but he didn't want that. He wanted me to come to a House." East finally got Barrett to the Ronald McDonald House in Houston. She immediately fell in love, she says. "He knew it would take only one visit. Once he got me in there, he knew I would be sold for life."

*Southwest Airlines and its employees contributed $739,292 to help support Ronald McDonald Houses in 1996, including $33,830 in cash donations from the company and $302,462 worth of free air travel for families staying at Houses on the Southwest system.*

East got Kelleher involved next. "It has been a love affair of the heart since I first stepped inside," Kelleher says. "Nothing depicts Southwest's love theme more than the Ronald McDonald Houses." It didn't take long for Captain East to recruit the entire airline.

"He started with a huge dream and his dream has come true," Barrett says of Dick East. Today, Southwest employees spend countless hours sharing love and compassion with children at every Ronald McDonald House on the Southwest system. What makes Southwest so special to the Ronald McDonald House program is that employees have completely immersed themselves in it. It isn't the type of thing where the company writes out a check once a year and is done with it. Southwest employees roll up their sleeves and get involved. Throughout the year, they and their families visit the children in the Houses, cook meals, and become involved in their lives. Southwest employees know that, in most cases, they can't eliminate the problems these children face, but they also understand that love isn't always conveyed by doing things *for* people. They know that sometimes love is powerfully expressed by just being *with* people and being there *for* people who are lonely and afraid.

Southwest's Houston employees were the first company employees to cook monthly dinners at a Ronald McDonald House. Since 1983, monthly dinners have been added to the services employees donate in Dallas, Phoenix, San Antonio, and Fort Worth. In June and November each year, employees cook dinner in every Ronald McDonald House in Southwest's system. Southwest set a precedent; now Ronald McDonald Houses all over the country have organizations cooking for these families almost every night of the week.

Each year over one hundred Southwest employees volunteer their time to put on the LUV Classic Golf Tournament and Party in Dallas, which raises over $403,000 for Ronald McDonald Houses across the Southwest system. They also volunteer thousands of hours to Camp Ronald McDonald for Good Times. When Southwest was invited to Chicago in 1989 to be one of five companies honored by McDonald's for its contribution to the Ronald McDonald House Charities, Dick Darman, a public relations executive for McDonald's, said to the audience, "One company that I regard as very special is Southwest Airlines, because people give of their time and themselves, not just their money." In view of the fact that some of the other companies had given millions of dollars, Kelleher was astounded by Darman's statement.

Tonda Montague, director of employee communications, talks about her special relationship with Shea Runnels, the little girl who was filmed with Herb in 1985, in a letter written to *LUV Lines*. This excerpt exemplifies Southwest employees' active participation with the Ronald McDonald children and their families:

> *Due to my involvement with the Ronald McDonald House, I was one of the Employees asked to be in the commercial Southwest was filming at the Fort Worth Ronald McDonald House. On that day, I met the person who taught me the most about life—the person who touched my heart and made me realize the greatest joy one can experience is sharing with others and to get the most out of life each and every day because life can be so uncertain.*
>
> *It still amazes me how much I learned from that vivacious five-year-old who bounced into my life that day. We became instant friends, and during the next three years we did indeed learn a lot from each other. One thing Shea taught me was to*

*never feel sorrow—she was too spunky for that. With Shea, every day was a celebration of life.*

*I visited her often at M. D. Anderson Hospital, and through all that pain she always asked about Herb and all her friends at Southwest. We celebrated her sixth, seventh, and eighth birthdays at the Houston Ronald McDonald House, and I will never forget the time we gave her family a $3,000 check of donations from Southwest Employees, and as they drove off, Shea yelled: "Thanks for the million dollars." Or the time she barreled over the table as the Houston mechanics presented her with a bicycle. She was so appreciative of all we did for her.*

*In my heart, I never believed she would leave us. And I guess she really hasn't, because I feel her presence each and every day.*

As is usually the case when people give themselves and their love unselfishly, Southwest employees feel that they have received much more from their Ronald McDonald House experiences than they have given. Without exception, they say that the opportunity to help ease the emotional and financial pain of these families is very rewarding.

## LOVE IS AN ART

Great artists invest tremendous time, energy, and attention in practicing their art. Through discipline, hard work, and, in many cases, sacrifice, the talented artist eventually becomes proficient. And after more than twenty-six years of practicing in a particular art, you get pretty good at it.

People visit Southwest Airlines from all over the world to find out how to create a work environment that is loving and humane. Many leave disappointed when they learn that there is no secret formula. As "artists," the people of Southwest Airlines work hard at perfecting their art and doing things that create love and build relationships. Serving people is an act of love, but it is often an inconvenience. Another expression of love, exercising patience, can be a hardship—particularly when you have a very busy schedule. Going out of the way to celebrate people's victories and mourn their losses requires discipline and commitment. Remembering holidays, birthdays, and special events in people's lives is no doubt a joy, but it takes a lot of extra time and energy—just ask Colleen Barrett.

Southwest has shown us that creating an organization in which love flourishes is hard work. Love doesn't just happen. Love is a work of art that Southwest creates. It demands constant care. Companies that are unwilling to put forth the effort deny their people one of the most precious gifts an organization can give—loving relationships, formed over time through acts of affirmation and patience, kindness and generosity, grace and forgiveness.

So what kind of results does Southwest achieve from all this

*Employee communications director*
*Tonda Montague holding Shea Runnels*

## GOODBYE, LITTLE FRIEND

*In September 1988, Shea Runnels lost her battle with leukemia. Her loss had a profound impact on Southwest Airlines. In a tribute to the love and courage Shea spread throughout the Southwest system, Tim McClure of GSD&M wrote a farewell poem:*

> *Good-bye, little friend*
> *Tiny crusader against the odds.*
> *You, who have taught us so much—*
> *About living,*
> *About loving,*
> *About the temporary nuisance of pain*
> *And the timeless strength of hope.*
> *Even as we lift you on our heartwings*
> *To the waiting wings of angels,*
> *Your smile lives on—*
> *In those of us you touched*
> *Oh so fleetingly,*
> *And forever.*

## DEAR MR. KELLEHER

*This past weekend I had the pleasure of crewing for your airline's balloon at the River City Roundup and Rodeo in Omaha. . . . Greater than the balloon ride was meeting your fine young employees and realizing that your coming to the Omaha market isn't just dollars for Omaha, but brings us the addition of these lovely people. . . . Omaha is fortunate and Southwest is too.*

MARY FOGARTY MONSON
OMAHA, NEBRASKA

love? We could talk about the abundance of trust and confidence Southwest employees have in each other and the company. We could talk about the deep sense of loyalty people feel toward their coworkers and about the company's low turnover rate. Certainly, we could argue that love softens people's defenses and opens the communication channels so that information flows more freely and problems surface more quickly at Southwest Airlines. We could tell you that love is the foundation for building an extraordinary corporate culture, one in which it is safe for people to experiment and take risks to grow and mature.

We could also talk about love as the reason conflict doesn't escalate into costly grievances and drawn-out legal disputes. We could talk about the sense of cohesiveness that's generated when a skycap and a flight attendant are working next to a pilot and a provisioner who are working next to a marketing manager and a secretary as they all cook a meal to benefit a school for children at risk. Finally, we could talk about Southwest's immense goodwill and customer allegiance in every community it serves. Each of these results has a practical, bottom line impact on the airline's success, and each emanates from the art of love as practiced at Southwest Airlines.

We could expand on each of these practical results, and many more, but we would not be accurately conveying the true spirit with which love is given by Southwest's employees. At Southwest Airlines, love is not a sophisticated form of manipulation designed to get people to do things that increase the company's profitability. As the people we interviewed in our research told us stories about how love is expressed at Southwest, we continued to see the links between these acts of love and their value to the organization. Each time we described the relationship between love and the phenomenal business results it creates, we were met with a warning from our interviewees: "Yes, there are bottom line benefits to what we do, but that's not why we do it. We do it because we work in an environment where we have truly been loved. Having had this experience, the gratitude we feel naturally draws us to love others in return."

The people who shared their stories with us wanted to make sure we understood that when they do things for each other and the communities they serve, they don't expect anything in return. Certainly, they are thrilled with the practical benefits that result from their acts of love, but that's not what motivates them. The people of Southwest Airlines seem to be motivated by love itself. Perhaps this is why, since the very beginning, when the company is challenged and tested it always comes down on the side of what's good for people. Even if the costs are significant.

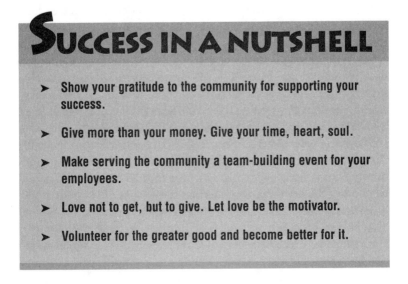

# Success in a Nutshell

- ➤ Show your gratitude to the community for supporting your success.

- ➤ Give more than your money. Give your time, heart, soul.

- ➤ Make serving the community a team-building event for your employees.

- ➤ Love not to get, but to give. Let love be the motivator.

- ➤ Volunteer for the greater good and become better for it.

## CHAPTER 18

# UNCONVENTIONAL ADVERTISING

## BENDING THE RULES TO BREAK A GREAT STORY

*The scene:* the Sportatorium, a dark, smelly, run-down wrestling palace somewhere in Dallas, March 1992. The restless murmur of the crowd, punctuated by the shouts and chants of cheerleaders, crescendoed quickly to hoarse yells and piercing whistles as, from the darkness at the top of the aisles, the two contenders marched toward the ring. Down one aisle strode a burly thirty-seven-year-old weightlifter, dressed in slacks and a dark-colored muscle shirt. He wore a menacing sneer and displayed the tattoo "Born to Raise Capital" on his massive right arm. Down the other, to the hair-raising trumpet blasts of the theme from *Rocky*, strutted a skinny, white-haired, sixty-one-year-old lawyer decked out in a white T-shirt and gray sweat pants under shiny red boxing shorts. He had a sling on his right arm and a cigarette dangling from his jaunty grin and was accompanied by a handler wearing a bandolier holding rows of airline-size bottles of Wild Turkey.

It was "Malice in Dallas," the match of the decade!

Actually, it was just a friendly contest between Southwest Airlines, represented by Herb Kelleher, and Stevens Aviation, championed by chairman Kurt Herwald, to decide the rights to an advertising slogan.

Stevens, an aviation sales and maintenance company in Greenville, South Carolina, had been using "Plane Smart" as its slogan at least a year before Southwest unknowingly began running its "Just Plane Smart" ad campaign. After bringing this to Southwest's attention, Stevens Aviation proposed that, rather than paying teams of lawyers to hash out the dispute over many months and under cover of hundreds of thousands of dollars in fees, the companies send their top warriors to battle it out, one-on-one, in an arm-wrestling tournament before an audience of their employees and the media. The best two out of three matches would win the rights to the slogan—and the loser of each match would donate $5,000 to a charity of the winner's choice.

Naturally, Herb accepted the challenge. And, naturally, he appointed himself to defend the honor of Southwest Airlines. It would be "Smokin'" Herb Kelleher versus "Kurtsey" Herwald—and let the world watch in anxious wonder.

Round One took a rapid turn for the ugly as Kelleher, reading a legal opinion conveniently provided by Texas Supreme Court Justice

John Cornyn, sent in a ringer, sixty-three-year-old one-time Texas arm-wrestling champion J. R. Jones. Before the match could proceed, however, Kelleher suddenly lunged at Herwald and had to be restrained. Jones then bested Herwald, and the Southwest faction roared its approval.

Round Two did not go so well. Kelleher was quickly trounced by Herwald's designated ringer, Annette Coats, a tiny customer service rep. It was the South Carolinians' turn to cheer. Kelleher complained loudly that his fractured wrist, injured while saving a little girl from being hit by a bus, had hampered his performance. "Herb, Herb, Herb!" chanted the disgruntled Southwest partisans.

## *At Southwest, advertising and marketing are used to both create and reinforce the company's nutty image.*

Finally it was Kelleher against Herwald. The two combatants took their positions and glared at each other over the cigarette-burned table. Their hands touched, gripped, locked. Knuckles cracked. Brows furrowed. Muscles strained. Sweat poured. It seemed to go on forever.

Actually, it took only ten seconds.

Kelleher blamed his defeat on a hairline fracture in his wrist, combined with a weeklong cold, a stubborn case of athlete's foot, and having accidentally overtrained by walking up a flight of steps. In the end, the event was clouded by allegations of a fix: Herwald announced shortly after his victory that he had decided to let Southwest keep using the slogan "Just Plane Smart."

So—had it all been done just for the publicity? Said Kelleher as he was carried out on a stretcher, "Why, I never even thought about it in those terms."

### THE POWER OF A GREAT STORY

"Malice in Dallas" is now an epic, a story thousands of people inside and outside Southwest Airlines know almost by heart. This rambunctious alternative to a drawn-out, boring, lawyer-enriching, half-million-dollar courtroom battle was exactly the sort of antic that Americans have come to associate with their favorite maverick airline.

Everybody won: the companies got great publicity, the media had a field day, and charity got $15,000—a $10,000 check was presented to the Muscular Dystrophy Association and a $5,000 check went to the Cleveland Ronald McDonald House. Everybody had a blast.

Most companies have stories to tell, but most are not good storytellers. When an organization doesn't tell its stories well, it limits its influence in the marketplace and misses out on opportunities to reinforce perceptions of what makes it special. Southwest has a tremendous presence in the markets it serves because it has built a strong personality and culture and has a canny ability to find novel ways to perpetuate them. The company is a master at using the storytelling power of marketing and advertising to make its persona come alive.

At Southwest, advertising and marketing are used to both create and reinforce the spirit of this nutty blend of people, planes, and performance. "People do not buy because marketing is glitzy," says Jay Conrad Levinson, author of *Guerrilla Marketing Excellence*, "but because marketing strikes a chord in the mind of the prospect that makes that person want the advantage of what you are selling." In other words, Southwest's marketing does not work because it sells

## DEAR HERB

*"Malice in Dallas" got even President Bush's attention.*

March 23, 1992

Dear Herb,

Just *Plane* Terrific! Your clever arm wrestling match with Kurt Herwald was a win/win, not to mention great comic relief to serious watchers of nightly news.

Congratulations on your "loss," and best wishes.

SINCERELY,
GEORGE BUSH

flights and destinations; it works because it helps people realize the merits of flying Southwest Airlines.

With the help of its two advertising agencies, GSD&M of Austin and Cramer-Krasselt of Chicago, and its media-buying agency, Camelot Communications of Dallas, Southwest strategically and creatively tells and sells its story to the outside world. "What we try to do is move our customers . . . through a process of bonding, which begins with the way we advertise and communicate with customers in the marketplace," says Tom Kalahar, CEO and president of Camelot Communications. "When customers go to the airport, we want them to relate to our people, to our crews on the airplanes, to the baggage handlers, to everybody they touch in Southwest's system."

Through advertising, Southwest makes customers aware of its low fares, frequent flights, on-time arrivals, safety record, and fun attitude. In turn, marketing and promotions focus on getting customers to accept the story and wanting to fly Southwest. "If customers first buy into what the company stands for," says GSD&M president Roy Spence, "they in turn will buy what we sell."

The way Southwest tells and sells its story inside and outside the company reflects its fundamental values. Ten core principles guide its marketing and advertising:

1. Make advertising an invited guest.

2. Use advertising to keep the company's spirit alive.

3. Match the message and the media with the company's strategy and culture.

4. Take the competition seriously, but not yourself.

5. Make flying fun.

6. Make every employee a living advertisement.

7. Model the company's values for employees.

8. Underpromise, but overdeliver.

9. Make creativity a team effort.

10. Build credibility in everything you do.

## MEET THE "INVITED GUEST"

"Let's face it, people do not wake up in the morning and say, 'I'd like a cup of coffee and a Tidy Bowl commercial,'" Spence says. "That's why most advertising is an uninvited guest: people don't want us in their homes and cars and some of the most private moments of their lives." Southwest insists that its agencies create advertising that gets people to actually look forward to it.

To become an "invited guest," Southwest strives to do three things in its advertising. First, Southwest's ads aim to *intrigue* the audience, to captivate them in the first three seconds of a TV commercial or the headline of a print ad. "You don't get a second chance to hook the audience," says Spence, so Southwest tries to captivate people with the company's quirky personality (who it is) and the fact that it is *The* Low Fare Airline (what it stands for). Second, Southwest's ads aim to *entertain*. They must reward the audience for spending their time with the ads—make them smile, laugh, cry, or think. Finally, the ads must *persuade*. Every ad that is run must convince the customers that what Southwest has to offer is of genuine value to them.

*What Southwest stands for is as important as what it sells. It doesn't promise one thing and deliver another.*

Whether it is a straight promotional ad like Southwest's $19 sale or more image-oriented ads like the "Peanuts" spot, Southwest's advertising mission is to connect with the life experiences of customers so they'll want to see the ads again and again. In this sense, Southwest Airlines becomes a part of the fabric of its customers' lives, and that is the foundation of the amazing and special relationship the airline has developed with its customers through advertising.

## A WHALE OF A TALE KEEPS THE SPIRIT ALIVE

It was the brainstorm of GSD&M, championed by executive v.p. and chief creative officer Tim McClure. The mission was classified Top Secret. The trick was somehow to convince Sea World of Texas that Southwest Airlines had already approved this daring concept while at the same time making Southwest believe that Sea World had already

**ANNOUNCER:** Because most of our flights are short, this is what our meals look like on Southwest Airlines . . .

**ANNOUNCER:** . . . It's also what our fares look like.

*Southwest runs TV commercials like "Peanuts" to tell people about its low fares simply and persuasively.*

blessed it. George Becker, then chairman of Sea World of Texas, says, "When GSD&M was pitching the Sea World account to us, the real punch in the presentation was the unveiling of a huge model plane painted like Shamu." McClure says, "There was an audible gasp from everyone in the Sea World presentation room when we undraped the Shamu model. No one could believe that this was being proposed." Becker remembers saying to Spence, "Roy, can you really pull that off? I've never heard of an airline doing anything as bold as this before." "Yes, everyone at Southwest Airlines has approved it," Spence assured him. Well, that wasn't *exactly* the case . . .

The idea was to cement the Sea World–Southwest Airlines promotional partnership by painting a plane like a killer whale. But before the Sea World presentation, McClure was sent on a mission to share the idea with Colleen Barrett (the ad peoples' confidante and "point man" to Kelleher) and ask whether they needed to get Herb's approval. Colleen didn't blink: "No. Go pitch it to Sea World. If they like it, he'll like it."

When Kelleher finally found out about the idea, he more than liked it; he loved it. But it wasn't until Becker and Kelleher met privately to sign the pact that both learned the truth. Basking in the irreverence and creativity inherent in the way the project was handled, Kelleher told Becker, "I didn't know anything about the plane until we came down to San Antonio. It was only when McClure unveiled it that day that I saw it for the first time. I think what they were trying to do was entrap me, George, so I'd have to go along with the plan!"

*Boeing 737s and a lot of paint. Southwest's fleet of specialty planes had grown to seven by mid-1996.*

Only a handful of people knew the purpose of the project, code-named "Project Friend." The material needed for Project Friend was not insignificant—a brand-new Boeing 737 and a lot of paint.

Several 737s were already in production for Southwest. The production schedule was changed so that flight testing on one of the planes, normally one of the last procedures, was conducted before it was painted. Meanwhile, Sea World's director of zoology, Ed Asper, helped design the painting template so that the plane would accurately represent Shamu. GSD&M selected the design firm of Walter Dorwin Teague Associates, Inc., of Redmond, Washington, to execute the final mechanical design and generate the computer templates.

After three days of a sophisticated painting process in an isolated World War II–vintage B-52 hangar, *Shamu One*, a brand-new 737 painted to resemble a killer whale, emerged at midnight.

In the middle of the night on Monday, May 23, 1988, *Shamu One* was secretly flown to Ellington Air Force Base in Houston. Later that day, the flying killer whale made its debut in San Antonio by buzzing over Sea World of Texas at a breathtaking twenty-five hundred feet with hundreds of cheering Sea World employees below! *Shamu One*'s inaugural flight then continued to Houston and Dallas. Over the next six days *Shamu One* completed a twenty-seven-city, coast-to-coast tour that included each of Southwest's cities and New York.

Since *Shamu One*, Southwest has invested more than $165 million in airplane billboards—*Shamu Two* and *Three*; *Lone Star One*, painted to look like the Texas flag; and two other "flag" planes, *Arizona One* and *California One* and most recently *Triple Crown One*. *Shamu Two* and *Three* were commissioned when Anheuser-Busch bought the Sea World parks and August Busch said the flying billboard was one of the best advertising ideas he'd ever seen. *Lone Star One* was unveiled in 1991 to mark Southwest's twentieth anniversary. *Arizona One* and *California One* joined Southwest's fleet of "flag" planes in May 1994 and August 1995. In June 1996, Southwest unveiled *Silver One* to commemorate the company's twenty-fifth anniversary. From the tail painted in Southwest's signature gold, red, and orange, a thin white pin-stripe runs the length of the silver fuselage—a reminder, says Kelleher, "that Southwest encourages employees to color outside the lines."

A royal blue 737 draped with a Triple Crown medal is the eighth custom-painted jet. In 1995 Kelleher promised to put each employee's name on a plane if they won a fifth annual Triple Crown. In 1997 Kelleher said, "It is my pleasure to announce that as you board *Triple Crown One*, you will find the names of all 24,000-plus Southwest Airlines employees." *Triple Crown One* is dedicated to the people of Southwest Airlines who have done "whatever it takes" to win thirty-one monthly Triple Crowns and five consecutive annual Triple Crowns.

"Southwest's painted planes offer more than good PR value," says Tim McClure. "They have delighted people—children in particular—for years. And, while you generally don't think about the plane you're getting on, when people see these, they point them out. So I think it keeps the spirit alive out there. These planes speak to the

Spirit of Southwest. What other company would have the guts to take the lead in painting one of these big monsters and having fun with it?"

Southwest's flying billboards do much more than sell airplane tickets; they stir spirit in those who happen to look up and be touched by these inspirations in the sky. These planes also demonstrate the creative license that the advertising agencies have in their partnership with Southwest. The company's painted planes, like all its marketing and advertising efforts, are not gimmicks; they are celebrations. They are intended to touch people's emotions, whether through evoking the kid in all of us when we step into the belly of a killer whale, or by awakening our dormant patriotism. More than anything, painting planes is nuts! Truly "invited guest" advertising.

## ON STRATEGY, ON CULTURE

Most organizations focus all of their marketing energy on being "on strategy." And while being on strategy is essential, at Southwest there is something just as important. "We must never allow the marketing of Southwest Airlines to be so strategic that we lose our heart and soul," says Colleen Barrett. That's why Southwest is fanatical about being not only on strategy but "on culture" as well. Southwest gets people involved at an emotional level. Employees and customers alike tend to really love and commit themselves to the company behind the story. Southwest is more than a personality promoted by an ad agency. People commit themselves to Southwest because they sense that the company has a heart, that it truly cares about people, that it is more than willing to fight for people's best interests.

"Southwest Airlines is really not in the airline business at all," says Roy Spence. "This company has a much higher calling. Southwest is in the business of allowing people from every walk of life to see and do things they never dreamed of." Southwest directs all of its marketing muscle toward communicating that mission in a fun, zany, yet highly effective way.

## TAKE THE COMPETITION SERIOUSLY,
## BUT NOT YOURSELF

"This airline was marketing-driven from the very beginning," says Judy Trabulsi, GSD&M's executive vice president and media director.

# DEAR MR. KELLEHER

*I am currently flying on a Southwest flight to Austin, Texas, and I am taking the time to say a word of thanks to Southwest Airlines. I have flown on your airline fifteen to twenty times a year for fifteen years. I appreciate your service and attention to delivering a great product to your customers. However, that function is expected in this world of consumer service. I really am writing to you so that I can share a special moment that happened to me because of you.*

*Friday, I was driving home from work around 6:00 P.M. It had just rained in Dallas and there was a complete rainbow showering the city with vivid colors. Just as I stopped on Empire Central and Denton Drive, by Love Field, I turned on the radio and Ray Charles was singing "God Bless America." (Nobody sings it better.) Right at that very moment, with a perfect rainbow shining and Ray Charles singing, something very special occurred. Your* Lone Star *airplane flew under the rainbow arch for a touchdown at Love Field, spraying up water as she headed down the runway. The sun made the colors so vivid that the plane itself seemed to take on an image of unbelievable pride and greatness.*

*I pulled over to the side of the road and cried for all the things that are special freedoms in our lives. I thought of your Christmas commercials with the kids and cried some more. I thought of your billboards, Austin Auften, etc., and started to laugh. I thought of your TV commercials about all the flights at all the times of the day you fly, and laughed again. I guess you could say your marketing has worked on me.*

*Patriotism is "in" these days and it is great that we all are experiencing a renewed dedication to our country. Southwest Airlines was a proud, patriotic American/Texas company long before the Iraq war made so many others jump on the bandwagon. For that you are to be acknowledged.*

*In closing, I just want to thank you for doing what you do and while it was purely circumstantial, you were part of a perfect moment in my life.*

TYLER BROWN
DALLAS, TEXAS

"When the airline was launched, Lamar Muse was the creator of wacky yet aggressive marketing. He marketed the company with hot pants, bottles of liquor, and the Love Airline theme. Back then they needed to make a statement with very few dollars." And make a statement they did! Whether it was flight attendants in go-go boots and hot pants or ads that read, "No one is going to shoot us out of the skies for a lousy $13," Southwest told its story to the public and captured the attention and hearts of many. What evolved was advertising that reflected who they were—that "maverick upstart" that rocked the Texas skies and shocked the competition.

## *Southwest's advertising gets in the competition's face and kills them with humor.*

Southwest has overcome its upstart image, and most of its competitors now take the company very seriously. In May 1988 Southwest topped all three categories of the Department of Transportation's (DOT) monthly Air Travel Consumer Report for the first time—earning the highest rating in on-time performance, fewest customer complaints per passengers carried, and fewest mishandled bags during a single month—and started the tradition of the Triple Crown. Bob Kneisley, a Washington, D.C. attorney, sent the agency's monthly report to Susan Yancey, Southwest's manager of corporate information, with a cover letter pointing out Southwest's "Triple Crown." Yancey cleverly continued to use the term "Triple Crown" each time Southwest repeated the accomplishment.

In January 1990, after Southwest had earned three monthly Triple Crowns, the company decided it was time to tell its story. GSD&M had a Triple Crown trophy designed to use in an ad that touted Southwest's "Triple Triple." When Southwest earned its fourth monthly Triple Crown, a second ad ran in October 1990 hailing its "Quadruple Triple." Not too long after these ads ran, Colleen Barrett was on the phone with Phyllis Nunnery, then administrative assistant to American Airlines CEO Bob Crandall. Barrett and Nunnery were discussing arrangements for Crandall to introduce Kelleher at a dinner when Barrett heard Crandall say in the background, "What the !#@!* is a Triple Crown?!"

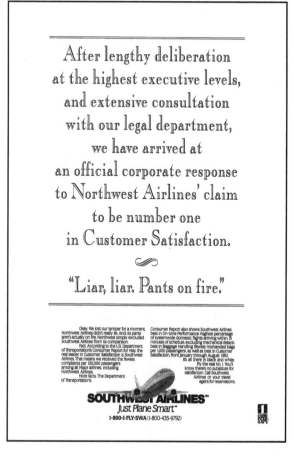

After lengthy deliberation
at the highest executive levels,
and extensive consultation
with our legal department,
we have arrived at
an official corporate response
to Northwest Airlines' claim
to be number one
in Customer Satisfaction.

"Liar, liar. Pants on fire."

Okay. We lost our temper for a moment. Northwest Airlines didn't really lie. And its pants aren't actually on fire. Northwest simply excluded Southwest Airlines from its comparison.

Fact. According to the U.S. Department of Transportation's Consumer Report for May, the real leader in Customer Satisfaction is Southwest Airlines. That means we received the fewest complaints per 100,000 passengers among all Major airlines, including Northwest Airlines.

More facts. The Department of Transportation's Consumer Report also shows Southwest Airlines best in On-time Performance (highest percentage of systemwide domestic flights arriving within 15 minutes of schedule, excluding mechanical delays), best in Baggage Handling (fewest mishandled bags per 1000 passengers), as well as best in Customer Satisfaction, from January through August, 1992.

It's all there in black and white. Fly the real No. 1. You'll know there's no substitute for satisfaction. Call Southwest Airlines or your travel agent for reservations.

**SOUTHWEST AIRLINES™**
*Just Plane Smart™*
1-800-I-FLY-SWA (1-800-435-9792)

Southwest created the Triple Crown campaign to transform boring DOT statistics into a coveted accomplishment. With the Triple Crown trophy and ad, Southwest playfully and publicly recognized its people and told its story to millions. When Northwest Airlines mounted a false claim to the Triple Crown, Southwest got serious—but in a fun way. In July 1992, Northwest ran print and TV ads claiming to have won the Triple Crown for May 1992. In tiny print, it ran a disclaimer that limited the field of comparison to the seven largest domestic airlines. In May 1992 Northwest placed first among the top seven in on-time performance (the company beat Southwest by two-tenths of a percentage point). It placed second behind America West in baggage handling, and second to Southwest in customer satisfaction (consumer complaints). Because Southwest was the eighth-largest airline in terms of passenger miles and America West was the ninth-largest, Northwest could claim the Triple Crown only by excluding Southwest and America West from the field.

Southwest didn't let Northwest get away with it. The company ran its "Liar, Liar" ad, developed by Cramer-Krasselt, to set the record straight.

At the heart of Southwest's marketing strategy is taking the competition seriously but killing them with humor. When America West ran a TV commercial accusing Southwest customers of being embarrassed to fly Southwest, the airline responded with a GSD&M TV commercial featuring Herb with a sack over his head. When American Airlines launched its ill-fated "value-pricing" strategy, Southwest responded with a full-page newspaper ad with the headline "To match their new low fares, we would have to raise ours."

*Original employees celebrating on-time arrival of Southwest's twenty-fifth anniversary.* **Left to right:** *Charlie Marcel, flight crew training instructor; Bob Pratt, captain; Dan Johnson, dispatcher; Willie Wilson, manager flight crew operations administration; Sam Cohn, captain; Gene Van Overschelde, captain; Scott Johnson, dispatcher*

## FLYING FOR THE FUN OF IT

"From the beginning, our ads have used humor that pokes fun at ourselves. I think that the most successful ads today are the ones that use some kind of humor," says Joyce Rogge. "We can't have something out there that doesn't convey our personality and the uniqueness of that personality."

Southwest has always been in the business of making flying fun. With its advertising, it wants customers to know that when they fly Southwest, they will have an experience like no other. Southwest markets its spirit loudly and proudly, and most of its advertising plays up the fun, spirited, and lively side of its culture.

It hasn't all been fun and games, though. "At one time it was all fun and zany," Judy Trabulsi says, "but we also went through a period when we didn't want to be just funny or zany. We had the fun people flying us; we needed business people flying us, too. So the question was, 'How do we keep that fun attitude without going way off into left field and upsetting or turning off the business travelers?'" The answer: Southwest markets to both by being humorous *and* direct. "The Company Plane" and "*The* Low Fare Airline" campaigns market the fact that Southwest has one of the best on-time records

---

THE UNKNOWN FLYER: "If you're embarrassed to fly the airline with the most convenient

| schedules and fewest Customer complaints, Southwest will give you this bag . . ." | ". . . If, on the other hand, Southwest is your kind of airline, we'll *still* give you this bag . . ." | ". . . for all the money you'll save flying with us." |

---

*The quirky, fun, and self-effacing Kelleher you see in Southwest's commercials is the same person you'd meet day after day in the office. Kelleher has always been willing to be in ads, as long as they are fun and not typical stuffy CEO spots.*

and the lowest fares in the country. These ads don't have to be crazy; they do have to radiate the Southwest personality and share its story in a direct manner. Cramer-Krasselt created the "Just Plane Smart" ads to play to the business traveler as well. These ads touted Southwest as the airline of choice for the fiscally responsible. The message is simple, but powerful—flying Southwest is smart, not only because Southwest is less expensive, but also because it's on time and its service is great.

## EMPLOYEES ARE LIVING ADVERTISEMENTS

Many companies think that if they purchase enough TV time, print space, or radio spots, consumers will eventually break down and buy simply because they're overwhelmed.

Southwest has a different approach. It uses communication in a much broader sense. Southwest's communication—its message—is its people. Every person in the company is a message. Southwest has twenty-five thousand employees spreading the word as missionaries who aren't afraid to be a little offbeat, work hard, and have a lot of fun. Customer service agents, operations agents, flight attendants, skycaps—anyone who has one-on-one contact with the customer—are some of the company's most powerful forms of advertising. In most cases, these people are the only memory customers will have of the company, and most Southwest people know this.

"Most of the time companies use money to legitimize themselves," says Peter Krivkovich, president of Cramer-Krasselt.

*Southwest Airlines uses—as trite as it sounds—the souls of its employees to legitimize the money. It's a reversal; it's a much harder thing to do because you have to have tremendous commitment over a tremendously long period of time to make it work. But when it works, it is so powerful. Southwest employees are what makes the advertising legitimate. It's not the advertising that is making employees legitimate, which is what so often happens in advertising communication. When people come in contact with Southwest's twenty-two thousand people, they experience the advertising. Employees give the advertising twice as much legitimacy as when you see XYZ company saying, "Oh, we're just a nice warm little company," but when you run into an XYZ employee, the experience is an "ouch!"*

Southwest employees work hard to minimize the "ouches!" Most understand that every interaction is an opportunity to promote goodwill and add value to the customer's experience.

## MODEL THE COMPANY'S VALUES FOR EMPLOYEES

Southwest's commercials and promotions are designed as much for employees as for customers. Southwest continues to reinforce its story with employees by highlighting important company values in its advertisements. Roy Spence says, "We understand a fundamental premise: our employees watch TV, too. So we role model to our people. When we create advertisements for Southwest, we know we are in the business of keeping love alive." When employees see Southwest commercials, they say, "Gee, that's who we're supposed to be," and they bring that reality to work with them the next day.

*"We have credibility because we tell people what we're going to do and then we do it."*

"I think that's one of the main reasons we're successful," says Tom Kalahar. "If we can energize our own people while building a relationship with our customers, we've accomplished two things. We've helped our customers feel more strongly about us. And we've helped our people because they're excited about what we're doing out there in the marketplace and they feel more strongly and more proud of who they are and what they are a part of."

By marketing and role modeling to employees, advertisements are able to protect and promote Southwest values—for example, "Doing whatever it takes." When the United Shuttle and Continental Lite began service, Southwest ran a "Battle Cry" ad in which one of the visuals was a series of energetic Southwest employees working to keep costs down so Southwest could continue its regular low fares. While telling a simple story to the public and the competition—Southwest is *The* Low Fare Airline—the company also sent a powerful message to its employees: because of their willingness to hustle, Southwest keeps costs down and fares low.

## UNDERPROMISE BUT OVERDELIVER

Southwest delivers on the promises its advertising makes. Unfortunately, not all marketing and advertising professionals can make this claim. *Guerrilla Marketing Excellence* author Jay Conrad Levinson notes that 53 percent of the American population has felt deceived by marketing. "A great deal of marketing exaggerates, primarily due to enthusiasm on the part of the company," Levinson says. "It is very

# THE ALL-TIME ON-TIME AIRLINE.

When you fly THE Low Fare Airline, you also get the #1 on-time performer.
Southwest Airlines has landed the #1 position in on-time performance for the overall
seven-year period the U.S. Department of Transportation has recorded the statistics.

# SOUTHWEST
### THE Low Fare Airline™

On-time ranking based on on-time arrivals of all reporting airlines, as published in DOT consumer reports. ©1994, 1995 Southwest Airlines

difficult to be believed in the marketing environment, even when you are telling the truth." Mark Boyter, captain with Southwest, illustrates: "It's funny, my friends see our advertising and they say, 'Is it really like that at Southwest? Are you having that much fun?' The answer is, 'Yes!' What you see is what you get at Southwest Airlines."

A company has integrity when it has a reputation for keeping its promises and doing what it says it's going to do. The real challenge lies in getting people to notice what you're promising. Southwest is very clever about getting people to pay attention to the promises it makes. Then, once it's got their attention, it delivers on those promises. "We know of no other clients who are so gutsy—who let the agency produce such outrageous advertising ideas. It is refreshing to work with Southwest, where all sorts of ideas come to life," says Cramer-Krasselt v.p. Cathy Beres.

So what does Southwest promise? Filet mignon? In-flight movies? First-class seating? No. Day in and day out, Southwest promises reliable, safe, frequent, low-cost air transportation—topped off with legendary service and a few nuts!

*Southwest's entertaining billboards reflect the company's fun and zany culture and still make a point. Others in the series are El Paso Pronto, Gumbo Jets, and Little Rock Around the Clock.*

"Southwest strives to deliver even more than its customers expect," Kalahar told us. "And then customers say, 'Gosh, these guys are different, they're special.' They have a feeling toward the company that causes them to want to fly Southwest whenever they can."

## MAKE CREATIVITY A TEAM EFFORT

The two marketing executives at Southwest, marketing and sales v.p. Dave Ridley and advertising and promotions v.p. Joyce Rogge, function as one. They have to because they have a big job: to take the best and the brightest advertising talent they can find, manage the egos, and get everyone focused on doing what's right for the company and its employees and customers.

Ridley and Rogge have done something that is almost unheard of in the advertising industry. They have built a creative partnership with three firms—GSD&M, Cramer-Krasselt, and Camelot Communications. The Three Musketeers, as they are fondly referred to, work with one another and Southwest to develop and communicate Southwest's story with a nutty flair. The three firms collaborate in a process that normally tends to be very proprietary: the creative development of marketing communications.

Peter Krivkovich of Cramer-Krasselt describes the way Southwest fostered this unique creative partnership:

> *It had a lot to do with the Southwest culture; it permeated its way into the outside agencies. In observing the way that Herb, Colleen, Joyce, and Dave work within the company—they are all very collaborative, and when you work with them, it is very contagious—we actually got to a point where we all sat down and said, "We all want the same thing in terms of the end result for Southwest." And Southwest never treated any of the agencies like a stepchild. It was more like "Hey, you guys are all here because you're part of the family and we are all in this together to give our customers the best value in the airline industry." It's that Three Musketeers kind of a thing.*

The result is extremely powerful. Southwest isn't just another client; each one of the Three Musketeers assumes ownership for Southwest's success as if it were their own company. Clearly, they've all bought into the crusade and they have learned over the years to put aside their egos and work as a powerful united front to fight for the cause.

## BUILD CREDIBILITY IN EVERYTHING YOU DO

Credibility builds on integrity and creates a powerful force in the marketplace. Because of its credibility, there is a perception that when Southwest comes to town, good things happen. "If you go to a mayor, a city council, a county commissioner, or a U.S. congressman and say, 'Southwest Airlines is coming to your town,' their reaction, generally, is 'Hallelujah!'" governmental affairs v.p. Ron Ricks told us. "We have credibility because we tell people what we're going to do and then we do it. We tell people we're about low fares and we offer low fares and give ordinary people an opportunity to do extraordinary things. There are airlines that match our low fares on a restricted basis, but there is no airline, low cost or high cost, that charges fares as low as Southwest across the board, consistently, all the time!"

"Not too many years ago, the economy in Texas was bleak, the competitive framework was desperate, and Southwest was very concerned. Southwest held a meeting to discuss the very survival of the airline," recalls Roy Spence. "After everyone voiced their opinions, Colleen Barrett said, 'The most critical issue we face is not pricing, costs, or the dismal state of the economy; it is whether we have the courage and will to keep love alive.' The room went silent."

It seems that the real secret to Southwest's marketing is its almost religious fervor to maintain and perpetuate the core values of the culture. Through the will of its chairman, the spirit of its employees, and the fun and irreverence of its advertising and marketing, this fun-loving band of mavericks, musketeers, and missionaries works hard to nurture Southwest's very special culture in the face of incredible growth and expansion. Southwest has made a serious commitment to keeping love alive. Spence says, "It's a full-time job. But, hell, someone's got to do it. And it might as well be the airline that's still nuts after all these years!"

## SUCCESS IN A NUTSHELL

- ➤ Market to employees, not just to your customers.

- ➤ Promote your culture as well as your product.

- ➤ Look for creative, unusual ways to tell your story.

- ➤ Collaborate with others in creating your story.

- ➤ Use your story as a way to build spirit, service, and performance.

- ➤ Have everyone play a part in keeping your company's advertising and marketing promises.

- ➤ Find ways to tell your own story. Use it to further your personal and professional success.

**CHAPTER 19**

# CUSTOMERS COME SECOND

## AND STILL GET GREAT SERVICE

The customer is not always right. Employees, not customers, come first. So readers learned when *Reader's Digest* ran this excerpt from Tom Peters in its July 1995 "Personal Glimpses" feature:

> *While Southwest Airlines CEO Herb Kelleher gives customers a terrific deal on an airplane seat, he makes it clear that his employees come first—even if it means dismissing customers. But aren't customers always right? "No, they are not," Kelleher snaps. "And I think that's one of the biggest betrayals of employees a boss can possibly commit. The customer is sometimes wrong. We don't carry those sorts of customers. We write to them and say, 'Fly somebody else. Don't abuse our people.' "*

Southwest employees go out of their way to accommodate customers with legendary courtesy and good cheer, but the company has also been known to encourage some of its not-so-pleasant customers to choose other carriers—Kelleher gives the example of a customer who thumped a customer service agent on the head with a stanchion.

Jim Ruppel, director of customer relations, and Sherry Phelps, director of corporate employment, tell the story of a woman who frequently flew on Southwest, but was disappointed with every aspect of the company's operation. In fact, she became known as the "Pen Pal" because after every flight she wrote in with a complaint. She didn't like the fact that the company didn't assign seats; she didn't like the absence of a first-class section; she didn't like not having a meal in flight; she didn't like Southwest's boarding procedure; she didn't like the color of the planes; she didn't like the flight attendants' sporty uniforms and the casual atmosphere. And she hated peanuts! Her last letter, reciting a litany of complaints, momentarily stumped Southwest's customer relations people. Phelps explains: "Southwest

**WE CAME. WE SAW. WE KICKED TAIL.**

Make that, tails. Head-to-head against all the major airlines in America, Southwest Airlines just won the first annual Triple Crown ever: Number One in On-time Performance, Number One in Baggage Handling, and Number One in Customer Satisfaction for all of 1992. How can an airline that specializes in low fares deliver such a consistently high level of Customer Service? Simple. We care! Southwest Airlines. Number One and still climbing.

**SOUTHWEST AIRLINES**
Just Plane Smart.

Based on on-time arrival, baggage handling and complaint data for all major airlines for January through December 1992, as published in DOT consumer reports. ©1993 Southwest Airlines

*Winning the Triple Crown five years in a row proves that even though customers come second at Southwest Airlines, they still get first-rate service.*

prides itself on answering every letter that comes to the company and several employees tried to respond to this customer, patiently explaining why we do things the way we do them. It was quickly becoming a volume until they bumped it up to Herb's desk, with a note: 'This

# BRAVO, HERB!

*Southwest received hundreds of positive responses to Kelleher's comments in* Reader's Digest. *One Southwest customer wrote this:*

Just a note to add my "Bravo!" to your company's policy regarding dismissing customers who abuse your employees (quoted in *Reader's Digest*). During my seven years as an Arizona desert rat, I flew Southwest as often as I could. There was just something about the demeanor of Southwest's people that set them apart from the usual airline employees. Their manner really picked me up and made me feel good all over. And now I know what it was—it was your affirmation of their worth as men and women. Wish you flew to New York so I could buy a "Quicket" and be treated right.

one's yours.' In sixty seconds, Kelleher wrote back and said, 'Dear Mrs. Crabapple, We will miss you. Love, Herb.'"

Kelleher received another letter of complaint, this time from a San Diegan who threatened never to fly Southwest again because the on-board lav had the toilet paper roll installed upside down with the loose end coming over the top! He complained, "If Southwest is so careless with the installation of its toilet paper, how can I possibly trust its maintenance?" Kelleher wrote back, "What the hell were you doing upside down in our lavatory?" The response was a big hit with the customer, who was less surprised by the response than by the fact that Kelleher himself had read his letter and responded.

Three things are for sure: at Southwest Airlines, customer service doesn't have to be serious, it isn't bound by rules, and the customer doesn't always have to be right. So how does Southwest keep winning awards and customers? "Anybody can do it," Kelleher said when Southwest won the Triple Crown the fourth year in a row. "All they have to have is the lowest fares, the highest frequency, and the best customer service from the most fun-loving, warm, welcoming, spirited, hospitable employees in the airline business." At Southwest Airlines, legendary service springs from the heart and soul of confident, loyal, and trusted employees.

## SERVICE IS A WAY OF LIFE

"Many organizations will fail in their quest for total quality service," says Karl Albrecht, author of *The Only Thing That Matters*, "not because their leaders don't understand the conceptual or technical requirements for achieving it, but because they don't realize that *the heart of the service journey is spiritual rather than mechanical.* They will bureaucratize the whole thing and make it look like every other program." At Southwest Airlines, service transcends techniques. Southwest's long-term customer satisfaction comes from service delivered from the heart, from choosing service over self-interest. Service is not the result of teaching employees to *act* like customers are important; it comes from employees who genuinely feel loved and who work in an environment that dignifies them by valuing their contributions. When employees feel they are being treated humanely, when *they* receive "legendary service," they provide the kind of customer service for which Southwest Airlines is so well known. Perhaps this is why their willingness to serve is not an act but, rather, a true expression of the heart.

*Treat your employees with care and concern if that is the way you want them to treat each other and your customers.*

Scott Gross's classic *Positively Outrageous Service* gives credence to the kind of service Southwest provides its customers and was an instant hit from the front line to the boardroom. The book didn't tell Southwest employees what to do; it affirmed what they had been doing all along. Whether you describe it as "legendary," "knock your socks off," "fabled," or "positively outrageous," service that makes customers come back again and again is a major contributing factor to Southwest's success. In 1993 Southwest wrote its own book—*The Book on Service*—to show employees what Positively Outrageous Service looks like. Inspired by the "service feats, legends, and near-miracles" of Southwest employees, it reminds employees that "service is a matter of choice. Service involves giving of your time and talent while performing your job; it is a true reflection of how you live your life day to day." Yet there is no formal script or series of steps that employees can follow to provide this type of customer service. The spirit of service that pervades Southwest Airlines is, in Albrecht's words, "an element of giving—a spirit of generosity that makes people give something of themselves, in addition to just doing the job." At Southwest, customer service isn't a label or a technique; it's a way of life.

The people of Southwest understand that service does not start at the beginning of each workday, nor does it end when they go home. It is a very real part of who they are, what they think, and how they feel every moment of their lives. People are invited to join the Southwest family when this attribute is recognized in them. To serve and be kind, to entertain and have fun, defines the kind of personality Southwest Airlines looks for. The company's job, then, is to maintain a culture that draws from its employees that which is already in them.

### The Commitment to Service Must Be Personal

Whether it's responding to the needs of a coworker, taking personal responsibility for addressing a customer's problem, or joining an employee group in a community project, Southwest's leaders are personally involved in serving others. It's not unusual to see an officer of the corporation jumping on an airplane with a cadre of excited employees to go remodel a break room at one of Southwest's stations. Most of these people are doing it on their day off and without pay. It's

## DEAR MR. KELLEHER

*I fly to Phoenix on business and, to be honest, I'm usually very tired and a little cranky on the way home. I was not looking forward to the flight due to the length, stops, time difference, etc. However, the good part (finally) was the two flight attendants. They were the best I've ever seen. Professional, friendly, and sincere. They really made a difference and I enjoyed them both.*

*You can tell when someone actually likes their job and meeting people. It was the kind of service you can't teach or force.*

MICHELLE FULLEN
INDIANAPOLIS, INDIANA

one small way of saying to the employees who work at that station, "You're important and we care."

Embedded within Southwest's culture is the notion that service depends heavily on employees' ability to build strong and caring relationships. Since you can't build strong relationships without a high level of personal involvement, all employees at Southwest are expected to be available to one another. Jeff Sullivan, former director of people development, shared an interesting interaction he had with one of Southwest's station managers:

> *While I was out in the field visiting one of our stations, one of our managers mentioned to me that he wanted to put up a suggestion box. I responded by saying, "Sure—why don't you put up a suggestion box right here on this wall and then admit that you are a failure as a manager?" Our theory is, if you have to put up a box so people can write down their ideas and toss them in, it means that you are not doing what you are supposed to be doing. You are supposed to be setting your people up to be winners. To do that, you should be there listening to them and available to them in person, not via a suggestion box. For the most part, I think that we have a very good sense of this at Southwest. I think that most people employed here know that they can call any one of our vice presidents on the telephone and get heard, almost immediately.*

The station manager's intentions were understandable and admirable. As an organization grows larger, managers often feel they have less time to devote to one-on-one communication with their subordinates. A suggestion box becomes a tempting alternative. But for Sullivan, a suggestion box just didn't make sense in the context of personally responding to employees' concerns: "The suggestion box gives managers an out; it relinquishes their responsibility to be accessible to their people, and that's when we've gotten in trouble at Southwest Airlines—when we can no longer be responsive to our flight attendants or our customer service agents, when they can't gain accessibility to somebody who can give them resources and answers. Then, what they invariably do is turn to the next person who will serve them in a responsive manner." At Southwest, managers understand that they need to spend at least one-third of their time out of their office, walking around. This is not just an exercise in observation and critiquing the work of others; it's doing the work and spending enough time to truly understand and appreciate the difficulties people face in doing their jobs.

Southwest believes that the better you treat your people, the better they perform. You have to treat people well because you want to, however, and because you care about the people who work for you. Loyalty is something you earn. It is not an entitlement. Southwest managers and executives must earn the loyalty of employees; employees must earn the loyalty of supervisors; and this is done through service. It is a reciprocal phenomenon. Tom Burnette, president and business manager of the Teamsters Local 19 in Grapevine, Texas, says, "Let me put it this way. How many CEOs do you know who come into the cleaners' break room at 3:00 A.M. on a Sunday, passing out donuts or putting on a pair of overalls to clean a plane? If employees feel like they are respected and dignified, cared for and loved, then they will take good care of outside customers." Burnette has a good point. When people become committed to personally serving each other, a mutual respect and trust develops that enables them to earn the loyalty of customers.

### Service Springs from Sincerity

It's difficult to provide service that is sincere when you operate in an environment that is superficial, cold, and unfriendly. A lot of companies say they treat people with dignity and respect; Southwest actually does it. Company executives are very approachable, not at all into creating barriers between themselves and other members of the organization.

One customer service agent remembers meeting Jim Parker, vice president and general counsel, at a ticket counter. The agent said, "Hello, Mr. Parker." He responded, "Please, call me Jim!" Kathy Pettit, director of customers and a former Braniff flight attendant, remembers the first day she met Kelleher. She was working the ticket counter and Kelleher appeared from out of nowhere, kissed her on the cheek, and told her that Southwest was really lucky to have her. He welcomed her aboard and then went on his way. She turned to her training agent and said, "Who was that guy?" "Oh, that's Herb," she said. "Isn't he just the neatest thing?" When Pettit found out who "Herb" was, she was stunned. More importantly, she was proud to be recognized in such a personal way. Once asked by the CEO of another company how he could emulate Southwest's friendly corporate culture, Kelleher suggested that he start by saying "Hello," after noticing that the CEO neither recognized nor acknowledged two of his own employees as they got on an elevator with him. Winston Churchill said that the key to a leader's impact is sincerity: "Before you can inspire with emotion, you must be swamped with it yourself. Before you can move their tears, your own must flow. To convince them, you must yourself believe." Leaders set the tone for service that is genuine, sincere, and authentic.

### Serving the Good and the Bad

In a lot of organizations the willingness to serve gets smothered because people are no longer passionate about what they do. Cumbersome systems, bosses who are too controlling, boring routine, and endless competition exhaust people and cause them to feel indignant or indifferent. When customers bump into exhausted, indignant, indifferent employees, disgruntlement is what they see. It's hard to feel passionate when you don't feel supported.

Kathy Pettit remembers what it was like working for the original Braniff:

> *When we got good letters from customers (we called them passengers), I didn't see them for six months or so. Mysteriously, copies would arrive in my files. Sometimes there would be ten; sometimes there would be three; but it was always clear to me that somebody in customer relations had cleaned off his desk. There was also a time that I got one complaint in my fourteen years of flying. I never got any recognition for the good letters, but this one complaint was a big deal. I got hauled in for a fact-finding.*
>
> *How can I be expected to do the right thing when I'm locked in a tube with hundreds of strangers, all the while knowing that if something happens to go wrong, my company will not back me?*

This company demonstrated to her, through just one incident, that employees didn't count.

Southwest tracks employee compliments and complaints to better serve not just its customers but its employees as well. The rationale is this: letters from customers are learning opportunities for employees. At Southwest, the process of looking into a customer complaint is not a fact-finding mission that might result in the employee's losing his or her confidence, loyalty, or even job. The procedure is an opportunity to say, "Gosh, what's going on? Is everything okay?" It's an opportunity for people to make adjustments. The company may find out that the employee has a sick child, or is in the midst of a difficult divorce, or has car problems and can't afford to fix them. Or, just maybe, the customer was wrong.

When employees receive complimentary letters from customers, they get a memo from Kelleher with words to this effect: "Here's a copy of the customer letter. I think you're great and my hat's off to you. Keep up the great work. I love you." The message is simple—treat your employees with care and concern if that is the way you want them to treat each other and your customers.

"People are capable of the highest generosity and self-sacrifice," says Ernest Becker, author of the Pulitzer Prize–winning book *The Denial of Death*. "But they have to feel and believe that what they are doing is truly heroic, timeless, and supremely meaningful. The crisis of modern society is precisely that people no longer feel heroic." By loving them, celebrating their accomplishments, encouraging them to assume ownership for the success of the business, and treating them with dignity and respect, Southwest Airlines has employees who feel heroic and passionate about what they do. The heroism and passion with which they work translates into exceptional customer service.

### Serving the Person behind the Need

At Southwest Airlines, personal commitment to service means getting beyond an intellectual understanding of a customer's dilemma. It means identifying with whatever emotions the customer is feeling so that it drives you to take action. This may be the feature that most distinguishes Southwest Airlines from other companies. Southwest's service is "positively outrageous" because employees understand that customers are people—human beings who think and feel physically, emotionally, spiritually, and psychologically.

Southwest people believe that customer service involves more than an objective understanding of the customer's need. It also means, in Karl Albrecht's words, "being attentive to the *person* behind the need, and responding to the *person* more than just responding to the need." It requires employees to listen from the heart and put themselves in the shoes of the customer. When a customer boards a flight and is disgruntled about a fare restriction, for example, it's up to the flight attendant not only to help that person understand the restriction (an intellectual exercise), but also to empathize with how the customer is feeling (an emotional exercise). Service is about reading the customer, identifying with his or her needs, and caring—just because it is the right thing to do. Since every customer is unique, this is a formidable task.

Southwest has learned that you can't script out service for your people and expect them to deal effectively with a wide variety of customer needs. What one customer expects may annoy another. For example, some business travelers want nothing more than on-time performance, a seat, and no hassles. On the same flight, there may be a family on vacation that chose Southwest because the airline is known for fun and games. Today, customer service is a highly individualized experience. With humor, compassion, and a big dose of personal attention, Southwest employees go out of their way to make sure that every customer is treated like a member of the family.

A young man and his girlfriend boarded a flight from El Paso to Dallas in March 1994. Soon after the plane began its taxi toward the runway, the man felt like a private part of his anatomy was on fire! He scrambled to the lavatory to cool himself off as the plane pulled out. The flight attendant banged on the door and pleaded with him to get back to his seat. When he did, she asked what was wrong. Despite his embarrassment, he confessed, "MY BALLS ARE ON FIRE!"

## DEAR MR. KELLEHER

*I fly all over the world on a lot of different airlines but between Oakland, Los Angeles, and Phoenix I always fly Southwest. It's not because your fares are low. It's because you're usually running on time, you get people to board the aircraft quickly, and the #1 reason—the great disposition of your flight attendants. They are the best flying today.*

A SATISFIED CUSTOMER
CALIFORNIA

"Excuse me?" she replied. He repeated himself and explained that someone had left some dried chili peppers on his seat and that they must have worked their way into his shorts. The flight attendant, biting her lip so she wouldn't laugh, took charge and immediately brought him the necessary first aid—a towel, an ice pack, and a blanket.

## *Service is about reading the customer, identifying with his or her needs, and caring—just because it is the right thing to do.*

Almost a year later, the man wrote to Southwest to share his story—first for therapy; second, to thank the flight attendant for treating him with dignity and compassion, in spite of the humorous circumstances; and, finally, to encourage the flight crew to "watch out for practical jokers leaving *%$# chili peppers behind!" Scott Moore, the Southwest customer relations representative who received the letter, took it upon himself to purchase a pair of satin chili pepper boxer shorts, which he sent to the customer with a funny poem to commemorate the experience.

By serving, caring, and not taking a terribly embarrassing situation too seriously, both the flight attendant and the customer relations representative were free to use their training and, at the same time, express their individuality, show genuine concern, and treat the customer like family. Both went above and beyond the call of duty to serve him Southwest-style. In the end, both did the right thing, even though there was no rule book or ten-step process directing their behavior. Each simply cared enough to respond to the person behind the need with a unique flair.

### SERVICE BEYOND SERVING

Southwest expects employees to express their personalities in their work; the company wants employees' individuality to flourish. Consequently, a lot of Southwest people don't see their work as work; they see it as a stage on which they can use their gifts and talents to make a difference in the lives of others. That stage may be a ticket counter, janitor's supply room, maintenance hangar, reservations

# CHILI PEPPERS: A MEMENTO

*'Twas the minute before takeoff,*
*And all through the plane,*
*Not a passenger was stirring*
*Until one had some pain.*

*The passengers were nestled*
*All snug in their seats*
*With visions of cocktails*
*And Southwest's peanut treats.*

*When out of the blue*
*There arose such a ruckus,*
*The flight attendant jumped up*
*To see what the fuss was.*

*But what to her wondering*
*Eyes should appear?*
*A man in the lav,*
*She thought, "Too much beer!"*

*She banged on the door*
*And said, "Back in your place!"*
*She noticed the panic*
*And terror on his face.*

*"I'm really not trying*
*To create such a drama*
*But I feel like I sat*
*In hot, molten lava!"*

*"You're breaking the law;*
*Don't deny it, I've seen ya.*
*Return to your seat,*
*Or we'll hear from Fred Peña."*

*He sat there in agony;*
*The minutes seemed long*
*Until the flight attendant said*
*"Umm . . . Sir, what's wrong?"*

*He couldn't respond;*
*She seemed far too sweet.*
*He'd die from embarrassment*
*If not from the heat.*

*"Do you have a husband?*
*Do you have a son?"*
*He was trying to discover*
*If she'd ever seen one.*

*"You see, its these SEEDS!*
*They've soaked through my pants!*
*And I feel like I've rolled*
*In a bed of fire ants!"*

*The flight attendant gasped;*
*Her brow rose higher,*
*"Goodness! Gracious!*
*GREAT BALLS OF FIRE!"*

*The passengers grew anxious;*
*They thought it amazin'*
*To be sitting by a man*
*Whose crotch was a-blazin'.*

*She brought him a towel,*
*A baggie of ice,*
*A blanket for cover,*
*"Oooh. . . . That feels so nice!"*

*The pain, it subsided,*
*He felt no more fire.*
*And that was just fine*
*With that FREQUENT FLYER.*

*As he deplaned,*
*We all heard him say:*
*"I LUV Southwest!*
*I'll fly again, someday!"*

*"I would've been arrested,*
*If I'd flown on another.*
*The flight attendant acted*
*Like she was my mother."*

*"The flight was on time;*
*The treats were delicious.*
*Just watch out for those SEEDS,*
*I tell ya they're vicious!"*

*They heard him exclaim,*
*"There're no ifs, ands, or buts.*
*I prefer the TRAIL MIX*
*Over roasted NUTS!"*

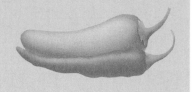

center, receptionist's desk, flight simulator, or the cabin or cockpit of a 737. This is why they experience service as a source of meaning, joy, and fulfillment, instead of something mundane, oppressive, or dehumanizing. For Southwest employees, service is about the daily celebration of having a job and working for a company they love.

The people of Southwest Airlines seem to have embraced Albert Schweitzer's observation: "We make a living by what we get, but we make a life by what we give." Service at Southwest is about giving, and, through giving, experiencing the joy and fulfillment of life like it's never been experienced before. It's a common occurrence to see energetic members of the ground crew running to meet the aircraft, just to turn a plane as fast as they can. Flight attendants willingly fly an extra leg of a flight because they've befriended an unaccompanied minor who is afraid to travel alone. Provisioning agents leave "LUV Notes" for flight attendants and assist the crew in cleaning up the plane for the next round of customers. Southwest does not underestimate the importance of creating an environment where employees feel passionate about what they do. The company has learned that passion, not techniques, is the key to legendary service.

When service is relegated to a technique or a program, it becomes nothing more than a sophisticated method of manipulating people to act in ways that accomplish organizational objectives. Unfortunately, the rewards for this type of service—advancement, money, and status—rarely deliver the sense of fulfillment and happiness they promise. True happiness is found in serving a cause that we believe has lasting significance. As we begin to serve the customers for which the cause exists, and thus embody the values and ideals inherent in the cause, our lives become more whole. Service that comes from a pure motive has the power to unite people, bring meaning to their lives, and enrich their humanness. Therein lies genuine happiness and one of the secrets to the spirit of service that distinguishes Southwest Airlines.

## SUCCESS IN A NUTSHELL

➤ Defend your people. The customer may not be right all the time!

➤ Make service a way of life, not just a business technique.

➤ Give people the flexibility to transcend rules and regulations to better serve the customer.

➤ Ask yourself, "Whom can I serve today?" Then do it.

➤ When it comes to serving others, make sure that "good enough" is never good enough.

➤ Treat your friends and family like your most valued customers.

**CHAPTER 20**

# EMPLOYEES COME FIRST

## GREAT SERVICE BEGINS AT HOME

In the first all-day Culture Committee meeting we attended at Southwest, the committee members kept referring to the company's "do the right thing" philosophy. When we got home, we continued to be puzzled by what we had seen. Many other employee groups we've interviewed and worked with over the years have expressed skepticism and apprehension when management offered this kind of discretion and empowerment. How did Southwest get its people to accept that freedom so enthusiastically?

> *"We are not an airline with great customer service. We are a great customer service organization that happens to be in the airline business."*

Since then, we've learned. The company believes that *employees come first*. When the systems, structure, policies, procedures, and practices of an organization are designed and lived out so that employees genuinely feel that they come first, trust is the result.

Southwest employees trust the company and love its leadership, so they are not skeptical or apprehensive when management says, "Do whatever you think is right."

## DO WHAT YOU ASK OF OTHERS

Kelleher loves to tell a story about Gigi Perry, a customer service agent at Love Field in Dallas. A seventy-year-old woman who had recently had heart surgery was bound for Amarillo, Texas. Her flight was grounded in Dallas because of heavy fog in Amarillo. Some two and a half hours after the bus had left to take the stranded customers to a hotel, Gigi noticed the woman outside the terminal, standing on the curb. Gigi drove the woman to the hotel and stayed with her the entire night because the elderly woman was afraid to be alone. The next morning, Gigi saw to it that the woman made her departure and then arrived in Amarillo safely. "Our people do that type of thing all the time," Kelleher says. "I mean, they have big, big hearts." Why did this customer service agent go out of her way for the elderly woman? In addition to her own sense of kindness, we think she did it because she knew that if Herb Kelleher, Colleen Barrett, John Denison, or any other Southwest executive had encountered this woman on the curb, that's exactly what they would have done.

We can't tell you how many times we've heard employees say, "Herb and Colleen would never ask us to do anything they aren't willing to do themselves." This is true of all the people in management at Southwest Airlines. They lead by example and *a*ffect change from the inside out. That is, they naturally model the behaviors they would like to see in others. They address their own responsibilities before asking employees to do the same. For Kelleher, Barrett, and the others, no job is too menial or mundane. While we were finishing up the research for this book in November 1995, we couldn't reach Kelleher on the Wednesday before Thanksgiving because he was at Love Field, doing what he does every year, working alongside the Dallas ground crew, loading bags and provisioning aircraft on the airline industry's busiest day. When company officers pitch in, the people of Southwest Airlines see the behaviors that are valued within the company. They also develop respect and love for their leaders because they know that Southwest's executives are willing to help out with jobs other senior executives might consider demeaning.

*Servant Leadership* author Robert Greenleaf says that we make a conscious choice to follow leaders "because they are proven and trusted as servants." One reason Southwest employees continue to provide legendary service is that they are led by leaders who know what it means to serve. By watching others, they see how the role of trustee is played out in an organization, and they learn how to practice stewardship—in Peter Block's words, "the willingness to be accountable for the well-being of the larger organization by operating in service, rather than in control, of those around us." Servanthood and stewardship are at the heart of Southwest Airlines' legendary service. Leaders at Southwest are passionate about taking care of the company, and they understand that the key to doing this is serving others.

# THE FIRST PLACE TO LOOK

*Southwest's mission statement is one of the first places employees look for direction about customer service. It's not some trendy wall hanging, designed to impress customers; it's a living, breathing document that provides guidance to every Southwest employee. The mission statement has two simple charters—it directs employees to express their individuality as they take care of customers and to become lifelong learners who take care of the company and each other. In full, it reads:*

Southwest Airlines is dedicated to the highest quality of Customer Service delivered with a sense of warmth, friendliness, individual pride, and Company Spirit.

We are committed to provide our Employees a stable work environment with equal opportunity for learning and personal growth. Creativity and innovation are encouraged for improving the effectiveness of Southwest Airlines. Above all, Employees will be provided the same concern, respect, and caring attitude within the Organization that they are expected to share externally with every Southwest Customer.

## THE MORE EMPLOYEES KNOW,
## THE MORE THEY CARE

"Communicate everything you can to your associates," Sam Walton said. "The more they know, the more they care." Armed with good information, employees have a wider range of alternatives for serving customers.

Southwest is known for saturating people with information that will help them better understand the company and its mission, customers, and competition. Information is power: it is a resource that equips people to do their jobs better. Unfortunately, many companies deny information to the very people who need it most—front-line employees. Southwest, on the other hand, is fanatical about making information readily available to the front line. Employees have the opportunity to learn every aspect of the business. Access to critical information grants customer-contact people the knowledge and understanding they need to take ownership and responsibility for doing the right thing. For example, a Southwest customer service agent who understands how the company makes its money, where profits come from and what they mean to the company, is in a better position to serve a customer who is making a special request. An agent who doesn't have access to this knowledge is limited by the company's rules and regulations.

Customers who deal with Southwest employees rarely get the runaround. Instead, they are likely to deal with a person who is well informed, makes sound decisions, and has a flexible, creative problem-solving approach. Their solid knowledge of the company gives the people of Southwest Airlines the confidence and power to truly make a difference in the lives of their customers.

## MAKE IT EASY FOR PEOPLE TO LEARN
## BY EXAMPLE

When employees witness, read, or hear about other people in the company modeling legendary service, they are influenced to do the same. Customer relations director Jim Ruppel says it another way: "Southwest equips people to do the right thing by giving them opportunities to learn through watching. Observation is the key to an employee's desire and willingness to do the right thing. When an

# THEY JUST DO IT

*A member of Southwest's frequent flier program—now called Rapid Rewards—was traveling with one of his customers on a special pass. The Rapid Rewards member worked for a company that imported fine wines from Italy. His companion and client was the owner of an exclusive winery in Italy. They finished their business early and hurried to the airport, just in time to make an earlier flight. When they got to the gate the customer service agent told them, "Sorry, you can't take the earlier flight. You have restricted tickets. I'd love to let you on, but I can't do it. We have a full flight today." The Rapid Rewards member said, "Well, I knew that, but you can't blame us for trying." So he and his client sat down in the lounge to wait for their scheduled flight. Not too long after, the agent walked up, handed each of them a gift certificate, and said, "I don't want you to be angry and I hope you understand." Neither traveler was angry and neither wanted to accept the gift. But the agent insisted. Amazed, the gentleman from Italy said, "I've never seen a company do anything like this. You would never see that on Alitalia. Who do you think gave her permission?" "Probably no one," the Rapid Rewards member said. "My girlfriend works for Southwest and they just do this kind of thing." The owner of the winery was so impressed that he took the gift certificate back to Italy, framed it, and hung it in his office as a reminder of the legendary service he experienced on this crazy, Texas-based airline.*

individual who is new to Southwest actually observes somebody taking that extra step or going the extra mile, it becomes contagious."

Doing the right thing is not something people do for a reward; they do it because that's who they are. Ruppel believes that everybody wants to do the right thing: "We all have that gene somewhere within us. Doing the right thing gives us pride in the work that we do, and we all have a need to feel good about what we do." Yet at one point or another, we all judge the effectiveness and appropriateness of our actions by comparing them with those of the people around us. Our perception of others' behavior directly influences our own. If we witness our colleagues day after day treating customers as interruptions, we soon grow to believe that customers are less important than other tasks we perform. In time, we behave accordingly—we treat customers as an inconvenience as well.

Southwest helps develop the spirit of service in new employees by matching them with senior people who are known for providing great service. New customer relations representatives, for example, go through a four-week learning-by-example process. To start, they get firsthand experience in ground operations. They spend time with the customer service agents selling tickets, issuing boarding passes, tagging bags—doing all the things involved in customer service at the airport. When the new reps return to the Customer Relations Department, they don't just read some standard training manual cover to cover; instead, they team up with senior reps for the next phase of watching and doing. The first week, they listen to the senior people talk on the phone and watch them use the computer system for online research necessary to assist customers. The next week they start learning the computer while they continue to listen to the more experienced reps handle incoming calls. Finally, the employee team reverses roles.

> ### *People at Southwest do the right thing because that's who they are.*

The new reps talk with customers and may even try using the computer system alone at that point. It takes about four weeks of this kind of coaching and mentoring before the new employees are equipped to do it on their own. Because there is no how-to manual, and because Southwest's customer relations philosophy is so individualized, supervisory and management staff continue to coach and guide when questions arise. During their four weeks of learning by example, new hires see great customer service up close and experience the company's principles in action. It doesn't take long for them to realize that their mission is to go the extra mile with creativity and flair.

## LET COMMON SENSE PREVAIL

Southwest employees know from history that when they use common sense to do what they think is right, the company will support them. "We never jump on employees for leaning too far in the direction of the customer," says Colleen Barrett. "They have to know that we stand behind them, and we do. The only time we come down on them pretty hard is when they fail to use common sense."

Common sense may sound easy enough, but it's a hard thing to define. Colleen gave us a clear example of what common sense *doesn't* look like: "When we say we are going to be an on-time airline and we

## TRANSCEND THE RULES AND REGS

*In 1989, when Colleen Barrett thought Southwest Airlines was becoming too rigid, she sent a memo to all station managers exhorting them not to use rules and regulations as a crutch when serving customers:*

No Employee will ever be punished for using good judgment and good old common sense when trying to accommodate a Customer—no matter what our rules are. Let's start leaning toward our Customers again—not away from them. Let's start encouraging our line Employees to be a little more flexible and to take that extra minute to try to accommodate special needs. Let's start encouraging our Supervisors to give our Customers the benefit of the doubt. I'll bet if those of us in top management started exhibiting some of that special WINNING SPIRIT that has contributed so greatly to our present success, those on the lower ends of the Management Group would be quick to jump in and follow suit.

*Barrett understands that when employees do not have the freedom to act on their own, they must hide behind the company's rules and regulations. The problem is that a company's rules rarely equip people to deal with every customer service problem they will encounter. Barrett's memo led to the company's Flexibility Program, in which all employees were given the freedom to handle customer service problems using their own judgment.*

are not holding planes for anybody, period, we have to use good judgment. We once had a situation where we slammed the door to a jetway because we wanted to push the plane on time. Fine. But when the passenger coming down the ramp is a paraplegic and can be seen by the operations agent in the jetway and has to sit in a wheelchair for four and a half hours for the next flight—that's not common sense."

Southwest's managers constantly reinforce the message that, whatever the situation, they have confidence in employees' abilities to make wise decisions and good choices. "I can't anticipate all of the situations that will arise at the stations across our system," Kelleher said in a 1991 *Nation's Business* interview. "So what we tell our people is, 'Hey, we can't anticipate all of these things; *you* handle them the best way possible. *You* make a judgment and use *your* discretion; we trust you'll do the right thing. If we think you've done something erroneous, we'll let you know—without criticism, without backbiting.'" Southwest believes that giving people flexibility empowers them to do what's right.

### *"We never jump on employees for leaning too far in the direction of the customer."*

People will work hard when they have the freedom to do their job the way they think it should be done. But take away their independence and choke them with rules—zap! You've stifled, if not killed, their creativity. No longer free to use their better judgment, they become less flexible. When employees are given a wide range of operational responsibilities without too many bureaucratic restrictions, they will operate like owners and entrepreneurs, rather than robots you wind up and micromanage.

### PEOPLE INSPIRE PEOPLE

For over two decades, Southwest has made living legends of employees who went above and beyond the call of duty to offer exceptional customer service. Through these stories of extraordinary service, employees quickly learn that the company encourages and recognizes flexibility and good judgment. Employees who see a col-

## LUV LINES SCENARIO

*December 17, 1994, was a cold and windy day. When Captain Brittan called in range, he advised us of a heavy offload of mail and freight. He wanted to make sure the ramp was given a heads-up to better prepare for the flight.*

*When the flight pulled into the gate, Captain Brittan was one of the first ones off. He smiled, waved, and disappeared down the jetway stairs to the ramp. I proceeded to board the flight, and when it was almost departure time, Captain Brittan reappeared from the ramp, still smiling. It wasn't until the flight pushed that I had learned what he had done.*

*Captain Brittan had climbed into the front bin to unload all of the mail and freight—with no gloves, knee pads, or coat—while the other ramp agents offloaded the bags in the back. With his assistance, the flight left on time. A heartfelt "thank you" goes out to Charlie Brittan for his Winning Spirit.*

A GRATEFUL EMPLOYEE

league offering Positively Outrageous Service are encouraged to write up the scenario for all to read in *LUV Lines*. Customer stories about great customer service also abound in the monthly "Scenario" section. What you see in this chapter is just a small sample.

## HELP ORDINARY PEOPLE DO EXTRAORDINARY THINGS

Southwest Airlines is committed to giving customers more than they pay for. This is a company that understands that anybody can provide low fares and poor service, and anybody can provide high fares and great service, but it's tough to provide low fares and great service. Giving more than expected and dignifying and appreciating the customer: these are a large part of what makes Southwest successful. Southwest people give more because they have more to give. The company has invested in their emotional bank accounts.

# LUV LINES SCENARIO

*I am a sales representative in the surplus sales department of Airborne Express. I was traveling with my wife in July to New Orleans on nonrevenue standby tickets I had purchased through Airborne Express. We started in Ohio, with stops in Chicago Midway, Louisville, and Birmingham.*

*We did fine until we reached Louisville, where we were called from the flight. My wife ended up getting the last seat and made it to New Orleans without any problem. I then flew to St. Louis and on to Houston Hobby. This is where I ran into the real problem. There were eight flights to New Orleans that evening, but I was told it was very unlikely that I would make any of them. I had no credit cards, and my wife had most of our cash. I knew I was doomed to spend the night at the airport.*

*I decided to fly to Dallas Love Field to catch an American Airlines flight. The flight was leaving Dallas/Fort Worth at 8:30 and I was at Love Field at 7:40. I was still in a dilemma. Then came Southwest Airlines Worker's Compensation Safety Specialist Tim Quarles.*

*Tim overheard me speaking to my nephew on the phone about the dilemma. He told me there was no time to take the shuttle, and he would drive me. He got me to the American terminal right at 8:00. I went in only to find that the ticket had not been paid for because American had my nephew on hold for over an hour.*

*Tim came back into the terminal and said that he had a feeling that I was still in trouble. After I explained the situation to him, he walked to the counter with me and, without hesitation, got out his VISA Gold Card and paid for my ticket. He explained that we didn't have any more time to try to get through on the phone. He then walked me to the gate and made sure that I got on the plane.*

*I arrived in New Orleans at 9:30 that evening. It was my wife's birthday, and she said Tim gave her the best present of all!*

*It is unheard of in today's world that someone would be so generous, especially to a complete stranger. It just goes to show that there are still good people in the world. You have an outstanding employee in Tim Quarles.*

JAMES MCINTOSH
SABINA, OHIO

Another factor, so fundamental it is sometimes forgotten, is this: Service Southwest-style helps customers realize their dreams by making flying more affordable. "Southwest Airlines is the standard bearer," Kelleher likes to say. "It is *The* Low Fare Airline!" Yes, other airlines may have promotional low fares, but Southwest has permanent low fares that help customers do things they never thought possible. Southwest made it possible for medical students living in Detroit to fly to a class in Chicago every Wednesday evening. When the students wrote to Kelleher and told him they were arriving fifteen minutes late to class, he changed the flight schedule to accommodate them. Mike Young, founder of Chuy's, a chain of Mexican restaurants based in Austin, plans to expand—but only to cities in Southwest's system. Southwest's ability to help him travel on short notice while keeping expenses low is essential to his expansion plans. Keith Harris, founder of Technosource Consulting, Inc., of Albuquerque, also plans to expand only into cities served by Southwest. "With a young family, I don't like to be away from home," Harris says. "Southwest makes it possible for me to fly to Phoenix, fly home that night, and return to Phoenix the next day for less than it would cost for a hotel stay. I'm grateful to Southwest for that."

Southwest's low fares make it possible for dual-career couples to have commuter marriages and for divorced parents to see their children more often. Southwest makes it affordable for people to travel to Houston's world-renowned M. D. Anderson Cancer Center to get the treatment they need. Because of more flight options, business travelers are able to get home in time for soccer games, dance recitals, and birthday parties. Grandparents can spend holidays with their families because even Southwest's regular fares are so inexpensive. With Southwest's Fun Fares and other special rates, families can go on vacations they could never afford otherwise. One Dallas customer fulfilled her dream of becoming an attorney because of Southwest. Once her children were established in school, she applied for admission to The University of Texas Law School in Austin. When she was accepted, she commuted every day because she didn't want to uproot the children. Southwest's schedule and fares made it affordable for her to go to school two hundred miles away.

# LUV LINES SCENARIO

*On the morning of February 7, 1995, I flew on a Southwest flight from San Antonio to Houston Hobby, on to New Orleans, and then to Birmingham. I travel weekly out of Oklahoma City to many areas and fly several airlines. Our company franchises Sonic Drive-In restaurants, and we feel very customer oriented. To those of us in the service sector, seeing outstanding service really is appreciated!*

*On this flight, all the flight attendants were very personable, fun, and extremely into their jobs. As sometimes I do on early trips, when the flight attendants asked what I'd like, I said "waffles, crisp bacon," etc., whatever came to mind. Chicago Midway Flight Attendant Michelle Bauer responded to my "waffle" request with "How about beignets at New Orleans?" I said, "Sounds good." This went on for a stop or two.*

*At New Orleans, I was waiting for the plane to reload when here came Michelle with a dozen hot, fresh beignets—much to my surprise. I thought Jackson Square was the only place you could get beignets. She gave them to me with napkins so I could share with the other customers who were also waiting for the plane to reload.*

*I thanked her and tried twice to give her some money for them, but to no avail. At this point, I said, "I'm going to write and get you a promotion." She said, "Thanks, but I don't want a promotion. I just love my job." What an answer, and what a special job she does.*

*Southwest is to be praised for the job you do with virtually all your people to instill service beyond the call of duty. I just felt an extraordinary feat should be recognized and get a special thanks. I really appreciated her extra mile of effort.*

H. Max "Chuck" Harrison
Oklahoma City, Oklahoma

# LUV LINES SCENARIO

*I flew from Oakland to Burbank on company business in December. Both flights were in the incomparable Southwest style, and I was delighted to see the flight attendants dressed in elf costumes, serenading us with Christmas songs.*

*Later that evening, I realized that I didn't have my purse. As I frantically tried to recall the last time I had it, I realized that I'd probably left it on the plane. I called Southwest, and Oakland customer service agent Tausha Johnson handled my call. She reported that the purse had not been turned in and then filled out a report. I returned to the airport after dinner, but the purse had not yet turned up. However, she traced the plane to Ontario and to Phoenix. She called Ontario, but no purse. She called Phoenix, and the flight had not arrived. She said she'd call me later. I went home in a very dismayed state, wondering how I could leave the next day for ten days in Atlanta. In my purse were my credit cards, ATM card, driver's license, keys, and other assorted important items.*

*Around 11:30 P.M., I got a call from Oakland customer service agent Suzann Koehler, who was working with Tausha. My purse had been found on the plane by the aircraft cleaners in Phoenix. They'd fly it back to Oakland by 9:00 A.M. Needless to say, I was overjoyed.*

*When I retrieved my purse the next morning, everything seemed to be there. However, when I opened my billfold, the $40 I had was gone. I thought to myself, "Oh, well, $40 is a small price to pay for such a foolish mistake on my part." Upon closer inspection, I found a check from Southwest Airlines for $41 to "replace cash found in lost purse."*

*I am completely overwhelmed by this experience! The extra special service that I received from these Southwest employees is so unusual in this fast-paced, hard-bitten world of ours. I've been a fan of Southwest Airlines for several years now, and this experience has turned me into a "DIEHARD FAN."*

A Diehard Fan
from California

"We are not an airline with great customer service," Colleen Barrett always says. "We are a great customer service organization that happens to be in the airline business." Reaching out to people with kindness and inviting them to be part of the Southwest family are practices now deeply embedded in the company's culture. Extraordinary customer service at Southwest Airlines is not about superficial techniques or trendy programs; it is a deep, rich, ongoing tradition. Now celebrated throughout the industry and around the world for its tradition of service, Southwest has attracted the kind of unselfish, other-oriented people who know what it means to serve. In this way, the tradition of legendary service is maintained and the legacy lives on.

# SUCCESS IN A NUTSHELL

- ➤ Do what you ask others to do.

- ➤ Inform your people. It teaches them to care.

- ➤ Make living legends out of your service heroes. Real examples might inspire others to offer legendary service too.

- ➤ Show people what legendary service looks like, then trust them to do the right thing.

- ➤ Publish stories of extraordinary service in your newsletter. If you don't have one, write them up in a letter to employees.

- ➤ Make it a practice to give everyone—customers, coworkers, friends, family—more than they expect.

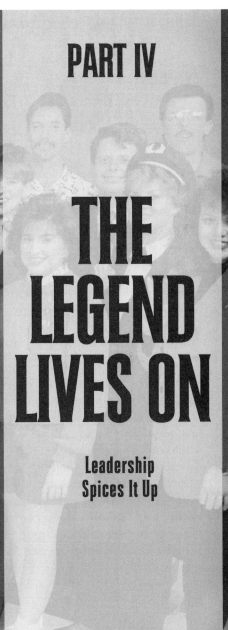

# PART IV

# THE LEGEND LIVES ON

Leadership
Spices It Up

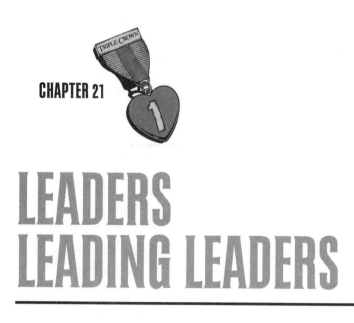

**CHAPTER 21**

# LEADERS LEADING LEADERS

As we think about what Southwest Airlines has achieved, we find ourselves asking, "What is the spark that ignites the heroic nature of this company? What makes this company able to sever the bonds that normally constrain us? What gives Southwest employees the freedom to think and act like nuts?" In a word, the answer is *leadership*. Turned-on, impassioned leadership is what makes the principles described in this book come alive. An organization rises to greatness when the otherwise latent talents and energies of its people are evoked by the power of leadership. At Southwest Airlines there exists a spirit of liberty and freedom that encourages people to use their imagination, express their individuality, and exercise leadership.

If leadership is the galvanizing force behind Southwest's recipe for success, what does it look like and how is it practiced? To answer this question we offer our definition adapted from Joseph Rost's *Leadership for the Twenty-First Century:*

> *LEADERSHIP is a dynamic relationship based on mutual influence and common purpose between leaders and collaborators in which both are moved to higher levels of motivation and moral development as they affect real, intended change.*

That *is* a mouthful, but the main elements in this definition describe leadership as it is practiced at Southwest Airlines. We hope it challenges you enough to consider the ways your own behavior might change if you were to adopt this philosophy.

## LEADERS COLLABORATE

At Southwest Airlines, leadership is practiced through collaborative relationships. The people of Southwest Airlines work in relationships where the roles of leader and collaborator are interchangeable. Essentially, leadership is something leaders and their collaborators do together.

At this point you may be asking, "Why use the word *collaborators* instead of *followers?*" We think that *collaborators* better describes the people of Southwest Airlines because, when it comes to leadership, they jump in with both feet! They are active and they are engaged, regardless of which side of the leadership relationship they are on. As GSD&M's Tim McClure explains, "Southwest has been building a company that has leaders within every rank and file of the business. They rise to the occasion at different points in their careers and at different times in the company's growth, but when they are there—*they are there!*" What you have at Southwest Airlines, at different times and in various ways, is leaders leading leaders.

The relationship between leaders and collaborators at Southwest Airlines is based on commitment, not compliance. Leadership isn't some sophisticated technique for getting people to do what *you* want them to do. Leadership is getting people to *want* to do what you want them to do because they share your purpose, vision, and values. When the interests of leaders and collaborators overlap, the result is long-term, sustained commitment. When people are committed, they are bound emotionally or intellectually to a purpose or course of action. They are in it with all their heart, soul, and mind. Compliant people simply go through the motions and put in their time; it's difficult for them to transcend the nine-to-five mentality because they have no emotional or spiritual attachment to the cause their work represents. Commitment doesn't come with position, and it can't be bought. Commitment must be earned. Leaders and collaborators are drawn to higher levels of commitment when both see that their personal agendas are encompassed by a purpose that is deeply held by everyone in the relationship.

## COLLABORATION IN ACTION

The collaborative nature of leadership at Southwest Airlines can be seen in many parts of the company. Perhaps one of the best examples exists in the Marketing and Advertising/Promotions Department.

When marketing and advertising v.p. Don Valentine left Southwest Airlines in 1992 to help Continental launch a Southwest clone, Dave Ridley (then director of marketing and planning) and Joyce Rogge (then director of advertising and promotions) got together and submitted an unusual proposal to their boss, Colleen Barrett. They wrote her a letter that said, "Each of us would be happy to work for the other, but we would prefer you do nothing rather than bring in someone from the outside." Against Kelleher's and other key officers' advice, Barrett agreed to give their proposal serious consideration. "I believe that this is a classic example of a culture that was willing to support something unconventional," Ridley says. "Colleen stuck her neck out because she believed in us." Barrett decided to accept their plan: Ridley and Rogge would remain directors and jointly be in charge of the department.

Joyce Rogge and Dave Ridley knew that if they were going to function as one, they would have to collaborate closely. Rather than debate or toss a coin over who would get Valentine's office, Ridley came up with another idea: "Why don't we get rid of the walls, put our desks out on the middle of the floor, and make ourselves accessible to the department?" Rogge thought it was an excellent plan. On New Year's weekend the construction crew came in and demolished Valentine's old office. In its place the crew built two small conference rooms for meetings and private phone calls. On Monday morning when everyone returned to work, the two directors' desks sat side by side in the open area in front of the two glass-front conference rooms.

The new physical arrangement communicated three important messages. First, it signaled that the department was under new leadership. Next, it said, "We're a team that is going to communicate openly and function as one." Finally, it indicated that Rogge and Ridley would be very accessible. Rogge says, "We wanted to make a statement to the marketing and advertising team that we were not going to jockey for Don's position. Dave and I have common goals for the people who work with us and a common vision for Southwest Airlines. My strengths are different from Dave's and that makes us even stronger together. But we don't find it threatening. What it really comes down to is respect and a real love for each other."

Like most working relationships, this one is not without conflict and tension. But it seems to work well because the two have held their egos in check. Ridley and Rogge have chosen to make serving the purpose of the organization more important than serving their own individual interests. Ridley describes how their roles are constantly changing in this collaborative relationship: "At times it is not as efficient as we would like. I'm more analytical and conservative than Joyce is. She tends to be more spontaneous and more tactical. Although she ultimately has responsibility for our advertising, if I don't like a storyboard or I don't think we have quite the right execution, she'll listen and she will often change it. Other times she'll say, 'No, I disagree with you,' and I'll back off. There's a very kindred spirit between us." Both Ridley and Rogge have been promoted to vice president, which speaks well for how their relationship works. "Dave and Joyce are absolutely different personalities," says Colleen Barrett, "but they've developed a partnership in that department."

## PREREQUISITES FOR LEADERSHIP

For leadership to be practiced at Southwest Airlines as a dynamic relationship between leaders and collaborators, two principles must be observed. First, leadership does not reside in one person (even if he is named Kelleher). Second, leadership is not a position of power and authority. These principles are important because they reveal a lot about the inner workings of leadership practiced the Southwest way.

### The Lone Ranger Is a Myth

In our yearning for heroes and our desire to better understand leadership, we are inclined to focus on the individual, a personality who embodies the attributes of a great leader. If you read the business literature, you are led to believe that Jack Welch single-handedly transformed General Electric, Anita Roddick built The Body Shop without any help, and Norman Schwarzkopf rallied the allied forces in Desert Storm all by himself. Intellectually, most of us would agree that no one person—no matter how great—does it alone. Yet we have been conditioned to think of leadership in terms of the heroic figure who comes to the rescue of people who are either too dumb or too weak to help themselves.

In *American Spirit: Visions of a New Corporate Culture*, Lawrence Miller describes some of the implications of defining leadership in term of the legendary hero. While humorous, Miller's parody indicts our traditional thinking about leadership:

> *Problems were always solved in the same way. The Lone Ranger and his faithful Indian companion (read servant of somewhat darker complexion and lesser intelligence) come riding into town. The Lone Ranger, with his mask and mysterious identity, background, and life-style, never becomes intimate with those whom he will help. His power is partly in his mystique. Within ten minutes the Lone Ranger has understood the problem, identified who the bad guys are, and has set out to catch them. He quickly outwits the bad guys, draws his gun, and has them behind bars. And then there was always that wonderful scene at the end. The helpless victims are standing in front of their ranch or in the town square marveling at how wonderful it is now that they have been saved, you hear hoofbeats, then* **The William Tell Overture,** *and one person turns to another and asks, "But who was that masked man?" And the other replies, "Why, that was the Lone Ranger!" We see Silver rear up and with a hearty "Hi-ho Silver," the Lone Ranger and his companion ride away.*

The Lone Ranger image—the idea that one heroic person is out in front taking charge while everyone else passively follows—just isn't what happens. Hear us loud and clear—Kelleher doesn't do it alone, even though many continue to describe him in Lone Ranger terms. When a problem arises "down on the ranch," Southwest employees are encouraged to solve it. The company believes that those closest to the problem are the most capable of fixing it. Even if they fail a few times in coming up with an acceptable solution, this is the way the people of Southwest Airlines learn and lead.

The image of a leader who hides behind the mask of anonymity doesn't fit the company either. Southwest people are anything but detached. Employees who wear masks and avoid the kind of intimacy that many consider a sign of vulnerability and weakness don't last very long at Southwest Airlines—the company culture won't allow it.

**Position Power Is Not Leadership**

Isn't it interesting that people who have participated in some of the greatest change efforts in history have done so without the backing and power of status, money, armies, or nuclear weapons? People may hold the title of chief executive officer, head coach, commissioner, mayor, or general, but their positions do not necessarily make them leaders. Nor does the absence of fancy titles prevent people from exercising leadership.

*Leadership is based on mutual influence. Leaders both shape and are shaped.*

"Leadership is not determined by position or title to any extent, shape, or form," Kelleher says. "Our people have determined not to regard title or position as especially important because they wouldn't be as free to make things happen." Titles have a smothering effect on leadership; they tend to make people cautious and too analytical. Employees spend too much time worrying about how the person behind the title will react to their initiatives instead of doing what's right for the company and its constituents. When employees who participated in the Fuel from the Heart program took pay reductions to offset escalating fuel prices, they didn't seek permission from someone in a position of power—they just did it. When Southwest employees came up with the idea for ticketless travel, they didn't write a proposal and present it to senior executives—they just went to work on it. This is not to say that the people of Southwest Airlines never rely on positional authority to get things done. They do, but using position power to accomplish their objectives is not their standard mode of operation.

## LEADERS INFLUENCE ONE ANOTHER

In an organization where titles are downplayed and leadership is not dependent upon position, it should come as no surprise that influence flows back and forth between leaders and collaborators. This means that influence does not always originate with the executive officers of Southwest Airlines. As John Gardner suggests, leaders both shape and are shaped. The result is mutual influence. The implication is that anyone, at any level within a company, has the opportunity to influence the system. At Southwest Airlines, you don't have to hold the title of chairman or chief executive officer to feel you can make a difference.

At Southwest, influence comes from all directions. For example, the pilots influenced people at all levels of ground operations to support the Cutting Edge Team. The result? Systemwide, Southwest's already speedy turnaround times were stepped up to save hours of ground time every day. Members of the company's Culture Committee persuaded senior management that Heroes of the Heart was the right thing to do and produced a major change in Southwest's reward and recognition system. Remember the Fuel from the Heart program? Employees in ground operations influenced thousands of their coworkers to take payroll deductions to offset the cost of skyrocketing fuel prices. In each of these major changes, influence initially came from somewhere other than the executive offices.

## HOW TO INFLUENCE PEOPLE

If you are interested in expanding your scope of influence, consider the following.

### 1. Walk your talk.

Influence comes from integrity. Integrity means doing what you say you are going to do and being the person you say you are. Integrity gives you trust and credibility, without which you can have no influence. You expand your influence in an organization when people believe that you can be trusted and that you are credible. The reason Southwest pilots were willing to enter into a landmark union contract with the company is that they believe that leaders on both sides of this agreement have integrity. The simple fact that Southwest people follow through and keep their promises creates an environment where everyone is more open to being influenced. Employees are then more willing to shape and be shaped because they are comfortable and secure in their relationships with their coworkers and bosses.

In an industry riddled with broken promises and unmet expectations, suppliers and customers also believe that with Southwest people, their word is their bond. "They ask you to be their partner,"

# WOW! YOU REALLY <u>WERE</u> THE PRESIDENT!

*"There is no caste system at Southwest Airlines," says Howard Putnam, Southwest's president and CEO from 1978 to 1981. On a recent flight from Houston to Dallas, Putnam stopped a flight attendant coming down the aisle and said, "Excuse me. Can you tell me who the captain is tonight?" The flight attendant rattled off the captain's name and then asked Putnam why he wanted to know.*

"Well, I used to work for the company and I thought I might know him."

"Oh yeah? Were you a flight attendant?"

"No, I didn't have enough hair to be a flight attendant."

"Were you a pilot?"

"No, I wasn't a pilot."

"What did you do?"

"I was in management."

"So, what did you do in management?"

"I was your president."

*Putnam says, "I got this look like, I'll bet you were." Nevertheless, the flight attendant introduced herself, got Putnam's name, and went straight to the cockpit. Pretty soon, as she made her way back down the aisle, she didn't even pause. She just hit Putnam on the arm as she went by and said, "You're right."*

says GE's chairman, Jack Welch. "And their word means everything— I mean they have the highest integrity." In its advertising the company promises consistently low fares, legendary service, and lots of fun. By simply keeping these promises, Southwest enjoys credibility with customers in every market it serves. Legislators representing constituents in areas where Southwest has dramatically reduced the average fare give people like governmental affairs v.p. Ron Ricks immediate access. Why? Because the company has a reputation for doing what it says it's going to do. Whether the fight is over FAA reform, a jet-fuel tax, or a government-subsidized bullet train, many of these lawmakers readily offer their enthusiastic support because they have been moved by Southwest's integrity.

## *Expand influence by focusing on things you can control.*

### *2. Focus on things you can control.*

Southwest employees rarely feel powerless to influence the system. For the most part, they are the kind of people who make things happen by concentrating on things they can control.

In December 1990, Southwest found that its on-time performance had slipped to an all-time low. Customer service coordinator Harry Ehmann sent a memo to Jim Wimberly, vice president of ground operations, in which he passionately expressed the need for Southwest employees to respond collectively to the challenge of improving on-time performance. To show how serious the issue was, Ehmann's memo went to the home of every Southwest employee. It set off an avalanche of recommendations from concerned people at every level in the company. Within a few months Southwest had improved on-time performance dramatically, and by July 1991, just eight months later, the company had regained its number-one standing in the Department of Transportation statistics.

Certainly, the change in on-time performance was not the result solely of Ehmann's memo. Changing schedules, rerouting aircraft, and building in catch-up time for the equipment also contributed substantially. However, Ehmann's choice to focus on something he could control, as opposed to simply complaining, shows how one person can influence a whole system.

### *3. Be prepared.*

When Southwest people take a position on a controversial issue, you can count on the fact that their argument has been thoroughly researched and their facts are in order. Roy Spence says, "Herb and his team have always succeeded on merit because they are well prepared—they do more research than anyone." Several years ago Kelleher testified before a congressional hearing to oppose a federally subsidized high-speed rail system in Texas. Jim Parker, Ron Ricks, and Kelleher constructed the testimony in such a way that every time Kelleher made a factual assertion there were several footnotes to substantiate what he had just said. His testimony was so loaded with supporting footnotes that it was difficult to read. However, the highest-ranking member of the congressional committee, a supporter of high-speed rail when the hearing started, directed his staff to check out every factual assertion and each and every footnote. At the end of the hearing the congressman said, "If the facts check out as Southwest argued, the proposed bullet train in Texas will receive no federal subsidies."

### 4. Sharpen your political skills.

"Politics has gotten a bad name in America," Kelleher says. "But politics really means dealing with people. Being politic is something everybody should be because it means learning what motivates people, what concerns people, what scares people, what inspires people in order to have them act affirmatively and effectively." Organizations operate in a political world; Southwest is no exception. The people of Southwest Airlines, a low-cost carrier, must compete for limited resources to get things done and advance the purpose of the company. To ignore politics is not only naïve, it's foolish. Kelleher and Barrett firmly believe that leadership is also, to some extent, a political process—not in the sense of covert manipulation and undermining, but rather in the sense of influencing people overtly through an aggregation of passion, sound judgment, and reasoned argument.

## Influence comes through <u>positive</u> political skills.

Southwest employees have learned that in order to influence others they must build a good, solid case for what they are trying to do and then argue that case with conviction and enthusiasm. If your case is strong enough, if you present it with contagious excitement, you can often persuade people and build commitment.

At Southwest Airlines politics doesn't mean scheming or arm twisting. It has nothing to do with distorting or withholding information to gain leverage in a situation or to jockey for position. At Southwest, influence is about building loyalty and trust by letting people know where you stand. It means being open, authentic, and aboveboard. It means using power to serve the purpose of the organization as well as the larger, common good of the society in which the organization operates.

### 5. Love people into action.

Love conquers the defensiveness that closes people to influence. When people feel loved, the walls come down. Southwest has discovered, almost by accident, that when people look out for their colleagues' interests, their colleagues are more open to accepting new ideas and behaving in prescribed ways. A lot of other people at Southwest Airlines believe that the reason Herb and Colleen have so much influence within the company has less to do with their positions than with the way that they consistently demonstrate their love for employees. You've probably heard the cliché, "People don't care how much you know until they know how much you care." Leading through love means you've got to care. Love is a source of influence.

### 6. Listen for more than you hear.

Listening is powerful because it shows a genuine desire to understand the unique needs and feelings of others. As with many other employees at Southwest Airlines, Kelleher's influence with people stems from his willingness to be influenced by them. People in the field, for example, are less resistant to change and more open to new ideas that come from the executive offices because they know that Herb, Colleen, and others will *listen* to what they have to say. More importantly, these people know that the company's executives will be influenced by what they hear. Listening that evokes some type of action or emotional response essentially shows people that they have been influential. People who feel they have been heard are more willing to hear others.

## LEADERS SHARE PURPOSE, VISION, AND VALUES

If you study the people who participate in dynamic leadership relationships, you will find that the majority of them never set out to be great leaders. Rather, they set out to pursue a purpose, a cause, or a calling that was worthy of giving it everything they had—in some cases, even their lives! Their power is the power of purpose. Whether it's chasing an exciting new opportunity or fighting an injustice, their belief in the cause gives them the strength to persevere when they come up against seemingly insurmountable odds. In their efforts to build relationships and rally people around the cause, they are engaging in the act of leadership.

## *People rise to leadership through a calling or a cause.*

This is what happened with the original employees at Southwest Airlines. Their perseverance took the form of a protest against the injustices levied by Braniff, Texas International, and Continental. Their fight was the fight for freedom. When confronted by the injustices of the bigger carriers, their resolve grew stronger, they became more unified, and more people got caught up in their cause. Those who opposed Southwest Airlines underestimated the power of purpose. They grossly misjudged the steady resilience and indomitable spirit of perseverance of people who are bound by a common purpose.

Southwest's original employees certainly shared the will to survive, but more importantly, they shared the vision of building an airline of their own choosing—an airline that allowed them to be themselves, use their brains, have fun on the job, and provide highly valued service to customers. It was a vision that allowed many of them to shape their future and create something they had never had the opportunity to create before. Today, the vision of Southwest Airlines is rooted in their deeply held personal visions. Southwest's employees have not just bought into an idea originally presented to them by Rollin King and Herb Kelleher; they are committed to Southwest Airlines because they see in the company's vision an opportunity to pursue personal aspirations. They feel intellectually, emotionally, and spiritually connected to this vision. Granted, as the company has expanded, this commitment to a bigger vision is not what draws everyone to Southwest Airlines, but it truly separates the short-timers from those who join the company because they see in it an opportunity to fulfill some of their dreams.

Many employees of Southwest Airlines are also committed to a set of values that are shaping Southwest's destiny and thus their joint destinies. If leaders and collaborators are not clear about what values form the basis of their relationships, those principles for which they truly stand, then how can they ever expect to lay the foundation for leadership, let alone have the capacity to effect change? Southwest's direction as a company is controlled by the gravitational pull of its values. They form the basis for what the company has become. Today, these values shape the beliefs Southwest employees have about who they are and what they are capable of doing. Strength of character and a sense of identity rooted in deeply held values enable Southwest employees to stay the course and exercise leadership as radical changes in the U.S. airline industry continue to unfold.

## LEADERS ARE SERVANTS BY NATURE

It has become rather fashionable in management circles to talk about the concept of service or servant leadership. Robert Greenleaf's magnificent book *Servant Leadership* has become a landmark in the management and leadership literature. It makes sense. After all, the idea has been tested for a couple of millennia. The concept suggests that inherent in the act of leadership is the natural desire and corresponding choice to *first* serve others. The defining element lies in a person's first inclination: is it to lead or is it to serve? The first inclination of great leaders is servanthood. Most people are drawn to leadership because they feel compelled to serve a purpose larger than themselves.

What seems to be missing from the mainstream discussions about servant leadership is the tremendous sacrifice that often comes with choosing to be a servant first. The people of Southwest Airlines have not achieved great success without paying a significant price. What goes on behind the scenes is a tremendous amount of hard work and self-sacrifice. Barrett and Kelleher routinely put in sixteen-hour days and regularly work seven days a week. While they don't require that level of commitment from others, the travel schedules and workloads are grueling for most people at Southwest. For some the sacrifice is offset by how much fun they have at work. However, we would be remiss in not telling you that, for some Southwest employees, something is forfeited.

Some people are uncomfortable with the idea of leadership as servanthood. They may see it as oppressive. For others who have been conditioned to view leadership as a tough, macho thing, servanthood may seem submissive or weak. Despite its alien feel, servanthood is a form of leadership particularly well suited to today's business world. First, servanthood sets people free. Servanthood means helping people remove the obstacles in their way and helping them acquire the tools they need to do their jobs better. It means jumping into the trenches and being willing to do whatever you ask of others. Think about it. There's dignity in contributing to another person's freedom. There's a sense of significance and a feeling of accomplishment when you know that you've played a small part in lightening the load of a colleague who is overwhelmed. These acts of servanthood are dignifying, not demeaning.

Second, servanthood is anything but weak. We seriously doubt that former Braniff CEO Harding Lawrence or former Texas International CEO Frank Lorenzo view Herb Kelleher as soft or weak. Yet, ask people inside or outside the company and they will tell you that Herb's first inclination is to subordinate his own interests to those of Southwest Airlines. This is certainly consistent with Kelleher's own philosophy: "Leadership is being a faithful, devoted, hard-working servant of the people you lead and participating with them in the agonies as well as the ecstasies of life." We are certain that it's not fame and fortune that keeps Kelleher at Southwest Airlines. It's that he gets a kick out of serving a cause and the people he cares deeply about.

## *Leadership is inherently oriented toward servanthood.*

Many of the people we talked to at Southwest Airlines believe that their company exists to serve a purpose, not just to make a profit. They are not focused on themselves, their individual departments, or the work associated with their functional area. Their focus is on serving the legitimate wants and needs of the people they care about, even if this involves some pain and self-sacrifice. It's as though they understand that their own needs will be met, not as a result of pursuing self-interest, but rather as a result of serving a cause they hold to be noble and heroic. In their lives this cause becomes tangible every day. Leadership, leaders leading leaders at all levels within the company, is the key ingredient in Southwest Airlines' recipe for success.

# CHAPTER 22

# LEADERSHIP FROM THE INSIDE OUT

Today people of all ages are searching for a deeper sense of meaning and significance in their lives. The workplace is no exception. Because we spend so much time there, work has become a place where we seek a sense of meaning and identity. Unfortunately, for much of the work force, work is a big letdown. Trapped in jobs they perceive as meaningless, many people go home at night emotionally drained. Having spent eight, ten, twelve hours in a job that exhausts them, they have nothing left to give their families and friends at the end of the day. The energy and motivation they long for escapes them in the absurdity of work that appears to be mundane. Deprived of meaningful work that satisfies their search for significance, people lose their reason for existence.

> *To know that our work matters, that our labor counts for something, is to know that <u>we</u> count.*

Southwest Airlines is different; its employees see themselves as leaders who make a difference. They believe their actions help create a work environment that is motivating and morally uplifting. Through leadership, Southwest employees have built a community known for drawing out the best in people.

# LEADERSHIP INSPIRES MOTIVATION

Southwest employees have an uncanny ability to sustain high energy levels for long periods. We suspect this is because they have come to see on-time performance, baggage handling, and customer service as a source of self-respect. They see the relationships they have with each other as a source of joy. They see the mutual trust and love that forms the basis for these relationships as a virtue to be protected. They are proud to be a part of a corporate culture that values them not as dispatchers, flight attendants, or provisioners, but as people. They see the competition with other low-fare carriers as an invigorating challenge. And they believe that their job security is inextricably tied to the company's well-being. These are the forces that motivate the people of Southwest Airlines. The role of leadership is to protect these sources of motivation and draw upon them to invigorate and revitalize people who temporarily lose hope.

### Make a Commitment

You've heard over and over that, for the majority of employees, Southwest Airlines is more than a business, it's a crusade. How does this relate to motivation? When work becomes a cause, our lives take on meaning and significance. We are moved to higher levels of motivation because work, no longer seen as a vocation, becomes an avocation. Gary Barron says, "Southwest Airlines is enough fun that it almost makes you feel guilty to call it work."

The organizing force behind this crusade is leadership. Leaders and collaborators are the champions of this concerted movement. Their commitment is to the cause and to the relationships they've established in pursuing the cause. Make no mistake; it's commitment that creates meaning in their work and it's meaningful work that motivates them to be the most productive work force in the U.S. airline industry.

### Honor People's Efforts

At Southwest Airlines, leaders raise people to higher levels of motivation by showing them how their individual contributions are linked to the major purposes of the organization. This is done by acknowledging people's contributions in spectacular celebrations, by publishing heroic feats in *LUV Lines*, and by simple "thank yous" that say, "What you did made a difference."

Leaders use just about any means available to show people the importance of what they do. As a result, people begin to see how they can make a difference. It's the pilot who concentrates on fuel burn rate every minute in the cockpit. It's the flight attendant who takes the time to show the company how it can save money by taking the logo off the trash bags. It's the director of technical services who decides that he can build computers more cost-efficiently than he can buy them. People become energized when they understand the significance of their contributions. It activates within them an inner drive to contribute more.

### Believe in People

When people believe in you, they help you blossom; they help you become a bigger, stronger, more capable person. Leaders show their belief in people by giving them assignments that are often way outside the boundaries of their normal job descriptions.

"Most organizations think you have to have an expertise in something before you can be a leader," Barrett says. "Of course you're going to have your failures along the way, but we're really very flexible in our thinking about who might be able to lead a particular effort. Most of the time it has very little to do with their technical expertise."

> *Motivation comes from showing people*
> *that you believe in them.*

Barrett believes that a person's capabilities and potential are not inextricably linked to experience or education. Kelleher says, "Colleen has a tremendous imagination as to how to get the most out of people and not compartmentalize them. She refuses to slot people by saying, 'For all time this is where you belong'; she puts people where they can have a positive impact and grow."

Perhaps this is what led Southwest to send Kathy Pettit, former director of corporate communications, who does not have degrees in engineering or interior design, to work with Boeing on the cabin design of the new 737-300. Or to tap Milt Painter, a pilot and the director of in-flight training, to negotiate the deal when Southwest purchased a new $12 million flight simulator. Southwest believed in their ability to do the right thing.

From a leadership perspective, this has two very important consequences. First, Southwest employees align themselves with the image the company has of them and behave accordingly. Second, when the company acknowledges the gifts people bring to the table, they work harder to develop and apply their gifts. As a result, the impact of their gifts expands because they use them more frequently and more effectively.

## LEADERSHIP ENRICHES THE HUMAN CONDITION

The true test of leadership is to ask the questions, "Are those who would participate in leadership equipped to serve the common good? Are they encouraged to learn and grow as human beings? In an organizational sense, is the firm a better firm, and is the community in which the firm operates a better place, as a result of having been exposed to both the process and end result of leadership?"

Leadership is the practice of helping people envision, and then participate in, creating a better world than the world they came into. It means raising individuals, organizations, and communities to higher levels of moral development—the obligations, responsibilities, and rights associated with bettering the human condition in a just and civil society. It means using the collective wisdom, knowledge, and experience of leaders and collaborators to further the welfare of others. What kind of community raises people to higher levels of moral development? The following examples characterize the community that leadership has built at Southwest Airlines.

### A Community That Honors the Sacredness of the Person

Southwest Airlines does not differentiate people by their organizationally prescribed roles. For Southwest, building community begins with something as simple as honoring the sacredness of each person who comes to work for the company. "It's very important to value people as individuals, not just employees," Kelleher says. "I don't use the word *employees* very much, and I never use the word *management*. I just refer to the people of Southwest Airlines, and we really try to treat them as people and recognize each one's individuality."

People at Southwest are encouraged to relate to the person, not just the ramp agent, secretary, operations agent, or executive. The difference is not just semantic. When people are dealt with as categories, the nature and outcome of their interactions with the company—in union negotiations, for example—are predictable. A category can be replaced without worry. A category can be moved without significant disruption. But when that category becomes someone's wife or son, when that category has a mortgage to pay and a family that counts on her, when that category is a living, breathing person with feelings and needs, it becomes a very different story. People on the other side of the negotiating table become family members with underlying interests that represent other people who care deeply about those interests, and the whole perspective changes.

## *Leadership raises people to higher levels of moral development.*

Why do Southwest people go out of their way to perform some of the extraordinary services for customers that you've read about in this book? It's because they don't view customers as categories or objects. They view customers as, to use Martin Buber's term, *sacred thous* who should be treated with dignity. When the customer is a category, you say, "I'm sorry, there is nothing more I can do for you." When the customer is a sacred thou, you scour the gate area for the lost teddy bear; you park his car when he's running late for a flight; you get out your credit card and pay for her ticket when she's lost her purse; and, yes, you even take him off the streets and give him a job. In exercising this form of leadership, Southwest has found that people become healthier, wiser, freer, and more human.

### A Community That Relates to the Whole Person

Most of us know that it's impossible to completely shut out our personal lives when we come to work and to turn off our work lives when we go home. Leaders understand that people bring every aspect of their humanness to the workplace. That is why the work and personal lives of Southwest employees are so closely integrated. The lines are always blurred between the two. Southwest recognizes that one dimension of a person's life is affected by all others and discourages people from compartmentalizing their lives. Sandra Bogan, one of Southwest's original flight attendants, described how well she and her family were taken care of during her son's illness. Her son, Tony, had leukemia and, during the first of his two bone marrow transplants, she and Tony lived in Houston for six months. Southwest Airlines gave Tony's father (Bogan's ex-husband) and Tony's girlfriend—in essence, the extended family—unlimited passes to fly back and forth to see Tony. Southwest reached out to help family members who had a personal need. Bogan feels that "there's not anything that I could ask for that Southwest wouldn't do. I'm well paid; I'm well taken care of; and I don't mind working a bit!"

### A Community That Cares

Leadership is moral in that it expresses and demonstrates a care and concern for the welfare of others. Through profitsharing, through its no-furlough policy, and through its stalwart defense of employees when customers are wrong, the company demonstrates its concern for the welfare of employees. Dale Foster, manager of standards/training of flight dispatch, told us a story about the Southwest art of caring: "My mother was sick. She called me and asked, 'Do you know someone by the name of Herb Kelleher?' I said, 'Yeah, he's the president of the airline. Why?' She said, 'I just got some flowers from the guy and I don't even know this man.'" Foster was taken aback. He had been out of town to visit her and didn't think that Kelleher and Barrett even knew he was gone, but they had sent his mom some flowers because she was sick. Foster continued, "She got two bunches of flowers from Southwest and it just blew her mind. She couldn't believe it. I called Colleen and I thanked her for it. I said, 'You know, in a little town in Northern Indiana, it's going to be the talk for the next year. Things like that just never happen.'"

The Southwest Employees Catastrophic Assistance Charity exemplifies how much employees care about each other. Formed through donations, recycling efforts, and creative fund-raising events and managed entirely by Southwest employees, the charity has given over $1 million to employees who have suffered serious illnesses, deaths in the family, accidents, and other catastrophic events. Sunny Divjak, manager of culture activities and a member of the committee that manages the fund, says, "It's run as a completely separate organization from Southwest Airlines. It's one of my favorite things here. We meet twice a month and we take all the applications we have and sometimes we even write a check on the spot! It makes me proud that

# ONE OF THE FINEST THINGS EVER

*In his final remarks in his Message to the Field a few years ago, Kelleher told Southwest Employees this:*

> When you're sitting around with your grandchildren, I want you to be able to tell them that being connected to Southwest Airlines was one of the finest things that ever happened to you in your entire life. I want you to be able to say, "Southwest Airlines ennobled and enriched my life; it made me better, and bigger, and stronger than I ever could have been alone."
>
> And if, indeed, that happens with your grandchildren, then that will be the greatest contribution that I could have made to Southwest Airlines and to its future.

our employees care enough about each other that they would donate to the charity and do extra work to raise money for it."

## A Community That Learns

Leaders are learners who teach. In order to equip employees to serve the common good, a company must become a learning community that taps into people's natural inquisitiveness. This means encouraging them to ask questions and challenge the system. Leaders understand that teaching people how to learn is much more important than conveying content. Yes, content is crucial, but in a world of warp-speed change it quickly becomes obsolete. Perhaps the most morally uplifting thing leaders can do for people is to help them learn how to learn. In doing so, people grow and become more wholly integrated, functional adults capable of equipping themselves to handle future challenges. This is based on the same philosophy that says, "If you give a person a fish, you feed him for a day. If you teach a person to fish, you feed him for a lifetime." The Day in the Field, Helping Hands, Walk a Mile, and other culture exchanges have all been designed to inspire organizational learning, sharing, and improving.

## A Community That Is Generative and Self-Renewing

Leadership is self-renewing in that leaders demonstrate a deep sense of concern for the future of the community. Leaders invest themselves in others to help them become the next generation of leaders. Leaders help people grow and mature so that they can lead big, enriched, and full lives. In this sense, leaders are as concerned with what happens to people in the process of affecting change as they are with the changes themselves. Perhaps the best example at Southwest Airlines is the story of Colleen Barrett. Barrett started working with Herb Kelleher in 1967 as a legal secretary in his San Antonio law firm. Her leadership and superlative organizational skills are surpassed only by her passion for keeping the Southwest Spirit alive and well and for nurturing the next generation of leaders. Today she is the company's corporate secretary and executive v.p. for customers who oversees a group of five hundred people in seven departments.

# LEADERSHIP INFLUENCES CHANGE

There is no doubt: leaders are in the business of change. Driven by curiosity, opportunity, outrage, and even fear, leaders make changes that are both deliberate and meaningful, that come from a gut-level desire to make a difference. Leaders affect change by helping people act on their expressed and unexpressed needs. They help transform people's needs into hopes, expectations, and ultimately demands.

Although the changes that leaders intend are not always successful, they are always aimed at achieving broad human purposes that reflect the common good—not just the common good of the people who make up Southwest's corporate community, but the common good of the nation as a whole. Whether you define the "common good" as the single father who can now afford to visit his children on weekends, the Southwest employee who sees work as a morally uplifting crusade, the family that is grateful for the comfort of the Ronald McDonald House, the Boeing employee who works on the assembly line of the Boeing 737, or the cities of America that have reaped the social and economic benefits of the company's low-fare, high-frequency service, Southwest Airlines has contributed to advancing the welfare of individuals, organizations, and societies. In doing so, Southwest has not only changed the U.S. airline industry, it has fundamentally changed the way people think about doing business.

**CHAPTER 23**

# GO NUTS!

When we first talked about writing a book about Southwest Airlines, we decided that it wouldn't be another corporate biography. We wanted it to be a book that gave people tools they could apply in their personal lives as well as in their businesses. Our hope is that you have found in *NUTS!* an interesting story about a fascinating company and some principles to enrich your life and make your business more successful. We understand that Southwest Airlines' culture and approach to doing business may not be for everyone. Yet there are ingredients in Southwest's recipe for success that can work for you regardless of the kind of person you are or the type of business you are in. We think there is a little bit of Southwest Airlines in all of us screaming to get out. We also think more of us would express our Southwest-like tendencies if only we had permission, from ourselves and from our organizations.

The malady of our time is that so many people have lost their sense of meaning, purpose, and dignity. Alienated and empty, these people go home exhausted and dehumanized. We are not suggesting that work can or should completely replace the emptiness many people feel in their lives. But work does play a significant role in determining our level of fulfillment. Our hope is that the story of Southwest Airlines' success will give you and your organization permission for new patterns of behavior, for living more freely, for new hopes translated into a new vision, and, ultimately, for a new organization.

## FIND A PURPOSE YOU'RE CRAZY ABOUT

There are no heights to which the human spirit can't rise when people see that their work has meaning and purpose. People *want* to make a difference. They *want* to know how they contribute to the success of an organization. When we know that our work is meaningful, we still have energy at the end of the day because the sanctity of our labor has been affirmed. The people of Southwest Airlines don't work there just because the company is thriving; they work there because they see how the company's fight to survive is tied up in their own need to make a difference in society. They know that their corporate philosophy of frequent, low-cost flights allows people all over the United States to do things they never dreamed of doing. Many of the people who work for Southwest Airlines feel that they are engaged in a purpose that reflects their own vision and values.

Find a purpose that you're crazy about, a purpose to which you are willing to give the totality of who you are, and who knows? Your work may become an avocation. You may recapture your idealism in a world that often gives little reason for being idealistic. You may even find a purpose so captivating that it awakens the collective energies of the people with whom you work and inspires them to soar.

## MAKE YOUR LIFE AND WORK AN ADVENTURE

Don't fall into the trap of believing that the vivaciousness and enthusiasm demonstrated at Southwest Airlines are beyond your reach. That's nonsense! The people of Southwest Airlines live above the level of mediocrity because they are adventurous and playful. They work at turning routine into festivity. They get more out of life because they *expect* more out of life. They find extraordinary qualities in people because they take the time every day to rediscover the people they know. Like treasures waiting to be discovered, people will teach us all kinds of things that make life exciting if we are only willing to explore. One of the reasons people gravitate toward Herb Kelleher is that, around him, life is adventurous. For Kelleher life is a process of discovery. When you're always learning something new it's difficult to get bored or burned out.

So, decide today to become more curious, interested, and inquisitive. If you've been sleepwalking through life, wake up and start seeking new challenges. Refuse to settle for mediocrity in yourself or in others. Make every moment count by giving yourself permission to work with fewer inhibitions and live just a little bit more adventurously. What have you got to lose? If you work in a company that doesn't seem to tolerate nuts, maybe it's time to lead by example and start a revolution in the part of the organization that you control or influence. If you've been there and done that, maybe it's time to muster the courage to leave. Life is too short and we work too much of it to be emotionally and spiritually dead.

## BELIEVE IN PEOPLE AND THEY WILL BELIEVE IN THEMSELVES

Southwest Airlines has demonstrated an age-old truth: When you believe in people, they will rise to greatness. Our hope is that this book inspires you to step up to one of the greatest challenges a leader ever faces: helping people believe in themselves. People who have self-confidence develop the creativity to dream, the boldness to venture into the unknown and pursue their dreams, and the courage and persuasiveness to summon help along the way. Because affirmation runs deep within the organization and young people with little experience are given big opportunities, Southwest has created a corporate environment in which people have a strong sense of self. We are talking about an authentic, deeply felt kind of affirmation that causes people to see their strengths more vividly and trust their capabilities. When this happens, the effect on the organization can be dramatic. People rise to the occasion and take charge of the future because they believe that they can shape and mold it through their own efforts.

Look beyond the surface and find the undeveloped potential in the people with whom you work. Take a moment to see them not as they are, but as they can be. When you do, our bet is that two things will happen. First, they will act and perform according to the image you have of them, and, second, your faith in the potential of the human spirit will be restored.

## DON'T TAKE YOURSELF TOO SERIOUSLY

Most of us take ourselves too seriously. When we're wrapped up in protecting our egos and holding onto life too tightly, it's easy to become rigid and boring. Think about the people you have the most fun being around. Are they people who can laugh at themselves? Are they people who can make you laugh by making light of their idiosyncrasies? Do yourself, your family, and your organization a big favor— lighten up. If Southwest's corporate culture teaches us anything, it's that employees and customers will love us for creating an environment where they can have fun. But the permission they get to loosen up must come from our example. There is a spirit of liberty and freedom among people who don't take themselves too seriously. If you haven't experienced it yet, take a cue from the people of Southwest. Check your ego at the door and quit pretending that you're always calm, cool, and collected. If you do something stupid, foolish, or clumsy—and you will—it won't be the end of the world. Laugh about it and move on.

## DARE TO DREAM

Dreams stimulate our senses and awaken our entrepreneurial spirit. They fuel our imagination, release our creative energy, and draw forth a deep sense of commitment to action. It's difficult to take action toward something you can't envision. It's almost impossible to envision something you don't have permission to dream about. People who lose their dreams have nothing to hope for and, without hope, they have nothing to live for. Dreams help us experience the richness of life.

There will always be people who respond to your dreams by saying, "You gotta be kidding! Are you *nuts*?" Remember Albert Einstein, though, who said, "Great spirits have always encountered violent opposition from mediocre minds." Dreams come true because people refuse to let disappointment permanently discourage or derail them. The story of Southwest Airlines is a story about unconventional people with an irrational faith in their ability to make a dream come true—a dream that eventually changed the course of aviation history. An indomitable spirit of perseverance and the raw determination to stay the course have a lot to do with Southwest's success. Those of us who admit we don't dream enough would do well to remember that most significant achievements in this world begin in the minds of those who have the courage to follow their dreams.

## BE YOURSELF

With the people of Southwest Airlines you get a refreshing dose of authenticity. Overcome the temptation to put on an act for others, particularly people you want to impress. Be yourself and express your individuality. It is the greatest asset you bring to every business and personal relationship. At the same time, let the individuality of others energize you rather than make you defensive and insecure.

## DARE TO BE DIFFERENT

Southwest Airlines is a legendary business today because its people dared to be different. It made room for the untried, the unpredictable, and the unexpected. When people who think differently hit you with a fresh idea that makes sense, go for it! If it bombs, learn from it. If it works, celebrate like crazy. But in either case, remember to keep looking for the new, the unconventional, the unfamiliar way of doing things. Not only is this a key to success in a world of change, it's a lot less stressful and more exciting way to live. Daring to be unconventional certainly has its risks, but, as Southwest has learned, the financial and spiritual payoffs can be immense.

## PURSUE LOVE BEFORE TECHNIQUES

In our quick-fix, instant-gratification society, we have fallen in love with techniques. Whether it's losing weight, toning the abs, or motivating a work force that is shell-shocked from being downsized, we want techniques that are simple, fast, and effective. Yet the technique-driven business system we have created in this country is failing to inspire people. Techniques have little meaning for those who have not been inspired to use them. This is why so many TQM, empowerment, and reengineering efforts fail. There is no spirit, no heart, and no love behind the techniques. Without love, techniques are simply another form of sophisticated manipulation with which we exploit people. If there is an overarching reason for Southwest Airlines' success, it is that the company has spent far more time since 1971 focused on loving people than on the development of new management techniques. The tragedy of our time is that we've got it backwards. We've learned to love techniques and use people. This is one of the reasons more and more people feel alienated, empty, and dehumanized at work. Many organizations today would be surprised at how much more people would be willing to give of themselves if only they felt loved.

*The tragedy of our time is that we've got it backwards. We've learned to love techniques and use people.*

When people feel loved, they love in return. Often this love is expressed in hard work, in kindness and generosity, and in sacrificing self to serve others. Sometimes it is even manifested in a willingness to genuinely and enthusiastically embrace new techniques. Love is the most important emotion there is because it's the one that allows us to enjoy—even to consider—all aspects of life. But we'll warn you up front. If a spirit of love and passion is going to pervade your life and your organization, you must work at it. It may start with getting over the outdated idea that expressing love is for wimps. It might even start with making yourself just a little more vulnerable around the people with whom you work. We're not suggesting that you give up the fight for good management tools and techniques. They are crucial to your success. We are simply saying, resist the temptation to let these things usurp love.

## CHOOSE SERVICE OVER SELF-INTEREST

Another key to Southwest's success is that its employees, starting with Herb Kelleher, see themselves as servants of the people. They seek to serve rather than to be served because they are most interested in the

# THE RESULTS SPEAK FOR THEMSELVES

*By practicing the principles outlined in this book, Southwest Airlines has achieved a phenomenal track record. Do these principles work? The results speak for themselves.*

## Southwest Airlines' Growth

|  | 1971 | 1996 |
| --- | --- | --- |
| Size of fleet | 4 | 243 |
| Number of employees at year-end | 195 | 22,944 |
| Number of customers carried | 108,554 | 49,621,504 |
| Number of cities served | 3 | 50 |
| Number of trips flown | 6,051 | 748,634 |
| Total operating revenues | $2,133,000 | $3,406,170 |
| Net income (loss) | ($3,753,000) | $207,337,000 |
| Stockholders' equity | $3,318,000 | $1,648,312,000 |
| Total assets | $22,083,000 | $3,723,479,000 |

freedom and welfare of others. America would be a lot better off and people would be a lot more fulfilled if we could only learn that true happiness is not found in self-interest and self-service, but rather in giving ourselves to purposes that transcend self. This country needs bold images of leaders who dignify the role of servant. Where do we begin? The examples at Southwest Airlines would tell us to start by listening more than we talk, by taking action based on what we learn, by leaning on our role as models more than on the power of our titles, by doing what we ask others to do, and by giving more than we take.

## MAKE SPIRIT YOUR COMPETITIVE ADVANTAGE

Southwest Airlines possesses very few unique technologies or material assets, yet the company is unique in the way it uses its assets. In an industry where every carrier has access to the same kind of equipment, Southwest's real competitive advantage is the spirit of its people. This is why we think it will be very difficult to replicate Southwest Airlines in its entirety. Those who come close will have focused more on what Southwest has done to unleash the human spirit than on its techniques for turning airplanes quickly.

In doing the research for *NUTS!* it wasn't surprising to see that the overwhelming majority of articles in the business press focus on the operations of Southwest Airlines, not on the spirit of its people. Perhaps this is because spirit is hard to define; operational techniques are much more tangible and therefore easier to learn and replicate. Dealing with the people issues is often messy and complex. We suspect this is why many people choose to spend their time on the tangibles. Unfortunately, America can't afford it anymore. What makes this country different from any other is our spirit. If America is willing to nourish the human spirit, our nation will release the tremendous energies of its people. The result will be unsurpassed levels of productivity, a better quality of life, and a higher standard of living.

## THE CHOICE IS YOURS, THE TIME IS NOW

The people of Southwest Airlines have shown us that we can laugh and celebrate more often, pursue purposes that give us a sense of heroism, simplify things without invalidating ourselves or our work, take more risks and think more unconventionally, express the off-the-wall part of ourselves more freely, and live and work in a way that is lovelier and more loving. This is why they are so alive. It is also why they are often accused of being nuts.

There will always be those who lounge in the safety of convention, who criticize you for daring to live life authentically in order to justify themselves. These are the same people who are off seeking permission while the rest of us are pursuing our dreams.

At this point you have a choice. You can treat this book as an entertaining story that you will refer to from time to time, or you can energize your life and work by going NUTS.

# EPILOGUE

# WHEN VISION BECOMES THE BOSS

It's fun and inspiring to read about the courage and charisma of very successful people. Of course, when a colorful personality is so tightly associated with the success of an organization, the question then becomes, "What happens when that person is gone?" This is the question the press has been asking for years about Herb Kelleher. Is there life for Southwest Airlines after Herb? Can Southwest survive without his brilliance and dynamic personality? Never mind that these questions imply a false notion—that leadership revolves around the Lone Ranger, alias Kelleher. What's the answer? *Is* there life for Southwest Airlines after Herb? We think so. Here's why.

First, the people of Southwest Airlines have an uncompromising dedication to a cause—a movement—they deeply believe in. Yes, they love Herb Kelleher. His charisma, his intellect, his charm, and his love for life and people make Herb one of the most extraordinary characters in American business today. But Southwest employees are not loyal only to Herb the man; they are devoted to the movement and the vision he helped inspire. It's true that Herb personifies much of what the company stands for. But the purpose, the culture, and the spirit of Southwest Airlines transcend Herb Kelleher's personality.

Second, Southwest Airlines has raised customer consciousness across America. As the standard-bearer of low fares, Southwest has made it possible for people all over the country to travel more conveniently and more affordably. Whether Herb Kelleher is there or not, the people of Southwest Airlines have too much integrity to let the American people down. Driven by a sense of duty, new leaders waiting in the wings at all levels of the organization will emerge to continue Southwest's legendary service at low cost and protect what they helped create.

Third, the model of leadership that we've presented shows that the success of Southwest Airlines is a collaborative effort. Kelleher has surrounded himself with many very capable people who run the airline today. They have been groomed in the fires of competition and have seen the airline through good times and bad. When we asked Jack Welch if there is life for Southwest after Herb, he said, "There has to be, or there wouldn't have been the success over this period of time. You can't be twenty-five thousand people and have the success they have without lots of great people out making it happen every day. The institution is infinitely more than one person." Boeing's CEO, Phil Condit, had a slightly different answer: "Southwest has the capability of augering into the ground if, when Herb disappears, they believe they can't fly anymore. On the other hand, they can do superbly if they believe they were doing this thing all along. It's what people believe that's going to make the difference."

In the Academy Award–winning movie *Braveheart*, William Wallace struggles to help the Scottish people believe enough in themselves and the cause of freedom to stand against the formidable powers of their English oppressors. In the end, Wallace dies for the cause, but in the wake of his death the people of Scotland develop the courage to stand together in the fight for freedom. Their commitment and loyalty were not to Wallace the man, but rather to the cause that he helped inspire. Even though the man was heroic, the cause outlived him.

A worthy cause is always bigger than the individuals who create it. Time will have to be the judge, but we suspect that Kelleher's departure from Southwest Airlines could have the same effect on employees. The people of Southwest Airlines are a courageous and capable bunch. They know in their hearts that they have what it takes to carry on the legacy left by Kelleher and others. They also know that the cause is worth fighting for. Together, these two beliefs create a powerful force that can give Southwest Airlines the momentum it needs long after Kelleher has left the scene.

# NOTES

Quotes from current and former Southwest Airlines employees and business partners are from personal interviews or survey responses unless noted here.

*Page*   **Chapter 1: Nuts? . . . You Decide**

4   ***The company has been praised for its leadership and customer service:*** See, for example, Chip R. Bell, *Customers As Partners: Building Relationships That Last*; Peter Lynch and John Rothchild, *Beating the Street: The Best-Selling Author of One Up on Wall Street Shows You How to Pick Winning Stocks and Mutual Funds*; James Ott and Raymond E. Neidl, *Airline Odyssey: The World's Turbulent Flight into the Future*; Tom Peters, *The Pursuit of WOW! Every Person's Guide to Topsy-Turvy Times*; Betsy Sanders, *Fabled Service: Ordinary Acts, Extraordinary Outcomes*; Michael Treacy and Fred Wiersema, *The Discipline of Market Leaders: Choose Your Customers, Narrow Your Focus, Dominate Your Market*; Richard Whiteley and Diane Hessan, *Customer Centered Growth.*

5   ***Investment guru Peter Lynch:*** Lynch and Rothchild, *Beating the Street*, p. 185.

5–6   ***According to Patrick Murphy:*** Remarks before the Chicago '95 Conference, Chicago Hilton and Towers, November 2, 1995, by Patrick Murphy, deputy assistant secretary for aviation and international affairs, U.S. Department of Transportation.

6   ***In 1993 the DOT . . . found:*** Randall D. Bennett and James M. Craun, "The Airline Deregulation Evolution Continues: The Southwest Effect,"p. 1.

7   ***The company services twice the number of passengers per employee:*** Whiteley and Hessan, *Customer Centered Growth.*

7   ***For equivalent aircraft stage lengths:*** Stage lengths are the average distance a carrier flies in its route system. When determining costs based on distance, short distances cost more because it costs just as much to reserve and ticket customers, take off and land (e.g., in fuel burn and airport fees), maintain facilities, and advertise for shorthaul flights as for longhaul flights.

7   ***Southwest is considered . . . one of the best companies to work for:*** Robert Levering and Milton Moskowitz, *The 100 Best Companies to Work for in America.*

8   ***Southwest Airlines is the only carrier in the United States to win the industry's "Triple Crown":*** DOT tracks performance in all three categories for U.S. major carriers (baggage handling, on-time performance, and consumer

complaints). When an airline achieves the highest ratings in all three categories in a given month or year, it is said to have achieved a "Triple Crown"— a triple win, in other words.

8    ***In terms of the number of flights operated:*** Gary Stoller, "The World's Safest Airline," p. 80. Southwest was also named a charter member of the International Airline Passengers Association's Honor Roll of Airlines as one of the world's safest airlines.

10    ***Roy Spence, president of GSD&M:*** Spence has known Kelleher since 1974, when the two were running congressional campaigns for opposing candidates. Spence ran an ad campaign that basically said, "Are you going to let the ten most powerful people in your community [like Herb Kelleher] handpick your next U.S. Congressman?" To the surprise of many, Spence's underdog candidate won the race. Nevertheless, Kelleher took an immediate liking to Roy's spirit and enthusiasm. The two have been friends ever since.

## Chapter 2: Goliath Meets David

15    ***They were also far enough apart:*** As an intrastate carrier, the new upstart would not be subject to the jurisdiction of the federal Civil Aeronautics Board (CAB), which regulated the economic aspects of interstate air transportation until it was abolished in the early 1980s by the federal Airline Deregulation Act. The Federal Aviation Administration (FAA) regulates the safety aspects of all air transportation.

16    ***On November 27, 1967, Kelleher filed Southwest's application:*** The application was made with the state (Texas Aeronautics Commission) and not the federal agency (the Civil Aeronautics Board) because Southwest wasn't going to fly outside of Texas. See previous note this chapter.

16    ***The day after the TAC voted:*** Unlike in California, where interstate airlines were not authorized to participate in administrative proceedings involving intrastate carriers, Texas statutes allow interstate airlines to be intervenors in an intrastate proceeding.

17    ***Braniff, Continental, and Texas International argued that the markets Southwest wanted to serve were already saturated:*** What the major carriers didn't understand was that Southwest's cost structure and low fares would enable people to fly who could never have afforded to fly previously. This means that the markets entered by Southwest are expanded.

18    ***I will continue to represent . . . and I'll postpone any legal fees:*** How could Kelleher afford to do this? The answer, very simply, is long hours and little sleep. The legal community thinks it's extraordinary when a lawyer bills a couple of thousand hours a year. Kelleher was putting in twice that much between Southwest Airlines and the rest of his legal practice, simultaneously.

21    ***He decided on a writ of mandamus:*** A writ of mandamus is an extraordinary writ, or order, issued from a court to an official to compel performance of an act that the law recognizes as an absolute duty, as distinct from acts that may

be at an official's discretion. It was a very unusual procedure to invoke in Southwest's situation, almost without precedent.

22    ***Through private investors ... Southwest was bleeding money:*** By the end of 1972, after eighteen months of operation, the company had lost over $5 million.

26    ***The amendment means that Southwest cannot advertise:*** However, because of Southwest's low fares and convenient schedule some customers bypass Wright Amendment restrictions by combining two or more scheduled flights. This is the customer's prerogative and, although Southwest does not promote the practice, if customers initiate an inquiry it does carefully advise that they will have to deplane, claim their luggage, and then recheck themselves and their bags at the intermediate destination.

## Chapter 3: The Battle Heats Up

29    ***King, Kelleher ... launched a campaign to garner local support:*** Initially, many in the business community were reluctant to assist Southwest in the Valley because TI had threatened to pull out if Southwest started service. The Southwest team finally persuaded Harlingen furniture-store owner and former mayor George Young to support its proposal. Young gave them the names of other business owners throughout the Valley, and Southwest soon developed a network of supporters.

29    ***TI didn't get its restraining order:*** On October 28, 1976, Judge William R. Meyers announced that the TAC order granting Southwest Airlines authority to serve the Rio Grande Valley was sustained.

30    ***To do this, Southwest applied the concept of price elasticity:*** The economic concept of "price elasticity" as manifested in the airline business is illustrated by charging 50 percent less than the normal fare but gaining a 125 percent increase in customers as a result of the lower tariff. Because its fare per passenger goes down 50 percent on a given flight but the number of passengers increases by 125 percent on that same flight, the airline's gross revenue is increased.

33    ***The plane became a financial burden:*** With no money for appeal, this would be the only case Kelleher would lose for Southwest in over ten years of litigation.

34    ***Franklin, like Muse, was a man of action:*** Barrett and Kelleher are quick to point out that, although the authoritarian style that Muse, Franklin, and the original station managers used to get things done wouldn't wash in today's environment, they were exactly the right people to have for that time in the airline's history.

35    ***The ten-minute turn became Southwest's signature:*** The ten-minute turn also showed Southwest that productivity can pay big dividends in terms of reducing costs. Today, because of airport congestion, larger aircraft, and cargo and mail loads, Southwest turns planes in fifteen to twenty minutes. If Southwest further increased its turn times by only ten minutes, it would require twenty-five more airplanes at approximately $30 million apiece to

operate its present schedule. At an interest rate of 10 percent, the added yearly cost of twenty-five additional airplanes would be $75 million.

### Chapter 4: A Maverick Emerges

39 ***Howard Putnam, the former group vice president:*** On March 28, 1978, Lamar Muse resigned as president and chief executive officer. Herbert D. Kelleher was appointed interim president, chief executive officer, and chairman of the board. On July 25, 1978, Southwest's board of directors unanimously elected Howard D. Putnam to be president and CEO, and Putnam came on board August 21, 1978. The directors asked Kelleher to remain permanent chairman of the board.

### Chapter 5: Flying in the Face of Conformity

48 ***Early on . . . "noninterlining" traveler:*** As a noninterlining carrier, Southwest does not make reservations, issue tickets, or transfer baggage for travelers who connect to other carriers. For example, a customer cannot make a reservation from San Diego to Phoenix, then connect to another carrier for Phoenix to New York through Southwest Airlines' reservations system.

48 ***Howard Putnam, then Southwest's president and CEO:*** On September 22, 1981, Howard D. Putnam announced his resignation to become president and chief operating officer of Braniff International. Southwest's board of directors asked Kelleher to serve as acting president and chief executive officer while continuing as chairman of the board. The board of directors announced on February 23, 1982, that Kelleher had agreed to serve, on a permanent basis, as president, chief executive officer, and chairman of the board of Southwest Airlines.

52 ***Phil Condit . . . uses the concept of "average velocity":*** Condit was inspired by *The Machine That Changed the World*, by James Womack, Daniel Jones, and Daniel Roos.

54 ***From the start . . . it can bring fares down:*** A 1993 Department of Transportation study found that the overall reason industry average prices declined in relation to the Standard Industry Fare Level (SIFL—a biannual pricing index tracking the lowest unrestricted coach fare in each market since July 1, 1977) is the low fares in Southwest's markets (Bennett and Craun, "Airline Deregulation Evolution Continues").

55 ***Sticking with the 737 series:*** In 1997, Southwest will launch Boeing's newest aircraft in the 737 family—the 737-700. This aircraft will expand Southwest's arsenal and provide the company with substantial flexibility. With the range to fly transcontinental routes, the 737-700 enables Southwest to enter longer-haul markets if necessary. Doing so would cause Southwest to supplement, rather than supplant, its core strategy. However, it would not surprise us to see the company take on a competitor in the longerhaul markets that has challenged Southwest on some of its shorthaul routes. Kelleher's position is very clear: "Even with respect to our core strategy, we

have to be alert and creative to take advantage of the opportunities that exist. We plan to stay within our niche. We don't want to visit our arsenal of long-range planes on anyone, but if we have to, we will. And we've got the capability." By operating only the Boeing 737, Southwest has been able to tightly control costs; this could potentially be a key competitive factor if Southwest enters the longhaul markets with its traditionally low fares.

57    ***If passenger boardings . . . Positively Outrageous Service:*** For a discussion of the basics, see T. Scott Gross, *Positively Outrageous Service.*

### Chapter 6: "Professionals" Need Not Apply

64    ***When Kelleher . . . charged the People Department:*** This is the department that other organizations usually call human resources or personnel.

64    ***"Terminal professionalism":*** C. W. Metcalf and Roma Felible, *Lighten Up: Survival Skills for People under Pressure.*

67    ***As "The High Priest of Ha Ha":*** Kenneth Labich, "Is Herb Kelleher America's Best CEO?"

67    ***Southwest has tailored:*** Targeted Selection is a selection system developed by Development Dimensions International, Bridgeville, Pennsylvania. For more about Southwest's interviewing and hiring practices, see Levering and Moskowitz, *The 100 Best Companies to Work for in America.*

71    ***Yes, we occasionally receive complaints from Customers:*** Several years ago, Southwest Airlines decided to capitalize the words *Customers* and *Employees* in all correspondence to honor these groups and note their pivotal role in the company's success. Today, the company has extended this practice to other key terms (for example, *People* and *Company* when referring to Southwest). Any quotations from Southwest publications and documents have preserved this style.

### Chapter 7: Kill the Bureaucracy

74    ***On November 13, 1990:*** When Chicago's Midway Airlines went into bankruptcy, Southwest got into a bidding war with Northwest Airlines for Midway's assets. Unwilling to pay premium rates, Southwest lost out. Northwest quickly acquired the lease on Midway's gates, but decided not to buy the rest of the assets, causing Midway Airlines to fold. However, Southwest soon discovered a loophole in the lease, whereby the City of Chicago could allow another carrier to use unoccupied gates. This was particularly good news because, at this time, Northwest was not using its Midway gates.

75    ***The company was able to capitalize:*** Southwest eventually worked out a deal in which it traded Northwest Airlines some surplus airplanes for the leases on the Midway gates.

78    ***As in small companies, communication is . . . always on a first-name basis:*** Kelleher is known for his talent for remembering names—by the thousands.

On many occasions we've heard employees say, "He only met me once, and when I saw him again a year later, he remembered my name." The combination of a photographic memory and a genuine love for people explains his uncanny ability to recall names.

83    *A Wall Street analyst recalls having lunch:* Labich, "Is Herb Kelleher America's Best CEO?" p. 4.

84    *When we look back at the last twenty years: Strategic Investment Newsletter* 11(1), p. 1 (published by Agora, Inc., Baltimore, Md.).

90    *In the beginning, Southwest employees*: David Vice, vice-chairman of Northern Telecom, has said, "The nineties will be a decade in a hurry; a nanosecond culture. There will be only two kinds of managers: the quick and the dead" (Tom Peters, *Liberation Management: Necessary Disorganization for the Nanosecond Nineties*, p. 59).

### Chapter 8: Act Like an Owner

100    *Profitsharing . . . is an expense:* Leigh Strope, "Kelleher: Southwest Will Stay on Top," p. 2.

103–4  *I think any company that's trying to play in the 1990s:* Noel Tichy and Sherman Stratford, *Control Your Destiny or Someone Else Will: Lessons in Mastering Change—The Principles Jack Welch Is Using to Revolutionize General Electric*, p. 305.

107    *Ten years is unheard-of . . . the pilots agreed to freeze their wages:* The amount of stock a pilot can purchase depends on his or her seniority on the date the contract was signed. Essentially, the most senior employees get options to purchase about ten thousand shares over a ten-year period.

108    *If you assign people heavy responsibilities:* Price Pritchett, *Firing Up Commitment during Organizational Change*, p. 14.

### Chapter 9: Learn Like Crazy

112    *Arthur Schlesinger, Jr., sums up: The Cycles of American History*, p. 11.

### Chapter 10: Don't Fear Failure

136    *The spirit of adventure is the fuel:* Doug Hall, *Jump Start Your Brain*, p. 49.

138    *Customers gain the convenience of ticketless:* Ticketless travel also allows customers to book their reservations individually. Direct-access booking means that a customer can call Southwest Airlines on a personal computer via the Internet, book a reservation, pay by credit card, and just show up at the gate.

### Chapter 11: One Great Big Family

144    **Fortune *ranked Southwest number one:* The factors used to measure corporate reputations in *Fortune* magazine's thirteenth annual survey were

quality of management; quality of products or services; innovativeness; long-term investment value; financial soundness; ability to attract, develop, and keep talented people; responsible use of the community and the environment; and use of corporate assets. *Fortune* surveyed 395 companies in 41 industries and ranked Southwest Airlines number one in the airline industry and forty-second in the cross-industry comparison (Rahul Jacob, "Corporate Reputations"; Anne B. Fisher, "Where Companies Rank").

## Chapter 12: Keeping the Spirit Alive

159  ***In organizations where relationships are based on covenants:*** In *Leadership Is an Art*, Max De Pree distinguishes between contractual and covenantal relationships. In a contractual relationship, employees operate out of a fair day's work for a fair day's pay; this is a transactional paradigm or worldview. Contractual relationships foster compliance. In contrast, covenantal relationships are built on commitment—a promise between leaders and followers—and rest on a shared belief in similar ideas, values, goals, and philosophy.

159  ***Southwest is more than just a successful organization:*** Thomas Sergiovanni has noted that all organizations have cultures, but not all organizations are communities. To think of an organization "as a community suggests a kind of connectedness among members that resembles what is found in a family, a neighborhood, or some other closely knit group, where bonds tend to be familial or even sacred" (*Moral Leadership: Getting to the Heart of School Improvement*, p. 47). In the organizations with which we have consulted over the years, few corporate cultures compare to the community or sense of connectedness we've experienced at Southwest.

164  ***Leaders create cultures:*** Edgar Schein, *Organizational Culture and Leadership: A Dynamic View*, p. 313.

164–5  ***Every family, every college:*** De Pree, *Leadership Is an Art*, p. 72.

## Chapter 13: The Art of Celebrating Milestones

177  ***Seduced by the mentality that says business:*** In his 1969 classic, *The Feast of Fools*, Harvey Cox observes that we have purchased prosperity at the expense of losing our own souls. Cox suggests that many people have lost the vital elements of life—the capacity for genuine revelry and joyous celebration. It strikes us that what Cox asserts may be more true today than when he made his case almost thirty years ago.

186  ***Celebrations nourish the spirit of an organization:*** Cathy DeForest, "The Art of Conscious Celebration: A New Concept for Today's Leaders," p. 224.

186  ***Celebration is not always festive:*** Katie Soles defines a celebration as a "deliberate intervention, only sometimes festive, often solemn, always meaningful, that honors and respects the culture and spirit of the organization" ("The Mourning After: The Use of Conscious Celebration during Downsizing," p. 2).

### Chapter 14:  Celebrating People with Big Hearts

190   *Celebration makes the spirit of the organization visible:* Soles, "The Mourning After," p. 2.

192   *Each recipient is invited:* A positive-space pass guarantees you a seat on the flight, as opposed to flying on a space-available basis.

198   *Whether the event is big or small:* The three roles—imagineer, artist, and evocator—are from DeForest, "Conscious Celebration."

### Chapter 16:  LUV

216   *We are interested in people who externalize:* James Campbell Quick, "Creating an Organizational Culture: Herb's Hand at Southwest Airlines," p. 52.

217   *The greatest disease in the West today:* Mother Teresa, *A Simple Path*, p. 79.

223   *Love starts in the heart:* Ken Blue, *Healing Spiritual Abuse*, p. 137.

### Chapter 17:  Compassion for the Community

234   *Love chooses . . . service:* Peter Block, *Stewardship: Choosing Service over Self-Interest*, p. 9.

236   *The Grinch:* Jonathan Eig, "The Grinch Tried to Steal Christmas, but the People of Dallas Swiped It Back."

### Chapter 18:  Unconventional Advertising

248   *"Malice in Dallas" is now an epic:* The media had a field day with Malice in Dallas. For months leading up to the event and on the actual day of reckoning, the *Wall Street Journal* and hundreds of newspapers across the United States ran articles, and the local TV stations, plus ABC, NBC, CNN, and the BBC, covered the event. The story made it around the world: Southwest's executive v.p. for corporate services, John Denison, read about it in Singapore, and Bob Joedicke, formerly of Shearson Lehman Brothers, saw it on television in Tel Aviv.

249   *People do not buy:* Jay Conrad Levinson, *Guerrilla Marketing Excellence: The 50 Golden Rules for Business Success*, p. 11.

257   *Barrett and Nunnery were discussing arrangements:* It didn't take long for the award of Southwest's making to catch on. In 1992 Southwest earned its first *annual* Triple Crown, and by that time the designation was well established. In February 1997 the industry learned that Southwest had won it, on an annual basis, for five years in a row.

258   *With the Triple Crown . . . Southwest playfully and publicly recognized its people:* The advertising value of the Triple Crown is important, but the

company sees its primary significance to be the inspiration it gives employees to excel. Giving a name to their accomplishment set a specific service standard that Southwest employees could strive to achieve. The company's recognition of their achievement inspires them to deliver top-notch service, month after month, year after year.

### Chapter 19: Customers Come Second

268    ***While Southwest Airlines CEO:*** Peters, *The Pursuit of WOW!* p. 165, as quoted in "Personal Glimpses," *Reader's Digest,* July 1995, p. 137.

270    ***Kelleher received another letter:*** Kelleher used to read every customer letter, but, as the company has grown, that is no longer possible. He does read everything that is addressed to him, and he takes a weekly sampling of letters from Customer Relations just to get a fix on what customers are saying.

270    ***Anybody can do it:*** The Triple Crown refers to statistics kept by the Department of Transportation for on-time flights, best baggage handling, and fewest customer complaints. It is essentially an airline's report card. No other carrier has won the coveted Triple Crown for even one month, let alone for five years in a row.

271    ***Many organizations will fail:*** Karl Albrecht, *The Only Thing That Matters: Bringing the Power of the Customer into the Center of Your Business,* p. 87 (emphasis his).

271    ***Whether you describe it as "legendary":*** See, for example, Chip R. Bell and Ron Zemke, *Managing Knock Your Socks Off Service*; Sanders, *Fabled Service*; Gross, *Positively Outrageous Service.*

271–2    ***The spirit of service that pervades:*** Albrecht, *The Only Thing That Matters,* p. 88.

275    ***Winston Churchill said:*** Sanders, *Fabled Service,* p. 105.

276    ***People are capable of the highest generosity:*** Ernest Becker, *The Denial of Death,* p. 6.

276    ***It also means, in Karl Albrecht's words:*** *The Only Thing That Matters,* p. 88.

280    ***Albert Schweitzer's observation:*** Peggy Anderson, *Quotes from Great Leaders,* p. 33.

### Chapter 20: Employees Come First

283    ***They lead by example and affect change:*** When we describe leadership, we are very purposeful in our use of the word *affect* versus *effect. Affect* means to influence, to change, and to touch the emotions of—this is the very essence of leadership. Leaders and collaborators influence (affect) change through a dynamic emotional commitment to each other and the cause that draws them together. Leadership does not produce change, as the word *effect* implies; instead, it influences transformation.

284    **Servant Leadership** *author Robert Greenleaf:* Servant Leadership: A Journey into the Nature of Legitimate Power and Greatness, p. 10.

284    *By watching others:* Block, *Stewardship*, p. 10.

285    *Communicate everything you can:* Sanders, *Fabled Service*, p. 1.

286    *A member of Southwest's frequent flier program:* The name was changed from the Company Club to Rapid Rewards in 1996.

289    *I can't anticipate all of the situations:* Charles A. Jaffe, "Moving Fast by Standing Still," p. 59.

292    *With a young family:* Todd Painter, "Frequent Flyer: Keith Harris, Founder, Technosource Consulting, Inc.," p. 120.

### Chapter 21: Leaders Leading Leaders

298    *LEADERSHIP is a dynamic relationship:* We are indebted to our longtime friend and colleague for his postindustrial definition of leadership. Joe has both challenged our thinking about a difficult subject and inspired many of the ideas developed in this chapter. For one of the most comprehensive critiques of the leadership literature, see Rost's *Leadership for the Twenty-First Century.* See note for page 283 for the significance of the word *affect.*

301    *Both Ridley and Rogge have been promoted:* In addition to their own partnership, Ridley and Rogge, in concert with their employees, their two advertising agencies, and their media-buying agency, have developed one of the most effective marketing and advertising efforts in the U.S. airline industry. Like their own relationship, the relationships Dave and Joyce have with these collaborators are very dynamic. During the various phases of developing a marketing and advertising campaign, representatives from any one of these groups will assume the interchangeable roles of leader and collaborator. What emerges is a conjunction of ideas that form the basis for the creative ads and fun promotional activities Southwest customers have grown to love and come to expect.

302    *Problems were always solved:* Lawrence Miller, *American Spirit: Visions of a New Corporate Culture,* p. 54.

303–4  *As John Gardner suggests:* On Leadership, pp. 1, 31.

### Chapter 22: Leadership from the Inside Out

316    *They view customers as ... sacred thous:* Martin Buber asserted that all relationships could be classified in terms of I-it relationships and I-thou relationships. In I-it relationships, people are objectified. They become things we label, categorize, and use to accomplish our goals. Buber contrasted these relationships with I-thou relationships. An I-thou relationship exists when people are treated as "sacred thous" (*I and Thou*).

# SOURCES

## INTERVIEWS

All interviews conducted by Kevin Freiberg or Jackie Freiberg from March 1995 to May 1996 unless otherwise noted. Number in parentheses indicates how many interviews, if more than one. An asterisk indicates an original employee.

### Employees (current and former)
Bailey, Rita, Director Employee Development.
Balfany, Mike, First Officer.
*Bardo, Joy, Senior Administrative Coordinator, Ground Operations.
*Barrett, Colleen C., Executive Vice President Customers and Corporate Secretary (12).
*Barron, Gary, Executive Vice President Operations.
*Bogan, Sandra, Flight Attendant.
Bordelon, Helen, Executive Assistant, Executive Office, interviewed by Wendy Paris.
*Bostic, C. J., Flight Attendant.
Boyd, Fawn, Employee Development Training Team Leader.
Boyter, Mark, Captain.
Bruce, Anne, Manager Employee Learning and Development.
Bruner, Ron, Reservations Agent.
Buckley, Matt, Director Central Baggage Services, Cargo, and Mail.
Campbell, Bruce, Flight Attendant.
Campbell, Laura, Customer Service Agent.
Cielak, Stan, Station Manager, Ground Operations.
*Cohn, Sam, Captain.
Denison, John, Executive Vice President Corporate Services.
Divjak, Sunny, Manager Culture Activities, interviewed by Wendy Paris.
Dowlearn, Julie, Executive Assistant, Ground Operations, interviewed by Wendy Paris.
*Druckamiller, Karson, Lead Shop Mechanic.
*Eldredge, Jim, Lead Stock Clerk, Ground Equipment.
*Force, Sandra, Flight Attendant.
*Franklin, Deborah, Flight Attendant.
*Goins, Mary, Flight Attendant.
Goodwin, Mark "Squidd," President, Ramp, Operations, and Provisioning Association.
*Gruslin, Brenda, Flight Attendant
Hardage, Ginger, Vice President Public Relations and Corporate Communications.
Jarvis, Art, Captain.
*Johnson, Dan, Dispatcher.
*Johnson, Scott, Dispatch Specialist.
Jones, Rod, Assistant Chief Pilot.
*Keith, Camille, Vice President Special Marketing.
*Kelleher, Herbert D., Chairman, President, and Chief Executive Officer (15).
Kelly, Gary, Vice President Finance and Chief Financial Officer.
*King, Rollin, Co-Founder and Board Member.

Lang, Chic, Captain.
*Lardon, Dennis, Director Flight Attendants.
*Lawrence, Bill, Ground Maintenance Mechanic.
Littenberg, Craig, Captain.
*Marcell, Charlie, Maintenance Controller.
*Martiniano, Frank, Operation Supervisor, Ground Operations.
Millard, Terry "Moose," Captain.
Miller, Ari, First Officer.
*Miller, Bill, Vice President Inflight Services.
*Mitchel, Mike, Operations Agent, Ground Operations.
Montague, Tonda, Director Employee Communications (3).
Montgomery, Bob, Director of Properties.
*Ordner, Karen, Travel Agency Administrative Coordinator.
Orgill, Pam, Flight Attendant.
Parker, James F., Vice President General Counsel.
Pettit, Kathy, Director Customers.
*Phelps, Sherry, Director Corporate Employment.
*Phillips, Ray, Lead Line Mechanic.
*Pinka, Linda, Flight Attendant.
*Puckett, Jerry, Lead Shop Mechanic.
Putnam, Howard, former President and Chief Executive Officer.
Reynolds, Tona, Flight Attendant (1986).
Ricks, Ron, Vice President Governmental Affairs.
Ridley, Dave, Vice President Marketing and Sales.
Rogge, Joyce, Vice President Advertising and Promotions.
Ruppel, Jim, Director Customer Relations.
Sartain, Libby, Vice President People.
Shuler, Vickie, Executive Assistant, Executive Office, interviewed by Wendy Paris.
*Stembridge, Deborah, Flight Attendant.
*Sturdevant, M. A., Flight Attendant.
Sullivan, Jeff, former Director People Development.
Tree, Jon, Chief Pilot.
Turner, Richard, Captain.
*Van Overschelde, Gene, Captain.
Vidal, Jack, former Vice President Maintenance and Engineering (deceased).
*Warrell, Carl, Station Manager.
Ways, Rodger, Captain.
Wenzell, Jim, Captain.
*Wilson, Willie, Manager Administration, Flight Operations.
Wimberly, Jim, Vice President Ground Operations (3).
Wright, Mickey, Captain.
Yeaton, Jim, Captain.

## Business Partners

Condit, Philip M., President and CEO, The Boeing Company.
Groseclose, Doug, Sales Director, The Boeing Company.
Kalahar, Tom, President and CEO, Camelot Communications.
Krivkovich, Peter, President, Cramer Krassalt.
McClure, Tim, Executive Vice President and Chief Creative Officer, GSD&M.
Milano, MaryEllen, Vice President and Account Director, GSD&M.
Spence, Roy, President, GSD&M (3).
Trabulsi, Judy, Executive Vice President/Media Director, GSD&M.
Welch, Jack, Chairman and CEO, General Electric.

### Other Interviews
Crandall, Robert L., Chairman and CEO, AMR Corporation/American Airlines.
Lewins, Steve, Analyst, Gruntal Investment Research.
Maldutis, Jr., Julius, Analyst, Salomon Brothers, Inc.

## SURVEY, INTERNAL INFORMATION, AND CONFIRMATION SOURCES
Ackerman, Debby, Associate General Counsel.
Carter, Laurie, Manager Rapid Rewards-Customer Relations.
Corona, Bobbi, Coordinator Corporate Information.
Devereaux, Wally, Houston Area Marketing Manager.
Donelson, Audy, Ground Operations.
Montague, Tonda, Director Employee Communications.
Rickard, Kathy, Executive Assistant, People Department.
Riley, Terry, Employee Communications Services Representative.
Romo, Tammy, Director Investor Relations.
Shubert, Jon, Manager Executive Office Communications.
Turnipseed, John, Director People Services.
Villalba, Naomi, Administration Specialist, Executive Office.
Yancey, Susan, Manager Corporate Information.

Also, respondents to written surveys sent to 102 Culture Committee members, 49 Station
     Managers, and 15 Provisioning Managers.


## INTERNAL SOUTHWEST AIRLINES' MATERIAL
*Annual Reports 1971–1995.*
*The Critical Difference* (video), 1991.
Culture Committee meeting minutes and reports.
*Employee Update* 1995–1996.
"Ground Operations Customer Service Principles and Practices."
*Halloween Tour* (video), 1995.
*Herb's Message to the Field* (videos), 1991–1996.
"Inventive Incentives: Keeping the Spirit Alive through Employee Recognition and Reward
     Programs."
Kelleher, Herb. "Commmencement of Hostilities" (letter to employees), August 30, 1994.
Kelleher, Herb. "Letter to Employees," March 8, 1993.
Kelleher, Herb. "Year 1994 and Continuation of Hostilities" (letter to employees), February
     15, 1995.
*LUV Lines* 1986–1996.
People Department: Public relations literature; hiring pamphlets.
*Plane Tails* 1995, 1996.
*Southwest Airlines History.*
*Southwest: Keepin' the Spirit Alive* (video), 1995.
*Southwest Shuffle* (video), 1992.
*The Book on Service: What Service Looks Like at Southwest Airlines,* 1992.
*The Winning Spirit* (video), 1983.
*This Week with David Brinkley* (video), 1993.
*20 Years of Love* (video), 1991.


## ARTICLES
"Aerospace Laureates–Commercial Air Transport: Herbert D. Kelleher." *Aviation Week &
     Space Technology,* January 25, 1993: 18.

Andersen, Katya. "Southwest Makes the Best of Bad Times." *Airline Executive International*, June 1991: 3–7.

Baiada, R. Michael. "Southwest Airlines: Below the Surface." *Airline Pilot*, July/August 1994.

Barrett, Colleen. "How I Did It: Pampering Customers on a Budget." *Working Woman*, April 1993: 19–22.

Barrett, Colleen. "Service Begins at Home." *Sales & Marketing Management*, March 1994.

Boisseau, Charles. "Southwest's Pilot." *Houston Chronicle*, March 10, 1996.

Bovier, Connie. "Southwest Airlines: The Rah-Rah's for Real." *Career Pilot*, November 1991: 20–39.

Brown, David A. "Southwest's Success, Growth Tied to Maintaining Original Concept." *Aviation Week & Space Technology*, May 27, 1991: 75.

Burke, Linda. "Into the Wild Blue Yonder." *Dallas Times Herald*, September 4, 1991.

Burke, Linda. "Tough Act to Follow." *Dallas Times Herald*, October 5, 1991.

Cardona, Mercedes M. "Long and Short of It." *Travel Agent*, July 13, 1992: 16–18.

Cardona, Mercedes M. "Secret of Success." *Travel Agent*, January 4, 1993: 9.

Castandea, Laura. "Southwest Leads Way in Getting There on Time." *Dallas Morning News*, February 17, 1995.

Chakravarty, Subrata N. "A Model of Superb Management: Hit 'Em Hardest with the Mostest." *Forbes*, September 16, 1991: 48–51.

Cross, Robert. "Time Flies When You're Having Fun." *Chicago Tribune*, November 28, 1993.

Donlan, Thomas. "The State Bird of Texas: Southwest Airlines' Herb Kelleher Has the Right Stuff." *Barrons*, October 19, 1992.

Eig, Jonathan. "The Grinch Tried to Steal Christmas, but the People of Dallas Swiped It Back." *Dallas Morning News*, December 4, 1993.

"Eighteenth Annual Air Transport World Awards. Airline of the Year: Southwest Airlines." *Air Transport World*, February 1992: 51.

Elsworth, Peter. "Southwest Air's New Push West." *New York Times*, June 16, 1991.

Fairbank, Katie. "How Kelleher Keeps Airline Flying So High." *Houston Post*, March 8, 1995.

Fisher, Anne B. "Where Companies Rank in Their Own Industries." *Fortune*, March 1996.

Friese, Richard. "The Music Man" (publisher's letter). *Travel Agent*, April 27, 1992: 6–7.

Gardner, Hugh. "Southwest: Flying Folks for Fun and Profit." *Airline Executive International*, August 1990: 12–17.

"Getting High on Love and Laughter." *Reputation Management*, July/August 1995: 61–66.

Gilchriest, Gail. "A Day in the Life of a Southwest Flight Attendant." *Houston Metropolitan*, October 1991: 50–54.

Hamilton, Martha M. "Short-Haul Airline Is Sitting Tall." *Washington Post*, August 8, 1991.

Hamilton, Scott. "Kelleher Most Influential of 1994." *Commercial Aviation*, January 1, 1995: 8–12.

Hamilton, Scott. "Southwest's Performance Makes Lenders Pause." *Commercial Aviation*, March 15, 1992: 16–17.

Hamilton, Scott. "Southwest Takes on the Big Guys." *Commercial Aviation*, March 15, 1992: 14–15.

Hamilton, Walter. "High Flier." *Los Angeles Daily News*, October 11, 1992.

Hayes, Thomas C. "A Bright Future at Southwest Air." *New York Times*, May 26, 1992.

Henderson, Danna. "Southwest Luvs Passengers, Employees, Profits." *Air Transport World*, July 1991.

Jacob, Rahul. "Corporate Reputations." *Fortune*, March 6, 1995.

Jaffe, Charles A. "Moving Fast by Standing Still." *Nation's Business*, October 1991: 57–59.

Jarboe, Jan. "A Boy and His Airline." *Texas Monthly*, April 1989: 98–155.

Jennings, Mead. "Staying the Course." *Airline Business*, February 1992: 52–55.

Jones, Del. "Baltimore Moves to Southwest." *USA Today*, September 17, 1993.

Jones, Del. "Low-Cost Carrier Still Challenges Industry." *USA Today*, July 10, 1995.

Jones, Del. "Southwest Flies High with Cut-Rate Niche." *USA Today*, May 7, 1992.

Jones, Kathryn. "Managing the Best Little Airline in Texas." *Biz Magazine*, May 1994.

Kaye, Ken. "High Spirits." *Sunshine*, May 12, 1996.

Kelleher, Herbert D. "CEO Interviews." *Wall Street Transcript*, September 25, 1995.

Kelleher, Herbert D. "Executive Corner: Sitting Pretty." *Spirit*, April 1991: 12.

Kelleher, Herbert D. "Flying High with Herb Kelleher." *Scoreboard*, Third Quarter 1994.

Knudson, Max B. "Flamboyant Southwest Chief Flying High in a New Direction." *Deseret News*, October 9, 1994.

Kohn, Bernie. "Just Plane Smart." *Charlotte Observer*, August 21, 1994.

Labich, Kenneth. "Is Herb Kelleher America's Best CEO?" *Fortune*, May 2, 1994.

Lee, Bill. "Southwest Airlines' Herb Kelleher: Unorthodoxy at Work." *Management Review*, January 1995: 9–12.

Levere, Jane, and Mead Jennings. "Staying at the Top." *Airline Business*, March 1994.

Lippert, John. "Southwest's Radical Ideas: Listen to Workers, Reward Them." *Tulsa World*, August 21, 1994.

Maxon, Terry. "Herb Kelleher's Jet Set." *Dallas Life Magazine (Dallas Morning News)*, January 12, 1992: 8–18.

Maxon, Terry. "Rising from Others' Ashes." *Dallas Morning News*, February 2, 1992.

McCartney, Scott. "Airline Industry's Top-Ranked Woman Keeps Southwest's Small-Fry Spirit Alive." *Wall Street Journal*, November 30, 1995.

McDonald, Michele. "Southwest Flying High but CEO Keeps Feet on Ground." *Scottsdale Progress Tribune*, June 11, 1994.

McGee, William J. "The World According to Herb: Southwest's Kelleher Grapples with Growth and Government." *Business Travel News*, March 7, 1994.

McGowan, Dan, and Tim Searson. "The Making of a Maverick." *Spirit*, June 1991: 37–40.

Meier, Barry. "A No-Frills Airline Has Few Complaints." *New York Times*, February 8, 1992.

Miller, Robert. "Davis, Kelleher Will Share Aviation Achievement Award." *Dallas Morning News*, February 17, 1994.

Nabers, William. "The New Corporate Uniform." *Fortune*, November 1995.

Painter, Todd. "Frequent Flyer: Keith Harris, Founder, Technosource Consulting, Inc." *Spirit*, April 1996: 120.

"Personal Glimpses." *Reader's Digest*, July 1995: 137.

Peters, Tom. "Air Travel's Greatest (Profitable) Show on Earth: Southwest Airlines." *The Business Journal*, week of October 7, 1994.

Peters, Tom. "Low Costs, Personality Key to Airline's Success." *Baltimore Sun*, September 26, 1994.

Proctor, Jon. "Everyone Versus Southwest." *Airways*, November/December 1994: 22–30.

Quick, James Campbell. "Creating an Organizational Culture: Herb's Hand at Southwest Airlines." *Organizational Dynamics* 21 (Autumn 1992): 45–56.

Reed, Dan. "High-Spirited Southwest Taken Seriously by Analysts." *Fort Worth Star-Telegram*, February 17, 1995.

Reed, Dan. "Industry Watershed." *Fort Worth Star-Telegram*, November 19, 1994.

Reed, Dan. "Who's Laughing Now?" *Business Travel Management*, May 1992: 28–31.

Rowe, Jeff. "Southwest Airlines Finds the Secret of Faster Flying Is Hustle on Ground." *Seattle Times*, June 1, 1994.

Sánchez, Jesús. "Just Plane Profitable." *Los Angeles Times*, November 23, 1992.

Sartain, Libby. "Airline Relies on Its Culture, Not Compensation, to Make Service Fly." *ACA News*, October/November 1994.

Sexton, Jim. "The Zany Captain of Southwest." *Best of Business Quarterly*, Fall 1990: 8–15.

Shulins, Nancy. "High-Flying Success." *Daily Southern* (Chicago), May 26, 1996.

Smith, Murray. "Southwest Gives Customers What They Want." *Professional Pilot*, November 1992: 40–45.

Sperry, Paul. "Southwest's Herb Kelleher: Flying High Despite the Airline Industry's Profit Tailspin." *Investors Business Daily*, June 2, 1993.

Stoller, Gary. "The World's Safest Airline." *Condé Nast Traveler*, July 1990.

Strope, Leigh. "Kelleher: Southwest Will Stay on Top." *Dallas Business Journal*, April 21, 1995.

Sunoo, Brenda Paik. "How Fun Flies at Southwest Airlines." *Personnel Journal*, June 1995.
Teitelbaum, Richard. "Southwest Airlines: Where Service Flies Right." *Fortune*, August 24, 1992.
Thurston, Scott. "Southwest's Wacky, Low-Cost World." *Atlanta Constitution*, July 17, 1994.
Turner, Mike, and Carren Newson. "Herb Kelleher on Life and Success." *Professional Review*, Fall 1994.
Underwood, Elaine. "Just Plane Hot." *Brandweek*, August 24, 1992: 16–18.
Weintraub, Richard. "The Southwest Revolution." *Washington Post*, September 12, 1993.
Wells, Edward O. "Captain Marvel." *Inc.*, January 1992: 44–47.
Werner, Debra. "Herb Kelleher. Chairman and Chief Executive Officer, Southwest Airlines." *Commercial Aviation News*, May 1993: 24–30.
Winstead, Nancy. "Colleen Barrett: Southwest's Untraditional VP." *Today's Dallas Woman*, April 1993: 6–7.
Woodbury, Richard. "Prince of Midair." *Time*, January 25, 1993.
Zellner, Wendy. "Striking Gold in the California Skies." *Business Week*, March 30, 1992: 48.
Ziemba, Stanley. "Secret of Southwest's Success: Fun." *Chicago Tribune*, April 13, 1992.

## BOOKS

Albrecht, Karl. *The Only Thing That Matters: Bringing the Power of the Customer into the Center of Your Business*. New York: Harper Business, 1992.
Alderson, Wayne, and Nancy Alderson McDonnell. *Theory R Management*. Nashville, Tenn.: Thomas Nelson, 1994.
Anderson, Peggy. *Quotes from Great Leaders*. Lombard, Ill.: Celebrating Excellence Publishing, 1990.
Autry, James A. *Love and Profit: The Art of Caring Leadership*. New York: Morrow, 1991.
Becker, Ernest. *The Denial of Death*. New York: Free Press, 1973.
Bell, Chip R. *Customers As Partners: Building Relationships That Last*. San Francisco: Berrett-Koehler, 1994.
Bell, Chip R., and Ron Zemke. *Managing Knock Your Socks Off Service*. New York: AMACOM, 1992.
Block, Peter. *Stewardship: Choosing Service over Self-Interest*. San Francisco: Berrett-Koehler, 1993.
Blue, Ken. *Healing Spiritual Abuse*. Downers Grove, Ill.: InterVarsity Press, 1993.
Buber, Martin. *I and Thou*. Translated by Walter Kaufman. New York: Charles Scribner's Sons, 1970.
Buhler, Rich. *Love: No Strings Attached*. Nashville, Tenn.: Thomas Nelson, 1987.
Campolo, Tony. *Carpe Diem*. Dallas: Word Publishing, 1994.
Campolo, Tony. *Everything You've Heard Is Wrong*. Dallas: Word Publishing, 1992.
Cox, Harvey. *The Feast of Fools*. Cambridge, Mass.: Harvard University Press, 1969.
DeForest, Cathy. "The Art of Conscious Celebration: A New Concept for Today's Leaders." In John D. Adams, *Transforming Leadership: From Vision to Results*. Alexandria, Va.: Miles River Press, 1986.
De Pree, Max. *Leadership Is an Art*. New York: Doubleday, 1989.
Farkas, Charles M., and Phillippe DeBacker. *The World's Leading CEOs Share Their Five Strategies for Success*. New York: Henry Holt, 1996.
Gardner, John. *On Leadership*. New York: Free Press, 1990.
Goddard, Larry, and David Brown. *The Turbo Charged Company*. Shaker Heights, Ohio: York Publishing, 1995.
Greenleaf, Robert. *Servant Leadership: A Journey into the Nature of Legitimate Power and Greatness*. New York: Paulist Press, 1991.
Gross, T. Scott. *Positively Outrageous Service*. New York: Warner, 1994.
Hall, Doug. *Jump Start Your Brain*. New York: Warner, 1995.
Kabodian, Armen J. *The Customer Is Always Right*. New York: McGraw-Hill, 1996.

Levering, Robert, and Milton Moskowitz. *The 100 Best Companies to Work for in America.* New York: Doubleday, 1993.

Levinson, Jay Conrad. *Guerrilla Marketing Excellence: The 50 Golden Rules for Business Success.* Boston: Houghton Mifflin, 1993.

Lynch, Peter, and John Rothchild. *Beating the Street: The Best-Selling Author of One Up on Wall Street Shows You How to Pick Winning Stocks and Mutual Funds.* New York: Simon & Schuster, 1994.

Metcalf, C. W., and Roma Felible. *Lighten Up: Survival Skills for People under Pressure.* Reading, Mass.: Addison-Wesley, 1993.

Miller, Lawrence. *American Spirit: Visions of a New Corporate Culture.* New York: Morrow, 1984.

Mother Teresa. *A Simple Path.* New York: Ballantine Books, 1995.

Nair, Keshavan. *A Higher Standard of Leadership: Lessons from the Life of Gandhi.* San Francisco: Berrett-Koehler, 1994.

Ott, James, and Raymond E. Neidl. *Airline Odyssey: The World's Turbulent Flight into the Future.* New York: McGraw-Hill, 1995.

Peters, Tom. *Liberation Management: Necessary Disorganization for the Nanosecond Nineties.* New York: Knopf, 1992.

Peters, Tom. *The Pursuit of WOW! Every Person's Guide to Topsy-Turvy Times.* New York: Vintage, 1994.

Pritchett, Price. *Firing Up Commitment during Organizational Change.* Dallas: Pritchett & Associates, 1994.

Ries, Al. *Focus: The Future of Your Company Depends on It.* New York: Harper Business, 1996.

Rost, Joseph C. *Leadership for the Twenty-First Century.* New York: Praeger, 1991.

Sanders, Betsy. *Fabled Service: Ordinary Acts, Extraordinary Outcomes.* San Diego: Pfeiffer & Co., 1995.

Schein, Edgar. *Organizational Culture and Leadership: A Dynamic View.* 2d ed. San Francisco: Jossey-Bass, 1992.

Schlesinger, Jr., Arthur. *The Cycles of American History.* Boston: Houghton Mifflin, 1986.

Sergiovanni, Thomas. *Moral Leadership: Getting to the Heart of School Improvement.* San Francisco: Jossey-Bass, 1992.

Slater, Robert. *Get Better or Get Beaten: 31 Leadership Secrets from GE's Jack Welch.* Homewood, Ill.: Irwin, 1994.

Tichy, Noel, and Sherman Stratford. *Control Your Destiny or Someone Else Will: Lessons in Mastering Change—The Principles Jack Welch Is Using to Revolutionize General Electric.* New York: Harper Business, 1993.

Treacy, Michael, and Fred Wiersema. *The Discipline of Market Leaders: Choose Your Customers, Narrow Your Focus, Dominate Your Market.* Reading, Mass.: Addison-Wesley, 1995.

Walton, Sam. *Made in America: My Story, Sam Walton.* New York: Bantam, 1992.

Whiteley, Richard, and Diane Hessan. *Customer Centered Growth.* Reading, Mass.: Addison-Wesley, 1996.

Womack, James; Daniel Jones; and Daniel Roos. *The Machine That Changed the World.* New York: Harper Perennial, 1990.

## OTHER

Bennett, Randall D., and James M. Craun. "The Airline Deregulation Evolution Continues: The Southwest Effect." Washington, D.C.: U.S. Department of Transportation, Office of Aviation Analysis, 1993.

Soles, Katie. "The Mourning After: The Use of Conscious Celebration during Downsizing." 1994.

# ACKNOWLEDGMENTS

There are so many people who contribute to the final product in a project of this magnitude. Our greatest fear is that someone will go unmentioned on these pages. Our deepest and heartfelt gratitude to the unselfish family, friends, colleagues, and clients who both directly and indirectly made *NUTS!* possible.

## Herb Kelleher and Colleen Barrett

To Herb Kelleher and Colleen Barrett for providing us unlimited access to the people and inside documents of Southwest Airlines. Because of this latitude we were able to make public an insider's view from an outsider's perspective. Over the course of many philosophical discussions with Herb and Colleen about business and about life, we have discovered that Herb's real calling in life is that of philosopher and writer—he just happens to carry out this calling under the guise of lawyer, chief executive officer, and Southwest's beloved court jester. Although she moonlights as executive vice president customers and corporate secretary, Colleen Barrett's true identity is the Queen of Hearts. She is ambassador for the employees and customers of Southwest Airlines and the creative heart and soul behind the company's spirited culture.

We are especially grateful for their unrestrained and enthusiastic support of this work. In true Southwest form they chose to cooperate with two relatively unknown authors when the world was knocking at their door to write this story. Generously, they each invested more than one hundred hours putting up with our marathon questions and trying to help us better understand the inner workings of Southwest Airlines. Thank you for your unyielding faith in us, for being such outstanding examples of passion, integrity, and commitment, and for the gut-busting laughs we had along the way. We cherish your friendship.

## The People of Southwest Airlines

Years ago, Southwest flight attendant Tona Reynolds' love and enthusiasm for Southwest Airlines led Kevin to our initial introduction to Herb and Colleen. Tona, had it not been for you we would have missed the party.

To Sunny Divjak, a wealth of information and contacts, a grand master at throwing corporate parties (and at Southwest that's really saying something), and a woman who truly lives the Southwest Spirit every day of her life. Herb and Colleen are very fortunate to have you on their team! Thank you for being so responsive to our daily requests—you never stopped giving. We love working with you!

To Ginger Hardage, for ensuring that Herb and Colleen knew where they were supposed to go and that they got there. Southwest has one of the best public relations efforts in the business. After working with you we know why. Thank you for opening your heart to this project and working tirelessly to coordinate a multitude of schedules and meetings. Without your willingness to step up and do whatever it takes, our production deadlines would never have been met.

To Joyce Rogge, who exemplifies in every way the leadership described in this book. For giving us access to years of Southwest's humorous and witty print ads, television commercials, and radio spots; for offering your great ideas; and for pushing us to think outside the box when it came to a title for the book.

To Tonda Montague for producing the best corporate communications pieces in the history of the world. For possessing that rare combination of being incredibly well organized and ultracreative. The fact that you and your staff could find a particular story to illustrate a point or that one perfect picture out of literally thousands is a tribute to

the archive you've built. Without you, the unique character of this book would not have been possible.

With twenty-six years of names, dates, numbers, and other details to chronicle, accuracy can be elusive. Four people made our job much less daunting and helped us get our facts right: Susan Yancey, Tammy Romo, Jim Parker, and Kathy Pettit checked and rechecked the accuracy of our information. You are *our* Heroes of the Heart!

Every year Southwest receives thousands of customer letters. The difficulty was not in finding the right letters to illustrate our points, but rather in having to leave so many wonderful ones out. We are grateful to Jon Shubert who pored through hundreds of these letters to help us narrow down the field.

To Vickie Shuler, Sylvia Gillean, Naomi Villalba, Helen Bordelon, Toni Crayton, and all of the Executive Office staff who routed our phone calls, dug up memos, pointed us in the right direction, and basically took care of us. Thank you for making us feel like family.

To all of Southwest's original employees who met with us in Dallas and came to our home in San Diego. You delighted us with your contagious enthusiasm, entertained us with your memorable stories, and gave us a sense of history. Without your indomitable spirit of perseverance, loyalty, and dedication, we would have nothing to write about.

To Captain Moose Millard and his wife, Allene, for opening their home in Albuquerque to us and rallying the fired-up group of Southwest pilots we interviewed. Without your hospitality we would never have learned about the rigors of flying for a company that believes that you're not just a pilot, you're an advocate of the highest safety standards, a businessperson, a public relations agent, and a customer service representative all in one.

To Chief Pilot Jon Tree and Assistant Chief Pilot Rod Jones for giving us an intimate look at flight operations and to vice president Paul Sterbenz for empowering them to do so. You helped make this research both fun and exciting.

To the members of the Executive Planning Committee, each of whom we respect immensely for their leadership at Southwest Airlines. To Gary Barron for your dry wit and good humor. To John Denison for being a true gentleman. To Jim Parker, who is the ultimate example of stewardship. To Jim Wimberly for embracing change and trusting us. To Gary Kelly for your kindness and patience in helping us understand the complexities of corporate finance and for masterfully communicating Southwest's philosophy to the rest of the world. To Ron Ricks for your steadfast passion in the fight for freedom. Thanks for your support and your friendship.

## Our Friends at GSD&M

To Roy Spence for encouraging Southwest to participate in this project and for stirring up enthusiasm everywhere you go. You are one of the true visionaries in corporate America! Thanks, friend, for being such a tremendous source of inspiration, compassion, and support.

To Tim McClure for turning on your "computer" and allowing your innovative ideas to spill out all over the jacket design. We admire your creative genius and we are grateful that you chose to share it with us. To MaryEllen Milano, who provided invaluable insight, ideas, and constructive criticism to the process. Thanks for your candor and your commitment to a better product.

To Marty Erhart for your patience and responsiveness with the numerous changes we made on the jacket design. Thanks for hanging in there with us.

## The Team at Bard Press

It was important for us to find a publisher that would fit the spirit of this book. We found that person in Ray Bard. For tapping into your vast network and assembling an incredibly talented team, for adding your wisdom and encouragement, and for bringing an entrepreneurial, creative, and unconventional approach to the publishing process, we are deeply indebted. Thank you for your careful guidance and direction, without which *NUTS!* would not exist.

When we started this project we had no idea what a gift a great editor is. Leslie Stephen masterfully threaded the needle between making the manuscript eminently more readable and maintaining the integrity of what we were trying to say. She is a woman with tremendous intelligence, insight, and architectural skills. We are honored to be associated with one who brings such personal attention and sheer competence to book editing. Thank you for your tenacious, can-do spirit, your consistent affirmation, and for being such a dynamo!

To Scott Bard for leading the aggressive marketing effort that has given this book a lot of exposure. Thank you for your continuous enthusiasm and for getting the good folks at National Book Network fired up about the book.

To Suzanne Pustejovsky, a fabulous art director. With *NUTS!* you've done a remarkable job of coloring outside the lines—bravo! You did it: you captured the spirit of Southwest through the look of the book. Thank you for adding the pizzazz this book called for.

To Steve Lux for your creative text design. You have made such a significant contribution to the uniqueness we wanted to create in *NUTS!*

To Kathy Bork and Jeff Morris for your copyediting skills. Thank you for your flexibility and for adopting an unconventional approach to meet our deadlines.

To over forty readers who gave us very valuable feedback on the first draft. Your candor and honesty were a gift and have clearly made it a better book. A special acknowledgment to Chip Bell and Frank Basler, who

provided the special hope and encouragement we needed during a time when the writing process was particularly difficult. Thanks, guys, for believing in this project and going the extra mile to express your enthusiasm.

To all of the people who attended to production. Your attention to the details of composition, photo reproduction, proofreading, and indexing reminded us just how much of a team effort it is to publish a book. We salute you.

## San Diego Consulting Group Associates

To Joe Reynolds for referring us to the professional team at Bard Press.

To Jenny Offner, our machine gun–speed typist. You're our angel. Thank you for transcribing thousands of pages of interviews, always in record time. Your faithful heart, esprit de corps, and incredible talent have touched this book in many significant ways. Jenny, we couldn't have done it without you! We love you.

Our thanks to Michelle Corbett, who helped us with the research for *NUTS!* Michelle spent countless hours labeling and categorizing hundreds of articles written about Southwest Airlines.

To Peter Stark, for your inspirational phone calls, your unselfish support, your innovative ideas, and your consistent model of lifelong learning. You are a great friend.

To Bill Keane, a photographer who really knows how to color outside the lines. Thank you for your graciousness and your creative insight. It was fun to watch a master at work.

## Influential Mentors

We owe an intellectual debt of gratitude to our friend, colleague, and mentor, Joe Rost. No one has stimulated and challenged our thinking about leadership the way you have. You consistently held us to higher standards of thinking and in the process inspired us to be better than we ever thought we could be. You have been the catalyst in building one of the truly cutting-edge doctoral leadership programs in the world. We are very thankful to be a part of that community and to work with an individual of your caliber.

To Tony Campolo for introducing us to the works of Ernest Becker, Victor Frankl, and Martin Buber many years ago. Through your passion and insight you have taught us to create meaning in our lives, find the heroism in what we do, and look for the dignity and worth in every person. By your example, you have challenged us to make our faith more relevant by enriching the human condition. Our hope is that this book is yet another step toward that end.

To our dear friend Ken Blue, whose integrity, loyalty, and unconditional love never waver, and whose insight and advice are always right on. You are wise beyond your years and we are eternally grateful for your friendship and the impact you have had upon our lives.

## Our Friends and Family

To Cheryl Emerson for your prayerful support and for being a faithful, devoted friend. Thank you for being such a bright light.

To Wendy Paris, who juggles the multiple priorities of our extremely fast-paced office with grace and poise. Your devotion and commitment to the manuscript revisions while managing the details of the San Diego Consulting Group were nothing short of extraordinary. Thank you for helping us maintain the integrity of our vision and blessing our lives through your rock-solid commitment to the real Chairman of the Board.

To Louie Freiberg for having the boldness and courage to pursue things others are afraid to try. Thank you for passing on your hard-charging, "never take no for an answer" spirit of intensity. Words aren't enough to express our gratitude for your generosity and years of sacrifice on our behalf. Thanks for believing in us.

To Judy Portle, who believed in the San Diego Consulting Group before we had a track record to stand on. We are so thankful for your consistent faith in us, your unselfish support, and the unconditional love you've extended over the years. Judy, you've given us the gift of comfort—to know that the girls were in your hands while we traveled granted us the peace of mind we needed to pursue this project. Thank you for always being there!

# INDEX

Abundance mentality, 110–111

Ackerman, Debby, 74

Acknowledgments of employees, 161–164, 289–290, 291, 313–314

Action orientation, 78, 87–94, 217, 308

Ad hoc committees, 152

Adaptiveness, 84–85

Adventurous spirit, 135–139, 321–322

Advertising. *See also* Camelot Communications; Cramer Krassalt; GSD&M; "Battle Cry" ad, 262; collaborative relationships in, 265–266, 300–301, 339; Company Plane campaign, 260; credibility in, 263–265, 266; employees as living advertisements, 261–262; examples of ads, 32, 43, 54, 94, 104, 109, 137, 145 204, 252, 259, 260, 258, 263–265, 269; in first year of SWA operation, 38, 257; goals of, 251; humor in, 255–260; integrity in, 263–264; "Just Plane Smart" ads, 261; "love" campaign, 38–40; and loving attitude, 267; *The* Low Fare Airline campaign, 54, 94, 260; "Malice in Dallas" armwrestling event, 9, 246–249, 337; on strategy versus on culture, 255; painted planes, 206, 251–255; principles of, 250; recruiting ads, 69–70, 204; as role modeling of SWA values to employees, 262; for RUSH PLUS, 132; *Shamu* airplanes, 206, 251–255; slogan, armwrestling to settle, 9, 246–249, 337; strategy of, 249–250; summary of successful approach, 267; $13 fare war, 32–33; timeline for, 90; Triple Crown campaign, 257–258; TV commercial featuring Kelleher with sack over head, 260; word-of-mouth approach, 38

Affirmation, 221–223, 224

Air California, 15

Air Southwest Company, 16. *See also* Southwest Airlines

Air traffic controllers, 101

AirCal, 84

Airline Deregulation Act, 25, 331

Airplanes

 age of SWA fleet, 8; *Arizona One*, 254; average hours per day in flight, 51; Boeing 737s, 55–56, 60, 87, 176, 180–181, 333–334; *California One*, 254; celebration of delivery of Boeing 737-300s, 180–181; cost of, 60; "flag" planes, 254; *Jack Vidal*, 188; *Lone Star One*, 175, 176, 254; number of employees per, 80; purchase of first airplanes, 19; *Shamu*, 206, 251–255; *Silver One*, 254; *Spirit of Kitty Hawk*, 181; *Triple Crown One*, 254

Airports. *See also* specific airports and cities avoidance of congested airports, 52–53; building of gates in Phoenix, 140–141; congestion in, 8, 52–53; cost of delays in, 8; SWA station openings, 90, 91–92; terminal construction, 90

Albrecht, Karl, 271–272, 276

Albuquerque, 26, 92, 138, 204

Altruism, 133, 150

Amarillo, 191

America West, 5, 62, 63, 258–259

American Airlines, xix, 10, 20, 35, 50–51, 84, 206, 257, 259

American Society of Travel Agents (ASTA), 136

*American Spirit: Visions of a New Corporate Culture* (Miller), 302

Anheuser Busch, 254

Announcement routine, in-flight, 65–66, 209–210

Annual Awards Banquet, 192–193

Apollo reservation system, 136

Approval, 228

*Arizona One* airplane, 254

Armwrestling to settle advertising slogan, 9, 246–249, 337

Arnold, Janice, 38

Arnold, Rusty, 191

Art, love as, 242–245

*As the Plane Turns* video, 170

Asper, Ed, 253

Assets, protection of, 100–102

ASTA. See American Society of Travel Agents (ASTA)

ATVM, 139

Austin, 30, 115, 134, 174, 250, 292

Authenticity, 324

Authority, questioning, 130

Automated ticket vending machine (ATVM), 138–139

"Average velocity," 52

Awards

 Annual Awards Banquet, 192–193; Community Relations Extraordinaire Award, 193–194; Founder's Award, 192, 193; Good Neighbor Award, 194; Leadership Award, 193; President's Award, 192–193; Sense of Humor Award, 194; special awards for unique contributions, 193–194, 230; Top Cleaner program, 197; Top Wrench program, 197; Triple Crown, 8, 205, 254, 257–258, 270, 330–331, 337–338; Winning Spirit Awards, 190–192

Balfany, Mike, 102

Baltimore/Washington International Airport, 179–180

Bardo, Joy, 37, 109

Barrett, Colleen

 and authors' research on SWA, xvii–xix; on celebration, 200; and collaboration in leadership, 300, 301; on common sense, 287–289; and cost-cutting strategies, 130; on crusading spirit of SWA, 26–27; on culture, 145; curiosity of, 113; on customer service, 295; on early financial difficulties of SWA, 19; on employee motivation, 105; and employees' creativity and maverick spirit, 128–129; and Gore's visit to SWA, 129; and costume parties, 67; on humor, 71; and interior decorations for headquarters, 126–127; on Kelleher's love of SWA, 26–27; leadership of, 283, 307, 308, 310, 319; and legal battles, 24; lobbying activities of, 25; and loving attitude, 221, 227, 228, 231–232, 242, 267, 308, 317; on low fares, 55; on marketing approach, 255; and Ronald McDonald Houses, 239; and RUSH PLUS, 131, 132; and *Shamu* airplane, 252; and Southwest Spirit, 156, 161–163; on ten-minute turn, 34; and Triple Crown, 257; in twenty-fifth anniversary ad, 145

Barron, Gary
    on ownership attitude, 97; and cash-register receipts as tickets, 56; on characteristics of SWA, 75; community relations and, 234, 236; easy access to, 83; on employee motivation, 313 humility of, 232; on marketing, 255; on profitsharing, 100; and reorganization of maintenance department, 77; and Rio Grande Valley service, 29, 30; on trust, 107–108, 109; in twenty-fifth anniversary ad, 145

"Battle Cry" ad, 262

Bauer, Michelle, 293

Becker, Ernest, 276

Becker, George, 252

Belief in people, 314–315, 322–323

Beres, Cathy, 264

Block, Peter, 234, 284

Bloom Agency, 32, 38

Blue, Ken, 223

Boarding passes, 81

Boarding process, 79, 81–82

The Body Shop, 301

Boeing, xviii, 19, 34, 52, 80–81, 85, 106, 314, 319, 329, 333–334

Boeing 737s, 55–56, 60, 87, 176, 180–181, 314, 333–334

Bogan, Sandra, 43, 44, 316–317

Bogan, Tony, 317

Bombing in Oklahoma City, 235–236

*Book on Service, The*, 271

Bottom Wrench Award, 197

Boyter, Mark, 116

Braniff
    Dallas–San Antonio fare of, 54; flight attendants' uniforms, 39; former employee of, 274; and Hobby Airport, 23; loan of ground equipment to SWA, 42; opposition to founding of SWA, 16, 17, 19, 20, 23–26, 28, 309, 311; policy on employee compliments and complaints, 275; Putnam hired by, 79, 333; termination of Dallas–Houston Hobby Airport service, 33; and $13 fare war, 31–33

Brittan, Charlie, 290

Brown, Barry, 74

Brown, Eric, 191

Brown, Tyler, 256

Bruner, Ron, 219–220

Buber, Martin, 316, 339

Buckley, Matt, 131–133, 135, 229–230

Bureaucracy versus entrepreneurship, 76–77

Burnette, Tom, 274

Bush, George, 249

CAB. *See* Civil Aeronautics Board (CAB)

*California One* airplane, 254

Camelot Communications, 220, 250, 265

Camp Ronald McDonald for Good Times, 241

Campbell, Bruce, 202

Case studies for learning, 119–120

Celebrations
    Annual Awards Banquet, 192–193; artist's role in, 198–199; benefits of, 178–188, 199–201; Community Relations Extraordinaire Award, 193–194; cost effectiveness of, 200; definition of, 336; evocator's role in, 199; Founder's Award, 192, 193; Good Neighbor Award, 194; guidelines for, 197–200; Heroes of the Heart program, 194–197, 304; of holidays, 184–185; imagineer's role in, 198; Kelleher on, 190; Leadership Award, 193; of milestones, 174–189; motivation and, 185; for mourning losses and deaths, 186–188, 243; need for, 176–177, 190; for new hires, 186; as norm, 152 of one-millionth customer, 181–182; for opening new facilities, 179–180; of passengers' anniversary, 182; of people with big hearts, 190–201; President's Award, 192–193; relationship building and, 178; self-confidence and, 186; and sense of history, 178–179; Sense of Humor Award, 194; special awards for unique contributions, 193–194, 230; "Still Nuts Party," 254; stress reduction and, 183–185; summaries of successful approach, 189, 201; Top Wrench program, 197; twentieth anniversary of SWA, 157, 174–176; and vision for future, 179–180; Winning Spirit Awards, 190–192; You, Southwest, and Success (YSS) program, 186

Central Airlines, 18

Challenging convention, 130

Chance, Kathy, 108

Chancellor, Jim, 175

Change and leadership, 319, 338

Chicago, 53, 55, 74–75, 179, 225, 241, 250, 335

Chicago Bears, 183

Chili peppers episode, 277–280

Christmas holiday, 184, 225–227, 236, 238

Churchill, Winston, 169

Chuy's, 292

Cielak, Stan, 58

Civil Aeronautics Board (CAB), 19, 20–21, 25, 28, 331

Cleveland, 55, 179–180, 237, 249

Clothing, 38–40, 202–205

Coats, Annette, 248

Coble, Larry, 169

Cockpit procedures, 20

Cohn, Sam, 259

Collaboration, 265–266, 299–301, 329, 339

Columbus, Ohio, 55

Commission concerns, 120

Commitment, 171–172, 299, 309–310, 313, 315

Committees, 152, 164–166

Common sense, 88–89, 150, 287–289

Communication
    access to key people, 83; consistent, ongoing nature of, 170–172; entrepreneurship and, 107–108; face-to-face communication, 77–78; on first-name basis, 78, 334–335; information and customer service, 285; learning through dialogue, 124–125; listening and, 308; Southwest Spirit and, 170–172; streamlining of, 82–83

Community
definition of, 336–337; development of, within
SWA, 159–172, 178, 315–319
Community relations
award for, 193–194; Christmas gifts for needy
children in Dallas, 236; compassion and,
234–245; "Home for the Holidays" program,
238; Loma Prieta earthquake, 235; and love as
art, 242–245; Oklahoma City bombing, 235;
Ronald McDonald Houses, 147, 161, 238–242,
249, 319; San Francisco project, 237; St. Louis
flood relief, 237; summary of successful
approach, 245
Community Relations Extraordinaire Award,
193–194
Company Club, 339
Company Plane campaign, 260
Compassion. *See also* Love
for the community, 234–245; love as, 223–227
Complaints from customers, 7–8, 71, 122–123,
269–270, 275–276
Completion factor, 8
Computers
building from parts, 138, 139; Internet, 70,
335; reservations systems, 56–57, 136–137,
333, 335
Condit, Phil, xix, 52, 80, 81, 164, 329
Conservative balance sheet of SWA, 5
Continental Airlines
Chapter 11 and, 5; Continental Lite, 9–10,
136, 262, 300; daily flights in Dallas-Houston
market, 50; Dallas-Houston daily flights of,
50–51; opposition to founding of SWA, 16, 17,
26, 28, 309; reservation system of, 136; SWA's
sublease of gates from, in Little Rock, 91
Continental Lite, 9–10, 136, 262, 300
Contractual relationship, 336
Convention, challenging, 130
Cope, Butch, 183
Corporate challenges, xxi
Corporate culture. *See* Culture
Corporate structure
and access to information, 82–83; and access to
key people, 83; action orientation of, 78,
87–94; adaptiveness and, 84–85; committees,
152; communication and, 77–78, 82–83; disad-
vantages of bureaucracy, 76; entrepreneurship
versus bureaucracy, 76–77; and future scenario
generation, 85–87, 152; and imparting urgency,
90–94; leanness of, 76–77; and Midway Airport
negotiation, 74–75; paperwork minimized, 152;
for promoting action and flexibility, 87–89;
reorganization of maintenance department, 77;
simplification, 79–82; small-company atmosphere, 77–79; speed and, 33–35, 43, 57–60,
80–81, 89–92, 153–154; summary of successful
approach, 95
Corpus Christi, 30
Cost-cutting strategies, 55, 62–63, 130, 138, 139,
333, 334. *See also* Profitability
Court cases. *See* Legal battles
Courtesy, 220
Covenants, 159, 336
Cox, Harvey, 336

Cramer-Krasselt, 250, 259, 261, 264, 265
Crandall, Bob, xix, 35, 206, 257
Creativity and humor, 212, 214
Credibility, 263–264, 266, 304–306
Credit rating of SWA, 5, 63
Crusading spirit, 10–11
Cubic Corporation, 139
Culture. *See also* Customer service; Leadership
advertising and, 255; altruism, 150; celebrations, 152, 174–201; common sense/good judgment, 88–89, 150, 287–289; communication
and, 170–172; community, 159–172, 178,
315–319; Culture Committee, 164–166, 194,
282, 304; "Dare to Dream," 157; Day in the
Field experience, 167–168; definition of,
144–145; egalitarianism, 149; employee commitments, 171–172, 299, 309–310, 313, 315;
family atmosphere, 147–148, 158–161,
167–168, 187, 200; fun, 42, 64–66, 69–73, 148,
202–215; gifts and acknowledgments, 161–164,
289–290, 291, 313–314; hard work, 148, 176;
Helping Hands program, 168–169; individuality, 40–41, 72, 149, 154, 324; legendary service,
41, 149; love, 148, 216–233; low cost, 147;
norms, 151–154; ownership, 96–111, 149; perpetuation of, 156–173; philosophy of SWA,
150–151; photos and memorabilia, 159–163;
profitability, 4, 23, 49–50, 61, 62, 63, 121–123,
147; simplicity, 56–57, 79–82, 150; Southwest
Spirit, 69, 154, 156–173; storytelling, 164;
summaries of successful approach, 155, 173;
values of SWA, 146–150, 262, 308–310; Walk
a Mile in My Shoes program, 166–167
Culture Committee, 164–166, 194, 282, 304
Culture Exchange meetings, 171
Curiosity, 113–114
Customer complaints, 7–8, 71, 122–123, 269–270,
275–276
Customer letters, 56, 62, 65–66, 71, 80, 91, 108, 205,
212, 218, 244, 256, 269–270, 272, 277, 291, 293,
294
Customer service
Barrett on, 295; celebration of one-millionth
customer, 181–182; celebration of passengers'
anniversary, 182; chili peppers episode, 277–
280; common sense in, 287–289; and complaints by customers, 7–8, 71, 122–123, 269–
270, 275–276; customers coming second,
268–281; "do the right thing" philosophy of,
282–287; emphasis on legendary service, 41,
149; and employees as living advertisements,
261–262; and employees coming first, 282–295;
helping ordinary people do extraordinary
things, 290–295; highest ratings on, 7–8, 257;
information to support, 285; inspiration for,
289–290; and learning by example, 285–287;
number of customers per employee, 80; personal commitment to, 272–274, 276–280;
Positively Outrageous Service (POS), 71, 149,
169, 214, 271–272, 276, 289–290; service
beyond serving, 278, 278–281; serving person
behind the need, 276–280; sincerity and,
274–275; summaries of successful approach,
281, 295; and tracking of employee compli-

ments and complaints, 275–276; as way of life, 271–278

Customer/profit statistics, 121–123

Cutting Edge program, 114–116, 117, 304

*Cycles of American History, The* (Schlesinger), 112

Daily flights. *See* Flights

Daley, Richard M., 74–75, 179

Dallas, 236, 241. *See also* Love Field (Dallas)

Dallas–Fort Worth Regional Airport (DFW), 23–27, 53

"Dare to Dream," 157

Darman, Dick, 241

Day in the Field experience, 167–168, 318

De Pree, Max, 165, 336

Deaths of employees and friends, 186–188, 243

Debt of SWA, 5

Deicing procedure, 134–135

Delta, 10, 136

*Denial of Death, The* (Becker), 276

Denison, John, 11, 63, 74, 208, 337

Denver, 53

Department of Transportation. *See* U.S. Department of Transportation (DOT)

Desert Storm. *See* Gulf War

Detroit, 292

DFW. *See* Dallas–Fort Worth Regional Airport (DFW)

Dige, Brian, 115

Discipline
avoidance of congested airports, 52–53; avoidance of diversification, 55–56; basic strategy of, 48–49; daily flights, 50–51; driving prices down, 54–55; frugality, 62–63; with humility, 60–61; knowing what you do best, 60–62; lowest fares, 53–54; market share and, 49–50; point-to-point system, 51–52; shorthaul trips, 50–51; simplicity, 56–57; summary of successful approach, 63; thinking ahead, 62–63

Diversification, avoidance of, 55–56

Divjak, Sunny, 192, 317–318

Dlouhy, Joe, 166

Doane, Gregory, 181–182

Documentation, 77, 78–79

Donelson, Audy, 139, 211

Dorsey, Darla, 126–127

Dorsey, Robert, 126–127

DOT. *See* U.S. Department of Transportation (DOT)

Dreams, 323–324

Dress. *See* Clothing

Druckamiller, Karson, 44, 104

Dyer, Rachel, 225–227

Earthquake, 235

East, Dick, 239

Eastern Airlines, 5, 102

Eating crow, 131–133

Edens, Dave "Bubba," 115

Egalitarianism, 10–11, 149

Ehmann, Harry, 306

Einstein, Albert, 323

El Paso, 26, 30, 193

Elderly, 238

Eldredge, Jim, 104

Elliott, Dick, 20, 38

Elvis impersonators, 69, 70, 180, 204

Empathy, 114–116

Employees. *See* Work force

Endriss, Mark, 197

Entrepreneurship
communication and, 107–108; engaging employees hearts and minds, 103–105; hiring entrepreneurial self-starters, 98–99; integrity and, 110–111; laying out SWA guiding principles, 105–106; letting employees know they make a difference, 103; of pilots, 98–99, 101–102, 108–109; profitsharing and, 99–101; and protecting SWA's assets, 100–102; summary of successful approach, 111; thinking like an owner by employees, 96–99; trust and, 107–109; versus bureaucracy, 76–77

Esprit de corps, 27, 44–45. *See also* Teamwork

Executive assistants, 76–77

FAA. *See* Federal Aviation Administration (FAA)

Failure. *See* Fear of failure

Families of employees, 148, 239, 316–317

Family atmosphere, 148, 158–164, 167–168, 187, 200

Fares
Fun Fares, 292; high fares of major carriers, 28–29; low fares of SWA, 5–6, 11, 28–35, 53–55, 62, 147, 292, 295, 333; Standard Industry Fare Level (SIFL), 333; SWA strategy of driving prices down, 54–55, 333; $13 fare war, 31–33; two-tier fare system, 30–31

Farry, John, 200

Fear of failure
avoiding, 128–141; eating crow and, 131–133; forgiveness and, 133–135; removal of, 131–135

*Feast of Fools, The* (Cox), 336

Federal Aviation Administration (FAA), 8, 20, 34, 99, 117, 126, 331

Federal Express, 131

Felible, Roma, 64

*Firing Up Commitment during Organizational Change* (Pritchett), 108

"Flag" planes, 254

Fleet Services Union, 218–219

Flexibility, 87–89

Flight attendants
celebration of passengers' anniversary, 182; clothing of, 202–205; contract negotiation with, 83; customer service by, 41, 276–280, 293; and Day in the Field experience, 167–168; flexibility in job responsibilities, 57, 60; hot pants of first flight attendants, 38–40; humor of, 6, 65–66, 209–211; original flight attendants, 36–38, 43, 45; response to Putnam as former president, 305; Winning Spirit Award for, 192

Flight simulator, 314

Flights
airplane's average hours per day in flight, 51; daily flight statistics, 50–51; hub-and-spoke system of, 51–52; Ogden's development of flight procedures, 20; point-to-point system of, 51–52; printed schedule of, 130; profit per flight, 121

Flood relief in St. Louis, 237

Football team logos, 128–129

Force, Sandra, 43, 45
Forgiveness, 133–135, 227–228
Fort Worth, 238, 241
Foster, Dale, 317
Founder's Award, 192, 193
Fourth of July, 185
Franklin, Bill, 20, 34, 37, 40, 41, 43, 138–139, 332
Franklin, Deborah, 41, 43
Freiberg, Aubrey, xiv
Freiberg, Jackie, xiii–xiv, xvii–xxi
Freiberg, Kevin, xiii, xvii–xxi
Freiberg, Taylor Grace, xiv, 131
Front Line Forum, 77
Frontier Airlines, 20, 33
Frugality, 62–63, 200. *See also* Cost-cutting strategies
Fuel burn rate, 101–102
Fuel from the Heart program, 303, 304
Fuel prices, 62, 101–102, 156, 303
Fullen, Michelle, 272
Fun. *See* Celebrations; Humor
Fun Fares, 292
Furloughs, 7
Future scenario generation, 85–87, 152

Gardner, John, 303
Gates, Bill, 84
Gatlin, Larry, 175–176
Gatlin Brothers, 175–176
General Electric (GE), xix, 80, 103, 301, 304
Generosity, 219–220
Gifts for employees, 161–164
Gile, Ken, 121, 236
Gobernatz, Tony, 104
Goins, Mary, 43
Golden, Mike, 138, 139, 140
Golden Rule, 133, 150, 151
Golf tournament, 241
Good Neighbor Award, 194
Goodwin, Mark "Squidd," 218–219
Gore, Al, 129, 132–133
Grace, 227–230
Grapevine, Texas, 274
Greenleaf, Robert, 284, 310
Grieving, 186–188, 243
Groseclose, Doug, 80–81
Gross, Scott, 271
Ground operations
    average turnaround time for SWA, 57–60;
    can-do attitude of, 42, 43–44; cost of, 51–52;
    Cutting Edge program for pilots, 114–116,
    117, 304; deicing procedure, 134–135;
    ground equipment in first year of operation,
    42; ground support team, 166–167; industry
    average turnaround time, 57; maintenance,
    34, 44, 77, 197; minute-by-minute log of,
    58–59; simplicity and, 80–81; ten-minute
    turn, 33–35, 43, 57, 332–333; tugs with football
    team logos, 128–129; turnaround time, 33–35,
    43, 57, 57–60, 80–81, 332–333; Walk a Mile in
    My Shoes program, 166–167
Growth of SWA, 5, 78, 196, 326
Gruslin, Brenda, 43
GSD&M, 10, 131–132, 165, 175, 199, 213, 220, 243,
    250–253, 255, 257, 259, 265, 299

*Guerrilla Marketing Excellence* (Levinson), 249, 263
Guidi, Rudy, 58
Gulf War, 62, 102, 156, 301

Haggard, Judy, 193, 236
Hall, Doug, 136
Halloween, 184–185
Hancock, Ann, 199
Hansen-Pole, Cheryl, 237
Hardage, Ginger, 123
Harlingen, Tex., 29
Harris, Keith, 292
Harrison, H. Max "Chuck," 293
Hauer, Jack, 24
Hawaiian Airlines, 20
Hayenga, Karen, 235
Hefner, Hugh, 38
Heizer, Ned, 17
Helping Hands program, 168–169, 318
Herman Miller, 164–165
Heroes of the Heart program, 194–197, 304
Herwald, Kurt, 9, 246–248
High-speed rail system, 306–307
Hinna, Jim, 229–230
Hiring. *See also* Work force
    for attitude and training for skills, 66–69, 152,
    216; of entrepreneurial self-starters, 98–99;
    humor's importance in, 42, 64–66, 69–73;
    interview process, 66–69; of loving people,
    216; and new kind of professionalism, 65–66;
    recruiting strategies and, 69–70, 72; statistics
    on applications, interviews, and hirings, 72;
    summary of successful approach, 73; and
    Targeted Selection, 67, 334; unselfishness
    as important in, 67–68, 216
Hobby Airport (Houston), 22–23, 24, 26, 34, 53, 193, 224
Holiday celebrations, 184–185
Holley, Rhonda, 130
Holloway, Gary, 235
"Home for the Holidays" program, 238
Honesty, 231–232
Hooper, Kathy, 226
Hope, Bob, 181
Hot pants for flight attendants, 38–40
Houston, 241. *See also* Hobby Airport
Houston Intercontinental Airport, 22–23, 24, 25, 53
"How Do We Rate" feature of *LUV Lines*, 123–124
Howling, Kirkland, 58
Howze, Peggy, 38–39
Hub-and-spoke system, 51–52
Humility, 60–61, 232–233
Humor
    in advertising, 255–260; in announcement rou-
    tine, 65–66, 209–210; benefits of fun, 212, 214;
    casual and unique clothes, 202–205; complaints
    from customers about, 71; creativity and, 212,
    214; of flight attendants, 6, 65–66, 209–211;
    fun attitude of work force, 42, 64–66, 69–73,
    148, 202–215; games and contests for passen-
    gers, 211; guidelines for, 213; importance of,
    42, 64–65, 323; practical jokes, 6, 210–211,
    230; in recruiting, 69–70, 72; Sense of Humor
    Award, 194; *Shamu* airplanes, 206, 251–255;
    summary of successful approach, 215

Hunnicutt, Cookie, 197

I-it relationship, 339
Incredible Productions company, 174, 175
Individuality, 40–41, 72, 149, 154, 324
"Industry News" feature in LUV Lines, 124
Influence
    and focus on what a person controls, 306;
    guidelines on, 304–308; integrity and, 304–306;
    of leaders on one another, 303–304; listening
    and, 308; and loving people into action, 308;
    political skills and, 307–308; preparedness and,
    306–307
Informality, 153, 202–205
Information. *See also* Communication; Learning
    access to, 82–83; customer service, 285; as
    power, 116–125
Integrity, 110–111, 263, 304–306
International Airline Passengers Association, 331
Internet, 70, 335
Interviewing. *See* Hiring
I-thou relationship, 339

*Jack Vidal* airplane, 188
Jackson, Cynthia, 226
Jarboe, Jan, 206
Jefferson, Judy, 185
Joedicke, Bob, 337
Joel, Billy, 175
Johnson, Dan, 41, 259
Johnson, Scott, 41, 259
Johnson, Tausha, 294
Jones, C. C., 194
Jones, J. R., 248
Jones, Rod, 88, 110
*Jump Start Your Brain* (Hall), 136
"Just Plane Smart" ads, 261

Kalahar, Tom, 220, 250, 265
Keating, Frank, 235
*Keepin' the Spirit Alive* video, 153, 154, 171
Kegley, Jan, 194
Keith, Camille, 45, 76
Kelleher, David, 113
Kelleher, Herb
    ability to recall names, 334–335; activities of,
    reported in *LUV Lines*, 124; on adaptiveness,
    84, 85; appreciation of, from employees, 224;
    armwrestling in advertising slogan dispute, 9,
    246–249; author's request for interview with,
    xvii; on Boeing 737s, 333–334; casual and
    humorous dress of, 67, 69, 70, 204; and cele-
    brations, 190, 199; on corporate structure, 76,
    77; crusading spirit of, 10, 26–27; on culture,
    145, 154; and customers coming second, 268, 269–270; egalitarianism of, 10;
    and employee characteristics, 130, 216; and
    employee compliments, 276; and employee
    mistakes, 131–134; on employee responsibility,
    289; eulogy for Jack Vidal, 188; on family
    atmosphere, 158; friendship with Spence, 331;
    on fuel costs, 102; on furloughing people, 7;
    humility of, 232; humor and, 67, 69, 70, 204,
    206, 213; incorporation of Air Southwest Co.,

16; integrity of, 110–111; as interim president,
    333; and King's idea for SWA, 15; as lawyer in
    San Antonio, 15; on laying out SWA guiding
    principles for employees, 106; leadership style
    of, xvii–xix, xx, 27, 283, 302, 303, 308, 310,
    311; legal battles at beginning of SWA, 16–18,
    20–21, 23, 24, 26–27, 331–332; "Letter to
    Shareholders" by, 222–223; letters read by, 338;
    lobbying activities of, 25; on low fares, 54; on
    management, 315; on market share and prof-
    itability, 49; "Message to the Field" from, 171,
    221, 318; on Midway Airport, 75, 179; on
    Muse, 18; and number of passengers on early
    flights, 22; and Phoenix gates built, 140; on
    point-to-point system, 52; on politics, 307; as
    president on permanent basis, 333; and printed
    flight schedule format, 130; on professionals,
    65; on profitsharing, 100; and recruiting ads,
    69; relationship with employees, 83, 221–223,
    274–275, 276, 317; *Triple Crown One* air-
    plane, 254; and reorganization of maintenance
    department, 77; and Rio Grand Valley service,
    29; and Ronald McDonald Houses,
    238, 239; and RUSH PLUS, 131–133; sense of
    urgency created by, 92–94; and *Shamu* airplane,
    252; and *Silver One* airplane, 254; on small-
    company atmosphere, 78, 79; and Southwest
    Spirit, 154, 161, 164, 165, 171; on speed, 90;
    on strategic planning, 85–86; on success as
    dangerous, 60–61; succession following, 164,
    328–329; testimony against high-speed rail sys-
    tem, 306–307; on thinking ahead and frugality,
    62; and $13 fare war, 32; and ticketless system,
    136–137; and *Triple Crown One* airplane, 254;
    on truth telling, 231; in TV commercials, 260;
    at twentieth-anniversary celebration, 175–176;
    unions and, 83, 110–111, 218; and Winning
    Spirit Awards, 192; on Wright Amendment, 26
Kelly, Gary, xviii–xix, 5, 208
Kerans, Gary, 110
Kilgore (Texas) Rangerettes, 174, 175
Kindness, 219–220. *See also* Love
King, Rollin
    and beginnings of SWA, 14–17, 24, 151–152,
    309; on encouraging difference, 40–41; on
    ground operations, 43; and Muse management
    team, 20, 40; relationship with employees, 41,
    42; and Rio Grande Valley service, 29; at
    twentieth-anniversary celebration, 176
Kiwi, 9
Klopfenstein, Robert L., 91
Kneisley, Bob, 257
Krivkovich, Peter, 261, 266

Labich, Kenneth, 83
Labor contracts. *See* Unions
Lang, Chic, 98, 101, 103, 193
Lardon, Dennis, 34, 41, 44
Lardon, Joanne, 130
Larrea, Mercedes, 226
Las Vegas, 26, 53, 167
Laughter. *See* Humor
Lawrence, Bill, 104
Lawrence, Harding, 311

LAX. *See* Los Angeles and Los Angeles International (LAX)

Layoffs, 7

Leadership
and belief in people, 314–315; and caring community, 317–318; change and, 319, 338; collaboration and, 299–301, 329, 339; commitment and, 313, 315; community built by, 315–319; definition of, 298–299; and employee learning facility, 125; and enrichment of human condition, 315–319; by example, 283–284; and focus on what a person controls, 306; and generative, self-renewing community, 318–319; and honoring people's efforts, 313–314; importance of, 312–319; influence guidelines, 304–308; influence of leaders on one another, 303–304; integrity and, 304–306; and learning community, 318; listening and, 308; and Lone Ranger myth, 301–302; and loving people into action, 308; as moral, 317; motivation and, 313–315; political skills and, 307–308; position power as not leadership, 303; preparedness and, 306–307; prerequisites for, 301–303; and relating to whole person, 316–317; and sacredness of person, 315–316; servant leadership, 310–312; and sharing purpose, vision, and values, 308–310; and University for People, 125; and walking your talk, 304–306

Leadership Award, 193

Leadership development, 125, 164

*Leadership for the Twenty-First Century* (Rost), 298

*Leadership Is an Art* (De Pree), 336

Leanness, 76–77

Learning
about competitors, 123–124; curiosity and, 113–114; customer service and, 285–287; through dialogue,124– 125; empathy and, 114–116; employee learning facility, 125; by example, 285–287; experimentation necessary for, 131; about industry averages, 123–124; information as power, 116–125; as key to SWA survival, 112–113; leadership and learning community, 318; through life, 119–120; through metaphor, 118–119; about milestones, 123; about profitability, 121–123; stretching and growing to activate, 125–127; summary of successful approach, 127; as way of life, 125

"Learning Edge" feature of *LUV Lines,* 118–119

Legal battles
over charters outside of Texas, 33, 332; and crusading spirit of SWA, 27; over Harlingen service, 29; over Love Field, 23–25; restraining order to keep SWA from flying, 21; over SWA certificate to fly, 16–18

"Letter to Shareholders," 222–223

Letters from customers. *See* Customer letters

Levering, Robert, 7

Levinson, Jay Conrad, 249, 263

*Lighten Up* (Metcalf and Felible), 64–65

Listening, 308. *See also* Communication

Little Rock, 91–92

Loma Prieta earthquake, 235

Lone Ranger myth, 301–302

"The Lone Star Is Flying High," 175–176

*Lone Star One* airplane, 175, 176, 254

López, Rudy, 193

Lorch of Dallas, 39

Lorenzo, Frank, 311

Los Angeles and Los Angeles International (LAX), 50, 53, 58–59, 169, 180, 225–227

Love
as action oriented, 217, 308; advertising and, 267; as affirming, 221–223; approval and, 228; as art, 242–245; caring community and leadership, 317–318; community relations and, 234–245; as compassionate, 223–227; as courteous, 220; forgiveness and, 227–228; grace and, 227–230; hiring of loving people, 216; humility and, 232–233; as kind and generous, 219–220; need for, 216–217; as patient, 218–219; pursuit of, before techniques, 324–325; summary of successful approach, 233; as tough and gutsy, 231–232; tough love, 231–232; as value of SWA, 148

"Love" campaign, 38–40

Love Field (Dallas), 23–26, 27, 35, 53, 126, 159, 181, 211, 283

Love Field Compromise, 26

Low–cost fares, 5–6, 11, 28–35, 53–55, 62, 147, 292, 295, 333

*The* Low Fare Airline campaign, 93, 260

Loyalty, 274

Lubbock, 30

LUV Classic Golf Tournament and Party, 241

*LUV Lines,* 71, 82, 107, 118–125, 157, 167–168, 170, 184, 187, 188, 191, 192, 193, 196, 225–227, 241–242, 290, 291, 293, 294, 313

Lynch, Peter, 5

Lyons, Bill, 136

M. D. Anderson Cancer Center, 292

Maintenance. *See also* Ground operations
crew members, 34, 44; reorganization of maintenance department, 77; Top Cleaner program, 197; Top Wrench program, 197

"Malice in Dallas" armwrestling event, 9, 246–249, 337

Marcel, Charlie, 259

Market share, 6, 49–50

Marketing. *See* Advertising

Martin, Tracie, 193–194

Martiniano, Frank, 109

Mascot of SWA, 184, 185

Maverick spirit, 40–41, 72, 153–154, 324

McAlister, Lowell, 138–139

McClure, Tim, 175–176, 199, 243, 251–252, 254–255, 299

McDonald's, 241

McIntosh, James, 291

Meal service, 57, 62

Media, 4, 337

Meetings
action-oriented meetings, 78; Culture Exchange meetings, 171; future scenario generation during, 86; "Message to the Field," 171, 221, 318

Metaphor, learning through, 118–119

Metcalf, C. W., 64

Meyers, William R., 332
Microsoft, 84
Midland-Odessa, 30
Midway Airlines, 5, 74, 179, 197, 334
Midway Airport (Chicago), 53, 74–75, 197, 225, 334
Mike's Tronics, 138, 139
Milano, MaryEllen, 199, 220
Milestones, celebration of, 123, 174–189
"Milestones" feature in *LUV Lines*, 123
Millard, Terry "Moose," 88, 99, 163, 178
Miller, Bill, 196
Miller, Lawrence, 302
Milwaukee, 55
Mission statement, 107, 118, 130, 284
Mistakes. *See also* Fear of failure
    eating crow and, 131–133; forgiveness and,
    133–135
Mitchell International Airport (Milwaukee), 55
Mitchell, Mike, 109
Monson, Mary Fogarty, 244
Montague, Tonda, 207, 241–242, 243
Montgomery, Bob, 133–134, 135, 140–141
Montoya, Elizabeth D., 62
Moore, Scott, 278
Morris Air joinder, xvii, 78–79, 87
Moskowitz, Milton, 7
Motivation
    celebrations and, 185; leadership and, 313–315;
    of work force, 103–105, 185, 313–315
Mourning of losses and deaths, 186–188, 243
Murphy, Charles, 17
Murphy, Patrick, 6
Muscular Dystrophy Association, 249
Muse, Lamar
    hired as CEO of SWA, 18–19; leadership style
    of, 27, 35, 40, 41, 332; legal battles of, 21, 24;
    management team of, 19–20, 40; marketing
    and, 257; resignation of, 333; and Rio Grande
    Valley service, 29–30; and $13 fare war, 31–33;
    and two-tier fare system, 30–31

Nabers, William, 202–203
Nashville, 53, 85
Negley, Alfred, 16
Negley, Joan, 15
New hires, 186
Newsletter. See *LUV Lines*
Noninterlining carrier, 48, 333
Norick, Ronald, 235
Norms of SWA, 151–154
Northern Telecom, 335
Northwest Airlines, 258–259, 334
Nunnery, Phyllis, 257
"Nutty" approach. *See also* Culture; Southwest Spirit
    application of, to personal lives, 320–327; of
    Southwest Airlines, 2–4, 38–41

Oakland, 53, 128–129
Oakland Raiders, 128–129
Office of Aviation Analysis, DOT, 6
Ogden, Donald, 20, 40
O'Hare Airport (Chicago), 53
Oklahoma City bombing, 235–236
Olsen, Milton, 118

Omaha, 244
Omission concerns, 120
*Only Thing That Matters, The* (Albrecht), 271
Ontario, 55
On-time performance, 306
Ordner, Karen, 37–38, 41
*Organizational Culture and Leadership* (Schein), 164
Organizational structure. *See* Corporate structure
*Our Colorful Leaders*, 208–209
Ownership attitude, 96–111, 149

Pacific Southwest Airlines (PSA), 15, 84
Painter, Milt, 314
Paipa, Speedy, 187
Pan Am, 5, 9
Paperwork, 152–153
Parker, Jim, 11, 74–75, 138, 208, 274, 306–307
Parker, John, 14, 17
Parties. *See* Celebrations
Passengers. *See also* Customer service
    and Hobby Airport, 23; number of, by 2005, 8;
    number of, on early SWA flights, 22
*Passion for Excellence, A* (Peters), xv
Patience, 218–219
Peace, John, 16
People Department, 64, 334. *See also* Hiring; Work
    force
People Express, 62
Pérez, Ricardo, 58
Perry, Gigi, 283
Perryman, Tommy, 97–98
Personal applications
    adventurous spirit, 321–322; authenticity, 324;
    belief in people, 322–323; dreams, 323–324;
    humor, 323; individuality, 324; love before
    techniques, 324–325; of "nutty" approach,
    320–327; purpose, 321; service over self-
    interest, 325–326; spirit as competitive
    advantage, 326–327
Peters, Tom, xv, 4, 222, 268
Pettit, Kathy, 106, 274, 275, 314
Phelps, Sherry, 40, 42, 219, 269
Phillips, Ray, 44, 104
Philosophy of SWA, 150–151
Phoenix, 26, 50, 53, 83, 85, 140–141, 181, 191, 225,
    226, 235, 241, 272
Photos and memorabilia, in corporate headquarters,
    159–163
Pilots
    Cutting Edge program for, 114–116, 117, 304;
    with entrepreneurial spirit, 98–99, 101–102,
    108–109; flexibility in job responsibilities, 57,
    60, 88; hiring process for, 68–69, 98–99; origi-
    nal pilots, 44; productivity of, 79–80; profit-
    sharing and, 101–102; 737-Type Rating for,
    98–99; stock purchases by, 335; ten-year con-
    tract signed by, 107–109, 304
Pinka, Linda, 43, 44
Plaque of SWA's beginning, 15
Point-to-point system, 51–52
Political skills, 307–308
*Positively Outrageous Service* (Gross), 271
Positively Outrageous Service (POS), 71, 149, 169,
    214, 271–272, 276, 289–290

Praise, 221–223, 224
Preparedness, 306–307
President's Award, 192–193
Presley, Elvis, impersonators, 69, 70, 180, 204
Pratt, Bob, 259
Price elasticity, 30, 332
Pricing. *See* Fares
Pritchett, Price, 108
Professionalism, 64–66, 71
Profitability, 4, 23, 49–50, 61, 62, 63, 121–123, 147
Profitsharing, 99–101
Project Friend, 253–254
PSA. *See* Pacific Southwest Airlines (PSA)
Puckett, Jerry, 104
Purdue Airlines, 43
Purpose, 308–310, 321
Putnam, Howard, 39–40, 42, 44, 48–49, 79, 305, 333

Quarles, Tim, 291
Questioning authority, 130
Quicket Machine, 139

Ramp agents, 114–116, 117, 191
Ramp, Operations, and Provisioning Association (ROPA), 218–219
Rapid Rewards, 286, 339
Reagan, Ronald, 238
Reavley, Thomas, 21
Recruitment, 69–70, 72, 204. *See also* Work force
Red Cross, 237
Reno Air, 8
Reservations systems, 56–57, 136–137, 333, 335
Rhodes, Ann, 219
Ricks, Ron, 11, 50, 266, 306–307
Ridley, David, 113, 265–266, 300–301, 339
Rio Grande Valley, 29–30, 332
Risk tolerance
    adventurous spirit and, 135–139; and challenging convention, 130; eating crow and, 131–133; employee creativity and, 128–130; forgiveness and, 133–135; making mistakes and, 131–135; and playing to win, not playing not to lose, 139–141; and questioning authority, 130; and removing fear of failure, 131–135; summary of successful approach, 141
Roddick, Anita, 301
Rogge, Joyce, 130, 208, 237, 260, 265–266, 300–301, 337
Romo, Tammy, 100
Ronald McDonald Houses, 147, 161, 238–242, 249, 319
ROPA, 218–219
Rost, Joseph, 298, 339
Runge, Laura, 185
Runnels, Shea, 238, 241–242, 243
Ruppel, Jim, 269, 285–286
RUSH PLUS, 131–133
Russell, Mrs. W. A., 218

Sacramento, 55
Sacred thous, 316, 339
Sacredness of the person, 315–316
Safety, 8, 20, 331
Safety announcements, 65–66, 209–210
St. Louis, 53, 55, 237
St. Patrick's Day, 185

Salvation Army, 236
San Antonio, 97–98, 241
San Diego, 53, 90, 209
San Diego Consulting Group, Inc., xiii, xiv, xxi, 364
San Francisco, 237
Sartain, Libby, 66, 208
"Scenario" feature of *LUV Lines*, 119–120, 290, 291, 293, 294
Schein, Edgar, 164
Schlesinger, Arthur, Jr., 112
Schnobrich, John, 110
Schwarzkopf, Norman, 301
Schweitzer, Albert, 280
Sea, Marty and Dianne, 182
Sea World of Texas, 206, 251–255
Seat reservations versus seat assignments, 81–82
Self-confidence, 186
Self-starters, 98–99
Senior citizens, 238
Sense of Humor Award, 194
Sergiovanni, Thomas, 336–337
Servant leadership, 284, 310–312
*Servant Leadership* (Greenleaf), 284, 310
Servanthood, 284, 310–312, 325–326
Service. *See* Community relations; Customer service
Service over self-interest, 325–326
*Service with Soul* video, xv, 221–222
737. *See* Boeing 737
*Shamu* airplanes, 206, 251–255
Shearson Lehman Brothers, 337
Sherman Antitrust Act, 25
Shorthaul niche of SWA, 50–51, 85
Shubert, Jon, 120
SIFL. *See* Standard Industry Fare Level (SIFL)
*Silver One* airplane, 254
*Simple Path, A* (Mother Teresa), 217
Simplicity and simplification, 56–57, 79–82, 150
Sincerity, 274–275
Sky Harbor International Airport (Phoenix), 26, 50, 53, 83, 85, 140–141, 181, 191, 225, 226, 235, 241, 272
Skycaps, 97–98, 224–225
Slaughter, Cliff, 114, 116
Slogan of SWA, 11
Small-company atmosphere at SWA, 77–79
Snack service, 57
Soles, Katie, 186, 190, 336
Southern Airlines, 18
Southwest Airlines. *See also* Kelleher, Herb; Muse, Lamar; Putnam, Howard
    authors' research on, xvii–xxi; and avoiding fear of failure, 128–141; beginnings of, 14–27, 145–146, 331–332; celebrations of, 152, 174–201; community relations and, 234–245; corporate headquarters of, 126, 159–163; corporate personality of, 36–45; corporate structure of, 74–94; crusading spirit of, 10–11, 26–27; culture of, 144–155; disciplined approach of, 48–63; early financial difficulties, 19, 22, 332; emulation of, by start-ups, 9; entrepreneurship of, 76, 96–111; financing of, 16, 19, 22; first day to fly, 21; first interstate route of, 25; first public stock offering of, 20; *Fortune* ranking of, 144, 335–336; frequent flyer program, 286, 339; fun image of, 65–73,

148, 202–215; future of, after Kelleher, 164, 328–329; growth of, 5, 78, 196, 326; hiring by, 64–73; incorporation of, 16, 18; learning and, 112–127; legal battles of, 16–18, 20–21, 23–27, 29; loving attitude and, 148, 216–233; low fares of, 5–6, 11, 28–35, 53–55, 62, 147, 292, 295; mascot of, 184, 185; mission statement of, 107, 118, 130, 284; "nutty" approach of, 2–4, 38–41, 320–327; philosophy of, 150–151; profitability of, 4, 23, 49–50, 61, 62, 63, 121–123, 147; shorthaul niche of, 50–51, 85; slogan of, 11; success indicators of, 4–10; summaries of successful approach of, 63, 73, 95, 111, 127, 141, 155, 173, 189, 201, 215, 233, 245, 267, 281, 295; Triple Crown won by, 8, 205, 254, 257–258, 270, 330, 331, 337–338; twentieth anniversary of, 157, 174–176; University for People, 125; values of, 146–150, 262, 308–310; vision of, 49, 61, 63, 151–152, 308–310
Southwest Airlines Pilots' Association (SWAPA), 107, 110
*Southwest Airlines Plane Tails*, 206, 207
Southwest Employees Catastrophic Assistance Charity, 317–318
*Southwest Shuffle* video, 171, 183
Southwest Spirit. *See also* Celebrations; Culture as "Battle of Britain mentality," 171; communication and, 170–172; community, 159–172, 178; Culture Committee, 164–166; "Dare to Dream," 157; Day in the Field experience, 167–168; employee commitments, 171–172, 299, 309–310, 313, 315; family atmosphere, 148, 158–164, 167–168, 187, 200; gifts and acknowledgments, 161–164, 289–290, 291, 313–314; Helping Hands program, 168–169; ingredients of, 69, 144–154; Kelleher on, 154, 171; perpetuation of, 156–173; photos and memorabilia, 159–163; storytelling, 164; summary of successful approach, 173; Walk a Mile in My Shoes program, 166–167
Spears, Dave, 140
Speed corporate structure and, 89–92; importance of, 335; ten-minute turn, 33–35, 43, 57; in turnaround time, 33–35, 57–60; as value, 153–154
Spence, Roy, 10, 165, 213, 250, 251, 255, 262, 267, 306, 331
*Spirit*, 196
Spirit as competitive advantage, 326–327
*Spirit of Kitty Hawk* airplane, 181
Spokane, 134–135
Stacy, Gary, 138–139
Stage lengths, 7, 330
Standard Industry Fare Level (SIFL), 333
Stapleton Airport (Denver), 53
Steagal, Red, 174–176
Stembridge, Deborah, 43
Sterbenz, Paul, 196
Stevens Aviation, 9, 246–248
Stewardesses. *See* Flight attendants
"Still Nuts Party," 254
Stock performance of SWA, 5, 100
Stock sales, 20, 21, 335
Storytelling, 164

Strategic planning, 85–86, 152
Stress reduction, 183–185
Structure. See Corporate structure
Sturdevant, Mary Ann, 43
Success summaries application of, to personal lives, 320–327; of Southwest Airlines, 63, 73, 95, 111, 127, 141, 155, 173, 189, 201, 215, 233, 245, 267, 281, 295
Suggestion box, 273
Sullivan, Jeff, 273
Supreme Court. *See* Texas Supreme Court; U.S. Supreme Court
SWA. *See* Southwest Airlines
SWAPA. *See* Southwest Airlines Pilots' Association (SWAPA)

T. J. LUV (mascot), 184, 185
TAC. *See* Texas Aeronautics Commission (TAC)
Tagorda, Randy, 166–167
Targeted Selection, 67, 334
Taylor, William, 24
Teamsters, 274
Teamwork, 37, 42–45, 57, 60, 88, 118–119, 299–301
Technosource Consulting, Inc., 292
Ten-minute turn, 33–35, 43, 57, 332–333
Teresa, Mother, 217
"Terminal professionalism," 64–65
Texas Aeronautics Commission (TAC), 16, 23, 29, 30, 331
Texas International (TI), 16, 17, 19, 20, 23–26, 28, 29, 40, 309, 311, 332
Texas Supreme Court, 18, 21
"Thank You, America" tour, 235–236
Thanksgiving holiday, 184, 283
Thomas, J. B., 191
TI. *See* Texas International (TI)
Ticker symbol of SWA, 216
Ticketing. *See also* Fares automated ticket vending machine (ATVM), 138–139; cash-register receipts as tickets, 56; costs of, 138; restricted-fare tickets, 139
Ticketless travel, 136–138, 335
Toffler, Alvin, 112 Top Cleaner program, 197
Top Wrench program, 197
Tough love, 231–232
Trabulsi, Judy, 255, 260
Trans Texas, 16, 20, 34. *See also* Texas International (TI)
Transportation Department. *See* U.S. Department of Transportation (DOT)
Trash bags with logo, 130
Tree, Jon, 115
Triple Crown, 8, 205, 254, 257–259, 270, 330–331, 338
*Triple Crown One* airplane, 254
Trust, 107–111
Truth telling, 231–232
Tucker, Barri, 167–168
Tugs with football team logos, 128–129
Tulsa, 211, 224–225
Turnaround time industry average, 57; simplicity and, 80–81; SWA average, 57–60, 332–333; ten-minute turn, 33–35, 43, 57, 332–333
Turnipseed, John, 157

Turnover for SWA, 7
TWA, 5
Twentieth anniversary celebration, 157, 174–176
Twenty-fifth anniversary, 254
Two-tier fare system, 30–31

Undhjem, Debra, 191
Uniforms, 38–40, 202–205
Unions, 57, 83, 107–110, 218–219, 274, 304
United Airlines, 9–10, 39, 44, 87, 92–93, 136
United Shuttle, 9–10, 87, 92, 136, 168, 204, 262
U.S. Department of Transportation (DOT), 6, 8, 123, 257, 330, 333
U.S. Justice Department, 78–79
U.S. Supreme Court, 18, 23, 24
Universal Airlines, 18
University for People, 125
University of Texas Law School, 292, 295
Unselfishness of employees, 67–68
Urgency, sense of, 90–94
USAir, 84, 85–86

Valentine, Don, 90, 300
Valentine's Day, 196
Values of SWA, 146–150, 261–262, 308–310
ValuJet, 9
Van Overschelde, Gene, 44, 259
Vice, David, 335
Vidal, Jack, 20, 34, 40, 42, 188
Videos, xv, 154, 170–171, 183, 222
Vision of SWA, 49, 61, 63, 151–152, 308–310

Walk a Mile in My Shoes program, 166–167, 318
Walking your talk, 304–306
Walter Dorwin Teague Associates, Inc., 253–254
Walton, Sam, 285
Warrell, Carl, 40, 109
Warrior spirit, 10–11, 152. See also Adventurous spirit
Weems, Wila Mae, 238
Weigold, Lisa, 225
Weiss, Donelle, 80
Welch, Jack, xix, 80, 103, 107, 301, 304–305, 329
Wells, Greg, 83
West, "Silver Dollar" Jim, 19
West, Wesley, 19
Western Pacific, 9
"What if?" questions, 86–87
Williams, Calvin, 58
Williams, J. D., 25
Wilson, Willie, 259
Wimberly, Jim, 58, 81, 83, 109, 134–135, 208, 229–230, 306
Winning attitude, 139–141, 171–172
Winning Spirit Awards, 190–192
Winter, Dugald K., 56
Wood, Karen, 209–210
Work force. See also Flight attendants; Pilots
    adventurous spirit of, 135–139; advertising for modeling company's values to, 262; altruism of, 133, 150; authority and responsibility of, 105–106, 125–127, 287–289, 314–315; belief in, 314–315; can-do attitude of, 42, 43–44, 57, 60, 88; celebrations of people with big hearts, 190–201; challenging convention by, 130; clothing of, 38–40, 202–205; as collaborators,

299–301; commitments of, 171–172, 299, 309–310, 313, 315; common sense of, 88–89, 150, 287–289; communication and, 77–78, 82–83, 106–107, 124–125, 170–172, 285; community and, 159–172, 178, 315–319; as crusaders, 10–11; customer compliments and complaints about, 275–276; Day in the Field experience, 167–168, 318; determination of, 36–38; difference encouraged in, 40–41, 72, 154; employees comes first, 282–295; engaging employees hearts and minds, 103–105; esprit de corps of, 27, 42–45, 57, 60, 88, 118–119; families of, 148, 239, 316–317; as family, 148, 158–164, 187, 200; flexibility of, 87–89; fun attitude of, 42, 64–66, 69–73, 148, 202–215; furloughing of, 7; gifts and acknowledgments for, 161–164, 289–290, 291, 313–314; hard work done by, 148, 176; Helping Hands program, 168–169, 318; hiring of, 64–73; informality of, 153, 202–205; inspirational nature of, 289–290; integrity and, 109–111; Kelleher's relationship with, 83, 221–223, 274–275; and leadership by example, 283–284; learning and, 112–127, 285–287; letting employees know they make a difference, 103; as living advertisements, 261–262; loving manner of, 148; management's relationship with, 41, 42, 83, 221–223; mission statement and, 118; mistakes made by, 131–135; motivation of, 104–105, 185, 313–315; new hires' celebration, 186; number of customers per employee, 80; number of employees per aircraft, 80; original employees, 36–38, 43, 44–45, 104, 109, 145, 259, 309; outrageousness of, 38–40; ownership attitude of, 96–111, 149; photos and memorabilia of, 159–163; praise for, 221–223; previous jobs of, 43; productivity of, 7, 212; profitsharing for, 99–101; and protecting SWA's assets, 100–102; questioning authority by, 130; and relating to whole person, 316–317; resourcefulness of, 42; and sacredness of the person, 315–316; as self-starters, 98–99; size and growth of, 153, 326; trust and, 107–111; and Triple Crown One airplane, 254; turnover rates of, 7; unselfishness of, 67–68; Walk a Mile in My Shoes program, 166–167, 318; willingness and ability of, 43–44, 57, 60; winning attitude of, 139–141, 171–172
Worldspan reservation system, 136
Wright, Jim, 25–26
Wright Amendment, 26, 332
Wright Brothers, 181
Writ of mandamus, 21, 331–332

Yancey, Susan, 257
Yarbrough, Dave, 134
Yeager, Chuck, 181
Yeaton, Jim, 101–102
Yeh, Willis, 212
York, Jackie, 43
You, Southwest, and Success (YSS) program, 186
Young, George, 332
Young, Mike, 292
YSS (You, Southwest, and Success) program, 186

*This page constitutes an extension of the copyright page.*

*Photos and Illustrations*

Photos and illustrations in text copyright © and reprinted courtesy of Southwest Airlines except as noted: *p. xv* photo courtesy of The Tom Peters Group; *p. xvii* photo by Bill Keane, Keane & Harrison, San Diego; *pp. 60–61, 114* LAX ramp photos by Julie Markes; *pp. 142–143* part III opening spread photo courtesy of *The Dallas Morning News*/Erich Schlegel; *pp. 153, 156* character created and animation cell supplied by DNA Productions, Dallas; *pp. 144, 162, 217* greeting cards and illustration created and supplied by Briley & Stables Creative, Richardson, Texas; *p. 179* Chicago opening photo reprinted courtesy of *Chicago Sun-Times*/Rich Hein; *p. 236* Thank You, America Tour photo by Randy Bennett; used courtesy of City of Oklahoma City, Public Information Office. Materials graciously provided by GSD&M, Austin, and Cramer Krassalt, Chicago, to reprint advertisements, photos, and illustrations on *pp. vii, 43, 54, 64, 70, 94, 96, 104, 109, 137* (top right, bottom), *145, 202, 204, 252, 258, 259, 260, 263, 264, 265, 269, 296–297, 312, 320.*

Special thanks to the people of Southwest Airlines for their enthusiasm and support and most especially to Steve Heaser, Tonda Montague, Jon Shubert, John Turnipseed, and Susan Yancey for their help with photo research and materials, source documentation, and fact checking and to Debby Ackerman, Diane Camp, Karen Devine, Sunny Divjak, Tricia Furstenberg, Ginger Hardage, Joyce Rogge, Vickie Shuler, Cami Simonis, and Mary Stahl for everything they did to make this book possible.

# WE'D LOVE TO HEAR FROM YOU!

If you have a story about FUN, HUMOR, or CELEBRATION in the workplace;

If you have a story about how LOVE and COMPASSION are practiced at work;

If you know of companies who take their work seriously, but not themselves;

If you want to let us know what you or your organization is doing differently as a result of reading this book;

## OR

If you would simply like to tell us what you think about *NUTS!* we would love to hear from you!

Please write to:

> **Kevin and Jackie Freiberg**
> **SAN DIEGO CONSULTING GROUP, INC.**
> **4110 Palisades Rd.**
> **San Diego, California 92116-2043**

> **Phone:** (619) 624-9691
> **Fax:** (619) 624-9695
> **E-mail:** SDCGI@aol.com

Be sure to include your name, address, and telephone number so we can contact you for more details if necessary and properly acknowledge your contribution if it is used in future books. Thanks for sharing!

# THEY'RE GOING NUTS OVER

# NUTS!

❝If you're interested in making your employees and customers raving fans of your business, *NUTS!* is a must read. Kevin and Jackie Freiberg reveal Southwest's success ingredients for building a company where people take personal responsibility for legendary customer service.❞

**KEN BLANCHARD**
Coauthor of *The One Minute Manager* and
*Empowerment Takes More Than a Minute*

❝Required reading for every entrepreneur and aspiring entrepreneur! It's the colorful, brash, exciting, often amazing story of how one of the country's best managed businesses continues to be outrageously successful year after year while everyone from the top down has a blast.❞

**SCOTT DeGARMO**
Editor-in-Chief and Publisher, *Success* magazine

❝The story of Southwest Airlines is as much fun to read as it is reader friendly and useful. I promise you, it's a blueprint for all organizations that want to succeed—not just airlines.❞

**WARREN BENNIS**
Author of *On Becoming a Leader*
Distinguished Professor of Business Administration
University of Southern California

❝We study almost 3,000 companies. The Southwest Airlines story, told in colorful detail at last, is undoubtedly one of the most important lessons in corporate America today. Do one thing, do it well, do it over and over and over again, and be true to your spirit—and you can beat the established industry giants. There is no better example of the importance of a simple, clear, and consistent vision in business success.❞

**GARY E. HOOVER**
Founder of TravelFest, BOOKSTOP, and Hoover's, Inc.,
publisher of *Hoover's Company Profiles* and *Hoovers.com*

66If you want to be a winner, read and learn from *NUTS!* It will inspire you and challenge you to create the heart of a champion. 99

**RUDY TOMJANOVICH**
Coach of the Houston Rockets

66An original and innovative approach to business. Herb Kelleher and his team are responsible for one of the great success stories of this century. 99

**DAVID GLASS**
President and CEO, Wal-Mart Stores, Inc.

66*NUTS!* is a terrific read which chronicles the birth and path to prominence of an extraordinary organization. The Freibergs' account of this amazing success story should be required reading for all managers and directors. 99

**RICHARD C. WHITELEY**
Coauthor of *Customer Centered Growth*

66Dare to be different! Read this book and you'll learn that it's all right to be original. Discover the power of sharing and caring in a loving manner at work. The commitment of the management team to these principles comes through loud and clear. I would have been proud to have been part of this corporation. 99

**BETTY SINNOCK**
Trust Officer, The Havana National Bank
Coauthor of *The Beardstown Ladies' Common-Sense Investment Guide*

66Herb Kelleher is an extraordinary man. His leadership challenges people to grow and care about the people they work with and the communities they live in. It is a shining example for all leaders. 99

**ROBERT H. SCHULLER**
Founder and Senior Pastor
Crystal Cathedral Ministries

**NUTS!** will take you on a roller coaster ride of emotions, laughing and crying, as you learn Southwest Airlines' hot and spicy recipe for success. This exhilarating book is a wonderful treasure of information and inspiration for anyone—at any level in any organization. **"**

**CHIP R. BELL**
Author of *Customers As Partners* and
*Managers As Mentors*

**"**Operating a commercial airline is serious business, but that doesn't mean it can't be fun. Herb Kelleher and his colleagues at Southwest Airlines have proven that it can be fun *and* profitable. In some very turbulent times for airlines around the world, Southwest blazed its own trail to success. This people-friendly airline is worthy of study by any enterprise. **"**

**PHIL CONDIT**
President and CEO, The Boeing Company

**"**A manual on leadership from the heart—a primer on how to deliver high-value service. The take-aways are clearly communicated. It shows how to bring a corporate strategy to life. The Freibergs have captured the spirit of a remarkable organization. **"**

**JAMES L. HESKETT**
UPS Foundation Professor of Business Logistics
Graduate School of Business, Harvard University

**"**The family spirit and dedication to community service rings true. The people at Southwest are special people who have a loving relationship with the 'house that love built.' *NUTS!* shows why Southwest is the 'airline that love built.' **"**

**KEN BARUN**
President and CEO, Ronald McDonald House Charities

66 Gives chapter and verse! A well-structured account of how to identify a market niche, jump on it, and concentrate on its success. An encouragement to those who believe that people give their best when you let them have a go and trust them. 99

### DIPL.-JNG. JÜRGEN WEBER
**Chairman, Executive Board, Lufthansa German Airlines**

66 A great book! I loved the recipes. Full of practical advice from one of America's true success stories. It helps the reader get behind the headlines to truly understand how they pulled it off—and continue to pull it off. Shows how you can go *NUTS!* and dominate your market. I recommend it to anyone and everyone who runs an organization. 99

### JAMES A. BELASCO
**Professor, San Diego State University**
**Author of *Teaching the Elephant to Dance***
**and *Flight of the Buffalo***

66 An excellent look at a company that shows how the funny line and the bottom line can intersect. There is a lot of love and laughter in the air at Southwest Airlines. *NUTS!* cracks the code to understanding every dimension of this out-of-sight company. 99

### JOEL GOODMAN
**The HUMOR Project, Inc.**

66 Managers wanting to lead and motivate people will find this book very informative and a lot of fun. It was a true pleasure to read about Southwest's pure concern for their employees, pride in their employees, and trust in their employees. 99

### DAVID GROOMS
**President, Kyocera America, Inc.**